AF560121

Forest Economy and Environmental Management

Forest Economy and Environmental Management

Dr. Arvind Kumar

RANDOM PUBLICATIONS
NEW DELHI (INDIA)

Forest Economy and Environmental Management

ISBN 978-93-5111-832-9

Published in 2016 in India by

RANDOM PUBLICATIONS

4376-A/4B, Gali Murari Lal, Ansari Road
New Delhi-110 002
Phone : +9111-43580356, 011-23289044, 011-43142548
e-mail: sales@randompublications.com,
info@randompublications.com, randomexports@gmail.com

Reprint 2022

Type Setting by : Friends Media, Delhi-110089
Printed at : Replika Press Pvt. Ltd.

Preface

It presents the basic principles of economics in a forestry context, dealing in great detail with basic economic concepts such as the production function, supply and demand, the market, competition and trade. It also takes the reader to more advanced applications in forest management, covering such issues as valuation of a property, rent and stum page, the forest management firm, economic rotation, multiple product management and government intervention.

The existence of a wood economy, or more correctly, a forest economy (since in many countries a bamboo economy predominates), is a prominent matter in many developing countries as well as in many other nations with temperate climate and especially in those with low temperatures. These are generally the countries with greater forested areas. The uses of wood in furniture, buildings, bridges, and as a source of energy are widely known. Additionally, wood from trees and bushes, can be employed in a wide variety, including those produced from wood pulp, as cellulose in paper, celluloid in early photographic film, cellophane, and rayon (a substitute for silk).

Forests cover about a third of the earth's land area and are essential to the health of our environment. For example, trees and forests absorb and store much of the carbon dioxide that otherwise would be contributing to climate change. Forests are home to about 80 percent of remaining terrestrial biodiversity. Forests also regulate water cycles, maintain soil quality, and reduce the risks of natural disasters such as floods.

The book would hopefully make indispensable ready for all planners, economists, environmentalists and the university students studying environmental science.

– Author

Contents

1

Introduction

ECONOMY OF FOREST MANAGEMENT

Forests play many roles in the development of a country, and especially in securing the livelihoods of people who live in and around them. Forest ecosystems are one of the greatest sources of biodiversity, but they are more fragile than many know. In particular, the natural forests of South and Southeast Asia, Africa, and Latin America are rapidly vanishing.

Although the international community has issued policy responses for sustainable forest management, forest degradation has not been halted in most developing countries. This situation requires a comprehensive analysis of the political economy of forest governance and an examination of the underlying causes of deforestation. Pakistan's forestry sector serves as an interesting case study for such an analysis in the South Asian context.

Deforestation in Pakistan is one of the highest in the world, despite rigourous institutional changes in forest management paradigms. This chapter attempts to provide an exploratory analysis of forest governance and deforestation and its consequences in Pakistan, to examine the interaction between forests and local livelihoods, and to identify the factors responsible for deforestation and the ineffectiveness of state forest management strategies. The paper argues that some of the main barriers to effective and sustainable forest management are a lack of understanding of local livelihood strategies, lack of political will on the part of state actors, lack of a sense of ownership of forests by the local communities, and the presence of powerful timber smugglers.

GLOBAL CONTEXT

Over the past few decades, the international community has discussed the global problem of deforestation and forest policy issues. In 1992, the United Nations Conference on Environment and Development in Rio de Janeiro served to catalyze debate and develop a vision of sustainable forest management. It is widely recognized that the forestry sector carries potential for achieving many of the Millennium Development Goals for poverty reduction. The World Summit on Sustainable Development, the Kyoto Protocol, and the Intergovernmental Panel on Climate Change all recognize that forests are imperative to achieving overall sustainable development, reducing poverty, improving the environment, compensating for general biodiversity loss, mitigating the impacts of climate change, and ensuring food security. Despite these positive developments and a policy climate that advocates sustainable forest management at global, national and local levels, deforestation continues.

Development practitioners, donors, and policymakers must keep working to find sustainable solutions. Apprehensions about forest degradation and deforestation in many countries and regions throughout the world have given rise to numerous research studies about its causes and effects. There is a growing realization that unsustainable forest management strategies and insecure and conflicting land tenure and property rights are some of the main underlying problems of forest degradation.

Deforestation is one of the most significant global environmental problems. Patterns of forest degradation are particularly visible in many parts of Asia and Africa. According to the Food and Agriculture Organization of the United Nations, some South and Southeast Asian countries, including Cambodia, Indonesia, Nepal, Pakistan, the Philippines, and Sri Lanka are losing forests at rates exceeding 1.4 per cent per year. These are among the highest rates of forest loss in the world.

Within South Asia, the rate of forest depletion is highest in Pakistan, despite intensive support from international donor agencies and numerous global and local initiatives for forest conservation, policy formulation, and improved governance. In fact, most of the national governments of South Asia have launched major initiatives since the 1980s to decrease deforestation through structural reforms in the forestry sector, decentralization of governance, and community forestry initiatives, with a similar lack of success. Deforestation always brings negative consequences. In September 1992, Pakistan experienced the worst floods in the country's history, and the vanished forests in the northern watersheds were regarded as one of the main possible causes. Therefore, the federal government imposed a complete ban on logging in 1993. But the ban did not take into account the country's own timber needs, and the ban not only triggered illegal logging there, but also led to smuggling of timber from Afghanistan into Pakistan, causing extensive deforestation in Afghanistan.

On October 8, 2005, Pakistan suffered its worst disaster in history, when an earthquake of 7.6 on the Richter scale struck South Asia, causing enormous destruction in the mountainous areas of northwest Pakistan. Massive landslides caused further loss to the region's inhabitants. The landslides occurred mostly in the denuded hills, whereas places with good forest cover suffered less destruction.

FORESTS OF OTHER COUNTRIES

According to statistics issued in 2006 by the Ministry of Finance and Economic Affairs, forests cover about 4.22 million hectares in Pakistan, only 4.8 per cent of the total land area. However, there is considerable controversy over the precise forest area in Pakistan, as different national and international agencies have published statistics based on different definitions of what comprises a forest. Areas designated as "forest areas" are merely lands under the administrative control of the provincial forest department.

Thus, officially designated forests may be devoid of trees while considerable tree cover may be found in areas other than the designated forests. There is a large variety of tree species because of the country's diverse physical geography and climatic contrasts. The important forest types are hill coniferous forests (46 per cent of the total forests), scrub or foot hill forests (28 per cent), irrigated plantations, farmland trees, and mangroves in the delta of the Indus River. Most of the forests are found in the northern part of the country, with 40 per cent in the Northwest Frontier Province (NWFP), 15.8 per cent in northern areas, and 6 per cent in Azad Kashmir. Eighty per cent of the forests in Pakistan are naturally distributed in the Himalayan, Karakoram, and Hindu Kush mountain ranges. Although Pakistan's forest resources are scarce, they contribute significantly to its economy.

These forests are imperative for the protection of the natural environment, production of various goods and services (such as timber, firewood, and medicinal plants), and the protection of land and water resources, particularly in prolonging the lives of dams, reservoirs, and the irrigation network of canals in the lowlands, where intensive agriculture is practiced.

Legal Classification of Forests

The provincial forest departments are charged with governing the forests, while the federal government is mainly responsible for policy formulation and international matters. The natural forests are managed according to their legal classification and tenure rather than according to species. These forests are divided between state and non-state forests. More than two-thirds of the total forests are state-owned and are generally divided into reserved forests and protected forests. In reserved forests, the local people have very limited rights.

They are only allowed to collect wood for fuel and extract timber for their personal needs. The main category of non-state forests is the subsistence (*guzara*) forests in which the owners or holders of exclusive rights are entitled to use the forest wood for domestic purposes. Others may be given permission by the owners for certain uses, such as grazing animals and collecting firewood. Provincial forest departments are responsible for management and planning of all types of state- and non-state-owned forests, except farm forest areas.

Forest Tenure as a Source of Conflict

There is a wide gap between the legal status of forests and the actual practice of forest management. In some areas, state control of the forests is never accepted by the locals, particularly in those forests where traditional rights have long been recognized. In some cases, local communities still claim ownership of these lands. An especially interesting case is that of the protected state forests. Based on traditional institutions such as customary land titles, many local people are of the opinion that they themselves own the forest. They do not accept legal ownership by the state, even as state authorities strive to assert their legally designated control. Such conflicting interests between the state and local communities have placed forests under continuous strain. Uncertainties and inequalities regarding tenure are a major cause of forest depletion. The local communities perceive the state to be in competition with their interests rather than being a mandated caretaker of the forests. Recent empirical studies have indicated a marked communication gap and distrust between the state and local stakeholders.

Illegal Logging

Timber harvesting from the mountain forests of northwest Pakistan has been banned since 1993, following the destructive floods of 1992, but illegal logging continued after the ban because of high demand for timber in the cities. Timber prices in Pakistan escalated after the ban, making illegal timber harvesting and smuggling from the highlands to the lowlands a very profitable business. The term "timber mafia," which came into common use after the ban, refers to a network of timber dealers, corrupt politicians, officials of the forest department, influential tribal leaders, and others who make money by illegally harvesting and smuggling trees from the highlands to the lowland cities.

They rely on bribing, bullying, political networking, and blackmailing. Powerful politicians, including members of Parliament, are believed to support or be part of the timber mafia. It is widely believed that these individuals can manipulate legislation to serve their interests and resist changes in forest law that would make forest management more participatory and sustainable. The civil society and media in Pakistan often accuse the forest department of being involved in illegal logging.

THE ECONOMIC DIMENSION OF TRANSITION IN FOREST

One way in which an economist familiar with cost-benefit analysis (CBA) may look at environmental impact assessment (EIA) is that EIA is a CBA requiring a large amount of information rigorously collect-ed and analyzed by a group of scientists of various disciplines. One can appreciate that the development of EIA has served to advance the systematic descrip-tion and quantification of environmental effects in a way which can only serve to improve the quality of

CBA undertaken. One can also appreciate that EIA constitutes a process, formalized through environ-mental legislation, regulations and procedures, which in turn reinforces the community participation re-quired for informed decision-makers seeking the common good. While CBA within EIA is a key gen-erator of information to the decision-makers, recog-nition should also be given that the EIA process is both a planning tool and an execution monitoring tool. Thus, the role of CBA is not as an intermediate step, but rather as an integrated parallel process.

Hence, the CBA should follow up, quantify and eval-uate the dynamic iterations created by the exhaustive search of alternatives, by the efficient inclusion of en-vironmental protection and mitigation measures and by the explicit valuation of preference and choice ar-ticulated by community, society and their representa-tives acting in the best interest of present and future generations.

VALUE OF CONSIDERING ENVIRONMENTAL EFFECTS

The main purpose of the economic analysis of a project is to ascertain whether the project can be ex-pected to create more net benefits than any other, mutually exclusive option, including the option of not doing it. Consideration of alternative options, therefore, is a key feature in proper project analysis. Often, important choices about alternative project options are made early on in the project cycle.

These options may differ considerably in their general eco-nomic contribution, and they may also differ greatly concerning their environmental impact. Therefore, including environmental effects in the early econom-ic analyses, however approximately, should improve the quality of future decisionmaking.

The CBA process-defining objectives, searching for alternatives, costing out the resources involved, speci-fying the effects of each option involved and compar-ing all the costs and benefits-normally requires considerable efforts. In the case of Cuba, we are faced with two joint families of economic valuation prob-lems: the "environmental" ones and those problems associated with the incipient transition from a cen-trally planned economy to a truly participative mar-ket based economic system.

In principle, economic analyses are to take into ac-count all costs and benefits of a project. With regard to environmental impacts, however, there have been two basic problems even in developed countries. First, environmental impacts are often difficult to measure in physical terms. Second, even when im-pacts can be measured in physical terms, valuation in monetary terms can be difficult. In spite of such dif-ficulties, a greater effort needs to be made everywhere to 'internalizes' as many environmental costs and benefits as possible by measuring them in money terms and integrating these values in the economic appraisal. The measurement in money terms are made even more difficult in countries undergoing market reforms. The environmental valuation problems can be sum-marized as follows:

VALUE OF ENVIRONMENTAL ASSETS

While man-made and human capital may be valued with relative ease by observing existing market sys-tems, where available; the existence value of clean wa-ter and air, tropical forests, wetlands, coral reefs and other environmental assets and their functions is much more difficult since not even market prices can reflect their full contribution to other economic ac-tivity and to human welfare. In particular, the mar-ket price of water does not reflect the various services it provides nor do market values can accurately re-flect what happens when irreversible loss or damage of natural resources occurs as environmental degrada-tion exceeds a critical threshold level.

COMPLEXITY OF ENVIRONMENTAL VALUATION

Complexity of environmental valuation also arises due to the multi-ple functions of being a source of raw materials and energy, being a sink for assimilating man-made wastes and providing other services such as recre-ational/tourism services, storage of genetic diversity and scientific and educational benefits.

The following classification is useful:

- Direct use values are derived from the economic uses made of the natural system's resources and services. Examples of these are outputs such as timber, game and recreation from forests or fish and scuba tourism from coral reefs.
- Indirect use values are the indirect support and protection provided to economic activities and property by the resource system's natural func-tions or environmental services. Examples of these are watershed protection and soil erosion prevention provided by forests, and beach sand and mooring facilities protection provided by coral reefs.
- Non-use values lie in the special attributes of the natural system as a whole, its cultural and heri-tage uniqueness; it includes both existence and option values. Existence values reflect public goods which can be enjoyed by more than one consumer without decreasing the amounts en-joyed by others such as clean air, beaches and forests. The existence value is the utility that consumers derive from just knowing the public good exists. A way of measuring that utility would be to measure the willingness to pay or the contingent value assigned if the public good were to disappear. Option values reflect what current generations wish to bequeath for future generations to inherit. They imply both an ethi-cal commitment to sustainabilty for the

children of our children and in a shorter time-frame the maintenance of options to solve current prob-lems. Examples of option values have been devel-oped for forests relating to biodiversity and the search for cures of cancer and AIDS-"if forest were to disappear then the options to find such cures will vanish" or "as long as the forest is pro-tected there is the option to find the cure".

Direct Effects Valued on Conventional Markets Some methods are directly based on market prices or productivity. This is possible where a change in environmental quality affects actual production or pro-ductive capability.

Change-in-Productivity: Development projects can affect production and productivity positively or neg-atively. The incremental output can be valued by us-ing standard economic prices where available. Loss-of-Earnings. Environmental impacts can signifi-cantly affect human health. In theory, the value of health impacts should be determined by the willing-ness to pay of individuals to maintain their health. In practice, one uses earnings lost upon early death, dis-ease or job absence. This approach is used in highway and industrial safety, and in air pollution studies. The "implicit value of human life" approach is rejected by many as dehumanizing since human life can be said to have infinite value. However, society, govern-ment regulations, insurance companies and judicial courts implicitly and explicitly place finite values on human life and health. This is a necessity reflecting limited resources to be allocated for health expendi-tures. The relatively high level of health expenditures in Cuba would indicate a high implicit value of hu-man life and health. However, one can also discern a political motivation and its attendant benefits behind it.

Preventive Expenditures: Individuals and governments invest in prevention measures to avoid or reduce un-wanted environmental effects. Environmental dam-ages, are often difficult to assess, but historical infor-mation on preventive measures and their costs may be interpreted as a minimum value for the expected benefits that the preventive measures seek. If it is found, for example, that there is a historical pattern of under investment in Cuba for natural disaster planning and prevention; then, it can be inferred that the benefits expected from such preventive measures have been very low. This conclusion would in turn imply that the loss of human life would be assigned a relatively low value. While this possible conclusion may appear to conflict with the high political priority for health expenditures, it can be observed that the level of damages or loss of lives caused by natural di-sasters cannot be easily attributed to government in-action and thus the political cost may be easily ex-plained away.

Potential Expenditure

Valued on Conventional Markets

Replacement Cost: Simply, the costs that would have to be incurred in order to replace a damaged asset. The estimate is not a measure of benefit of avoiding damage since the damage costs may be higher or low-er than the replacement cost.

Valuation Using Implicit (or Surrogate) Markets

Sometimes one must use market information indi-rectly. Approaches to be considered are the travel cost method, the property value approach, the wage dif-ferential approach, and uses of marketed goods as surrogates for non-marketed goods. Each technique has its particular advantages and disadvantages, as well as requirements for data and resources. One must determine which techniques might be applica-ble to a particular situation.

Travel Cost: This approach measures the travel cost which reflects the willingness of consumers or users can serve to measure the benefits produced by recreation sites (parks, lakes, forests, wilderness). It can also be used to value "travel time" in projects dealing with fuelwood and water collec-tion.

Property Value: This valuation method is based on the general land value approach and can determine the implicit prices of certain land areas. The property value approach can help analyze willingness to pay for properties with different pollution levels and infer the implicit cost of pollution. The method compares prices of houses in affected areas with equal size and similar neighborhood characteristics elsewhere in the same metropolitan area.

Valuation Using Constructed Markets

Contingent Valuation: When society's preferences as revealed in market prices are not available, the con-tingent valuation method tries to obtain information on individual preferences by posing direct questions about willingness to pay. It basically asks people what they are willing to pay for a benefit, and/or what they are willing to accept by way of alternate compensa-tion to tolerate an environmental cost. This process may be achieved through a direct questionnaire/sur-vey. Willingness to pay is difficult to measure and de-pends on the income level of the sample subjects, and involves problems of designing, implementing and interpreting questionnaires. While its applicability may be limited, there is now considerable experience in evaluating the quality of supply of potable water and electricity services. Artificial Market: Such markets can be constructed for experimental purposes, to determine consumer willingness to pay for a good or service. For example, a home water purification kit might be marketed at various price levels, or access to a game reserve may be offered on the basis of different admission fees, thereby facilitating the estimation of values placed by individuals on water purity or on recreation facilities.

THE DISCOUNT RATE

Discounting is the process by which costs and bene-fits occurring in different time periods may be com-pared. The discount rate to be used has been a gener-al problem in cost-benefit analysis, but it is particularly important with regard to environmental issues, since some of the associated costs and benefits are very long-term or irreversible in nature. In stan-dard analysis, past costs and benefits are treated as "sunk" and are ignored in decisions about the present and future.

Future costs and benefits are discounted to their equivalent present value and then compared. In theory, in a perfect market, the interest rate re-flects both the subjective rate of time preference (of private individuals) and the rate of productivity of capital.

Higher discount rates may discriminate against fu-ture generations. This is because projects with social costs occurring in the long term and net social bene-fits occurring in the near term, will be favored by higher discount rates. It is often argued that discount rates should be low-ered to reflect long-term environmental concerns and issues of intergenerational equity. However, this would have the drawback that not only would eco-logically sound activities pass the cost-benefit test more frequently, but also a larger number of projects would generally pass the test and the resulting in-crease in investment would lead to additional envi-ronmental stress.

Many environmentalists believe that a zero discount rate should be employed to protect future genera-tions. However, employing a zero discount rate is in-equitable, since it would imply a policy of total cur-rent sacrifice, which runs counter to the proposed aim of eliminating discrimination between time periods-especially when the present contains wide-spread poverty.

In the case of projects leading to irreversible damage (*e.g.*, destruction of natural habitats, etc.), the bene-fits of preservation may be incorporated into stan-dard cost-benefit methodology using the Krutilla-Fisher approach. Benefits of preservation will grow over time as the supply of scarce environmental re-sources decreases, demand (fueled by population growth) increases, and possibly, existence value in-creases. The Krutilla-Fisher approach incorporates these increasing benefits of preservation by including preservation benefits foregone within project costs. The benefits are shown to increase through time by the use of a rate of annual growth. While this ap-proach has the same effect on the overall CBA as low-ering discount rates, it avoids the problem of distort-ed resource allocation caused by arbitrarily manipulating discount rates.

CONCLUSIONS

In order to achieve economically sustainable manage-ment of natural resources and environmental protec-tion, one must effectively incorporate environmental concerns into decision making through the EIA pro-cess.

This presentation has reviewed concepts and tech-niques for economic valuation of environmental im-pacts within EIA procedures. The process of internal-izing these environmental externalities can be facilitated by making rough qualitative assessments early on in the project evaluation cycle-the advantages of which would include:

- Early exclusion of alternatives that are not sound from an environmental point of view;
- More effective in-depth consideration of those al-ternatives that are preferable from the environ-mental viewpoint; and
- Better opportunities for redesigning projects and policies to achieve sustainable development goals.

In order to fully reflect society's values and preferenc-es about environmental values, non-market methods of estimation can be used and will enhance commu-nity participation through well designed and admin-istered questionnaires and surveys. Research and training about EIA and embedded economic analysis methods is needed in Cuba. As developing countries learn to successfully apply EIA methodologies the goals of sustainable development will become more attainable.

THE ECONOMY OF NATURAL ECOLOGICAL PROCESSES

The terms ecology and economy are rooted in the same Greek word 'oikos' or household. Yet in the context of market-oriented development they have been rendered contradictory: 'Ecological destruction is an obvious cost for economic development'-a statement which is often repeated to ecology movements. Natural resources are produced and reproduced through a complex network of ecological processes. Production is an integral part of this economy of natural ecological processes but the concepts of production and productivity in the context of development economics have been exclusively identified with the industrial production system for the market economy. Organic productivity in forestry or agriculture has also been viewed narrowly through the production of marketable products of the total productive process.

This has resulted in vast areas of resource productivity, like the production of humus by forests, or regeneration of water resources, natural evolution of genetic products, erosional production of soil fertility from parent rocks, remaining beyond the scope of economics. Many of these productive processes are dependent on a number of ecological processes. These processes are not known fully even within the natural science disciplines and economists have to make tremendous efforts to internalize them. Paradoxically, through the resource ignorant intervention of economic development at its present scale, the whole natural resource system of our planet is under threat of a serious loss of productivity in the economy of natural processes.

At present ecology movements are the sole voice to stress the economic value of these natural processes. The market-oriented development process can destroy the economy of natural processes by over exploitation of resources or by the destruction of ecological processes that are not comprehended by economic development. And these impacts are not necessarily manifested within the period of the development projects. The positive contribution of economic growth from such development may prove totally inadequate to balance the invisible or delayed negative externalities stemming from damage to the economy of natural ecological processes. In the larger context, economic growth can thus, itself become the source of underdevelopment. The ecological destruction associated with uncontrolled exploitation of natural resources for commercial gains is a symptom of the conflict between the ways of generating material wealth in the economies of-market and the natural processes. In the words of Commoner: 'Human beings have broken out of the circle of life driven not by biological needs, but the social organisation which they have devised to 'conquer' nature: means of gaining wealth which conflict with those which govern nature."

THE SURVIVAL ECONOMY

Modern economics and the concept of development cover a miniscule portion in the history of economic production by human beings. The survival economy has given human societies the material basis of survival by deriving livelihoods directly from nature through self-provisioning mechanisms. In most Third World countries large numbers of people are deriving their sustenance in the survival economy in ways that remain invisible to market oriented development. Within the context of a limited resource base the destruction of the survival economy takes place through the diversion of natural resources from directly sustaining human existence to generating growth in the market economy. Sustenance and basic needs satisfaction is the organising principle for natural resource use in the survival economy whereas profits and capital accumulation are the organising principles for the exploitation of resources for the market. Human survival in India even today is largely dependent on the direct utilisation of common natural resources."

Ecology movements are voicing their opposition to the destruction of these vital commons so essential for human survival. Without clean water, fertile soils, and crop and plant genetic diversity economic development will become impossible. Sometimes by omission and sometimes by commission formal economic development activities have impaired the productivity of common natural resources which has enhanced the contradiction between the economy of natural processes and the survival economy.

The organising principles of economic development based on economic growth renders valueless all resources and resource processes that are not priced in the market and are not inputs to commodity production. This premise very often generates economic development programmes that divert or destroy the resource base for survival.

While the diversion of resources, like diversion of land from multipurpose community forests to monoculture plantations of industrial tree species, or the destruction of common resources, or the diversion of water from staple food crops and drinking water needs to cash crops are frequently proposed as programmes for economic development in the context of the market economy, they create economic underdevelopment in the economies of nature and survival. Ecology movements are aimed at opposing these threats to survival from market based economic development. Thus in the Third World, ecology movements are not the luxury of the rich; they are a survival imperative for the majority of people whose survival is not taken care of by the market economy but is threatened by its expansion.

The political foundation of ecology movements lies in their capacity to enlarge the spatial, temporal and social bases for the evaluation of economic development projects-in their capacity to bring into the picture all the three economies described earlier. A new economics of development will emerge only when these three economies can be conceptualized within a single framework.

TECHNOLOGY CHOICE TOWARDS HOLISTIC ECOLOGICAL CRITERIA

When economic development programmes are viewed from the perspective of all the three economies, a clearer view of the political economy of conflicts over natural resources is expected to emerge. In the dominant mode of economic development, perceived within the framework of the market economy, mediation of technology is assumed to lead to the control of larger and larger quantities of natural resources, thus turning scarcity into abundance and poverty into affluence: Technology, accordingly is viewed as the motive force for development and the vital instrument that guarantees freedom from dependence on nature ' The affluence of the industrialized west is assumed to be associated exclusively with this capacity of modern technology to generate wealth.

The concept of technology *per se* as a source of abundance and freedom from nature's ecological limits are based in part on the limitations of the market economy in understanding in a holistic manner, the same resources which it exploits. Only when development processes are viewed in the holistic perspective of all the three economies can the scarcities and underdevelopment associated with abundance and development be clearly seen. Most resource-intensive technologies operate in the enclaves with enormous amounts of various resources coming from diverse ecosystems which are normally far away. This long, indirect and spatially distributed process of resource transfer made possible by energy-intensive long distance transportation, leaves invisible the real material demands of the technological processes of development.

The spatial separation of resource exhaustion and the creation of products have also considerably shielded the inequality creating tendencies of modern technologies. Further, it is simply assumed that the benefits of economic development based on these modern technologies will automatically percolate to the poor and the needy and growth will ultimately take care of the problems of distributive justice. This would, of course, be the case, if growth and surplus were in a sense absolute and purchasing power existed in all socio-economic groups. None, however, is correct. Surplus is often generated at the cost of the ecological productivity of natural resources or at the cost of exhausting the capital of non-renewable resources. For the poor, the only impact of such economic activity often is the loss of their resource base for survival.

It is thus no accident that modern, efficient and 'productive' technologies 'creased within the context of growth in market economic terms are associated with heavy social and ecological costs. The resource and energy intensity of the production processes they give rise to demands ever increasing resource withdrawals from the natural ecosystems. These excessive withdrawals in the course of time disrupt essential ecological processes and result in the conversion of renewable resources into non-renewable ones. Over time, a forest provides inexhaustible supplies of water and biomass including wood, if its capital stock, diversity and hydrological stability are maintained and it. is harvested on a sustained yield basis.

The heavy and uncontrolled market demand for industrial and commercial wood, however, requires continuous over-felling of trees which destroys the regenerative capacity of the forest ecosystems and over time converts these forests into non-renewable resources. Sometimes the damage to nature's intrinsic regenerative capacity is impaired not directly by over-exploitation of a particular resource but indirectly by damage caused to other natural resources related through ecological processes.

Thus under tropical monsoon conditions, over-felling of trees in catchment areas of streams and rivers not only destroys forest resources, but also stable, renewable sources of water. Resource-intensive industries do not merely disrupt essential ecological processes by their excessive demands for raw materials; they also destroy and disrupt vital ecological processes by polluting essential resources like air and water. In the words of Rothman: 'the private economic rationality of the profit seeking business enterprise is a murderous providence because it cannot guarantee the optimum use of resources for society as a whole. It cannot avoid continually creating situations which cause the pollution of an environment

In the context of resource scarcity where most resources are already being utilised for the satisfaction of survival needs, further diversion of resources to new uses is likely to threaten survival and generate conflicts between the demands of economic growth and the requirements of survival. It, therefore, becomes essential to evaluate the role of new technologies in economic development on the basis of their resource demands and conflict with the demands of survival. The productivity of 8 technology in the perspective of human survival must distinguish outputs in terms of their potential for satisfaction of vital or non-vital needs, because on the continued satisfaction of vital needs depends human survival. As Georgescu-Roegen points out. There can be no doubt about it. Any use of the natural resources for the satisfaction of non-vital needs means a smaller quantity of life in the future. If we understand well the problem, the best use of our iron resources is to produce plows or harrows as they are needed, not Rolls Royces, not even agricultural tractors. In the context of the market economy, the indicators of technological efficiency and productivity are totally independent of the difference between the satisfaction of basic needs and luxury requirements. between resources extracted by ecologically sensitive or insensitive technologies or of the nature of the contribution of economic growth to diverse socio-economic categories. In the context of a highly non-uniform distribution of purchasing power and scanty knowledge of or respect for ecological processes, economic growth depends on production and consumption of non-vital products.

The expansion of the formal sector of the economy for the production of non-vital goods often leads to further diversion of vital natural resources. For example, water-intensive production of flowers or fruits for the lucrative export market often results in water scarcity in low rainfall areas. In a world with a limited and shrinking resource base, and in the economic framework of a market economy, non-vital luxury needs are fulfilled at the cost of vital survival needs. The high powered pull of the purchasing capacity of the rich of the world can draw out necessary resources in spite of resource scarcity and resulting conflicts. This complete lack of recognition of the resource needs of the survival economy nature's economy in the current paradigm of development economics shrouds the political issues arising from resource transfer and ecological destruction. For the economic sector based on 'efficient modern technologies', this provides an ideological weapon for increased control of the sponsors of economic development over the total natural resource endowments of the countries concerned.

The ideological and limited concept of 'productivity' of technologies has been universalised with the consequence that all other costs of the economic process become invisible. The invisible forces which contribute to the increased 'productivity' of a modern farmer or factory worker emanate from the increased consumption of non-renewable natural resources. Lovins has described this as the amount of 'slave' labour at present at work in the world. According to him, each person on earth, on an average, possesses the equivalent of about fifty slaves, each working forty hours a week. Man's annual global energy conversion from all sources (wood, fossil fuel, hydroelectric power, nuclear) at present is approximately 8 x 10 (12) watts. This is more than twenty times the energy content of the food necessary to feed the present world population at the FAO standard per capita requirement of 3,600 cals per day.

In terms of workforce, therefore, the population of the earth is not 4 billion but about 200 billion, the important point being that about 98 per cent of them do not eat conventional food. The inequalities in the distribution of this 'slave' labour between different countries is enormous, the average inhabitant of the USA, for example, having 250 times as many 'slaves' as the 'average Nigerian'. And this, substantially is the reason for the difference in efficiency between the American and Nigerian economies: it is not due to the differences in the average 'efficiency' of the people themselves. There seems no way of discovering the relative efficiencies of Americans and Nigerians: If Americans were short of 249 of every 250'slaves' they possess, who can say how 'efficient' they would prove themselves to be.

The increase in the levels of resource consumption is taken universally as an indicator of economic development. If the present level of resource consumption in the USA is accepted as the development objectives of India, the total resource demands of 'developed' India can be calculated by multiplying the current resource consumption by a factor of 250. Neither our forests nor our fields or rivers can sustain such a 'development'. When per capita resource consumption is considered, the Malthusian argument relating population with resource scarcity does not hold good. More significant than the population factor is the total resource factor.

Thus, although many countries of the South have a much larger population than those of the North, the industrialized of the world consumes more grain than all the other three-quarters put together. This high consumption is due to the fact that intensive livestock production in industrialized countries accounts for 67 per cent of their total grain consumption. This Efficient' process of livestock management for the production of meat, as reported by Odium requires 10 calories of energy input to produce one calorie of food energy.

The energy subsidy provided by the capital stock of the earth's non-renewable resources makes a resource inefficient process appear as efficient in the market economy. It is interesting to note that even in the West, nearly a century ago one calorie of food was produced by using a fraction of a calorie of energy input. The same is true in the economics of water resources use in modern agriculture. When the production of high yielding varieties of seeds is evaluated, not on productivity per unit land (tons/ha) but per unit volume of water input (tons/le lit), these miracle seeds of the Green Revolution are seen as two to three times less efficient in food production than, say, the millets. The results of evaluation of the technological efficiency of processes associated with economic development, when reexamined on a holistic basis and optimised against all resource inputs, would generally lead to the conclusion that: 'the much talked of efficiency of widely practiced high technology is not intrinsically true.

They are, in fact, highly wasteful of materials and pollutive (that is, destructive to the productive potential of the environment)'. New technologies in the market economy are innovated for profit maximization and not to encourage resource prudence *per se*. The extent of inefficiency in the utilisation of natural resources with production processes based on resource-intensive technologies, can be illustrated with the production of soda ash, an important industrial material. In the Solvay process for the production of soda ash. the two materials used are sodium chloride and limestone.

The entire limestone used in the process ends up as waste material, 25 per cent of the sodium chloride is lost as unreacted salt. From the balance 75-80 per cent, the acidic half is lost and only the basic half goes into the final product. Therefore only 40 per cent of the raw materials consumed are actually utilised. The waste products pollute land and water resources systems.

The economy of the process is artificially made good by concessions in procuring limestone, salt and fuel and further concessions in respect of land, transport, etc. It is these subsidies for natural resources which make the counter-productive processes appear efficient.

Referring to the technology of production of frozen orange juice Schnaiberg made the following remarks:

What is true of the unobtrusive shift from fresh oranges to frozen orange juice is typical of most transitions from traditional to late industrial technologies. The majority of these become more energy intensive: the energy content of all the necessary production processes increases per unit produced.... The hall mark of modern technology is its typical labour saving quality-not its energy saving aspect."

Guided by a narrow and distorted concept of efficiency and supported by all types of subsidies, technological change in market economy-oriented development continues in the direction of resource intensity, labour displacement and ecological destruction. The long-term continuation of such processes will lead to the destruction of the resource base of the survival economy and to human labour being rendered dispensable in the production processes of the market economy.

The partisan assumptions of modern economic development which cannot internalise the economy of natural processes and the survival economy are thus being raised to the level of universality. As a result, with the expansion of economic development in Third World countries, the resource-intensive and socially partial development is leading to social instability and conflicts. While ecology movements in the industrially advanced countries are directed against more recent threats to survival like pollution, ecology movements in Third World countries have a much longer history related to resource exhaustion and ecological degradation of natural ecosystems. It is in these countries that the holistic ecological criteria for technology choice is needed most urgently.

The process of transformation and utilisation of natural resources for the satisfaction of societal needs determines the economic organization of human societies. At various stages of development, the dominant patterns of utilisation of natural resources have been guided by the dominant pattern of scientific knowledge, and through the generation and use of technologies that actually bridge the gap between natural resources and human needs and requirements.

A special characteristic of human societies is that they can make deliberate choices between different ways of using resources and satisfying needs. The existence of plurality of alternatives in resource use for economic development creates the need for a selection criteria to make rational decisions about the use of natural resources and technological change.

A dialectical relationship exists between the criteria of technology choice and the nature of science and technology developed in response to the criteria. Traditional societies as well as modern scientific-industrial societies have adopted different systems of science and technology which differ primarily in the criteria of choice or rationality that guides resource use patterns for human needs satisfaction. The characterization of certain societies as primitive and unscientific is, thus, sociologically and epistemologically unfounded. The fact that values and rationality criteria of one form of social organization generate a particular type of science and technology matched to a particular criteria of scientificity does not imply that other social organisations lack a scientific basis for their economic activities.

If sustainable utilisation is the objective that guides the criteria of choice for a development strategy, a resource prudent technological path (T.) is rationally chosen. If maximization of the growth of man-made processes and increasing the productivity of labour is the objective, then a more resource-intensive path (T2) which is the integration of a large number of smaller technologies (t1) and in which increased resource and energy inputs allows the increase in labour productivity, is rationally chosen. In this process a large amount of secondary resources (R2-R6) are additionally required.

Traditional societies in all their diversity have, in general, shared a common set of characteristics. They have used natural resources prudently to satisfy minimum needs sustainably over centuries. Such resource use was based on.

Resource flow in resource prudent t1 and resource.-intensive t2 technology chains

1. A knowledge system with an ecological understanding of nature.
2. A technological system for processing resources to satisfy human needs with minimum resource waste.
3. Rationality criteria for demarcating vital and non-vital needs and between resource destructive and resource enhancing technologies.

Traditional world views and practices deterred over-exploitation of natural resources at all levels. As they were based on ecological perceptions of nature and guided by restraints in resource use, they used technologies which prevented ecological disruption. Modernisation of traditional societies in its present form has, by and large, been taken as synonymous with the substitution of indigenous science and technology systems by the modern western system. In this manner the resource-intensive western pattern of resource use is thrust on non-western societies through modernisation.

Modern western scientific knowledge, however, differs from indigenous knowledge systems in three important ways:

1. Modern western scientific knowledge is reductionist and fragmented.
2. Modern western technological systems are based on reductionist science and are generally more resource-intensive.
3. There are no criteria of rationality or technology choices to evaluate modern science and technology on the basis of resource use efficiency or need satisfaction capability.

These characteristics of modern western science and technology systems breaks the chain, beginning with natural resources and ending in the satisfaction of human needs and demands, into small fragments of individually identifiable economic activities. This provides justification for the resource intensity of the dominant paradigm of economic development and technological change, and thus leads to ecological instabilities.

Ecological crises are thus inevitable products of economic activities which are propelled towards longer and more complex and resource-intensive technological chains (T2) for the satisfaction of older needs (N.). Only individual segments(l) of the whole technological chain are examined from the narrow criteria of labour productivity. The situation is best exemplified in the case of food production. While indigenous and traditional food production practices used about half a calorie of energy to produce 1 calorie of food, the present mechanised and chemical farming techniques use 10 calories of energy to produce 1 calorie of food. These characteristics of contemporary scientific industrial development are the primary causes for the contemporary ecological crises. The combination of eco!ogically disruptive scientific and technological modes, and the absence of rationality criteria for evaluating scientific and technological systems in terms of resource use efficiency, has created conditions where society is increasingly propelled towards ecological instability and has no rational and organised response to arrest and curtail these destructive tendencies.

Environmental Management

Environmental management is not, as the phrase could suggest, the management of the *environment* as such, but rather the management of interaction by the modern human societies with, and impact upon the environment. The three main issues that affect managers are those involving politics (networking), programmes (projects), and resources (money, facilities, etc.). The need for environmental management can be viewed from a variety of perspectives.

A more common philosophy and impetus behind environmental management is the concept of carrying capacity. Simply put, carrying capacity refers to the maximum number of organisms a particular resource can sustain. The concept of carrying capacity, whilst understood by many cultures over history, has its roots in Malthusian theory. Environmental management is therefore not the conservation of the environment solely for the environment's sake, but rather the conservation of the environment for humankind's sake. This element of sustainable exploitation, getting the most out of natural assets, is visible in the EU Water Framework Directive.

Environmental management involves the management of all components of the bio-physical environment, both living (biotic) and non-living (abiotic). This is due to the interconnected and network of relationships amongst all living species and their habitats. The environment also involves the relationships of the human environment, such as the social, cultural and economic environment with the bio-physical environment. As with all management functions, effective management tools, standards and systems are required.

An 'environmental management standard or system or protocol attempts to reduce environmental impact as measured by some objective criteria. The ISO 14001 standard is the most widely used standard for environmental risk management and is closely aligned to the European Eco-Management and Audit Scheme (EMAS). As a common auditing standard, the ISO 19011 standard explains how to combine this with quality management. Other environmental management systems (EMS) tend to be based on the ISO 14001 standard and many extend it in various ways:

- The Green Dragon Environmental Management Standard is a five level EMS designed for smaller organisations for whom ISO 14001 may be too onerous and for larger organisations who wish to implement ISO 14001 in a more manageable step-by-step approach
- BS 8555 is a phased standard that can help smaller companies move to ISO 14001 in six manageable steps
- The Natural Step focuses on basic sustainability criteria and helps focus engineering on reducing use of materials or energy use that is unsustainable in the long term
- Natural Capitalism advises using accounting reform and a general biomimicry and industrial ecology approach to do the same thing
- US Environmental Protection Agency has many further terms and standards that it defines as appropriate to large-scale EMS.
- The UN and World Bank has encouraged adopting a "natural capital" measurement and management framework.
- The European Union Eco-Management and Audit Scheme (EMAS).

Other strategies exist that rely on making simple distinctions rather than building top-down management "systems" using performance audits and full cost accounting. For instance, Ecological Intelligent Design divides products into consumables, service products or durables and unsaleables-toxic products that no one should buy, or in many cases, do not realize they are buying. By eliminating the unsaleables from the comprehensive outcome of any purchase, better environmental management is achieved without "systems". "Today's businesses must comply with many Federal, State and local environmental laws, rules, and regulations. It's vital to safeguard your company against compliance shortcuts. This approach leaves you vulnerable to violations of the law, in addition to missing important environmental liabilities. "Who Needs Environmental Management?

All businesses need a sound environmental policy, and effective implementation. Certain business sectors and activities have been mandated to have effective environmental management practices, limits on emissions, prevention, and emergency response systems. Worldwide as of April 2005, 88,800 organizations have achieved compliance and registration to the ISO 14001 environmental management standard. Japan has the most registrations, followed by China. USA is ranked 6th, and Canada is 12th. The number of ISO 14001 registrations per $ GDP or population are interesting statistics. In 2001, the USA had one registration per 200,000 people or one per $6000 million of gross domestic product (GDP). This compares to one registration per 23,000 people in Japan and one registration per $900 million of GDP in the United Kingdom.

For Canada as of August 1999, it is 34th in the world in terms of ISO 14001 certifications per unit of GDP, behind all major competitors, and behind such countries as Korea, Thailand, Brazil and Mexico. Clearly, North America is lagging behind the rest of the world in adopting ISO 14001. EMAS, the European environmental standard, has achieved similar recognition and adoption. The rate of growth in ISO 14001 registrations has been exponential since its start in Dec. 1995. Individuals also need awareness and limits on their polluting behaviours that affect others.

Dimensions of Environment Management

A fruitful approach to studying environmental management is the analysis of industry-government relationships. Policy is defined and translated into action in this context. We find that industrial managers legitimize government regulation of industrial water use.

However, the pattern of responses suggests that some of the support may be based on economic self-interest and industry's ability to control agency action. Managers legitimize a policy-setting role for federal agencies and an enforcement role for local and state government. Across the Asian region, natural resource exploitation is accelerating dramatically as countries, cities and small communities are ever more incorporated into the global economy.

Economic reform programmes that favour domestic and global market expansion rather than a social welfare agenda, policy responses to climate change, pressures associated with population growth and intensified geographical mobility, and urbanization and commoditization, are reconfiguring patterns of natural resource use and governance at both a national and local level and are having complex effects on peoples' lives.

These processes are themselves not innocent of gendered power relations: they are inflected with gender discourses that set in motion differentiated and unjust life opportunities and exclusions. At the same time, sustainable development policy initiatives that seek to ameliorate environmental degradation and its negative livelihood effects not only bring gendered impacts and responses, they also work through and produce particular framings of gender and gendered power relations.

The impact of this is apparent in the unintended consequences associated with sustainable development initiatives that target women as a homogeneous and undifferentiated social category, at times exacerbating social and gender injustices.

Related to this process of globalized marketization, natural resource management is embedded in the increasing diversification of livelihoods: a process buoyed by policies that support entrepreneurialism and appear to be producing individualized portfolio livelihood strategies across Asia.

The Challenge of Environmental Management

Before moving on to introduce the elements of management practice and strategy which will facilitate improved environmental performance in industry, it is important to relay some of the factors which together serve to encourage industry to respond to the environmental challenge.

Environmental Efficiency

Companies often strive to minimize the costs of their operations. This is especially relevant in relation to the efficiency with which they use their material inputs. As the ability of the environment to supply raw materials and accept waste is diminished, the costs of these services to industry will increase. As a result, more efficient raw material utilization and a decrease in the amount of waste generated are key factors which will encourage industry to minimize its environmental impact. Particularly in relation to waste products, companies are experiencing increasingly stringent legislation which increases the costs of waste management. Waste should be viewed both in terms of physical waste generated and the less tangible losses experienced through an inefficient use of resources. Avoiding these losses improves both the business and environmental performance of a company. As a result, many companies have pursued a strategy of waste minimization for a number of years and have experienced short payback periods on investment in waste management. In efforts to increase the efficiency of their operations, many companies have developed integrated management systems to reduce inefficiencies and the likelihood of errors. Most commonly to date, these have centered around the promotion of quality.

The Influence of Government

The main impact of government on the environmental performance of industry has been through the development of environmental legislation. Environmental considerations have been built into the legislative framework for many years. Initially, establishing rights of ownership over natural resources led to the development of a legal system to protect those rights. Subsequently, the impact of industrial activity on the health of employees and the surrounding community *kd* to the creation of public health and safety legislation.

Measures have also been introduced to control the use of products, processes and wastes which may harm the environment. The impact of environmental legislation on the operation of industry has been profound and is set to become ever more tough. As the strain placed upon the environment mounts and knowledge of the causes and effects of environmental degradation becomes more complete, the extent and impact of environmental legislation will continue to develop. Thus, industry must satisfy an increasing number of legal obligations in relation to the effect that its activities have upon the environment.

As a result, in all of its operations, industry must plan ahead to meet the demands of current and forthcoming environmental legislation. By developing proactive responses to legislative pressure, industry will reduce its costs and exposure to risk.

While in the short term, legal obligations undoubtedly increase the costs of production that fall upon the firm, it is up to each firm to comply with legislation in the most cost-effective way. The development of proactive strategic responses to the demands of legislation will reduce these costs. In parallel with the development of environmental legislation, governments are increasingly applying market instruments to achieve environmental objectives. Actions of this nature may include the imposition of taxes on environmentally damaging goods, subsidies on environmentally friendly goods or the provision of information relating to the environmental performance of companies or products. Market instruments are intended to channel the choice of consumers or other stakeholders towards the better environmental option. Thus through a combination of legislative and market instruments, by encouraging certain activities and discouraging others, governments seek to accelerate the structural change which encourages improved environmental efficiency in the economy as a whole.

The Development of Stakeholder Influence

Individual businesses interact with a number of stakeholders, all of whom have an interest in the performance of that company. Traditionally the main focus of stakeholder interest has been upon the financial performance of the company. Increasingly, however, stakeholder pressure is concentrating on the environmental performance of the company. The range of stakeholders which demand high environmental standards.

Customers

The relationship between a company and its customers is obviously of para-mount importance. In relation to environmental considerations, the potential importance of green consumerism cannot be overstated. The range of characteristics that underlay the purchasing decision are a fundamental consideration for all businesses. Increasingly, the environment is being accepted as one such characteristic by consumers. At present, however, the influence of green consumerism on most businesses is marginal. Of the myriad of products that each consumer buys, very few are chosen on the basis of their environmental credentials alone. Nevertheless, it is certain that credible claims relating to environmental performance constitute one positive element among the many characteristics upon which consumers base their purchasing decision. Companies which can validate and communicate the environmental performance of their products will enhance their competitive position. Governments are also seeking to increase the potency of green consumerism by providing the consumer with the information necessary to make an informed choice in relation to the environmental performance of each product within the product range. For this reason for example, we saw the introduction of the EC's eco-labelling scheme in 1993.

Trading Partners

Many businesses do not sell into 'end-consumer' markets and may therefore perceive themselves to be remote from any consumer pressures to improve their environmental performance. Increasingly, the pressure to improve environmental performance is emanating from trading partners rather than the ultimate consumer. In efforts to improve overall environmental performance, many companies are exercising their own rights both as purchasers and as vendors and are demanding that all of the companies within their supply chain seek to minimize their own environmental impacts. Hence, demands to improve environmental performance at all stages in the supply chain are being diffused beyond those companies that are directly exposed to the pressures of green consumerism. An increasing number of companies are preferring to buy their resources from or sell their products to companies which meet certain standards of environmental performance.

The provision of information on company environmental performance through standards such as BS7750, the British Standard on Environmental Management Systems, and the EC's eco-management and audit scheme will increasingly be written into contracts in the future. Increasing environmental concern and the improved provision of information relating to environmental performance will reward those companies which achieve and communicate high environmental standards with a competitive advantage.

The Community

Industry shares its surrounding environment with the local population. Increasingly this population is demanding a high level of environmental performance from its industrial neighbours, and seeks some degree of reassurance that they are not exposed to significant environmental risk due to a company's operations. This concern has been recognized for many years and was initially recognized in public health legislation. Trends towards freedom of access to environmental information will give greater power to local communities when they question the activities of local industrial co-habitants. In order to foster a positive working relationship, companies must improve their environmental performance and communicate their efforts to the surrounding communities. This is true both for future developments and existing operations.

Employees

The population in the community surrounding a company also includes the workforce of that company. The pressure to provide a healthy living environment is magnified within the workplace. Employees seek healthy and secure working conditions, and can draw on an established framework of health and safety legislation in this respect. However, employees' concerns relating to the environmental performance of their employers goes beyond the impact of operations on the working and living environment. Increasingly people wish to work for ethical and responsible companies. Companies that reflect the environmental concerns of the public will find it easier to attract, retain and motivate a quality workforce.

Investors and Insurers

The pressures to improve environmental performance also emanate from the investors and shareholders of a company. The rapid growth of ethical investment schemes in recent years reflects the desire of many investors only to lend their financial support to companies which behave in a responsible manner. There are also a number of very good business reasons why investors prefer to work with companies that have a proven track record of environmental integrity. The structure of legal liability for environmental damage dictates that any party that causes environmental damage may be fined and required to bear the costs of remediating that damage and to compensate the affected parties for any associated losses. It is increasingly difficult and expensive to obtain insurance to cover such issues. Consequently, companies associated with a significant environmental incident may suffer significant financial losses. These losses are then translated into reductions in the share price and the associated dividends.

Banks that lend to companies secure the loans on the basis of the physical assets of the company and often on the land upon which any investment takes place. Should the company cease to be viable, the bank assumes ownership of those assets which are then sold to cover any outstanding debts. However, should the physical assets of the company be contaminated, then the value of the assets is significantly reduced. Indeed, the banks may inherit any environmental liabilities that the liquidated company generated. Commercial lenders are therefore reluctant to lend money to any company which may develop any environmental liabilities or to secure loans on the value of an asset which may be eroded through contamination. As a result, companies which cannot demonstrate a high level of environmental performance associated with low environmental risks will find it increasingly difficult and expensive to attract and retain investment and insurance for their operations.

Media and Pressure Groups

A combination of increased public awareness of environmental issues and freedom of access to information on the environmental performance of companies will serve to magnify media and pressure group interest in the environmental performance of industry. In order to manage media and pressure group attention, companies must be able to state that they have made efforts to reduce their environmental impact. However, while it may be tempting to allow the PR or marketing departments to lead the way in convincing all stake-holders of this commitment, any shallow or spurious claims will soon be uncovered. Claims which cannot be substantiated are likely to be seized upon and will be very detrimental to a company's public image. Companies which seek to communicate responsible environmental performance must base any claims that they make to this effect on hard facts which they are willing to communicate.

Economic Development and Environmental Conflicts

A characteristic of indian civilization has been its sensitivity to natural ecosystems. vital renewable natural resources like vegetation, soil and water were managed and utilised according to well defined social norms that respected the known ecological processes. The indigenous modes of natural resources utilisation were sensitive to the limits to which these resources could be used

It is said that the codes of visiting important pilgrim centres Badrinath in the sensitive Himalayan ecosystem, included a maximum stay of one night so that the temple area would not put excess pressure on the local natural resources base. In the precolonial indigenous economic processes, the levels of utilisation of natural resources were not significant enough to result in drastic environmental problems. There were useful social norms for environmentally safe resource utilisation and people protested against the destructive use of resources even by kings. A major change in the utilisation of natural resources of India was introduced by the British who linked the resources of this country with the direct and large non-local demands of Western Europe. Natural resource utilisation by the East India Company, and later by the colonial rulers, replaced the indigenous organizations for the utilisation of natural resources, like water, forest and minerals, that were mainly managed as commons.

With the establishment of British colonial rule in India, the ever increasing resource demands of-the industrial revolution in England were largely met from colonies like India. Forced cultivation of indigo in Bengal and Bihar, cultivation of cotton in Gujarat and the Deccan led to large-scale commitment of land for the supply of raw materials for the British textile industry, the flagbearer of the industrial revolution. Forests in the sensitive mountain ecosystems like the Western Ghats or the Himalayas were felled to build battleships, or to meet the requirements of the expanding railway network.

Forests of the Bengal-Bihar-Orissa region were used for running wood fuel locomotives in the early stages of railway expansion. The latter stages of colonial resource utilisation and control included the monopolization. of water rights as in the Sambhar Lake of Rajasthan or the Damoda' Canal in Bengal. Colonial intervention in natural resource management in India led to conflicts over vital renewable natural resources like water or forests and induced new forms of poverty and deprivation. Changes in resource endowments and entitlements introduced by the British came into conflict with the local people's age old rights and practices related to natural resource utilisation As a result local responses were generated through which people tried to regain and retain control over local natural resources.

The indigo Movement in Eastern India, the Deccan Movement for land rights or the forest movement in all forest areas of the country, the Western Ghats, the Central Indian Hills or the Himalayas, were obvious expressions of protest generated by these newly created conflict's. Conflicts generated by the colonial modes of natural resource exploitation could not, however, grow with a local identity. With the progress of the anti-colonial people's movement at the national level, these local protests merged with the national struggle for independence. With the collapse of colonial rule internationally, and the emergence of sovereign independent countries in the Third World like India, resolution of these conflicts at the local level became a possibility. While political independence vested the control over natural resources with the Indian state, the colonial institutional framework for natural resource management did not change in essence. Where colonialism collapsed, the slogan of economic development stepped in. There was unfortunately no alternative institutional mechanism other than that of the classical model of development left by the British, with which the newly formed Indian state could respond to the accentuated aspirations of the Indian people for a better life.

The same institutions and concepts, nurtured and developed by the colonial rulers were applied to objectives which were exactly opposite to those of the colonial period. Concepts and categories relating to economic development and natural resource utilisation that had emerged in the specific context of capitalist growth and industrialization in the centres of colonial power were raised to the level of universal assumptions and applicability. The processes which led to deprivation were now entrusted with the responsibility of basic needs satisfaction. No serious thought was given to the fact that the historical specificity of early industrial development in Western Europe necessitated the permanent occupation of the colonies and the undermining of the local 'natural economy'.' This inexorable logic of resource exploitation, exhaustion and alienation integral to the classical model of economic development based on resource intensive technologies led Gandhi to seek an alternate path of development for India when he wrote:

God forbid that India should ever take to industrialism after the manner of the West. The economic imperialism of a single tiny island kingdom (England) is today keeping the world in chains. If an entire nation of 300 million took to similar economic exploitation, it would strip the world bare like locusts.

While Gandhi's critique was a forewarning against the problems likely to arise by following the classical path of resource-intensive development, at the time of India's independence, there was no clear and comprehensive work plan to realise the Gandhian dream of alternate development that would be resource prudent and would satisfy basic needs. The issues of resource constraints of economic development were, therefore, not highlighted at the theoretical level, partly due to the tremendous pressure of the enhanced developmental aspirations of a newly independent nation, and partly due to the lack of internalization of natural resource parameters within the framework of economics. As the scale of economic development activities escalated from one Five Year Plan to another, the disruption of ecological processes that maintain the productivity of the natural resource base started becoming increasingly apparent.

The classical model of economic development in the case of the newly independent nations resulted in the growth of urban-industrial enclaves where commodity production was concentrated, as well as rapid exhaustion of the internal colonies whose resources supported the enhanced demands of these enclaves. In the absence of ecologically enlightened resource management methods, the pressure of poverty enhanced the pace of economic development activities in the hope of a quick improvement in the standard of living for all, as in the case of Western Europe. For example, commercial forestry earned more revenue by making increasing amount of timber and pulpwood available in the market but in the process reduced the multipurpose biomass productivity or damaged the hydrology of the forests. People dependent on non-timber biomass outputs of forests like leaves, twigs, fruits, nuts, medicines and oils were unable to sustain themselves, in the face of the commercial exploitation of forests. The changed hydrological character of the forests affected both the micro-climate and the stream flows, disturbing the hydrological stability and affecting agricultural production.

There are similar examples from all parts of the country, related to almost all massive developmental interventions in India's natural resource system. Ecological degradation and economic deprivation generated by the resource insensitivity and intensity of the classical model of development have resulted in environmental conflicts, an understanding of which is imperative for the reorientation of our current development priorities and concepts. It is becoming in creasingly clear that these classical concepts and priorities are being used as an alibi to direct 'development' at the national level, while the educated minority elite is the main beneficiary of these 'development' processes.

The ecology movements that have emerged as major social movements in many parts of India are making visible many invisible externalities and pressing for their internalisation in the economic evaluation of the elite-oriented development process. In the context of a limited resource base and unlimited development aspirations, ecology movements have initiated a new political struggle for safeguarding the interests and survival of the poor, the marginalised, including women, tribals and poor peasants.

Ecology Movements and Survival

The intensity and range of ecology movements in independent india have continuously widened as predatory exploitation of natural resources to feed the process of development has increased in extent and intensity. This process has been characterised by the massive expansion of energy and resource-intensive industrial activity and major development projects like large dams, forest exploitation, mining and energy-intensive agriculture. The resource demand of development has led to the narrowing of the natural resource base for the survival of the economically poor and powerless, either by direct transfer of resources away from basic needs or by destruction of the essential ecological process that ensure renewability of the life-supportirig natural resources.

In the light of this background, ecology movements emerged as the people's response to this new threat to their survival and as a demand for the ecological conservation of vital life-support systems. The most significant life-support systems in addition to clean air are the common property resources of water, forests and land on which the majority of the poor people of India depend for survival. It is the threat to these resources that has been the focus of ecology movements in the last few decades. Among the various ecology movements in India, the Chipko movement (embrace the trees to oppose fellings) is the most well known.

It began as a movement of the hill people in the state of Uttar Pradesh to save the forest resources from exploitation by contractors from outside.' It later evolved into an ecological movement that was aimed at the maintenance of the ecological stability of the major upland watersheds in India. Spontaneous people's response to save vital forest resources was seen in Jharkhand area in Bihar-Orissa border region as well as in Bastar area of Madbya Pradesh where there were attempts to convert the mixed natural forests into plantations of commercial tree species, to the complete detriment of the tribal people.

In the southern part of India the Appiko movement, which was inspired by the success of the Chipko movement in the Himalayas, is actively involved in stopping illegal over-felling of forests and in replanting forest lands with multipurpose broad leaved tree species. In Himachal Pradesh the Chipko activists have intensified their opposition to the expansion of monoculture plantation of the commercial Chir Pine (Pinus roxburghii). In the Aravalli Hills of Rajasthan there has been a massive programme of tree planting to give employment to those hands which were hitherto engaged in felling of trees.

The exploitation of mineral resources, in particular the opencast mining in the sensitive watersheds of the Himalayas, the Western Ghats and Central India have also resulted in a great deal of environmental damage.

As a consequence, environmental movements have come up in these regions to oppose the reckless mining operations. Most successful among them is the movement against limestone quarrying in the Doon Valley. Here, volunteers of the Chipko movement have led thousands of villagers, in peaceful resistance, to oppose the reckless functioning of limestone quarries that is seen by the people as a direct threat to their economic and physical survival.'

While the Doon Valley instance has a long history of popular opposition to the quarrying of limestone and a Supreme Court order has restricted the area of quarrying to a minimum, examples of such success' of ecology movements are rare People's ecology movements against mineral exploitation in the neighbouring areas of Almora and Pithoragarh still seem to be ignored, probably due to the relative isolation of these interior areas. Beyond the Himalayas, the ecology movement in the Gandhamardan Hills in Orissa against the ecological havoc of bauxite mining has gained momentum and it draws inspiration from the Chipko movement. The mining project of the Bharat Aluminium Company (BALCO) in the Gandhamardan Hills is being opposed by local youth organisations and tribal people whose survival is directly under threat. The peaceful demonstrators have claimed that the project could be only continued 'over our dead bodies. The situation is more or less the same in large parts of Orissa-Madhya Pradesh region where rich mineral and coal deposits are being opened up for exploitation and thousands of people in these interior areas are being pushed to deprivation and destitution. This is also true of the coal mining areas around the energy capital of the country in Singrauli. In these interior areas of Central India, movements against both mining and forestry are becoming increasingly volatile and people's resistance is growing.

Large river valley projects, which are coming up in India at a very rapid pace, is another group of development projects against which people have organised ecology movements. The large-scale submersion of forest and agricultural lands, a prerequisite for the large river valley projects, always takes a heavy toll of dense forests and the best food growing lands. These have usually been the material basis for the survival of a large number of people in India, specially tribal people.

The Silent Valley project in Kerala was opposed by the ecology movement on the ground of its being a threat, not to the survival of the people directly, but to the gene pool of the Tropical Rainforests threatened by submersion. The ecological movement against the Tehri high dam in the UP Himalaya exposes the possible threat to people living both above and below the dam site through large-scale destabilization of land by seepage and strong seismic movements that could be induced by impoundment. The Tehri Dam Opposition Committee has appealed to the Supreme Court against the proposed dam by identifying it as a threat to the survival of all people living near the river Ganga up to West Bengal. Most notable among the people's movements against dams on the issue of direct threat to survival from submersion are Bedthi lcchampalli, Bhopalpatnam, Narmada Sagar, Koel-Karo, Bodhghat, etc.

In the context of the already overutilised land resources, the proper rehabilitation on a land-to-land basis of millions of people displaced through the construction of dams seems impossible. The cash compensation given instead is inadequate in all respects for providing an alternate livelihood for the majority of the displaced. Destitution is thus the first and foremost precondition for initiating large dam projects

While the process of construction of dams itself invites opposition from ecology movements, the functioning of water projects dependent on the constructed dams results in further ecological disasters and movements. People's movements against widespread water-logging, salinisation and the resulting desertification in the command areas of many dams have been registered. Among them are instances of protests against the Tawa, Kosi, Gandak, Tungabhadra, Malaprabha, Ghatprabha projects and the canal irrigated areas of Punjab and Haryana. While excess water led to ecological destruction in these cases, improper and unsustainable use of water in the arid and semi-arid regions generated ecology movements in a different way. The anti-drought and desertification movement is gaining momentum in the dry areas of Maharashtra, Karnataka, Rajasthan, Orissa, etc. Ecological water use for survival is being advocated by water based movements like Pani Chetana, Pani Panchayat, and Mukti Sangharsh. Another major movement originating from the ecological destruction of resources by growth based development is spreading all along the 7,000 km long coastline of India. It is the movement of the small fishing communities against the ecological destruction caused by mechanised fishing whose instant profit motive is destroying the coastal ecology and its long-term biological productivity in a big way.

No amount of threat to survival in India from environmental hazards can be complete without a reference to the Bhopal tragedy on 2 December 1984, in which several thousand people died and several lakhs faced serious health hazards following the leakage of poisonous Methyl Iso Cyanate from a pesticide plant of Union Carbide (India) Limited. People's movements for clean air and water are growing in ail parts of the country just as ecologically irresponsible industrialization is moving deeper into the hinterland in search of new resources.

Interactions and Intermediate Conditions

The forests described above are stereotypes that represent the ends of the range of variation. In practice, many forest types are intermediate in some respect, although their dynamics and composition can be related to the stereotypes. Some examples illustrate the range of possibilities.

- Forests in which partial stand destruction is commonplace can develop into complex mosaics of tolerant and intolerant species. An example is the *Pseudotsuga menziesii* forests of the Pacific North-west, where saplings and underwood are frequently burned but the overstorey is unaffected. Moreover, light fires tend to be patchy, burning some places but leaving other patches untouched. This allows the overstorey of *Pseudotsuga menziesii* to be infiltrated by *Abies amabilis,* which develops as patches in a mosaic with groups of younger *Pseudotsuga menziesii* in larger burned patches.
- Complex interactions can develop between disturbance regimes. For example, in the southeastern USA *Pinus* forests were maintained naturally by frequent fires. However, where stands happen to remain unburned, *Quercus* and other broadleaved species colonize, form an underwood and eventually dominate the canopy. Since the broadleaved stands are relatively fireproof they tend to remain undisturbed, thereby generating a patchwork of broadleaved and *Pinus*-dominated stands whose pattern is determined by disturbance history. This capacity for two forest types to develop on one site type is inherent

in any region where disturbance becomes less likely as succession proceeds.

- The characteristics of *Fagus sylvatica* in central Europe determines much of the forest pattern. Its capacity to coppice enables it to form distinctive low scrub woodlands with *Sorbus aucuparia* near the treeline, where wind and snow maintain a chronically disturbed environment. In this case, the *Fagus sylvatica* is effectively undisturbed. Elsewhere, in steep slopes in gorges, the stands are chronically destabilized by the fall of large trees growing on insecure rootholds, and this breaks the dominance of beech and enables a mixture of tree species to survive, including *Tilia, Ulmus* and *Fraxinus.*

Disturbances have long-term effects on forest composition. For example, drought rarely destroys stands entirely but confers an advantage on species that survive droughts. Ultimately this is expressed as a distinctive assemblage on drought-prone sites, such as outcrops and convex slopes with thin soils. In this instance, disturbance tends to generate adapted forests, which thus reduces the incidence of disturbance. Alternatively, species that depend on disturbance may both invite it and be ready to survive. The best examples are the fire-dependent *Pinus banksiana* and *Pinus contorta* forests, which are inherently inflammable, particularly those that exhibit serotiny, where long-lived cones release their seed only after fire and which falls into a seed bed free of litter and competing vegetation. A more extreme example is seen in the *Pinus mugo* of avalanche tracks, where repeated disturbance has provoked the evolution of a species that can withstand the disturbance.

The multitude of interactions between trees and disturbance regimes is expressed as different assemblages on different site types and as a range of successional states on each site type. Disturbance should be seen as an integral component of the forest type, not an external destructive force. Collectively, disturbances enhance regional diversity by creating distinctive forest types, maintaining a range of successional states, and by enhancing the amount of edge in the landscape.

Influence of People

The relationships described so far have dealt with natural conditions. In practice, most forest types are overwhelmingly influenced by people:

- Secondary successions to forest on land previously cleared are a response to severe disturbance, *i.e.* the complete loss of tree cover and the alternative use of land for cultivation or pasture. Pioneer trees are almost always intolerants. The pattern of secondary succession depends on seed sources, so that colonization may be extremely patchy. Colonization often takes place in waves, for example when initial colonization by wind-dispersed trees is followed by bird-dispersed trees once perches have been created.

- Coppice systems enable shrubs and intolerant trees to form a higher proportion of a stand than they would naturally maintain. Despite the constant disturbance of felling, individual trees can sprout again indefinitely and thus live well beyond their natural span. In terms of individuals and small-scale patterns, coppices are probably more stable than the natural forests from which they were derived.
- In woodland pastures, regeneration is inhibited by grazing and browsing, although established individuals have little competition and can expand to great sizes. Moreover, the constant lopping of branches for fuel and fodder, followed by regrowth from the pollard, enables individual trees to grow to great ages. Here, too, the effect of management disturbance is to generate unnaturally high stability.

Finally, there is the problem of *Quercus petraea* and *Quercus robur* in Europe. These are long-lived intolerant species that have been abundant in the pollen rain over very long periods, which implies that the forests were considerably disturbed, albeit at long intervals.

They have been maintained at unnaturally high levels by traditional management, which favoured them as timber trees in coppices and wood-pastures.

Under natural conditions it is possible that oaks were maintained by the high level of browsing and grazing imposed by populations of large herbivores, such as deer, horses and cattle. In fact, it has been proposed that natural forest was more like savannah before prehistoric hunters reduced and domesticated the larger herbivores.

However, this seems far from proven, although the possibility remains that herbivore populations maintained a controlling presence on the structure and composition of some types of temperate forest, particularly perhaps those on wet ground and heavy fertile soils (where ground vegetation would be vigorous) and steep dry slopes (where tree growth might be poor).

Forest Micro-Environmental Gradients

Canopy microclimate is ultimately determined by the stand macroclimate; the rhytms of change above and within the forest are set by the cycles of annual and diurnal heating and by the movements of air masses and clouds.

Very short term events (time scale of less than a minute) are important in exchange process and ventilation of canopy layers. Some environmental variables are influenced by broadscale canopy features (wind), whereas others (light) are depended on the local arrangements of elements.

The vertical pattern of microenvironmental conditions within forests is important because it influences the distribution of forest biota, behaviour of vertebrates, the development and growth of tree structures, amount of gas exchange and water release by forest leaves, infection potential for numerous tree parasites, invasiveness of lianas into tree crowns, growth and productivity of epiphytes, biological activity levels of microbes, and numerous other aspects of ecosystem function.

The forest influences microclimate, and microclimate influences how and where the forest will grow, so that the interaction of the two results in measured patterns in a dynamic state.

The three-dimensional microenvironment (light, humidity, temperature, and wind) of forests is spatially heterogeneous based on composition and structure of the forest. Wind, for example, has higher peaks in the upper canopy, than down near the forest floor. In general, wind is rapidly decelerated in the layer just above the forest The velocity profile in this layer is commonly described as though the wind were reacting to a rough surface displaced above the ground by a distance d.

This is equivalent to the mean height of the momentum absorption, with a gradient controlled by the roughness of the surface. Both the roughness and the displacement height of canopies depend on the amount and distribution of canopy material, and also on wind speed itself.

Estimates are often based on the canopy height. In some stands, wind speeds do not decline monotonically with depth, but have a secondary max in the lowermost canopy levels. This is seen in stands of simple structure that lack vegetation layers at the bottom, or at forest boundaries, where winds may blow through for distances equal to several canopy heights.

The canopy acts as a filter of high frequency gusts, arresting small-scale fluctuations, but permitting the penetration of large eddies. The depth to which eddys penetrate depends on canopy density, strength of the eddy, stability of the canopy air column. Much of the total transport occurs during a small fraction of the time. Periods of relative quiescence are punctuated with gusts that can penetrate deeply. With high-frequency sensors, rapid vertical motions and temperature deviations may be observed almost simultaneously at several canopy levels.

Trace gases and particle concentrations have relatively weak gradients within the canopy, but mean concentrations are typically lower in the understory than in the overstory. For CO_2, however, the active layer of the canopy is an enormous sink, and CO_2 concentrations are often slightly depressed in the overstory during the daytime. The ground is a source due to root and soil respiration and decomposition. A pronounced co2 max develops in the understory late at night, especially under stable conditions.

Light is perhaps the most influential and complex of all canopy microclimatic variables. Most microenvironmental factors correlate with light intensity. Therefore, the effect of microclimate on plant physiology and growth as well as on animal behaviour and occurrence is difficult to separate from that of light alone.

This makes light a suitable universal indicator for just about every aspect of forest canopy ecology, but it is very difficult to measure in three-dimensional space. Parker proposed a vertical subdivision of canopies into three zones based on the patterns of the mean and variance of vertical light transmittance; bright, transition, and dim.

The bright zone (upper canopy) is characterized by high transmittance and low variability, the transition zone (mid canopy) is where transmittance is most variable and the mean changes rapidly with height, while the dim zone (lower canopy) is characterized by low transmittance and variability.

Based on work by Parker an age class sequence of Douglas-fir forests near the WRCCRF, the bright zone is wide and dim zone narrow in older stands due to the vertical differentiation of the canopy with age.

Younger forests have a narrow bright zone and wide dim zone. Canopy soils are a particularly interesting habitat due to their patchy spatial distribution and vertical organization. Soils develop where there is a perch that allows the accumulation of litter, such as under and around epiphytes, on large branches, and in branch crotches.

DOM is especially interesting because it can capture incoming nutrients bystoring them on the negatively charged sites, lots of recalcitrant nutrients,and support of invertebrates, and its ability to store water for a long time.

Several studies have examined differences between canopy and forest floor soil - In Monteverde, compared nutrients and pH. Also studied differences in soil temperature and soil moisture soil temp. Not much difference for temperature, but striking idfferences for moisture. Severe drydowns occur in the forest canopy, not the soil. This could have a role in determining the composition and abundance of vertical gradient.

The Vertical Gradient as a Defining Feature of Biotic Communities

The vertical gradient is a defining feature of forests because increasing height causes structure and microclimate to be more obviously vertically organized. Height of the canopy and tree size are defining characteristics of forests yet smaller stature vegetation types all exhibit vertical patterns. The vertical plane is a simple and convenient way to visualize and organize concepts.

POLITICAL ECONOMY OF FOREST MANAGEMENT

TRADITIONAL FOREST MANAGEMENT PRACTICES

Historically, forest ownership in most South Asian countries (Bangladesh, India, Nepal, Pakistan, and Sri Lanka) was mainly communal, and the forests were generally managed by indigenous customary practices that varied from region to region. For example, in Pakistan, decisions related to access to resources and sharing of benefits and responsibilities were deeply rooted in sociocultural mechanisms such as customary practices (*riwaj*) and the council of tribal elders (*jirga*) system.

Forest ownership in most of the regions was held by the concerned landowners. Others in the community, including non-owners and the landless, held some privileges. They held free access to the forests of the concerned village for livestock grazing, cutting timber and collecting firewood for household purposes, cutting grass and lopping of trees for feeding cattle, and collecting minor forest products, such as mushrooms, honey, and medicinal plants.

The owners rarely interfered with the exercise of these rights. The local forest dwellers lived in harmony with the natural environment. Relatively small populations and the subsistence economy put limited pressure on the natural forests.

Institutional Changes—Toward a Participatory Approach

In the last several decades, decentralized and participatory or joint forest management have become major policy trends in the forestry sector of many South and Southeast Asian countries, including Bangladesh, India, Indonesia, Nepal, and Vietnam. In the forest-rich mountain areas of Pakistan, several participatory forest management programmes and projects have been implemented since the 1980s. Although most of the interventions were on a pilot scale, they opened the doors for institutional change on a larger scale. The process of institutional change in the forestry sector was initiated in 1996 by the Forestry Sector Project (FSP) in the NWFP, funded by the Asian Development Bank. The FSP, together with the Institutional Transformation Cell, a joint Dutch–Swiss-assisted project, devised a setup to improve decision making and participatory ownership of the institutional reforms in the forest department of the NWFP, making use of existing experiences and proposals generated by other projects.

The project commenced under a loan agreement between the Asian Development Bank and the government of Pakistan. The Dutch government, the German federally owned development company GTZ (Deutsche Gesellschaft für Technische Zusammenarbeit), and the Swiss Agency for Development and Cooperation also contributed to the project. It aims to protect and improve the hilly and mountainous environment of the NWFP.

Doing so would raise the productivity of private, community, and government lands that are suitable for trees, fodder, and other crops through active participation of beneficiaries in the design, planning, and execution of project-related activities. This project brought major reforms to the provincial forest department based on these principles and objectives:

- Institutionalization of the participatory forestry approach in the department

- Social organization and capacity building of local communities' organizations
- Creation of specialized management and enforcement units in important areas
- Increasing coordination, cooperation, and promotion of team-based management in the department
- Decentralization of planning and authority
- Redefining and reorienting the role of the forest department toward advisory functions
- Addressing gender concerns in the department
- Improving the training and education system of the department

These reforms provided considerable space for village-level institutions and joint forest management committees (JFMCs) to manage forest resources at the village level. The improvement of village infrastructure was also an objective of the FSP, in addition to the core objective of forest management. Within the provincial forest department, a new structure was developed to decentralize planning and authority (*i.e.*, by backstopping the JFMCs) and to increase coordination and cooperation within the department, thus enabling the department to actually implement the new participatory forestry approach.

A positive outcome of the participatory approach was the increase in awareness among the residents regarding forest protection, as indicated by the significant difference in the responses of residents of the project villages (*i.e.*, those villages where FSP had interventions and joint forest management was in practice) versus those in nonproject villages (no interventions by the FSP). A 5-point Likert scale was used to record perceptions of the respondents regarding the change of forest cover and illegal cutting (by the concerned villagers and outsiders) during the last five years. The Likert scale (5 = increased, 1 = decreased) is shown in table.

	Village	**N**	**Mean**	**t-test T**
Change in forest cover	Project	200	2.22	
	Nonproject	200	1.66	
	Both	400	1.94	7.081
Illegal cutting (by outsiders)	Project	200	2.65	
	Nonproject	200	3.66	
	Both	400	3.16	–10.09
Illegal cutting (by villagers)	Project	200	2.97	
	Nonproject	200	3.97	
	Both	400	3.47	–10.48

The data in the table reveal that, although forest cover decreased in both the project and nonproject cases, the rate of forest depletion was significantly higher in the nonproject villages. Illegal cutting by outsiders of the project villages decreased, whereas it increased significantly in the nonproject villages. Similarly, illegal cutting by the villagers concerned increased in the nonproject villages, while it decreased in the project villages.

These trends indicate the positive impact of participatory forest management. One of the reasons for this progress can be traced to the joint forest management process, in which the forest department used participatory rural appraisal tools, such as transect walks and group meetings, to inform local people of the forest's importance to their livelihoods and to future generations.

The negative consequences of forest degradation were also highlighted. For the majority of participants, such meetings were the first of their kind, and they understood that they would benefit from organized forest protection. In most cases, the JFMCs imposed fines on the transgressors, and the JFMC members themselves guarded the forests.

Colonial and Post-Colonial Forest Management Strategies

In South Asia, including in Pakistan, the forest management paradigms have been heavily influenced by the British colonial administration. After 1850, when the British came to rule this part of the globe, forest management became a centralized state function. The Indian Forest Act of 1878 brought the major part of the forests under government control and, as such, nationalized one-fifth of India's land area, while giving limited rights to the local people. Local people, who had once enjoyed customary rights over forest resources, were resentful. Although communities were granted some rights in 1923, and a new Forest Act was promulgated in 1927, local residents could no longer exercise their customary rights with the same freedom. In the case of reserved forests, for example, they could no longer cut trees, and they had to seek permission from the state authorities for subsistence and other access to protected forests.

Most of the forest policies and land regulations that were promulgated in colonial South Asia during the 19th century were retained by newly independent nations of the region. Pakistan was no exception. In 1947, at the time of independence, the policies, regulations, and hierarchies that administered the new nation's forests were largely left intact. The Indian Forest Act of 1927, which became the Pakistan Forest Act of 1927, introduced punitive sanctions against transgressors. The top-down, colonial approach of governance was also reflected in most of the national forest policies announced from time to time. Such nonparticipatory approaches failed to stop forest depletion, and Pakistan's deforestation rate became one of the highest in the world.

The policing efforts of the state forest department have hardly ever succeeded in protecting the forests; rather they have earned mistrust and provoked confrontation with local forest dwellers. This forced development practitioners, donors, and policymakers to push for a paradigm change, toward community participation.

2

Pricing Theory and the Financial Values of the Forest

In economic theory, the price of an item can represent one of three circumstances for the owner.

- The price could reflect the value of the item to the owner.
- The price could value the item at a level greater than the owner's subjective valuation. In this case the owner is likely to sell the item.
- Alternatively, the price of the item may be less than the value to the owner in which case the owner will refuse to sell.

The price of wood must also reflect the different type of values generated by the wood and the portion of forest which is altered by its extraction.

Hence, if the 'public citizen' 2 offers a logging coupe for sale, by definition the value anticipated from the sale must at least exceed the value expected from any alternative use. And additionally, the price needs to equal:

- The costs of the production of wood;
- Plus a return on the capital invested, with sufficient reward to cover the risk; and
- Total compensation for all non financial values (NFV's) lost in the process of an extraction of the timber.

This pricing method ensures that timber with values exceeding the market price will not be sold. However, the significance of NFV's is that they make up a considerable proportion of the value of timber. When NFV's are destroyed, the loss of value is not felt by one person alone, but is likely to be felt by every Australian citizen, every international citizen and everyone yet to be born. When logging occurs, each of these people experiences a change in the value they derive from the forest, and hence each should be compensated. The price of timber needs to be able to compensate all losers if policy is to be socially optimal. The pricing of timber is crucial to determining the pattern of logging in the forest. In order to implement a solution, the present approach of forestry commissions uses regulation to separate logging areas from non logging areas. This approach could be assuming one of two things. Firstly, it could be assuming that royalties are sufficient compensation for the loss of NFV's 3. In this case, it remains to be demonstrated by those who set royalty levels that they have evaluated the worth of the lost NFV's, and thus set royalty levels accordingly. In the absence of information about how NFV's are determined, it could be assumed that non financial values in the logged areas are considered insignificant to the extent that the Australian community will not require compensation for the losses in NFV's which result. In theory, logging will then occur, in the areas set aside, if the cost of production and capital makes it a financially rational exercise.

Pricing policy is, thus, conducted on a 'compartmentalised basis'. In other words the forest is surveyed for its values, and those areas where NFV's are deemed 'small enough' to avoid the need for compensation, are made available for logging. The remainder is put aside for conservation. Thus, if we use a 'compartmentalised' approach, timber is valued in a two stage process. The forest is allocated to different uses depending on the scale of NFV's in different areas. Forest that is to be subject to logging is then priced on a commercial basis. Pricing takes place on the assumption that the coupes have already been surveyed, and the NFV's have been found to be minor; ie very close to zero.

The worth of the royalties, of course, must also cover the costs of wood production, the return on capital required, and the financial opportunity cost of foregone uses. The Victorian Auditor General's report (1993) indicated the likelihood that the forestry operations in Victoria were making low profits (if any at all). Given that royalties must cover operating, capital and opportunity costs, this leaves very little room to compensate for lost NFV's. In such a circumstance, it is feasible that NFV's are being valued at a worth very close to zero. No evidence was identified to justify such a valuation.

PRICES OF FOREST TIMBER

Pricing of logs should, however, be offered on a normal commercial basis. It is fairly clear from the reports that have been reviewed that operations are not presently proceeding on a commercial basis.

Prices of forest timber are being distorted by a range of factors that are, in general terms providing a subsidy to the logging of native timber, whilst other factors are raising the costs of private plantations. Other factors such as the lack of rational markets for the pricing of water and other services, partly or wholly derived from forests, are raising the relative cost of alternative financial values.

The following distortions in commercial pricing of timber have been identified. The list has been 'cobbled' together from all the reports reviewed in this survey.

1. The lack of marginal cost pricing.
2. The non-existence of effective commercial accounting systems.

3. Long-distance transport subsidies.
4. Non-payment of rental for use of public land.
5. Low royalties; ie. low log prices for timber
6. Possible cross-subsidisation from community service obligations.
7. No liability for payment of a resource rental tax.
8. No liability for payment of a notional income tax (presumably meaning company tax).
9. No liability for local government rates.
10. No liability for sales tax on vehicles, plant and equipment.
11. Non, or low, payments of interest on borrowed capital.
12. Non-payment of dividends.
13. Low user charges for cost recovery from long-distance transport
14. The lack of commercial discipline due to lack of a corporatised commercial structure;
15. Serious deficiencies in the tax system for plantations;
16. Problems with planning, rating and exporting from plantations;
17. Problems with the small numbers of buyers and sellers of timber;
18. Problems with the purchaser behaviour of large buyers of timber;
19. The dominant market role of state forestry agencies;
20. Failure to properly account for non-financial values in pre-logging operations either by exclusion of areas or by forestry codes of practice.
21. Failure to adequately assess the potential financial contribution from sales of goods and services such as water from the native forest.
22. Failure to separate commercial operations from regulatory functions.

They also felt that the market price was too low and that international prices were not as significant in pricing native forest timber as was considered by the Commission. They felt that the native forest timber price should be raised to 'the point of indifference.' (?) and that the case for doing so was 'overwhelming'. This is even more significant when it is considered that 'the Forestry Commission sets these prices...the Commission is clearly a price leader.'

Inadequacies in Assessment Frameworks

The existing assessment framework is in a period of transition. The post-1945 charter of the forest agencies to push for economic development has changed. The capital resources of government and the Australian economy are scarce and need to be deployed for maximum financial benefit or for some clearly identified social 'good'.

Changes in social values are also placing pressure on the old system. These two forces, in combination, are leading to greater scrutiny of forest activities, and demanding greater levels of accountability. It is clear that assessment processes are lagging in their response to these issues.

Entrepreneurial Capture

The existing assessment process is vulnerable to 'capture' by entrepreneurs proposing one-o ff developments. This limits government ability to consider a range of project options as proposed by the OECD (1986) and the World Bank (1992) in particular. The existing Australian approach of having a single project option placed in front of decision-makers must be regarded as inferior, if not a structural distortion of the decision-making process.

Lack of Commercially based Accounting of Projects

The lack of commercially-based accounting data for project analysis means that it is not possible to accurately evaluate true project financial worth. This means that many unprofitable activities are slipping through the policy net adding to the economic burden already being borne by Australians. The effect of such methods is to inflate the relative worth of financial values vis a vis non-financial values. It also inflates the relative values of forestry operations vis a vis the alternative activities such as plantations and water production.

NFV's are not being Assessed

The most serious flaw is that it appears that assessment of non-financial values is simply not occurring. The concentration of reports on discussing aspects of how such analysis could be done, rather than a focus on how it is being done leads to the conclusion that serious analysis of the relative worth of non-financial values is yet to begin. It would seem fair comment that if relatively simple choices between wood and water production are not being evaluated, then other more complex interactions are also being neglected.

Lack of a Comprehensive set of Values Descriptions

The next major flaw in assessment processes is the lack of a complete set of values relating to forestry. Each report examined has mentioned a range of words that seek to describe, in particular, the non-financial values, but there has not been a report which systematically listed what society derives from the forest. It is little wonder then that assessment frameworks barely exist or function if the values are not even identified.

Lack of Focus on the Full Suite of Values

Where non-financial values are considered, they tend to relate only to the assessment of physical characteristics of the forests. All reports acknowledge the need to protect these physical characteristics, for example 'sustainable yield', yet there is evidence that they are not being protected, even at this rudimentary level (. If physical characteristics are only barely being protected, then it is reasonable to assume that other more abstract and intangible values of the forest are not being taken into account. The Dorrigo Management Area Environmental

Impact Statement does not mention any non-financial values other than soil, birds, animals and recreation. Ecological sustainability and existence values are barely considered at all.

Public Involvement: Preached by Some but not Practised

The practice of assessment seems to place too little stress on the need to obtain public review and input into forestry decisions. In an area where clashes over values are common, the need for representation by different values should be considered. As a result the political process is starved of information about social preferences. The OECD (1986) reveals a considerable commitment to public involvement, in particular their example of the 'Inner Valley Road Project'.

Future Generations Considered by Implication Only

The OECD (1986) report was not without its flaws. Its assessment framework gave little attention to considering the impact of future generations from any valuation assessment process. In economic theory it is impossible to internalise the interests of future generations simply by assessing the preferences of the present generation. Neither market processes or valuation techniques, in the face of irreversibility, are capable of 'looking after' the interest of future generations in any manner that can be relied upon. Fortunately the concept of ecological sustainability goes some way to achieving this goal. The internalisation of the interests of future generations requires explicit discussion.

Most reports steered clear of identifying procedures that would resolve the choices thrown up in the forestry debate. The RAC report (1992) went furthest in this regard but tended to educate by demonstration rather than explicit prescription. The ESD report (1991) had some brief comments, but if the assessment of these different values is to proceed satisfactorily, it is clear that the hard issue of 'assessment frameworks' must be dealt with honestly.

DIRECT EVALUATIONS OF NON-FINANCIAL VALUES

The OECD indicated that other nations are moving towards direct evaluations of non-financial values. Australia's approach would appear to be somewhat slower than average, though of course there are some institutions such as the World Bank that have acknowledged the need for change but are yet to make the practical changes that are required.

It was significant that the United States was acknowledged as having greater experience in the area of non-monetary evaluation. The experience was deemed to be due to the 1969 Environmental Policy Act which required quantification in non-monetary terms of all environmental impacts. The OECD concluded that it would seem that education and more valuation projects are a prerequisite for more effective utilisation of the techniques. A learning process is needed.. Valuation techniques, whether monetary or non-monetary, form the backbone of an assessment framework. The same learning process is required for assessment processes as well. Many OECD countries are learning but Australia does not appear to have started.

Assessing the Assessment Frameworks

A major difficulty with evaluating an assessment framework is the sheer scale of the task itself, as anyone who has read an Environmental Impact Statement will testify. The result is a tendency to focus on one or two key angles to the exclusion of other angles. To provide a systematic 'framework' for assessing assessment frameworks. A series of questions is provided, that an assessment framework, if it is to be successful, should be able to address. The existing Australian and international assessment practices are evaluated has been tested on actual reports, in this case the Victorian Auditor General's report as well as an analysis of the Dorrigo Management Area Environmental Impact Statement.

The native forest is capable of producing three major categories of values. These are:

- Financial values from timber production;
- Alternative financial values from other forms of forest use; and
- Non-financial values.

This report has sought to examine the issue of giving each type of value 'full and due consideration' in policy processes. Three themes have recurred throughout this study.

- There is a theme focusing on the analysis of technical comparisons between different values. That is the use and abuse of various techniques that quantify values.

The native forest is capable of producing three major categories of values. These are:

- Financial values from timber production;
- Alternative financial values from other forms of forest use; and
- Non-financial values.

This report has sought to examine the issue of giving each type of value 'full and due consideration' in policy processes. Three themes have recurred throughout this study.

- There is a theme focusing on the analysis of technical comparisons between different values. That is the use and abuse of various techniques that quantify values.
- Asecond theme revolves around the nature of the institutional arrangements that ensure value selection which is socially optimal.
- The major theme, however, is achieving a level playing field between the major types of values derived from the forest.

The emphasis on achieving a level playing field is in the spirit of the microeconomic reform process that has taken place over recent years, and continues with recent reports such as the Hilmer Inquiry. Sims described microeconomic reform as occurring when changes are made to achieve more output from a given level of inputs.. The output from the forests is intended to maximise the social welfare of the community. For this reason, microeconomic reform in the forest sector must seek to arrange the three sets of values above so that welfare is maximised.

NEED FOR MICRO-ECONOMIC REFORM

The implication of the need for micro-economic reform is that the sector is not making an optimal contribution to the quality of Australian life. This review of reports on the forest sector suggest that there is considerable potential for microeconomic reform in two dimensions.

- In broad social terms it would appear that the community is not maximising the social benefit from the forest resource.
- Secondly, within the social benefit the community receives, the financial value to be had from the forest resource is not being maximised, assuming that all other types of values remain unchanged (ceteris paribus 'All other things being equal.').

If the microeconomic reform process (optimising social benefits) in the forest sector is to succeed, the estimation of the worth of the three categories of value described above must be accurate. It would appear that estimation of these three categories of value is presently inaccurate. This inaccuracy would confound any attempt to derive optimal social benefits.

APPRAISING THE VALUES OF THE FOREST

On forests for their views on the appraisal of forest values. Each report was reviewed in order to gain an understanding of the value assessment problems in the forest sector. The reports were examined on the basis of four criteria:

- Identification of externalities.
- Identification of valuation methodologies.
- Identification of pricing/financial valuation practices.
- Identification of likely assessment frame works.

Problems in the Identification of Externalities

A representative example, of the values identified, is listed below. These values were derived from the Resource Assessment Commission (RAC) study. This study, amongst those examined, was the most comprehensive and thorough in its treatment of the issues. The weaknesses in its study were repeated, and magnified, in other studies.

Assessment Commission Inquiry into Forest and Timber

Conservation; wilderness; recreation; Financial values such as wood, tourism and water supply, oils, seeds, tannins, medicinal plants, sandalwood, bark products, fishing, hunting, wild foods, infrastructure corridors; Information via education, research; intrinsic values like aesthetic (different from visual), heritage, spiritual, biocentric, wilderness, lifestyle; Utilitarian values; 'pristinity'; landscape; scenic quality, public sensitivity, industry value by implication; existence values, option values, vicarious use values, bequest values, ecological sustainability, ethical values.

The main weaknesses in assessing the manner in which values had been surveyed were that:

- Values were not identified or listed in a systematic or comprehensive manner. The above extract from the RAC report was amongst the most comprehensive, but even so, lacked a systematic listing of values.
- Different value categories often overlapped. For example, ecological sustainability was repeatedly confused with 'environmental amenity'.
- There was also repeated confusion over the values we impute to an object, and the values we derive from that object as a result of our preferences. For instance, a forest site may have great scientific value, but not be of great aesthetic value. Conversely, a forest site may have limited scientific value, but great aesthetic value. In the latter case, a purely scientific view point would not reveal the aesthetic importance of the site. Similarly, there are other values-for example existence value-held subjectively by the public with respect to native forests. A study which evaluated objective characteristics only would not pick up the subjectively felt values. We have identified this as the 'object subject' tension.

Confusion over the type and source of 'values' will undermine the efforts to assess all values. It is therefore necessary to have an agreed list of all values, comprehensively and systematically ordered, in order to achieve the goal of optimising benefits to the community. The twentynine uses identified each provide seven different types of value which give their total worth. For example, use D 11 (craft industries) provides D 11.1 (direct use value), D 11.2 (option value), D 11.3 (quasi-option value), D 11.4 (existence value-sometimes known as industry value), D 11.5 (intrinsic value), D 11.6 (combination value) and D 11.7 (bequest value). Each of these seven components combines to give the total value provided by craft industries. In turn, the 'use' known as 'craft industries' can be combined with a package of other uses that will generate the total economic value of the forest.

While within a particular use, different components can be combined to provide a total value for that use-this does not imply that the relationships between each component are necessarily positive. They may in fact be inverse for a range of values. Similarly, the relationships between different uses can be positive, negative or zero-even though total economic value is additive of the components.

Identifying Suggested Valuation Techniques

Each report suggested, implicitly or explicitly, a range of valuation techniques for providing an 'objective' assessment of the values identified. Overall, the lack of comprehensive identification of values, common to all thirteen reports, subsequently inhibited the matching of valuation techniques to appropriate categories of value. This complicated the process of value assessment since it provided limited guidance about how various values should be measured.

On the positive side however, the Resource Assessment Commission report did provide an assessment of each evaluation technique, which marks a very useful first step towards providing a listing of techniques relevant to the assessment of each value. The Organisation for Economic Co-operation and Development references (OECD, 1986; 1992) also made a worthwhile contribution towards evaluating techniques.

In general, the reports provided only limited advice on the means by which different types of values should be evaluated. Moreover, with the exception of the RAC and the OECD reports, the techniques put forward were generally insufficient to measure the full range of values derived from the forest. For example, the reports would discuss techniques for measuring the scientific values of the forest, with out discussing other measures that evaluate the 'worth' of the non-scientific values.

Whilst some discussion of uncertainty was entered into by four reports, the issue was not raised sufficiently to provide guidance on how valuation techniques were to account for uncertainty. What is required is a more explicit discussion on the means by which 'uncertainty' should be handled in valuation processes.

The valuation techniques that were identified. While there will be some debate about whether these are all 'techniques' or 'management strategies', it is clear that the implementation of these processes leads to the de facto valuation of forests. For the purposes of this report, we have described them all as valuation techniques. Some of the techniques identified below were implicit in the various reports rather than explicitly described.

THE ASSESSMENT FRAMEWORK AND FOREST POLICY

Reviewing the various reports on the issue of forest policy has provided an insight into the process by which decisions are made. To summarise the inadequacies that have been identified in the respective assessment frameworks and processes.

Assessment Frameworks and Processes

There are several assessment frameworks used in Australia for forest decision-making. Most of the reports have only considered assessment frameworks in general terms, without specific reference to real examples. In order to evaluate these assessment frameworks, the report provides a 'checklist'. The 'checklist' provides a comprehensive series of questions which any worthwhile assessment framework should be able to answer. The 'checklist' approach facilitates identification of the broad strengths and weaknesses of existing or proposed assessment frameworks

A common theme in all reports (both Australian and international) was an underlying philosophical assumption that a 'technical', non-political choice process was possible, and to some extent desirable. This process was not challenged explicitly in any report, despite the obvious claim that the political arena is the desired place for settling value disputes (indeed it could be argued that this is the raison d'etre of politics). For the moment, however, this discussion accepts the premise that a 'technical' or 'black box' approach is feasible for value choices. So as to gain an understanding of international experience, the report has sought to review processes suggested by the OECD and the World Bank. These internationally-recommended approaches provide a benchmark for achieving 'world best practice' in this field. The report has also examined the type of system deployed by New Zealand under the auspices of the Resource Management Act.

The international reports reflect a worldwide concern over the assessment of environmental values. While it is now recognised that environmental values must be incorporated, it is not known how this should be achieved. The World Bank view is not unusual:

Externalities are thus clearly troublesome, and there is no altogether satisfactory way to deal with them. This is no reason simply to ignore them, however; an attempt should always be made to identify them and, if they appear significant, to measure them. This accurate, but unhelpful commentary is largely due to a neglect of environmental factors within economic analysis. This was noted by two internationally renowned economists in 1988, with respect to the field of development economics:

Environmental resources appear in this literature about as frequently as rain falls on the Sahara. They also noted, as recently as 1988, that one of the world's best known texts on development economics... simply has no discussion of environmental resources and their possible bearing on the development processes.'

This is symptomatic of neglect within the broad field of economic analysis. The OECD (1992) remarked that conventional cost benefit analysis would not include a number of environmental effects ...because of the lack of market price data or easily accessible direct proxy price data.'

Given this neglect the OECD report (1986) on the public management of forests, must be regarded as a landmark publication amongst the reports reviewed in this study. Overall, given that all economic activity centres on the idea of 'development', the general lack of incorporation of environmental issues is a serious omission. As a result the weaknesses identified in Australian assessment processes are not unusual when compared with 'world best practice'-though this does not make such deficiencies acceptable according to economic theory. Neo-classical economic theory would state quite clearly that on a worldwide basis, as well as locally, such an omission must be regarded as a threat to the economic well-being of society.

Existing Assessment Frameworks

Australia, with its federal political structure, has many different means by which choices over values are made. Rather than describe this diverse array of assessment frameworks, this book will provide a thumbnail sketch of the key features of assessment frameworks and processes. Along with the international examples cited, seem to point to three key characteristics of concern in any assessment: 'Who makes the decisions' is significant because it determines whose values are brought to the process. The economics profession has long argued that institutions tend to be captured by the values of specific groups, and that to expect any public institution to be value-free and working purely in the public interest is naive. From the perspective of assessment processes, it is important that advocates of differing values are given an equal voice in the process of analysis and decision-making.

The RAC Forest and Timber Inquiry report took some interest in the Victorian model which involved the Land Conservation Council in decisions about selection of forest logging coupes. The AHC-CALM model of joint survey work also received some favourable attention, though its joint deliberations were designed to identify values rather than make decisions. That no other systems were singled out for favourable comment, in the various reports reviewed in this study, seems to indicate that other processes may be lacking an adequate contribution from representatives of other values.

It is not unfeasible that an appropriately structured institutional process could make optimising decisions-given that the right information on values was available. The information provided, as outlined by the thirteen reports reviewed in this process, is inadequate for the task of making choices over values. The AHC-CALM model received some favourable comments for its process from the ESD and RAC reports Certainly, its assessment method is systematic and thorough. Its prime weakness is that it does not consider, in its own words, 'social values'. 'Social values' as defined by the AHC, appear to cover that group of values described by economists as existence value. As a result, it only acknowledges some of the values considered important in a total economic assessment. That it was commended as a model for others suggests that even analysis of 'non-social' values is deficient in existing assessment frameworks and processes.

Other reports such as the Victorian Auditor-General's report and the NSW Public Accounts Committee confirm the impression that only poor data is available on values.

Financial values are also a significant part of the analysis. A significant range of reports located deficiencies or made recommendations that pointed to opportunities to improve the gathering of financial data. The deficiencies in this regard extended to the data on both financial values generated by forestry and financial values generated by other activities. The existing assessment framework and processes were not being supplied with the relevant data because the necessary mechanisms such as appropriate accounting systems are not adequate.

Compare Different Values

Assessment frameworks must make choices between values. Few technical models were offered on how such choices should be made,outside the political process. The Victorian Auditor-General's report noted that the previous system in that State had used a committee of relevant officials, backed up by a requirement to find options, with a final 'safety valve' being provided by there being recourse to the Minister. No doubt similar methods are used elsewhere, though, what is required is a method that considers all values at the point of decision with appropriate systemic checks and balances.

The AHC-CALM model and the process offered by the RAC Forest and Timber inquiry were the closest Australian examples of technical approaches which are beginning to seek full consideration of all values. The OECD (1986) report is a benchmark in this field. Only the process implied in the RAC report comes close to this analysis. It is assumed that if there were another system, the RAC inquiry would have located it. The existing assessment frameworks, obviously, can be said to rely on the judgements of those who take the decisions and the information that they have been supplied with. There must be serious doubts that these existing frameworks have been properly structured. A assessment framework and process needs to specify who decides, with what value information and by what intervalue comparative techniques.

Inadequacies in Pricing/financial Valuation

The significance of non-financial values to the calculation of financial values is considerable. The forest agencies and all the reports reviewed in this study have adopted a compartmentalised approach to pricing. The compartmentalised approach assumes that assessment of choices between values occurred prior to the pricing of timber. If non-financial values are improperly assessed, then the resulting effect is that financial values will also be inappropriately founded. In this sense a compartmentalised approach to pricing is a practical manner of settling commercial pricing issues. In simple terms, if non-financial values are being compromised it is due to the lack of adequate assessment prior to the commercial pricing process.

THE THEORY OF TOTAL ECONOMIC VALUE

In any public decision over the net benefits of forests, externalities and public commodities, along with project and alternative financial values, need to be taken into account, as part of the value provided by a 'resource'. In analysing different resource options, a total listing and weighting of values, both private and 'externalised', must be provided for each option. When an economist is comparing alternative social arrangements, the proper procedure is to compare the total social product yielded by these different arrangements... In devising and choosing between social arrangements we should have regard to the total effect. This, above all, is the change in approach which I am advocating.

Coase refers to 'total social product' which we have renamed 'total economic value' in the tradition established by Pearce (1989). In order to compare the total economic value of differing policy options, it is necessary to aggregate for each option all the values (financial, aesthetic, spiritual, etc.) that would be produced for the community if a particular policy option were to be undertaken.

TRADITIONAL PROJECT EVALUATION

Traditional project evaluation normally compares one option against another option, and chooses that which has the most value. In the presence of market imperfections such as externalities, the total economic value (the project's total costs and benefits to society) can be severely miscalculated in at least two ways. First, proper economic evaluation needs to consider the financial impact that one project may have on other parties, not simply whether it is profitable when considered in isolation. Suppose, for example, that the government is requested to give its approval for the establishment of a factory on a river bank. Viewed in isolation, the proposal is attractive: it is expected to provide jobs for 100 local unemployed young people and will contribute an extra $5 million to tax revenues. Viewed from a wider perspective, however, the project's net financial value would be seen to be negative if the poisonous effluent it emits cause the bankruptcy of downstream fish farms and tourist resorts which together generate 200 jobs and $10 million in tax revenues. These 'down stream' financial values are often overlooked by traditional project evaluation methodologies.

The second weakness of the traditional evaluation approach is that it gives little consideration to non financial values. To continue with the illustrative example above, the factory's pollution may poison wildlife and household pets, ruin a picnic spot favoured by thousands of local residents, etc. These types of costs are real and relevant, notwithstanding the fact that they are of a 'non financial' nature. Resolving the first problem is easier, since it may be possible to obtain the relevant financial data if appropriate economic modelling is conducted. The second problem is more difficult because non financial values are not traded in markets. In other words, there is no 'objective dollar price' which can provide a yardstick with which to compare non financial and financial values. Environmental economists have been working on providing techniques to evaluate non financial values.

Economic Decision Making

As a society, and as individuals, we are constantly evaluating and rejecting options. A social cost benefit analysis is, in effect, the act of making choices. Social cost benefit analysis becomes a conceptual framework that expresses the less formal processes we use to make choices. While the National Forest Policy Statement leaves open the practical question of assessment, it identifies the need for evaluation of policy options. In Diagram 1 we have listed all the values, in the tradition of Pearce (1989) and Young (1992) that appear to be provided by the native forest. Type of value, and where relevant, their relationship to each other. Total economic value (TEV) analysis would require that each policy option would receive a 'score' in each cell of an evaluation matrix. Scores are aggregated by a means yet to be determined which then enables decisions over differing options to be made. Economic decision making seeks to choose between the differing options on the basis of determining that which provides the greatest net social benefit. The means of deciding which option has the greatest net social benefit where 'scores' cannot be aggregated into a single numeraire is, of course, highly contentious.

There are three channels through which resources can be allocated. These are the markets, institutional processes and executive decision making. Markets, however, as decision making institutions, are largely unavailable in the circumstances covered in this report because we are dealing specifically with instances of market failure. However, modified markets (ie. markets subject to government intervention) are included as a means of policy implementation. The choice between government modified markets and 'pure' market measures should be justified on the grounds of net social benefits.

The irony is that if market measures are to be chosen as the decision making process, then it is a decision that will have to be made by government anyway, and hence does not relieve the public decision making process of the need to evaluate the optimality of value flows from the forests under differing policy options.

In other words, choosing to 'do nothing' is as much a decision as choosing to 'do something'. The lesson is that if optimal social benefits are sought, then market failure automatically triggers government decision making processes-even if that results in a decision to 'do nothing'. The creation of a formalised process for considering environmental values and other externalities requires a clear understanding of the integrated structure of externalities, economic value and economic decision making. All values-financial, ethical, ecological, etc-must be accounted for, if different policy options are to be compared on a equal basis. The different values that comprise each policy option, need to be integrated in some manner which enables socially optimal choices to be made.

IMPACT OF MISCALCULATING FINANCIAL VALUES

The impact of miscalculating the financial value of timber production is significant for Australia's macro-economic performance. Firstly, it overestimates the financial worth of timber production vis a vis some other form of commercial activity. The Read Sturgess report (1992) made it clear that it was more financially valuable for the Upper Thomson catchment to supply water than to supply timber, and consequently more profitable for the economy. The overestimation of the worth of forestry would tend to hide this potential economic 'free lunch'. Other competing uses for the forest may be similarly affected. More generally, the over-valuation of forestry financial values disguises what may be net losses in this sector which are actually diminishing the wealth of Australia unlike other commercially viable industries. Failure to accurately value forestry also leaves the commercial operations of the forestry commissions vulnerable to an income shortfall in the event of corporatisation. Even without corporatisation, the poor measurement processes for forestry blind the commissions to other profit centres such as leasing forests to supply water to regional communities with expanding industries.

Over-valuation of forestry through poor input pricing, in addition to affecting competing uses of the forest, also undermines industries that provide substitutes for forest timber ranging from plantations to steel production. Inefficient input pricing in native timber production undermines all competing industries, all other things being equal. This report has focused on the 'collateral damage' caused to the plantation industry. However, what applies to the private plantation industry, also applies, probably on a lesser scale, to other industries that compete with native forest timber. The private plantation industry is one clearly visible victim of an 'unlevel' playing field in the forest sector.

The over-valuation of native forest harvesting undervalues, by definition, the product of plantations. This leads to lower levels of investment, employment and wealth creation than may otherwise have occurred. It prevents the development of value-added timber industries that can further develop on the basis of a plantation resource. This presents the Australian economy with a 'double loss'. T h e macro-economy loses, marginally at least, from harvesting native forests, and then loses again through the disincentive effects on plantations. Other industries may suffer as well. Finally, there is a third loss built into the playing field, which are the microeconomic distortions, such as poor taxation arrangements, identified by NPAC (1991), that inhibit the plantation industry. The microeconomic distortions in the plantation sector alter the financial calculus such that the value of native timber is enhanced relative to plantation timber. In addition these microeconomic distortions cause a further round of macro-economic losses from the plantation industry. The structural distortions within the forestry sector, and within other sectors both competing and substitute, compound the overvaluation of forest timber relative to other values. This causes a loss of income, jobs and a waste of capital as private agents respond to these inappropriate signals.

The Effects of Miscalculating NFV's

The second major impact of overvaluing forestry financial values, is felt on non-financial values. Over-estimating of forestry financial values also underestimates, by definition, the relative worth of non-financial values. Thus the process of evaluating non-financial values is seriously handicapped from the beginning. The significance of this was pointed out by Sims, in another context, when he stated

Clearly our objectives are broader than maximising GDP. For example pollution in our cities is of general concern. It might be that including externalities in prices would decrease environmental damage and decrease growth, but improve overall living standards.

Two points flow from the comments by Sims. Firstly, Sims appears to be giving emphasis to a commonly-held view that environmental improvement can only be achieved at a cost to the economy. This review has indicated, in a very clear manner, that in the forest sector financial gains can be achieved whilst making environmental improvements. The view espoused by Sims presumes that the 'balance' between environmental and financial considerations is 'efficient'; that is, in the context of this report, the evaluation of the financial worth of native forests has been accurately calculated. The evidence indicates that the balance is inefficient, because calculations of financial and alternative financial values, as well as NFV's are inaccurate. Therefore, this report indicates that improvement in environmental conditions, over a very large margin, will improve financial conditions as well.

At some point along the policy continuum, improving environmental conditions will negatively affect financial conditions-but the forest sector, along with many other sectors, is not at this point, and indeed is a long way from it. Microeconomic reform in the forest sector has the potential to bring environmental improvement in its wake by removing financial inefficiencies that have contributed to over-exploitation of the environment. The implication of financial 'inefficiency' in the sector needs to be clearly understood. It implies that society could be financially better off if certain microeconomic reforms were undertaken. The implication of 'economic' inefficiency is that, in the context of this report, the environment and the financial wealth of society, could be better off, leading to an unambiguous improvement in society's level of 'satisfaction'. In this sense, when 'financial inefficiency' is present, microeconomic reform and environmental policy can be complementary, and not competing policies.

Secondly, failure to evaluate non-financial values relative to financial values accurately is critically important to maximising 'overall living standards'. The benefits that are provided to Australians from NFV's can also be described as 'psychic income'. These benefits also have the fortuitous 'collateral' benefit of also attracting tourists, and hence contributing to the expansion of this critical export industry. Non-financial values provide direct inputs into the daily consumption of Australian citizens and even to foreigners through tourism, wildlife films and existence values. An assessment framework which seeks to optimise benefits to the community, but which does not recognise these non-financial values can generate financial flows that actually undermine community well-being. This happens because the source of much 'psychic income' (ie. the natural environment) has been lost and replaced by financial benefits that are too small to compensate.

If non-financial values are to be given their full and due consideration, then financial and alternative financial values must be correctly evaluated. This review has identified that there are significant inefficiencies in the estimation of value in the forest sector. The presence of these inefficiencies in the market activities of the forest sector is due to structural distortions.

FINANCIAL AND ENVIRONMENTAL PERFORMANCE

The structural distortions contribute to poor financial and environmental performance. There is a considerable social, environmental and financial dividend to be achieved by microeconomic reform in the forest sector. Microeconomic reform requires that a 'trilogy' of assessments be made: evaluate financial values (FV's), evaluate alternative financial values (AFV's) and evaluate non-financial values (NFV 's). Continuation of present practices such as failure to 'estimate value' accurately will cost Australia in lost jobs, lower incomes and a diminished environmental quality of life.

Here this report distinguishes between financial gains that contribute to the overall health of the financial economy, and economic gains that contribute to the overall state of social well-being. Improvements in financial well-being are commonly referred to as economic gains, for example improved resource allocation, because of the easy but methodologically sloppy habit of referring to the financial activities of the Australian society as the 'economy'. Accurately the economy is the process by which we gain 'welfare', a part of which is the financial gains offered by financial activity. In another circumstance, when a Treasury officer was asked to described the non-pecuniary benefits of working in Treasury, he called these benefits 'psychic income'.

3

Forest Resources

ACCESS TO FOREST RESOURCES

The divide in access to forest resources between those who live in the north of the Terai and those who live in the south is likely to become a major distributional and equity issue in the future. There are therefore a number of complex issues in relation to how communities are defined and the determination of what area and where community forestry may be established.

It is unlikely that the inequalities that have now been established can be resolved through reallocation of resources and the only possible route is a fiscal one, whereby communities that have gained control of valuable resources are appropriately taxed and the distribution of VDC expenditure deployed to address the existing inequities between communities with and without community forest resources and between communities that do have community forest. As matters stand in Nepal, this is likely to be a long and difficult route.

Legal or Encroachment Rights

This issue clearly matters more in the Terai than the hills and in closely related to (b). One's status as a 'user' at least in the view of the Department of Forests, clearly depends as to whether you have legal rights to the land on which you are settled.

In one case (in Devdaha) resistance by the District Forest Officer (DFO) to the establishment of a FUG was expressed in terms that it could not be done because it would give legal status to illegal encroachment.

The committee of FUGs do not appear to have adopted such a restrictive approach, although it must be recognised that encroachers and landless may well be amongst the poorest of households and the most dependent on forest resources for income, most notably through the collection and sale of firewood.

The processes by which FUGs come to be formed and established indicate a wide range in approach and participative mechanisms; these may have causal effects on the ways in which FUGs operate and deliver benefits although this is difficult to determine.

There is a strong contrast in the way in which community forest users group were established in Devdaha with heavy involvement of the NGO WATCH in the process of group formation and consultative processes and that of the HJAB FUG in Harpur which was essentially set up by the District Forest Office. Whatever the participative processes in bringing a CF group into being, there are at least two bureaucratic hoops through which all potential CF groups must go – the preparation and drafting of a constitution and the preparation and approval of an operational plan. The influence of these on the nature of the FUG is unclear, but the requirement that these documentary processes should be gone through put the District Forest Office in a strong position to regulate or control if and how the group is established.

There is not space here for a detailed textual analysis of the constitutions of the registered FUGs but a number of general points can be made. First is that they tend to be formulaic and have often been copied from other established FUGs. In Harpur the original name of the FUG from which the constitution (Hariyali CF in Rupandehi) had not been removed of the document. Second and related, the content of the constitutions largely address functions and structures following the listing of matters given in the 1995 Forest Regulations. The main headings required by the Forest regulations for User group constitutions and selectively illustrates these with extracts from the Dhuseri.

The extracts from Dhuseri, which do not differ substantially from other forest user group constitutions, are clear with respect to the stated objectives of the user group – the scientific management of the forest is the first amongst these, with meeting the demand for forest products by users the second. Dhuseri has established three membership categories, which relates to the way in which benefits are distributed. The rest of the constitution largely deals with rules, committee structure and responsibility. This includes a five-member board of directors that includes a Chief of Board, with four councillors each with responsibility for one of the divisions of protection, plantation, management and utilisation. In other words the constitution proposes a village level version of the Department of Forests. In the case of Dhuseri, the strictures on crimes and punishment are held over to the Operational plan rules.

The Forest regulations (Ministry of Forest and Soil Conservation, 1995) also establish what should be included within the workplan and the key headings are summarise. These regulations have since been backed up by Guidelines for the inventory of Community Forests (Ministry of Forests and Soil Conservation, 2000). These guidelines, which it is claimed have been developed to assist users and District Forest field staff in assessing the condition of the forests, are classic forest inventory. They are concerned with sampling design, stratification, sampling intensity, plot size and number, plot-layout, data capture, growing stock culminating in the estimations of annual increment and allowable cut.

But the exercise of estimating the annual increment and allowable cut is a fiction since a 1999 government order forbids the cutting of green wood, even though a later government order of May 2000 requires the calculation of annual allowable cut to be based on detailed calculations and estimates of annual increment. More to the point, and as Dhital et al (2003) have recently pointed out even the Department of Forests has limited capacity to implement these guidelines so how users groups can be expected to apply them is unclear. They found that of the 7048 community forests that had been handed over only about 21 per cent of these (1518) had actually had an inventory.

Managing the Forest

It is also evident from the details on the methods cited above that this information is simply not relevant or usable by those who are meant to be managing the forest – namely the FUGs. In short the requirement for an operational plan, and the stipulation that a new one needs to be approved every five years sets has, as again Dhital et al, ' created a significant delay in forest handover and the renewal of [operational plans]'

As matters stand at present given the requirement and design specifications for constitutions and operational plans, the scope for participatory processes and genuine authority sharing is very limited. These bureaucratic devices, in the name of scientific forestry, can only be seen as serious impediments to promoting livelihood opportunities.

Product and Protection or Livelihood Oriented

As will be clear from the discussion on the content of the operational plans and constitution, the plans and objectives of these community forests combine a mixture of product and protection objectives and do not systematically address livelihood needs or recognise employment or income generation objectives for different social groups. If anything with recent government orders, forest protection is taking precedence even over production objectives.

It could be argued that because the Department of Forests of disciplinary necessity takes a single sector view of planning and development, foresters cannot be expected to explore areas of convergence between forest management and other institutional management structures in communities. Such an approach cannot address the 'joined up livelihoods' of people, particularly poor people, and the trade-offs they make in the management of their own and communal resources.

The message from this chapter is clear: all the evidence on institutional processes over which the Department of Forests has jurisdiction points to attempts to gain greater control rather devolve authority for community forestry in the Terai. The higher value of the forests in the Terai means that there are greater stakes to play for and through various means – control over land areas (how much, where etc.) and procedural strategies (constitutions, operational plans) – attempts to set limits to community authority and governance outcomes have been made. However field level processes, involving both DFO-staff and communities and NGOs, are another level of engagement and it is to these that we now turn.

RESOURCES OF THE NATIONAL FORESTS

The Forest Service began in earnest the development of all the resources of the national forests. Mature timber was sold wherever there was a demand for it and the permanent welfare of the forests and protection of the streams permitted, but always so as to prevent waste, guard against fire, protect young. growth and ensure reproduction. Regulations were adopted which allowed small sales to be made without formality or delay. secured for the government the full value of timber sold and eliminated unnecessary routine.

Care was taken to safeguard the interests of the government and provide for the maintenance of good technical standards. The conduct of local business was entrusted to local officers. Large transactions with general policies were controlled from Washington, but with careful 2 = *District Boundaries and Numbers* provision for first-hand knowledge and close touch with the work in the field.

Business efficiency and the convenience of the public were carefully studied. In short, an organization was created capable of handling safely, speedily and satisfactorily the complex business of making useful a forest property of vast extent, scattered through sixteen different states of an aggregate area of over 1,50o,000 sq. m. and with a population of 9,000,000.

The growth since the 1st of July 1897 of the area of the national forests, of the expenditures of the government for forestry and of the receipts from the national forests, is shown by the statement which follows. Though the act of June 4, 1897, became effective immediately upon its passage, the fiscal year 1899 was the first of actual administration, because the first for which Congress made the appropriation necessary to carry out the law.

Forest is ripe for the axe, the demand is strong and control by trained men makes it safe to cut more freely. The increase is marked both in small and in large sales, but a score of sales for less than $5000 are made against one for more. The total cut is still far below the annual increment of the forests. As the demand grows restrictions must increase in order to husband the present supply until the next crop matures.

- The stumpage price would seem on the face of the figures to have risen from about one dollar to more than three dollars per thousand board-feet. The receipts, however, for any one year are not exclusively for the timber cut in that year, since payments are made in advance. In the year 1907 the average price obtained was something less than

$2.50 per thousand. It is therefore true that stumpage prices have risen greatly, although conditions new to the American lumbermen are im *Area of National Forests, Annual Expenditures of the Federal Government for Forestry and National Forest Administration and Receipts from National Forests, 1898-1909* Until 1906, the sole source of receipts was the sale of timber. In the fiscal year 1907, however, timber sales furnished less than half the receipts. The following statement concerning the timber sales of the fiscal years 1904-1907 will serve to bring out the change that followed the transfer of control to the forest service in the midst of the fiscal year 1905:

- A large excess each year in the amount of timber sold over that cut and paid for;
- Nine times as much timber sold at the end of the four-year period as at the beginning and three times as much cut;
- A much higher price obtained per thousand board-feet at the end of the period than at the beginning. Each of these matters calls for comment. The sales are of stumpage only; the government does no logging on its own account.

- More timber is sold each year than is cut and paid for, because many of the sales extend over several years. With increasing sales the amount sold each year for future removal has exceeded the amount to be removed during that year under sales of earlier years. Large sales covering a term of years are made because the national forests contain much overmature timber, which needs removal, but which is frequently too inaccessible to be saleable in small amounts. To prevent speculation the time allowed for cutting is never more than five years and cutting must begin at once and be continued steadily.
- The volume of sales has increased rapidly because much 1 The United States fiscal year ends June 30 and receives its designation from the calendar year in which it terminates. Thus, the fiscal year 1898 is the year July 1, 1897 - June 30, 1898.

Administration transferred to Bureau of Forestry, February I, 1905. Full utilization of all merchantable material, care of young growth in felling and logging and the piling of brush, to be subsequently burned by the forest officers if burning is necessary, are among these conditions.

Timber to be cut must first be marked by the forest officers. Sales of more than $100 in value are made only after public advertisement.

Only the simplest forms of silviculture have as yet been introduced. The vast area of the national forests, the comparatively sparse population of the West, the rough and broken character of the forests themselves and the newness of the problems which their management presents, make the general application of intensive methods for the present impracticable.

Natural reproduction is secured. The selection system is most used, often under the rough and ready method of an approximate diameter limit, with the reservation of seed trees where needed. The tendency, however, is strongly towards a more flexible and effective application of the selection principle, as a better trained field force is developed and as market conditions improve. One conspicuous achievement was the reduction of loss by fires on the national forests. During the unusually dry season of 1905 there were only eight fires of any importance and the area burned over amounted only to about 16 of 1% of the total area. In 1906 about 12 of 1% was burned. This was accomplished by efficient patrol, co-operation of the public and by preventive measures, such as piling and burning the brush on cut-over areas.

Since the beginning of 1906 the largest source of income from the national forests was their use for grazing. Stock-raising is one of the most important industries of the West. Formerly cattle and sheep grazed freely on all parts of the public domain. In the early days of the national forests the wisdom of permitting any grazing at all upon them was sharply questioned.

Unrestricted grazing had led to friction between individuals, the deterioration of much of the range through overstocking and serious injury to the forests and stream flow. The forests of the West, however, are largely of open growth and contain many grassy parks, the results of old fires and many high mountain meadows.

Under proper regulations the grass and other forage plants which they produce in great quantity can be used without detriment to the forests themselves and with great benefit to the stock industry, which often can find summer pasturage nowhere else.

Except in southern California grazing is now permitted on all national forests unless the watersheds furnish water for domestic use; but the time of entering and leaving, the number of head to be grazed by each applicant and the part of the range to be occupied are carefully prescribed. Planted areas and cut-over areas are closed to stock until the young growth is safe from harm and goats are allowed only in the brushland of the foothills.

The results of regulation, in addition to the protection of forest growth and streams, are the prevention of disputes, improved range, better stock, stable conditions in the stock industry and the best use of the range in the interest of progress and development. The first right to graze stock on the forests is given to residents, small owners and those who have used the range before. Thus the crowding out of the weaker by the stronger and of the settler by the roving outsider has been stopped. In 1906 the forest service began to impose a moderate charge for the use of the national forest range.

The following statement shows the amount of stock grazed on the national forests 1904-09 and the receipts for the grazing charge: - A work of enormous magnitude which has now begun is planting on the national forests. At present, with low stumpage prices and incomplete utilization of forest products, clear cutting with subsequent planting is not practicable.

There are, however, many million acres of denuded land within the national forests which require planting. Such planting is still confined chiefly to watersheds which supply cities and towns with water. The first planting was done in 1892, in California. Since then similar work has been done on city watersheds in Colorado, Utah, Idaho and New Mexico. Other plantations are in the Black Hills national forest, where large areas of cut-over and burned-over land are entirely without seed trees and in the sandhill region of Nebraska. Up to 1908 about 2,000,000 seedlings had been planted, on over 2000 acres - a small beginning, but the work was entirely new and presented many hard problems.

The nursery operations of the forest service are concentrated at seven stations, located in southern California, Nebraska, Colorado, New Mexico Utah and Idaho, where stock is raised for local planting and for shipment elsewhere. These nurseries are small. Their annual productive capacity is between 8,000,000 and seedlings. Each nursery is practically an experimental forest-planting station, at which a large variety of species are grown and various methods are tried.

The organization of the administrative work of the national forests is by single forests. On the 1st of January 1908 the total number of forests was 165 with a total area of 162,023,190 acres. In charge of each forest is a forest supervisor. Under the supervisors are forest rangers and forest guards, whose duties include patrol, marking timber and scaling logs, enforcing the regulations and conducting some of the minor business arising from the use of the forests. Guards are temporary employes; rangers are employed by the year. The supervisors report directly to and receive instructions from the central office at Washington.

In this office there are four branches - operation, grazing, silviculture and products - each of which directs that part of the work which belongs to it, dealing directly with the supervisor.

For inspection purposes, however, the forests are separated into six districts, in each of which is located a chief inspector with a corps of assistants. The inspectors are without administrative authority, but assist by their counsel the supervisors and through inspection reports keep the Washington office informed of the condition of all lines of administrative work in progress. Administrative officers alternate frequently between field and office duties.

The number of forest officers in the several grades on the 1st of January 1908 were: 6 chief inspectors, 26 inspectors, 106 forest supervisors, 41 deputy forest supervisors, 820 forest rangers and 283 forest guards. The total number of employes of the forest service on the same date, including the clerical force, was 2034.

Besides the administration of the national forests, the forest service conducts general investigations, carries on an extensive educational work and co-operates with private owners who contemplate forest management upon their own tracts. This last work is undertaken because of the need of bringing forestry into practice, the lack of trained foresters outside of the employ of the government and the lack of information as to how to apply forestry and what returns may be obtained. Co-operation takes the form of advice upon the ground and, on occasion, of the making of working plans.

The educational work of the service is performed chiefly through publications, the purpose of which is to spread very widely a knowledge of the importance of forestry to the nation and of the principles upon which its practice rests. The investigations which the service conducts extend from studies. of the natural distribution and classification of American forests. and of their varied silvicultural problems to statistics of lumber production and laboratory researches which bear upon the economical utilization of forest products. As examples of these researches may be mentioned tests of the strength of timber, studies of the preservative treatment of wood for various uses, wood-pulp investigations and studies in wood chemistry.

PLANTATION RESOURCES IN INDIA

Plantation resources have been generated and maintained in India over the ages. Emperor Ashoka (273-232 BC) is known to have had trees planted along long stretches of main roads in his vast empire. Emperor Shivaji (1630-1680) is reported to have encouraged plantation forestry within his empire. Sher Khan (1472-1545), who asserted his independence from the Mughal Emperor Humayun and built and ruled over a large empire, is known to have formally converted an old imperial highway spanning almost the entire north of the Indian sub-continent into the Grand Trunk Road and had large stretches of the roadsides planted with trees.

The earliest plantation of the colonial era in India is reported to be of a native species, teak (*Tectona grandis*), planted in 1840 in Nilambur, Kerala. Regular planting, mainly of teak, began in 1865 in many of the teak-growing central and southern provinces.

In 1910, *Eucalyptus* spp. was introduced in the Nilgiri Hills of the present Tamil Nadu. Planting of other native species was accelerated after the *taungya* system was introduced in 1911. These plantations, however, did not cover an extensive area until 1950.

Planned afforestation for soil conservation, industrial wood, fuelwood and fodder started in the late 1950s. The total plantation area to the end of 1972 was about 2.1 Mha. Establishment of plantations remained confined mostly to forest reserves until 1979. The plantation boom occurred when the social forestry projects (SFM Programmes) were launched in many states along with several other afforestation projects carried out with the assistance of external donors. The annual planting rate increased to about 1 Mha during 1980-1985. Most plantations have since then been established outside forest reserves in wastelands owned by the government or on community or private farmers' land. Plantation forestry received further impetus when a National Wasteland Development Board was created in 1985. The annual rate of planting increased to 1.8 Mha during 1985-1990. The area of plantations established during 1980-1990 was estimated by converting seedlings planted/distributed by a notional equivalence of 2,000 seedlings to one hectare.

Records of plantations established since 1991 are maintained for planted area and distributed seedlings separately, by the National Afforestation and Eco-development Board (NAEB) created in 1992 at the Union Ministry of Environment and Forests. The annual rate of planting since 1990 has been ranging between 1.4 to 1.6 Mha.

India has sizeable plantation areas of non-forest species. The total area to 1997 was about 15.3 Mha, of which rubber (*Hevea brasiliensis*) occupied $1.2x10^{-2}$ Mha and bamboo and cashew (*Anacardium* spp.) occupied 0.4 Mha and 0.1 Mha respectively.

Species Composition

A large variety of species are planted in the varied agro-climatic zones. However, detailed information about the composition of species in plantations is lacking. *Acacia* spp., *Eucalyptus* spp. and *Tectona grandis* occupy the greatest areas in the plantations.

Eucalyptus globulus, *E. grandis* and *E. tereticornis* are most common species, while among the Acacias, *Acacia auriculiformis*, *A. catechu*, *A. mearnsii*, *A. nilotica* and *A. tortalis* are common. Other commonly planted broadleaves are *Albizia* spp., *Azadirachta indica*, *Casuarina equisetifolia*, *Dalbergia sissoo*, *Gmelina arborea*, *Populus* spp. *Prosopis* spp., *Shorea robusta* and *Terminalia* spp. Survival rates of species differ and sal (*Shorea robusta*) is known for seedling dying-back disease.

Among conifers, *Cedrus deodara* and *Pinus roxburghii* occupy a major area. *Pinus patula* and *P. caribaea* have been planted to a limited extent.

Growth and Yield

Wood production from forest plantations at the national or sub-national level is not available. It is reported that productivity from plantations in general is quite low. For example, mean annual increment (MAI) for teak at the average rotation age of 58 years varies between 0.6 to 7 m^3/ha/yr with a mean of 2.5 m^3/ha/yr in Kerala, one of the major teak producing states. This recorded productivity may differ from real productivity on account of not taking into account the since smalltimber and fuelwood removal from forests is not taken into account. Productivity levels of some plantations, mainly of eucalyptus and poplar, raised by farmers under private ownership, is better.

Yield of selected species is as below:

- *Dalbergia sissoo*
- Rotation (years): 30 to 40
- Mean annual increment m^3/ha/yr: 4 to 6
- *Eucalyptus spp.*
- Rotation (years): 10 to 20
- Mean annual increment m^3/ha/yr: 8 to 12
- *Gmelina arborea*
- Rotation (years): 30 to 40
- Mean annual increment m^3/ha/yr: 10 to 15
- *Acacia nilotica*
- Rotation (years): 20 to 25
- Mean annual increment m^3/ha/yr: 3 to 4
- *Populus* spp.
- Rotation (years): 8 to 10
- Mean annual increment m^3/ha/yr: 20 to 25

NATURAL FORESTS

The forest area estimates described above include undisturbed forests, forests modified by humans through use and management (or 'seminatural' forests) and forests created artificially by humankind (*i.e.* forest plantations) by afforestation or reforestation. (Afforestation is defined as the establishment of a tree crop on an area from which it has always, or for a very long time, been absent. Reforestation is defined as the establishment of a tree crop on forest land.)

In most industrialized countries, particularly in continental Europe, forests are being managed in such a way that at management-unit level a continuum exists from low-intensity management, involving natural regeneration, through more intensive methods involving some artificial planting to highly intensive methods with complete planting and cultivation; this makes it difficult to isolate figures for natural forest and plantations. The distinction between natural or seminatural forests and forest plantations can more easily be made for developing countries and some industrialized countries such as New Zealand in which forest plantations have been established using introduced species.

Interest in natural forests, particularly their role in the conservation of biological diversity, has led to efforts to compare forests today with what is thought to be their original character and to give complete protection to areas of forests which have had no, or minimal, human interference. Although there are difficulties in identifying the extent of natural forest, compounded by problems of definition, some information exists that can be used as an indication of broad patterns of natural forests in various regions.

An attempt has been made by the World Wide Fund for Nature (WWF) to quantify the area of forests in western Europe that has been relatively undisturbed by humans or which has retained much of its natural character. Their report distinguishes between 'virgin forest', defined as 'forest ecosystems whose characteristics are determined exclusively by natural location and environmental factors... without human influences present or visible any more', and 'natural and ancient seminatural forests', which 'have not been planted or sown by man for the past two centuries' and 'which continue to have a large number of the natural elements'.

The study found that only a small proportion (probably < 1 per cent) of the total forest land in northern and western Europe could be considered as virgin forest, which has arisen since the last glaciation. Almost all was located in Sweden, Finland and Norway, with small areas in Greece, Austria and Switzerland and (according to another author) in France. In eastern Europe, Slovakia and Belarus have considerable areas of virgin forest while Poland and Croatia have small areas. In addition, in northern and western Europe, the WWF report identifies natural and ancient seminatural forests representing 2.1 per cent of the total forest cover (1990) of the 16 countries concerned. There are a further 3 million ha of land in the region in national parks and other protected areas and another 50 000 ha in small forest reserves (mostly for nature conservation and scientific research), whose use is tightly restricted.

The situation in temperate and boreal North America is quite different from that of densely populated Europe and Japan, where use and management of forests for many centuries have left very little of the original forest area untouched. 'Old growth forests', as they are called in North America, still cover extensive areas. On the lands managed by the US National Park Service alone, old-growth forests covered 1.97 million ha in 1988. Although not a direct measure of the extent of old growth forest, it may be noted that the area of forest included in national parks and other protected areas in North America (USA and Canada) was reported to be nearly 49 million ha in 1990.

The FAO Forest Resource Assessment 1990 did not distinguish between undisturbed and disturbed 'natural' forests in developing countries. However, the Forest Resource Assessment 1980 made estimates of the areas of undisturbed closed forests (primary forests and old secondary forests where there had been no logging for the last 60-80 years) and of closed forests that were included in national parks and other protected areas (thus relatively undisturbed, at least in theory).

At that time, these two categories together represented 60 per cent of the total closed forest area in the tropics, a proportion varying from 39 per cent in tropical Asia to 59 per cent in tropical Africa and 69 per cent in tropical America. These different proportions by region reflected a slower development of large-scale harvesting in tropical America compared with tropical Africa and Asia, and also the fact that, in tropical America, spontaneous colonization did not follow in the wake of logging as systematically as in the two other regions due to lower population pressure.

Although the two categories do not match the concept of 'virgin forests' of Europe and of 'old growth forests' of North America discussed above, the sum of the two categories nevertheless gives an indication of the amount of forest disturbance (or management, depending on the point of view of the observer) that existed around 1980 in the humid tropics. Although corresponding estimates for 1990 and 1995 are not available, it is likely that the share of undisturbed forests remains higher in the three tropical regions than in Europe and probably in North America too.

Forest Plantations

Recent data in this chapter are also available in *State of the World's Forests 1999,* which also discusses some of the issues concerned with forest plantations in more depth.

Early Development

By the seventeenth century the decline in the area of native forest in European countries led to the planting of trees, largely to provide alternative sources of timber supply. Sometimes plantations were established for the provision of services or other products than timber. They might be planted as shelterbelts, for dune stabilization, for amenity or for the supply of firewood. Plantations of native species were established at first in areas where forests occurred naturally, for example France, Germany, England and Scotland, but later also on previously unforested land. In France, for example, planting of *Pinus pinaster* was started on the sand dunes of the Landes and with *Pinus sylvestris* and *Picea abies* on former agricultural land in the Vosges; in Germany likewise agricultural land was planted with Norway spruce *(Picea abies)* in Saxony. In tropical countries such as Myanmar (then Burma), teak *(Tectona grandis)* was planted as a native species in the *taungya* system.

Teak was one of the first exotic forest plantation species to be used, being planted in Sri Lanka and the island of Java (Indonesia) from early in the nineteenth century. Exotic species, such as Douglas fir *(Pseudotsuga menziesii),* Sitka spruce *(Picea sitchensis),* Japanese larch *(Larix kaempferi),* lodgepole pine *(Pinus contorta)* and poplar *(Populus deltoides),* were introduced to Europe during the nineteenth century, when they began to play an increasingly important role in forest plantation programmes. Other exotic species, particularly the eucalypts *(Eucalyptus* spp.) and wattle *(Acacia* spp.) from Australia, were introduced as exotics in tropical and subtropical countries from the middle of the nineteenth century, while *Pinus radiata* was introduced from California to New Zealand and other countries such as Chile from the early years of the twentieth century. Box 1.3 describes in detail the experience with forest plantations in Denmark.

The main reason for the establishment of plantations remained the decline in natural forest area and a scarcity of wood, the conversion of woods and forests to agricultural and grazing use. In recent years increased areas of natural forest have been managed for nature conservation, recreation, wildlife parks, etc., and commercial wood production has been either reduced or eliminated. For example, over 25 000 ha of high-yielding hybrid poplar plantations have been established in the north-western USA between 1992 and 1997 in response to both increased demand for poplar wood for orientated-strand board and decreased supply from public forests. On the other hand, some new areas have become available in European countries as land is taken out of agriculture due to trade and market considerations.

Objectives

Forest plantations are tree crops that are in some, but not all, ways analogous to agricultural crops. They often have a simple structure, at least in youth, and are usually composed of one or a few species (but not varieties as in agriculture, except in a few cases such as the intensively bred poplars) chosen for their fast growth, yield of specified products and ease of management. When established for wood production they have a higher productivity of usable wood than natural forests, but due to the way they are managed they do not, indeed cannot, provide the full range of goods and services that natural, seminatural or even secondary forest can provide.

Although the objective of many plantations is the production of industrial roundwood and/or fuelwood, many are established for environmental protection or other services and some also provide non-wood forest products, such as fodder, various foodstuffs, medicines, etc.

Area

The area of forest plantations throughout the world started to increase in the 1970s as many governments became concerned about wood supplies for industry, and in developing countries fuelwood supplies, and has continued to increase since. However, there are no reliable global figures for plantation areas because forests of native species in several developed countries in the temperate and boreal regions, especially in continental Europe, are frequently regenerated naturally and it is not possible to distinguish those areas where supplementary artificial planting has been done.

Furthermore many countries consider their plantations as 'seminatural' forests over a certain age, because as stands mature the clear initial row layout of the trees is lost and other species naturally regenerate under the canopy. For example, Austria, Czech Republic and Finland, in responding to a questionnaire to collect data for the ECE/FAO Temperate and Boreal Forest Resource Assessment (TBFRA), stated that they had no plantations in their countries as defined by the TBFRA process. In 1995, an approximate estimate of the area of plantations in developed countries was 60 million ha, comprising 13.7 million ha in North America, 22.2 million ha in the Commonwealth of Independent States, 12.1 million ha in Europe and 13.2 million ha in Oceania (Australia, New Zealand, Japan). The most significant areas of plantations were in the Russian Federation (17.3 million ha, 2.1 per cent of the country's total forest area), the USA (13.7 million ha, 6.3 per cent), Japan (10.7 million ha, 44.4 per cent), Ukraine (4.4 million ha, 46.8 per cent) (FAO/ECE 1996), Spain (1.9 million ha, 14.9 per cent), New Zealand (1.54 million ha, 19 per cent of the total forest area in 1996, 91 per cent of which was *Pinus radiata)* and Australia (1.04 million ha in 1994, 85 per cent of which was softwood species, mainly *P. radiata).*

The estimated 'net' plantation area of 55 million ha in developing countries in 1995 was about 2.8 per cent of the total area of forests in developing countries. In 1980 the net plantation area was assessed at about 40 million ha. It has thus increased by about 15 million ha in 15 years, but even this figure may be liable to error. Many developing countries, especially those with large forest plantation programmes, provided updated information on their present plantation plans to FAO in 1996 and 1997 from which the reported annual rate of new plantations of 3 million ha was derived.

Note, however, that this is the reported or planned rate, which may not necessarily have been achieved. Most of the countries with large plantation estates indicated that they intended to double their plantation areas between 1995 and 2010.

It was estimated from reported figures that 57 per cent of the forest plantation area consisted of hardwood species and 63 per cent was established for industrial purposes. Nearly three-quarters of these plantations were in the Asia-Pacific region, where China (21 million ha) and India (20 million ha) dominate, while about 15 per cent were in Latin America and 10 per cent in Africa.

One of the trends in the tropics has been that the proportion of industrial plantations established in large blocks fell from 40 per cent of the total plantation area in 1980 to 35 per cent in 1990. The proportion of smaller plantations established through farm forestry or agroforestry programmes grew in importance during the period 1980-95, particularly in the Asia-Oceania region.

Unfortunately, the figures on small-scale private or community-owned forest plantations are even less reliable than for large-scale plantations. Some of these farm forestry or agroforestry plantations supply industrial wood markets for pulpwood. In many countries, particularly those with limited forest area, planted trees grown outside the formal forest area often provide the bulk of fuelwood, poles, construction wood, utility wood, as well as fodder and other non-wood forest products for household use.

Of the area of hardwood plantations planted for industrial use, 30 per cent or nearly 10 million ha consists of eucalyptus, followed by acacias (3.9 million ha or about 12 per cent of the hardwood area) and teak (about 7 per cent). Short rotation plantations of hardwood species such as the eucalypts, acacias and *Gmelina arborea* have been grown for many years by the private sector, but the establishment of plantations of teak or other valuable hardwood species has been carried out only by government forest services because of their slow growth and hence delayed returns.

However, the likelihood of reduced supplies of high-quality hardwood logs derived from natural forests, combined with increasing purchasing power and expected higher prices for logs, is leading to increasing interest in investment by the private sector in valuable hardwood species, especially teak, in a number of countries, for example India, Malaysia, Costa Rica and Ghana. Of the softwoods grown for industrial purposes, fast-growing pines such as *Pinus radiata, P. patala and P. caribaea* constitute about 25 per cent of the area while other, often slow-growing pines make up about 36 per cent.

Responsibility for the monitoring and regulation of plantation crops grown for food and certain other purposes has long been the job of the agricultural sector. In recent years, however, several of these crops (the main ones being rubber, coconut and oil palm) have been providing 'forest' products that have been used for wood and fibre. For example, rubber wood is now used for the manufacture of about 80 per cent of the furniture made in Malaysia, while coconut and oil palm trunks and the branches of rubber wood are used for various forms of reconstituted 'wood'. Rubber wood and coconut stems are derived from the conversion of old plantations formerly disposed of by burning, while oil palm fruit residues are used for medium-density fibre board. The development of these new markets has thus not only improved financial returns but also used the resources in an environmentally friendly manner.

The area of these species appears to have increased from the 14 million ha reported in 1990. The increase may be due to better coverage of the data, although it is known that oil palm areas are increasing rapidly, rubber tree areas are also increasing and coconut plantations are decreasing. Coconut plantations comprise the largest area (about 42 per cent of the total), rubber 36 per cent and oil palm 22 per cent. Most of the coconut plantations are in Indonesia (33 per cent of the area) and the Philippines (28 per cent); most of the rubber plantations are in Indonesia (34 per cent), Thailand (20 per cent) and Malaysia (18 per cent), while most of the oil palm plantations are in Malaysia (44 per cent) and India (29 per cent). Not all of the areas mentioned above are suitable or available for substitute 'timber' production but they illustrate the potential.

Contributions of Forest Plantations to Wood Supply

The continuing increase in the area of forest plantations which have been established for industrial wood supply has been to meet the reduction of outturn foreseen from natural forests arising from deforestation and changes in land use (largely in the tropics and subtropics) or from natural forest being taken out of production and devoted to service functions such as conservation. It has been believed that the outputs from forest plantations can help to reduce the pressure on natural forests as sources of industrial wood supply; while the logging of tropical natural forests is not the prime cause of deforestation, logging roads often provide the means for farmers to gain access to forests. The reduction of logging, combined with effective protection, may thus help to reduce deforestation in certain locations until land use and ownership are clarified. However, none of these palliatives will remove the underlying causes of deforestation: high rates of population growth, poverty, hunger and a shortage of fertile land to cultivate.

The potential of forest plantations to meet demand for industrial roundwood is considerable; it has been estimated that the present global demand for paper pulp could be met from an area equivalent to only 1.5 per cent of the world's closed forest area. No global estimates of current output of timber from forest plantations are available, although FAO's global fibre supply model (GFSM) estimated that the potential annual growth of industrial wood from forest plantations in developing countries was about 5 per cent of the increment of natural forests in 1995. In some countries, plantation production already makes a highly significant contribution to the industrial wood supply, for example in New Zealand 99 per cent of industrial roundwood in 1997 was grown in plantations, while in Chile the equivalent figure was 95 per cent, in Brazil and Argentina 60 per cent, and in Zambia and Zimbabwe 50 per cent.

Estimating the future contribution of forest plantations to wood supply is at present imprecise and is based on many more or less unreliable assumptions, particularly concerning the rate at which afforestation will continue. By the year 2010 the GFSM (op. cit.) estimated that the potential increment from forest plantations would be about 40 per cent of that from natural forests in Asia, Oceania and Latin America and about 15 per cent in Africa, under rates of deforestation and afforestation largely the same as today.

FOREST LAND SURFACE

The world's forests cover an area of 3454 million ha or approximately 26.6 per cent of the land surface, with 56.8 per cent of this area in developing countries, which are mostly tropical. Forest cover has largely stabilized in most industrialized countries but deforestation continues in many developing countries. Between 1990 and 1995, the area of natural forests in developing countries decreased by an estimated 13.7 million ha per year, although this rate of loss appears to be slightly less than in the period 1980-90. Furthermore, forest management is relatively little practised at present in natural tropical forests.

The extent and condition of the global forest resource are determined by many economic, social and political factors external to the forestry sector, including, in particular, continued population growth and higher rates of global economic growth. Population growth, which will occur mainly in tropical developing countries, will continue to be combined with urbanization, while global economic growth will continue to be combined with changing consumption patterns, especially in the regions with fastest economic growth.

In the coming decades, pressures for increased food production are expected to lead to continued conversion of forest land to agriculture in many developing countries. It is estimated that in developing countries 90 million ha of land, of which about half may be forest land, would need to be converted to arable crop production alone between 1990 and 2010.

Agricultural land expansion is projected to be faster in sub-Saharan Africa than in the past; given the unsuit-ability of much of this zone for agriculture, there must be a continuing threat to natural forest cover from agricultural expansion as land continually goes out of agricultural production. Infrastructure development will also contribute significantly to the continued loss of forests. In addition to deforestation in developing countries, large areas of forest worldwide are being degraded by overharvesting, overgrazing, pests, disease, wildfires and airborne pollution.

At the same time as forest cover globally is decreasing and forests are being degraded, demands on forests to supply wood and non-wood products and social and environmental services are increasing. Global consumption of wood increased by 36 per cent between 1970 and 1994, and is expected to increase by another 20 per cent by 2010.

Greater emphasis is being put on the services that forests and trees can provide, including soil and water conservation, sequestration of carbon for the mitigation of climate change, conservation of biological diversity, support in combating desertification, enhancement of agricultural production systems, improvement of living conditions in urban and peri-urban areas, and provision of educational and recreational opportunities.

Forests will remain an essential source of the livelihood of the poorer sectors of the world's population and a home to indigenous peoples for some time to come. The challenge of meeting the growing demand for forest products while safeguarding the ability of forests to provide a wide range of environmental services will increasingly be met through the planting of trees, either within the forest or outside. However, less natural or seminatural forest will be converted to plantations due to the emerging values of such ecosystems, and suitable land for plantation development will therefore be in short supply in many places. Governments will thus aim to encourage large- and small-scale landowners to plant trees outside forests, often integrated into agricultural systems, through policy measures including incentives.

There are likely to be moves towards making blocks of trees more 'natural' with a diversity of species, in some instances in order to provide a wider range of goods and thus serve as an insurance against the possibility of a single species failure or to guard against possible loss of soil fertility or site degradation, as well as to provide for improved amenity and recreational potential. There should be less emphasis on the area or quantity of forest cover and more attention paid to forest health and condition.

Forest cover in industrialized countries will continue to expand, and several newly industrialized countries will see their forest cover stabilize and even increase. Industrialized and newly industrialized countries will place greater emphasis on the conservation of natural forest where it still exists and on the conservation of seminatural forest. Plantation areas will continue to expand, either as intensively managed systems akin to farming practices or management will tend to move towards a more 'ecosystem' approach.

RESEARCH FOR PARTICIPATORY RESOURCE MANAGEMENT

Research for participatory resource management requires, but is not limited to, the use of participatory methods. In other words, PNRM does not mean that only participatory research approaches and methods can be used. A wide range of research methods, both participatory and non-participatory are combined and need to be understood as a spectrum of methods and approaches from which stakeholders – not just researchers – can choose. The cases analysed in this book illustrate how research for participatory management involves stakeholders in generating new information relevant to making decisions about the parameters and procedures for adaptive management. These parameters or procedures may include the boundaries of the ecosystem, the relevant actors, the physical and social spaces for intervention, the priority problems and opportunities, the alternative development paths, optional interventions (both technical and institutional) and the tradeoffs these entail for different stakeholders.

The Schreier case study in this volume illustrates the combination of geographic information systems (GIS) research with participatory management; Vaughan's case study in this volume shows how modelling is being integrated with participatory research methods; Martin and Sutherland explain how researchers' own institutional studies were used to inform participants in community meetings convened to vision new forms of devolving resource management. Snapp and Heong, in this volume point out that a major research challenge is to combine the various 'information bits' derived from different stakeholders, and distil these into decision rules that they can use.

A useful rule of thumb is: the more stakeholder 'buy-in' that is required – and the more diverse expertise needed to generate the information required to reach agreement – the more important it is to use participatory research approaches and methods for NRM. However, whether participatory or non-participatory methods of enquiry are used, research carried out for PNRM has to incorporate stakeholders' different research objectives and criteria for validity and credibility even if, for example, stakeholders are not involved in data collection and analysis. Then methods – both participatory and non-participatory – need to be agreed upon that meet these objectives.

PARTICIPATORY RESEARCH

It can be seen from the above discussion that participatory research is a collection of approaches that enable participants to develop their own understanding of and control over the processes and events being investigated. This is derived from the principle that greater understanding and power to use information results from being involved in its generation. Participatory methods for monitoring and evaluation help to make NRM more accountable to stakeholders, and to give participants greater confidence in the results. In the McDougall case study in this volume, easily understood criteria and indicators are developed by local communities, researchers and other stakeholders.

These provide a framework for later monitoring, and for assessing key factors and their direction of change. This monitoring process creates the opportunity to feedback information and learning into the community forest management system. It thus serves to guide future action, helping to increase the sustainability of community forest resources. In a different approach, Vernooy and McDougall show how creating a set of environmental monitoring indicators with stakeholder participation, and presenting these to local government decision-makers, raised awareness and provided a basis for action.

Participatory *action* research has the added objective of enabling participants to act more effectively based on their own improved understanding. Action research combines intervening in the process being studied with investigating the changes this action produces, and this approach is highly compatible with the concept of adaptive PNRM.

Different kinds of participation in research are possible and there are several typologies that distinguish along one or more dimensions (Arnstein, 1969; Biggs, 1989; Pretty, 1995). Empirical study of how different kinds of participation are being used in participatory research shows a huge diversity of practice in combining different types. Analysis of 150 NRM projects using participatory research shows that there is a definite pattern of using more empowering types of participation in the dissemination of results – ie, at a stage when conventional researchers are most comfortable in 'letting go' and relaxing conventional controls.

One of the fundamental differences among approaches to stakeholder participation in research for NRM is the way in which power relations among different stakeholder groups are structured. Natural resource management and research about it are embedded in power relations. These may encompass powerful international, national or regional interest groups and relatively powerless local people. And they may also include the relatively wealthy, high caste or male members of a community in contrast to the poor and those of low social status, such as women and minority ethnic groups. Information is one source of power in a changing NRM situation, and participatory research can purposively generate new information that changes the balance of power, and can strengthen the bargaining situation of less powerful stakeholders.

Processes to promote participation in the management of resources and in research that fail to examine how power relations affect, and are affected by, the participatory process are often superficial and transitory. For example, participatory rural appraisal (PRA) has been heavily criticized for failing to recognize the incentives for different interest groups to manipulate the appraisal process. The way in which power relations among stakeholders are handled in a participatory research process is intimately related to the issue of research quality. For example, gender relations affect the distribution of power in a participatory research process and bias results.

One way to assess quality in participatory research is to ask: 'How valid and reliable do the different stakeholders who are party to the research process judge the results to be?' In a PNRM process researchers are stakeholders who set research standards, but they are not the only ones. Thus standards for reliability and validity have to be negotiated with stakeholders.

Often researchers have to accept compromises. A variety of different standards will often have to be met for quality assurance. The way in which power relations shape results can make or break the credibility of both the research process and its conclusions. For example, Mosse (2001) describes a PRA sponsored by a State Forest Department in India in which an overwhelming preference for planting eucalyptus trees was identified among the villagers participating.

It turned out that villagers had little knowledge or experience of eucalyptus, but prioritized what they perceived the agency was able to deliver. The results of the PRA reflected the balance of power between the villagers and the State Forest Department, but did not provide a valid assessment of villagers' needs nor a conclusion that stands up to further analysis. Sutherland's case study in this volume reports that villagers did not distribute vetevier grass planting material from experiments to other communities because they did not have permission from the project that had paid them for growing these, illustrating how power relations also affect ownership and how research results are used.

One of the major threats to the validity of research occurs when stakeholders have not explicitly negotiated how control or ownership of a participatory research process is going to be managed. Ravnborg et al (1996) show how the exclusion of a key stakeholder group from a problem diagnosis led to a result that was fundamentally biased against them and towards an interpretation that ultimately damaged the agreed-upon collective reforestation programme. Only once a forum was created, in which the absent stakeholders were included, were new information and competing interpretations of the advantages and disadvantages of slash and burn practices aired. Only then was it possible to negotiate a viable plan for collective action, which was subsequently successfully implemented. The cases in this book illustrate the broad spectrum of approaches to managing power relations, control and ownership of participatory resource management and the research it involves. For example, the African Highlands Initiative (AHI) case did not negotiate power relations explicitly and this affected research quality as researchers began to drop out because of their loss of control.

The 'Landcare' process is quintessentially owned and driven by local groups, but managing the dynamics of power relations among different stakeholders within the Landcare groups or among groups, and how these affect research is not evident in the project strategy. In the Centre for International Forestry Research (CIFOR) case study reported by McDougall (this volume) researchers were flexible from the start in providing a framework for monitoring that enabled multiple stakeholders to develop their own indicators, and eventually to take over and adapt the framework. This approach focused on generating feedback and adaptive learning, making it easier for researchers to see the advantages of 'letting go', but the negotiation of power relationships among other stakeholders in the research process was less explicit. In all these cases, the motivation for the participatory research is researcher-driven, at least at inception.

A different approach is illustrated by the explicit negotiation of control in a PNRM process, which is secondary to and embedded in solving a compelling wetland management problem. This case initiated its process with a meeting in which a vision for the future of the wetland involved various 'stakeholders' presenting their individual views and negotiating a basic agreement on rules to be respected and activities to be carried out. Within this framework of agreed rules, stakeholders decided what research they needed and how to collect it in order to throw light on different resource management options.

In summary, research for NRM cannot be carried out as if it were independent of power relations among researchers, or between researchers and other stakeholders. For this reason, a capacity for organizational learning in research organizations is an important determinant of the outcomes and impacts of research, because organizational learning is essential for transforming power relations that otherwise become an obstacle to innovation in NRM, as the case study by Stroud in this volume illustrates.

The models or theories of participation and resource management that drive innovation in a research organization engaged in NRM are critical determinants of research practice. Many of the problems encountered in conducting participatory research are rooted in organizational behaviour rather than in the choice of methods or types of participation.

Common Organizational Problems in Participatory Research

- Lack of representation of key stakeholders in the research process.
- Participation is not developed around clearly specified rights, roles and responsibilities.
- Mechanisms of accountability among participants are lacking, especially the accountability of researchers.
- The process is corrupted by hidden agendas.
- Conflicts of interest are not made explicit nor negotiated.
- Transaction costs of participation exceed the benefits to the participants.
- Feedback mechanisms, such as monitoring and evaluation of the research process are not in place so that learning about how to improve the process is minimal or slow.

Models of participation in a research organization provide a means to structure and organize the research process, methods for decision-making, and the rules and behaviours of researchers. Models that are incompatible with adaptive PNRM make it difficult for the necessary learning to occur. When models of participation incompatible with adaptive PNRM prevail in a research organization, for example when research and development is the dominant model in contrast to research *for* development, most of the innovative research is done by an informal, or 'shadow', organization that develops as a way of circumventing the outmoded rules of the formal organization (Sherman and Schultz, 1998). Rocheleau, in this volume, analyses the world of isolated and undocumented participatory research outside formal research organizations and the institutional divides within formal research that are an obstacle to organizational learning.

In contrast, in a learning organization new models of how to conduct research *for* development are rapidly incorporated and innovations are readily undertaken. The idea of a learning organization arose in the private sector out of the need to be adaptive in the face of rapid change driven by intense competition, and the learning organization concept has several features in common with participatory methodology. The models of participation that drive organizational behaviour and research practice are based on underlying principles (defined as the ideas that are used to formulate models).

Principles are more important than rules or methodology: 'rule-generated behaviour doesn't work' (Sherman and Schultz, 1998). For this reason, an important focus of this book is the illustration of the underlying principles of participation that are more important than the specificities of one or another participatory methodology. One way of illustrating how principles are more important than methods is to examine how participation in research adds value to adaptive NRM.

RIGHTS OVER FOREST RESOURCES

The tribal people are facing serious problems with regard to utilisation and rights over forest resources. Due to the increasing pressure on forests by various interest groups, there is a corresponding pressure on the tribals to reduce their dependency on forests. This is creating serious situations of conflict, as tribal life is symbiotic with land and forests and their livelihood and culture are based on their relationship with the natural wealth around them. The tribals are being harassed for using forestlands and being evicted in many places. Such reports have come from places like Khammam, Visakhapatnam, Vizianagaram, Adilabad, Srisailam and other places. In Khammam in one particular village, the forest and police departments allegedly branded the tribals on their shoulders as an indication that they were destroying the forests. There are ambiguities in forest-revenue land demarcation. In some places like Nellore district, a lot of land on Velugonda hills is indicated as 'poramboku' in revenue records and as RF as per the forest department. These lands do not have any forest growth. The FD is taking up palm oil plantation in these RF lands (which is not a forest species). However, landless tribals are booked in criminal cases or prohibited from using these lands for agricultural cultivation. These lands should be given to tribals with pattas for cultivation.

In some areas like in Visakhapatnam district, the lack of clear forest boundaries is making tribals vulnerable to the exploitation of both the forest and revenue departments. A joint survey and demarcation of boundaries by both departments should be immediately taken up to arrest these conflicts. Such Joint surveys need to involve the villagers at various levels. The Forest-Revenue Boundary dispute is a perpetual problem in Adilabad and Warangal districts, leading to booking of cases by the Forest department and tension in these tribal villages.In Visakhapatnam Agency and Nallamala areas, there is the unique problem of Enclosure Villages. There were many tribal villages that were not enumerated in the forest surveys. Due to such sheer negligence, the villages were not given revenue status and to this day, they do not have pattas for their lands. They face constant harassment from local forest officials, as they do not possess land records. Recognising these enclosure villages and issuing pattas to tribals should immediately resolve this problem. In Buttapur (Adilabad district) and in Nellore Dt. (Yanadis), the tribals were given lands decades ago under the social forestry scheme and are cultivating there. But due to lack of pattas, they are being harassed by the police and forest departments and also do not have access to bank loans as they cannot prove their ownership. These tribals have to be given pattas as promised.

Attacks on tribals, their properties and livestock by wildlife are not compensated by the Forest Department. Several cases are pending where tribals have been either killed or disabled and yet have not received any monetary compensation as due to them under the Wildlife Act. The tribals should not be prohibited from entering the forests to collect NTFP for their domestic requirements, like firewood, medicinal herbs, food, or agricultural and housing material. The tribals should not be defined as 'encroachers', as is being projected by the forest department and also as indicated in the Circular of IG Forests, MoEF dated 3rd May 2002. In districts like Visakhapatnam, East Godavari and Vizianagaram, where there is high prevalence of podu cultivation, the tribals are facing threats of eviction from the forest department. There was a notification issued by the government of A.P in 1987 ordering that pre-1980 settlements will not be evicted until further orders. This should be implemented. The JFM programme now renamed as the Community Forest Management programme of the A.P Forest Department has caused grievous violations with regard to tribal rights. One major violation is the displacement of tribals from their podu lands by reclaiming them back into the forests through the JFM programme. The official reports of the forest department and the World Bank (which has funded the project) reveal that 37,000 hectares of forestland has been reclaimed back from the people§. The APFD further states its intention of displacing tribals in G.O. where it calls for voluntary surrender of lands by involving NGOs to motivate people under the CFM programme. The APFD has come up with a proposal for rehabilitation of tribals displaced from their podu lands through a monetary and schematic approach. This should be condemned as it bypasses the issue of eviction and rights of people over their podu lands. Their act of reclaiming lands under JFM programme and the APFD's forestry project under World Bank assistance has to be scrutinised closely by the Commission.

Samata and a few other NGOs raised this issue by writing to the World Bank on its violations of its own Operational Directives 4.2 and 4.3 in its financial support to the APFD. This has led to the Bank's insistence on an R&R policy to be proposed and implemented by the APFD in its CFM programme

In Srisailam area, the Rajiv Gandhi Tiger Sanctuary has led to eviction of tribals from their original homes. They have not been properly settled so far. The concept of EDC (Eco Development Committees) that was introduced is working to the detriment of the tribals, as the objective of this programme was to reduce the forest dependency of the tribals. The tribals are given income-generating programmes and alternate sources of firewood by the forest department. This is an artificial mechanism that is not sustainable in the long term.

In the Srisailam Tiger Sanctuary area, the Chenchus, who are traditional hunter-gatherers, go into the forest everyday for all their needs. They are being harassed by the forest department for trespassing into the sanctuary. The groups who came from the chenchu area felt that the Chenchus should atleast be given identity cards to prevent harassment from forest department and the police department who mistake them for naxalites.

Another serious problem with regard to Sanctuaries is the settlement of people's rights. The Settlement Officer is the Conservator of Forests whereas the forest department is one of the interested parties in the land acquisition for the sanctuary and hence it is not appropriate to make the forest officer the settlement officer**. It should be the revenue department (District Collector) who should be authorised to settle the people's rights. G.O.No.112 which calls for involvement of private industries like ITC, Reliance and others for taking up commercial plantations through the VSS should be withdrawn immediately, as this is a backdoor method of allowing private industries to enter forest and tribal lands. Such tripartite agreements between the government, the industries and the tribals can never provide a level playing ground for the tribal people and make them more vulnerable to the exploitation of private industries.

The historical injustices to the tribal people in this region and that of the tribals in southern Orissa due to construction of several 'development' projects and industries like Nalco, HAL, Sileru, Machkund and others which have displaced tribals in large numbers without any rehabilitation, and has forced them to migrate in search of livelihood. They are now being treated as encroachers and criminals in forestlands. This definition should be condemned and Commission should recommend proper mechanisms for resolution of conflicts. The Commission should strongly recommend the orders passed by the Ministry of Environment and Forests in 1990, on the recommendations of the Commissioner of Scheduled Castes and Scheduled Tribes, to ensure that such conflicts are resolved. Infact, the first two orders alone show a way forward to settle disputes concerning forestlands.

All the groups consulted strongly felt that the pressure on forests and the destruction of forests is taking place more due to increase in industries and private commercial activities like Mining, paper-mills, timber smuggling and the growing non-tribal population settling down in Agency areas, than due to the podu cultivation practiced by tribals. Eco-Tourism is also causing destruction of forests. For example, the A.P Tourism Department built huge infrastructure close to Farhanbad, near Mannanur (Srisailam) for Tourism purposes in the middle of the protected area and in Araku, Borra and Anantagiri (Visakhapatnam). While tribals are prohibited from entering these forests for their survival needs, it is totally unjust to allow tourism, which is causing a lot of degradation. Hence, the constitutional provisions of the Fifth Schedule, the Samatha Judgement and the PESA Act should be strictly implemented following the right spirit with regard to industries and non-tribal settlers, which includes the Tourism Department.

The Tourism Department also conducts tours through tribal villages, especially in Chenchu settlements, and exhibits them like museum pieces. The groups felt that this degrading exercise further underscored the lack of empathy among the various government departments towards the tribals.

Because of a shift in the policy of the government, profits to G.C.C. are more important than benefits to tribals. Although there are 32 items in the procurement list of GCC Ltd, it procures a limited number of commodities and at very low prices compared to the market rates. The tribals face several constraints in collection of NTFP and marketing these items because of the monopoly rights enjoyed by GCC Ltd.

They do not have the right to sell their produce to private traders even when their rates are higher. Hence, a long-standing demand has been for removal of the monopoly restriction of GCC Ltd and instead a minimum support price should be provided by GCC to protect the tribals from exploitation of traders. The monopoly of forest department over Beedi leaf collection and sale should be removed. The tribals or VSS should be given 100 per cent rights over income from beedi leaf and also the right of sale, with the forest department providing the support price.

THE IMPACT OF FOREST DEGRADATION ON FOREST RESOURCE USE

In some regions formerly plentiful supplies of wildlife, medicines and supplementary foods have practically disappeared. This is not to suggest that substitutes are not adopted or that cleared forest lands reap no harvests. The degradation of the forest quite naturally leads to a decline in resource use. However, in the West African region there are some forest "products" which cannot be readily replaced; those that serve cultural or symbolic functions are especially important (*e.g.* bushmeat, medicines, and housing material). For example, in Korang's (1986) study of the impact of forest conversion on surrounding residents, a diminished supply of locally valued forest resources was noted. These losses had not been replaced with substitute products from the plantations. Thus people had lost a source of income (sale of canes and chewing sticks), food (bushmeat), and medicine.

In some cases, deforestation has reduced the extent to which forest resources are used. Visser (1975) notes that among the Ando in Côte d'Ivoire a decline in knowledge regarding medicinal plants and their uses has resulted from a decline in actual forest resources. In the case of plant medicines this loss of knowledge is particularly troubling, as traditional medicine is the only health care available to the majority of those living in rural areas of this West African region.

In Western Cameroon, Koagne (1986) notes that there are many forest foods which are decreasingly exploited. He adds that almost all of the region's natural vegetation has disappeared. Traditional supplemental foods are not available in exploitable quantities and new foods that are imported from other regions have taken their place. Forest foods with particular social value are still consumed on ceremonial occasions though these products are often specially protected or produced on farms for such occasions.

The greatest amount of information on the impact of forest degradation comes from studies of wildlife decline. Several studies have shown that bushmeat consumption is limited by the supply of wildlife. In southern Cameroon Laburthe-Tolra (1981) asserts that the decline in bushmeat consumption, caused by reduced supply of wild animals, has resulted in a deterioration in the quality of people's diets. The risks associated with a continued decline in supply become particularity great when it is realised that, as discussed earlier, it is difficult to substitute for wild animals; livestock production is difficult in this region.

Fuelwood scarcity has led to a range of different problems. In the southern regions of Ghana, Ardayfio (1986) has found that fuelwood scarcity has forced households to purchase fuel at the expense of food (in one village household, fuelwood expenditures rose from 1 per cent to 16 per cent of total expenditures within a few months), cooking time is being reduced and, in some cases, different foods are being used. The additional time that must be spent collecting fuelwood has increased the negative health effects of fuelwood gathering, and women's income earning activities which require high fuelwood energy inputs, have, in some cases, been curtailed because the fuel costs have become prohibitive.

Use of Forest Tree Species on Farm Lands

In some areas the combination of declining forest resources and increasing market demand for certain products has resulted in increased use of forest trees on farm lands. This is occurring, to different degrees, throughout humid West Africa. Its predominance depends upon the amount of land pressure that exists, the quality of nearby forest resources, traditional tenure regulations, the extent of commercialisation, and the markets for forest products. In Nigeria, on-farm trees are valued for cash income, shade, fruit, fuelwood, wood for building material and agricultural implements, soil conservation, and palm wine. As nearby forests disappear it is not only trees with marketable products which are increasingly left on farms, trees with food crops or particular household uses such as those use for medicine production, are also being preserved and supplemented.

Generally it is believed that many of the West Africans from the region do not plant trees. Trees on farm lands are most commonly those that have been left and protected during forest fallow and cultivation periods, or transplanted wildlings. But, tree planting on farm lands is increasing. In southern Nigeria, where land pressure is at perhaps its highest in the West African region, the number of trees being planted on farm and fallow lands is increasing. Currently approximately 37 per cent of the farm and fallow land trees were planted.

In southeastern Nigeria, there is a considerable amount of research evaluating trees on farm lands. One hundred and seventy-one (171) common farm and fallow land forest tree species with edible products have been identified; the density of these species is often far greater on farm lands than in natural forests. On-farm trees serve a multitude of household functions while providing support to agricultural production (*e.g.* yam stakes and mulch) and a source of cash income. Okafor (1987) found that the tree species with the greatest number of household uses were often incorporated into compound farms while less frequently used species were found in outlying fields. In other parts of West Africa, tree planting also appears to be of growing importance. In Western Cameroon, Depommier (1983) notes that natural vegetation has almost disappeared. He finds that many useful forest species are protected and planted in hedgerows, especially those with market value. In Sierra Leone, Engel et al (1984) has also found that most farmers are interested in planting trees on their farms. The most valued species for planting are oil palm and other food trees.

Fruit trees are of growing importance. In an examination of agroforestry systems in southeastern Nigeria, Ijalana (1983) found that trees (especially fruit trees) were being incorporated into farms with increasing frequency. Trees were generally protected as wildlings though they were planted as boundary demarcations; generally those with long gestation periods were selected for this purpose, (*e.g.* Mansonia altissimaand Nauclea diderrichii).

In the Ho district (Ghana), approximately 75 per cent of the fallow field tree species have medicinal uses. In Nigeria medicinally valued trees are also predominant on farm and fallow lands. For example, the leaves of Jatropha curcas are used for treating ringworm (the seeds are used as a soup ingredient).

Okafor found that at least half of the produce gathered from on-farm and fallow land trees was consumed by the household rather than being marketed, though strong markets for these tree products did exist. Another study in southeastern Nigeria echoes Okafor's findings. It reveals that a great portion of the tree product harvest is consumed by the household rather than being sold: for example, 78 per cent of the Irvingia gabonensis fruit and seeds harvested from compounds are consumed by the household.

Changes in Usuary Rights to Forest Products

In addition to planting trees, changes in the commercial value of forest products has, in some cases, led to changes in traditional regulations over tree products. For example, in a rural community near Accra, in Ghana, Ocansey

(1985) found that the increasing market value of fuelwood led to severe exploitation of the woody vegetation, and changes in the rules associated with resource use. Fuelwood became a privatised commodity, and could now only be collected from people's own farm lands. Thus landless people in the community were forced to purchase their fuel.

In some instances changes in tree tenure systems may reflect increasing market demand for certain forest products and a rapid decline in resources themselves. This may be the case in Casamance, Senegal, where Pelissier (1966) writes that the traditional rights associated with forest products have changed with the decline of forest resources. Formerly, access to forests was "open", then rights to forest areas surrounding farm fields and especially the vast array of palm products from them, were restricted.

Increased tree planting can also be a sign of increased privatisation as it is traditionally a sign of ownership in some parts of humid West Africa. The introduction of a new technology for palm alcohol production in southern Benin catalysed changes in the management and value of raphia swamp resources. In village areas with considerable raphia resources a system of communal management has developed. However, in villages with good access to the Cotonou urban market, excessive overexploitation has sometimes led to privatisation of raphia groves.

In many cases, raphia groves have been divided among villagers who have been given permanent rights to parcels of grove. By tradition, raphia is never planted, it is seen as a gift of God. However, since the privatisation of these areas people have begun to plant young seedlings. Good seed trees are now protected and their seeds are distributed among the villagers who raise and transport them into the groves. In some cases the privatisation has led to clearing of the raphia groves for vegetable cultivation which, because it can be undertaken in the dry season, leads to higher profits. In both cases the increased marketability of a forest product has led to changes in the management of a formerly "free" resource.

As forest resources decline, their utility and value to local people may diminish. Some authors suggest that loss of knowledge about traditional foods, medicines and uses of surrounding resources are indications of cultural disintegration and impoverishment (Okigbo). There is, however, little concrete information on either the changing uses of forest resources or the differential uses of different forest types. The examples presented in this chapter highlight some apparent trends. They suggest that it may be possible to manage both forest and fallow land in such a way that the production of increasingly valued (both commercially and domestically) forest products is supplemented.

4

Forest Economy: Medicine and Drugs

IMPORTANT ECONOMIC AND MEDICINAL PLANTS

Survey of important economic and medicinal plants conducted in different forest localities of Hilkot Watershed area indicated that a number of them having good demand can be collected in sizeable quantities, while others are threatened with extinction due to their heavy use by ever-increasing population pressure. Key plant species of economic and medicinal value given as under:

PLANTS GROWING AND MARKETING

Acorus calamus (Bach), Arisaema tortosum (Sur-ganda), Cannabis sativa (Bhang), Chenopodium album (Bathu), Mentha longifolia (Jangli-podina), Nastrum officinale (Jangli-salad), Plantago major (Jangli Isabghol) and Verbascum thapsus (Gidar-tambaku).

Plants of Commercial Value

Anethum graveolens (Ajmod), Asparagus adscendens (Musli-sufaid), Carum copticum (Ajwain), Foeniculum vulgare (Sonf), Hyoscyamus niger (Ajwain-khurasini), Linum usitatissimum (Alsi), Malva parviflora (Sonchal), Punica granatum (Annar), Saussurea costus (Kuth) and Vernonia anthelmintica (Kali zeri).

Threatened Plants

Due to over-exploitation by locals resulted in the loss of plant population and need to be conserved. The threatened group of economic/medicinal plants categorized in three sub-groups.

i. *Endangered Species*: Distribution frequency of the following species is low in the visited localities and considered to be endangered with extinction. Angelica glauca (Chora), Aesculus indica (Bankhor), Celtis australis (Batkarar), Corydalis stewartii (Mamiri), Ficus palmata (Wild Injeer), Juglans regia (Akhrot) Paeonia emodi (Mamekh), Quercus sp. (Rien), Rheum emodi (Revand-chini) and Zizyphus vulgaris (Unab).

ii. *Rare Species*: These species have limited distribution in specific area. Their populations are decreasing in localized habitats and became endangered: Bergenia ciliata (Zakhm-e-hayat), Berberis lycium (Kashmal), Dactylorhiza hatagira (Salep-misri), Delphinium denudatum, Geranium wallichianum (Ratan-jot), Polygonum amplexicaule (Anj-bar), Skimmia laureola (Ner), Thymus serpyllum (Ban-ajwain), Valeriana jatamansi (Mushak-bala), Viola serpens (Banafsha) and Zanthoxylum armatum (Timar).

iii. *Extinct Species*: Elaeganus hortensis (Singli), Fraxinus excelsior (Sum), Fraxinus xanthoxyloides (Sum), Taxus baccata (Barmi) and Ulmus laevigata (Kain).

MEDICINAL PLANTS SECTOR IN INDIA

India has 16 Agro climatic zones, 45000 different plant species out of which 15000 are medicinal plants. The Indian Systems of Medicine have identified 1500 medicinal plants, of which 500 species are mostly used in the preparation of drugs.

The Indian Systems of Medicine, particularly Ayurveda, Siddha, Unani, and Homoeopathy medicine largely use plant base materials, minerals, metals, marine and products of animal origin. Our ancient texts had documented medicinal uses of a large number of plants. These plants are being used for preparation of medicines for centuries.

A new trend has, however, been noticed that foreign countries have evinced interest in medicinal plants available in India and well documented in our books indicating the formulation in which they are used. A number of medicinal plants and their uses have been patented by foreign countries. There has been criticism by the people and in the press on this growing trend of patenting of our medicinal plants and their uses. Some of the well-known plants Kala Zeera, Amaltas, Indian Mustared, Karela, Brinjal, Neem, Gudmar etc. have patents. Some of the patents have been successfully contested by India. These patents have been granted because the knowledge about the uses of these plants is not available in the format and manner which the patent examiners can have easy access. Therefore, it was considered necessary to bring the knowledge contained in ancient texts and in public domain in patent compatible format to prevent patenting by others.

Current trends all-over the world has shown that for one reason or the other, people are not only willing to try natural medicine especially those of plants based but are also actively seeking non-conventional remedies. As a result there is a global resurgence in the trade of herbal medicine. International market of medicinal plants is reported to be over 60 billion US dollars per year, which is growing at the rate of 7 per cent. India's contribution to this large pool is just to the tune of a few hundred crore rupees only which is expected to be raised to ₹.3000 crores by 2005.

There is thus an enormous scope for India to emerge as a major player in the global herbal product based medicines. But unfortunately various lacunae pertaining to quality of herbal drugs do exit which are the major hindrance to come up to the expected level of trade of these medicines both within and outside the country. This requires a grand strategic plan to augment the availability of quality raw materials and standardised finished products. In this context it seems important to find out ways and means of increasing availability of raw materials to ensure quality formulations and to invest in Research and Development.

THE ACTION PLAN OF THE BOARD ENVISAGES THE FOLLOWING ACTIVITIES

- Encouragement for cultivation of selected medicinal plants backed by buyback arrangements.
- Registering raw drugs traders.
- Simplification of Transit permit/legal procurement certificate for transportation of raw drugs.
- Thirty one (31) selected priority medicinal plants, like Ashwagandha, Brahmi, Atis, Guggal, Sanai, Musli etc., which are in great demand both in domestic and international market to be brought into cultivation status for the overall development of the medicinal plants sector.
- General and specialised surveys of the international market for medicinal plants and products to be undertaken for identifying niche areas.
- Registration of farmers/cultivators and traders of medicinal plants to be entrusted to the respective State Medicinal Plants Board/Vanaspati Van Societies.
- R & D studies in the areas of post harvest management shelf life, storage and simple agro techniques to be taken up through CSIR, NBRI, CIMAP, ICFRE, RRLs, DBT, Horticulture and Forest Department.
- Constitution of State Medicinal Plants Board in every State/UT of the country for overall development of medicinal plants sector.
- Efforts to create mass awareness about the importance of medicinal plants among the people and publish distribution material for the purpose.

The Medicinal Plants Board has formulated some schemes for funding the projects related to development, creating awareness about the therapeutic uses of plants, marketing and cultivation of some selected medicinal plants having assured market. The Operational Guidelines for funding the project proposals for above activities have been formulated by the Board

- *Promotional schemes would be related to*:
  - Research and Development in medicinal plants sector including drug-testing labs for validation and certification of farmers produce.
  - *In-situ* conservation and *ex-situ* cultivation of medicinal plants for restricted sustainable harvesting.
  - Production of quality planting material
  - *Extension activities*:
    a. Training/seminar/workshop
    b. Visit of growers to demonstration spots and research institutes.
    c. Extension material on agro-techniques
  - Marketing information service on medicinal plants for domestic as well as global market.
  - Survey and inventorization of medicinal plants.
- *Commercial schemes would be related to*:
  - Ensure supply of quality planting material in bulk to the farmers by way of appropriate technology *viz.* vegetative propagation, tissue culture etc.
  - Production of medicinal plants in bulk as per demand and supply position of most preferred species.
  - Area expansion for selected species in the specific agro-climatic zones.
  - Develop proper harvesting techniques.
  - Semi-processing of produces *viz.* collection, grading, drying, packing etc.
  - Develop innovative marketing mechanism.

ISSUES RELATED TO INTELLECTUAL PROPERTY RIGHTS

India is behind the rest of the world in patents both quantitatively and qualitatively, even when comparison is made with our neighbour China. The continued illiteracy and confusion about patents is a serious matter. Our pool of knowledge that is protected by patents, even in areas where we have a competitive advantage is rather poor. Take the area of herbal products, where so much emotion has been raised. The number of herbal patents between 1995-1998 was 1889, out of which China had a share of 889, and the Indian share was next to nothing.

Medicinal plants represent not only a valuable part of India's biodiversity but also a source of great traditional knowledge. Knowledge-rich companies and researchers from the developed world have been attracted to the wealth of the poorer countries have in their biodiversity and the traditional knowledge systems. Some argue that the access to such biodiversity and community knowledge by the industrially developed nations is necessary for the larger welfare of mankind as this advances knowledge and leads to new products which contribute to the well being of global consumers.

The point is that this access to the resources of the poor does not benefit in any way, while their natural resources and intellectual property continues to be appropriated and exploited.

We are on the verge of witnessing a convergence of proprietary knowledge-based scientific and technical invention and innovations making considerable impact on knowledge-based economies of the future. This has brought with it a compulsion to put intellectual property protection on 'top priority' of the international community. Over the last three decades, there has been a growing realization and concern for traditional knowledge (TK), encompassing a wide range of applications. This includes human health, medicine, treatment of animals and birds, conservation of water, increased productivity and the art that is associated to it.

The wealth of this traditional knowledge is almost unbounded and has provided solutions to diverse problems through the centuries, often involving new approaches, based on this knowledge. However, these invaluable functions of accumulated knowledge are mostly un-documented, and passed on from generation to generation through the spoken word, practical demonstrations and frequent improvements made over long periods of study and applications.

The absence of proper documentation of verbally expressed traditional knowledge, whether in codified or published form, has contributed to its vulnerability to large-scale exploitation by innumerable sources including multinational companies who conveniently tap its resources and subsequently patent some of them. This is the reason for which the world edges towards a deregulation of regional markets and, a proliferation of trade occurs with domestic and indigenous communities.

An increasing need is felt among these communities who are the actual store-house of this traditional knowledge and culture, as also among the intellectual property right (IPR) expert, that protect such communities from uncontrolled exploitation of their inheritance, heritage and creativity by outsiders and multiplication industrial interests must be bound under very clear contract laws.

The urgency for protection of the human, ethical and economic rights of the holders of traditional knowledge is gaining acceptance more, because of the improper and unchecked exploitation of this knowledge and the related natural resources base and, the resulting destructive depletion. This perspective has an unfathomable developing country, of commercial benefits accruing to multinationals big business house, mostly from the developed countries.

Therefore, finding effective measures to protect these areas of traditional knowledge, especially those from the developing countries like China, Latin,

America, India, South Africa, Indonesia, Sri Lanka and others which are known powerhouses in ancient histories, traditional knowledge and cultures is considered to day to be of prime importance.

TRADITIONAL KNOWLEDGE DIGITAL BANK

The government of India has set up a Traditional Knowledge and Digital Library (TKDL), namely, an electronic database of traditional knowledge in the field of medicinal plants. Such a database would enable the Patent Officers all over the world to search and examine any prevalent use/prior art, and thereby prevent incorrect grant of patent based on knowledge in public domain, including knowledge associated with medicinal plants. The issue had also been taken up at the international level in the Inter Government Committee of the World Intellectual Property Organisation to ensure that TKDL is prescribed as a non-patent literature and minimum PCT documentation to ensure that patent examiners are duty bound to search the said database for any prior art. The primary objective of TKDL is that of avoidance of grant of patent on the traditional knowledge of the country. Therefore, it is imperative to understand in detail the process relating to grant of patent in IP office and the requirements of a patent examiner.

The Task Force on TKDL found that out of 4896 references on 90 medicinal plants in USPTO patent database, 80 per cent of the references were on seven (07) medicinal plants of Indian origin. Of the 762 patents on medicinal plants studied, about 360 could be categorised as traditional.

The TKDL will have 35,000 Ayurvedic Slokas/Verses form identified books which are available in Indian Cosmetic and Drug Act and will have 1,40,000 pages of information in each language, which will be easy to retrieve. The TKDL will have the objective of preservation, protection and wealth creation.

The international acceptance of the TKDL project is promising. India's Traditional Knowledge (TK) database has been selected for pilot study by 170 member states. There is a need to document the indigenous knowledge related to Indian herbs and plants and their medicinal and other uses and convert it into easily navigable computerise data base for easy access and to secure patenting rights; to discourage other countries for patenting Indian heritage; to transfer knowledge to all sectors who are interested to know about our Indian Systems of Medicine; most of our knowledge is in Sanskrit, Arabic, Persian and other classical languages, which needs to be translated to other modern languages.

MEDICINAL PLANTS AND HERBS

Humans have used plants and herbs for medicinal purposes for thousands of years, and herbal medicine, or the use of herbal supplements for their supposed health benefits, remains very popular today. A 2007 survey cited by the National Centre for Complementary and Alternative Medicine, or NCCAM, found 17.7 per cent of Americans used a "natural product" supplement at some time in the last 12 months. It's important to note that herbal supplements are still not subject to the same regulations as pharmaceutical drugs, although in 2007 the U.S. Food and Drug Administration, or FDA, adopted more rigorous requirements that will take effect later this year.

CLASSIFICATION

Herbal supplements are classified as dietary supplements by the FDA, meaning that manufacturers do not generally need to register their products with the FDA or solicit approval before selling their wares. The Dietary Supplement Health and Education Act of 1994 holds manufacturers responsible for the product's safety but does not require that they submit to an FDA approval process.

If a product is found to be unsafe or adverse effects are reported, the FDA can take action against the manufacturer or restrict the sale of the product, but these steps are taken after the fact. Herbal supplements do not have to endure the rigorous testing process that's required for pharmaceutical drugs.

MISCONCEPTIONS

Since they are classified as dietary supplements, herbal medicines cannot be promoted that they will treat or prevent disease. The FDA considers claims of this nature to be "unauthorized" since the herbal remedy hasn't actually been through the drug approval process. Herbal supplement makers can, however, make "function claims" about how their product might affect the consumer's general well being as long as there is some evidence to support the claim.

For example, a seller might advertise that a product "helps support a healthy immune system" if there is some evidence to show that this is true and as long as they do not imply the product is meant to treat or prevent a disease. Manufacturers who use misleading or entirely unsubstantiated claims to sell products may be subject to penalties enforced by the Federal Trade Commission, or FTC.

WARNING

It's important to remember that just because a product is "natural" doesn't mean it's safe—poison mushrooms are entirely "natural," for example. Herbal supplements may contain many compounds whose activity is unknown or poorly understood. Moreover, some herbs can cause deleterious side effects; the herb kava, for example, can be bad for your liver according to the NCCAM. Herbal supplements could also interact with drugs or medicines you are taking in ways that might cause other side effects or reduce the drug's effectiveness.

CHANGES

In June of 2007, the FDA announced some changes to the rules on herbal medicines and other dietary supplements. After finding that some supplements were contaminated or contained different amounts of ingredients than indicated on the label, the FDA issued new rules establishing minimum standards or "good manufacturing practices" by which all supplement manufacturers must abide. These regulations had a three-year phase-in period and thus takes full effect in August of 2010.

POTENTIAL

Critics believe the regulations that govern herbal medicine are insufficient to ensure consumer satisfaction and safety; since herbal medicines aren't subject to an approval process, they may be completely ineffective or have unknown side effects. These critics argue for stronger regulation. On the other hand, while the evidence for the benefits of many herbal medicines is inconclusive, past research suggests that other herbs may indeed offer a variety of health benefits. Curcumin, a compound found in tumeric, and garlic are two examples of herbs or "natural remedies" that already seem to show health benefits in past studies, although further research is ongoing. Some critics therefore contend that herbal medicines are an alternative treatment that deserves more attention—and that the current drug approval process is ill-suited to the evaluation of herbal remedies.

CONSIDERATIONS

If you're thinking about buying herbal remedies, your best bet is to choose a reputable source for your information. Don't trust internet rumors or websites making wild claims; it's better to rely on published studies—you can use the website PubMed to search through past publications in scientific journals—or on sites like the NCCAM. It may also be a good idea to let your doctor know if you do take supplements and discuss the possible implications. As always, none of the above is intended as medical advice; if you have questions about the best treatment for your condition, please consult your physician.

HERBAL MEDICINES

Herbal medicines were in use from ancient past; however it suffered a severe set back with the introduction of modern medicine. Recently a reawakening in the interest on herbal medicines has necessitated a scientific knowledge on medicinal plants. The forests have been the source of many of the medicinal plants, but the destruction and degradation of their natural habitats has resulted in the extinction of many species.

The poor availability of raw drugs has also resulted in adulteration. To check the adulteration in raw drugs, the highly used medicinal plants have to be domesticated and cultivated. In the process of domestication, the most important step is the development of agrotechnology. For cultivation as sole crop or as intercrop in coconut, arecanut, rubber etc. and to increase the farm revenue, the medicinal plants such as *Kaemferia galanga, Piper longum, Plumbago indica, Indigofera tinctoria, Holostemma ada- kodien, Kaemferia rotunda, Alpinia galanga, Asparagus racemosus* etc. can be selected.

Systematic experiments were carried out at AMPRS, Odakkali for standardisation of agro- techniques of *Holostemma ada-kodien* (Adapathiyan), *Alpinia galanga* (Chittaratha), *Kaemferia rotunda* (Chengazhiner kizhangu) and *Curculigo orchioides* (Nilappana). Harvest of Holostemma is done at the end of second year which yield about 500 kg roots per hectare. *Alpinia galanga* can be cultivated as intercrop in coconut gardens and young rubber plantations and it yield about 2.5 t rhizome per hectare at the end of third year. In the case of *Kaemferia rotunda*, the crop can be harvested after seven months to give 12-15 t fresh rhizome per hectare. *Curculigo orchioides* prefers shade and grows best as intercrop. The dry tuber yield is 1-1.5 t/ha if harvested during first year. Double the yield is obtained if harvested during second year.

EVALUATION OF HERBAL DRUG/PRODUCTS

BIOLOGICAL PARAMETER (BIOASSAY)

It is well established that the biological potency of the herbal constituents is due to not one but a mixture of bioactive plant constituents and the relative properties of a single bioactive compound can vary from batch to batch while the biological activity remains within the desirable limits. Some of the examples are:

Evaluation of Adaptogenic Activity

Adaptogens help the body to come up with stress and enhance general health and performance. AVM is an herbal formulation. Composition- Emblica officinalis, Withania somnifera, Asparagus racemosus, Ocimum sanctum, Tribulus terrestris and Piper longum. AVM shows significant antistress, immunomodulatory and anabolic activities in different animal models there by proving a promising adaptogen.

A new test method for measuring the antioxidant power of herbal products, based on solid phase spectrophptometry using tetrabenzo-b, f, j, n, l, 5, 9, 13-tetraazacy- clohexadecin- Cu (II) complex immobilized on silica gel is proposed. The method represents an alternative to the mostly used scavenging capacity assays. The method was approved in the analysis of the most popular herbal beverages and drugs Echinacea determined spectrophotometrically.

Evaluation of Microbial Contamination Reduction

The technological process of raw material has many stages, generally, adverse to microbial growth, but its complete elimination depends on the initial and work condition utilized.

The aim of this work was to verify the microbial contamination, such as extractive solution (SE) and spray dried extract (PSA) with the purpose of evaluating the decrease of contamination after the decoction and the spray dry. The microbiological analysis of the products was performed by total plate count and MPN coliform.

Evaluation of Nitric Oxide Scavenging Activity of Selected Medicinal Plants used in Inflammatory Diseases

Four traditional medicinal plants, namely Ventilago madraspatana Gaertn., Rubia cordifolia Linn., Lanatana camara Linn. And Morinda citrifolia Linn. Were selected for a study on the inhibition of nitric oxide (NO), a key mediator in the phenomenon of inflammation, signifying the presence of effective anti-inflammatory constituents therein. Plant samples were extracted with different solvents for evaluation of their inhibitory activity on NO produced in vitro from sodium nitroprusside, and in LPS- activated murine peritoneal macrophages, ex-vivo.(20)

The lipid Peroxidation Inhibitory Activity

The reaction mixture contained mice liver homogenate (0.2 ml, 10% w/v) in 0.15 KCl, KCl (0.1 ml, 150 μm), Tris buffer (0.4 ml, Ph 7.5) and various concentration of test extracts. In vitro lipid peroxidation was initiated by addition of Feso4.7H2O (0.1 ml, 10 μm). The reaction mixture was incubated at 37o for 1 h. After the incubation period, reaction was terminated by addition of thiobarbituric acid (TBA-2 ml, 0.8%) and by heating the contents for 15 min. for development of coloured complex.

The tubes were then centrifuged at 4000 rpm for 10 min. and cooled. The% inhibition of lipid peroxidation was determined by comparing the results of test compound with those of control not treated with extracts by monitoring the colour intensity at 532 nm. Gallic acid was used as a positive control.

Evaluation of Marketed Polyherbal AntidiabeticFormulatios Using Biomarker Charantin

Charantin is one of the phytoconstituents present in Momordica charantia. It is well known to possess antihyperglycaemia, anticholesterol, immunosuppressive, antiulcerogenic, antispermatogenic and androgenic activities. HPTLC method is fast, precise, sensitive and reproducible with good recoveries for standardization of polyherbal formulations. The recovery values of charantin were found to be about 98.89%.

Vivo and in Vitro Evaluation of Hair Growth Potential

The leaves and flowers of Hibiscus rosa-sinensis are used as promoters of hair growth and as an aid in healing of ulcers. Petroleum ether extract of leaves and flowers of the plant was evaluated for the potential growth in vivo and in vitro methods. In vivo, 1% extract of leaves and flowers in liquid was applied topically over the shaved skin of albino rats and monitored and assessed for 30 days. The length of hair and different cyclic phases of hair follicles, like anagen and telogen phases were determined at different time periods. In vitro, the hair follicles from albino rat neonates were isolated and cultured in DMEM supplemented with 0.01 mg/ml petroleum ether extract of leaves and flowers. It is concluded that the leaf extract, when compared to flower extract, exhibits more potency on hair growth.

Clinical evaluation to assess the safety and efficacy of coded herbal medicine "Dysmo-off" versus allopathic medicine "Diclofenac sodium" for the treatment of primary dysmenorrhoea:–The clinical study on primary dysmenorrhoea to comparatively examine the coded herbal drug formulation "Dysmo-off" with authentic allopathic medicine "Diclofenac sodium".

A random controlled clinical trial was conducted. These evaluations were based on verbal rating scale so as to ascertain the rate of analgesic effects on dysmenorrhoeic pain. The patients were randomly allocated with the ratio of 1:2 for controlled treatment with (NSAIDS) (n=40) received Diclofenac sodium tablets twice daily for 4 days (50 mg one day prior to and three days after the menstruation), and test treatment with Dysmo-off (n=80) received powdered Dysmo-off twice daily for 4 days (5 g one day prior to and three days after the menstruation). Treatment lasted for 4 consecutive menstrual cycles. Haemoglobin, ESR and ultrasound were measured at baseline during study. All subjects were clinically studied.

Thermographic Evaluation

In the present study, the authors used thermography to evaluate the effects of herbal formulations based on "Sho" scientifically. In the cases that were suitable for Keishibukuryogan, the so called Keishibukuryogan Sho, a significant skin temperature rise was observed in the upper half of the body after the intake of Keishibukuryogan. In a case that was suitable for Hochuekkito, a marked elevation of skin temperature spread through the upper trunk. It suggested that thermography is useful for an objective evaluation of Sho in Kampo medicines, and for identification of the action site of the herbal formulation.

Biochemical Evaluation

Most of the herbal drugs are a mixture of a number of ingredients. Their cumulative effect increases the efficacy of the drug in curing the diseases. Muthu Marunthu is an herbal formulation comprising of eight various plant ingredients, and has been claimed to possess anticancer effect.

It was observed that the growth rate in rats was normal and there was no change in blood parameters such as glucose, urea, proteins, cholesterol and also in the activities of pathophysiological enzymes such as lactate dehydrogenase (LDH), gluconate oxaloacetate transaminase (GOT), glutamate pyruvate transaminase (GPT), alkaline and acid phosphatase after Muthu Marunthu administration. The tumor weight was found to be reduced in methylcholanthrene induced fibrosarcoma rats after Muthu Marunthu treatment.

Evaluation of Kutaj-Ghanavati for Alkaloidal Principles

Kutaj-Ghanavati is a reputed Ayurvedic preparation used in dysentery and diarrhea. It contains water extract of Kurchi bark and fine powder of aconite roots. It was evaluated quantitatively and qualitatively employing TLC and titrimetric method. In TLC study no interference of Kurchi and Aconite alkaloids with one another in their respective solvent systems. The formulation was found to contain all alkaloids of Kurchi and Aconite.

Organoleptic Evaluation

Organoleptic evaluation of food products plays an important role in judging the censoring acceptability or rejection of food items in the market. Effect of various treatments (blanching, pricking, and lye treatment), sugar concentration (50%, 60%, 70%) and storage on the colour scores; flavour scores; texture scores of intermediate moisture apricots. The overall acceptability of the products was significantly higher in 70% sugar syrup but these scores decreased as the storage period advanced. The subject of herbal drug standardization is massively wide and deep. There is so much to know and so much seemingly contradictory theories on the subject of herbal medicines and its relationship with human physiology and mental function.

For the purpose of research work on standardization of herbal formulations, a profound knowledge of the important herbs found in India and widely used in Ayurvedic formulation is of utmost importance.

Even when the chemical composition of a plant extract is known, the pharmacologically active moiety may not be. Environment, climate, and growth conditions influence composition, as does the specific part of the plant and its maturity. Monographs detailing standardization of active ingredients would improve the marketplace. Even if an herbal product is standardized to, for example, 4% of a constituent, the remaining 96% of ingredients is not standardized and may affect the product's solubility, bioavailability, stability, efficacy and toxicity. Just as controlled trials are necessary to establish safety and efficacy, manufacturing standards are required to ensure product quality. Now a days newer and advanced methods are available for the standardization of herbal drugs like fluorescence quenching, combination of chromatographic and spectrophotometric methods, biological assays, use of biomarkers in fingerprinting etc. Bioassay can play an important role in the standardization of herbal drugs and can also become an important quality control method as well as for proper stability testing of the product.

India can emerge as the major country and play the lead role in the production of standardized, therapeutically effective ayurvedic formulation. India needs to explore the medicinally important plants. This can be achieved only if the herbal products are evaluated and analysed using sophisticated modern techniques of standardization such as UV- visible, TLC, HPLC, HPTLC, GC-MS, spectrofluorimetric and other methods.

MARKETING SYSTEM AND TRADE OF MEDICINAL PLANTS

Markets of Batal and Chatter-plain area are trade centre of medicinal plants and black mushroom (Guchi). People collect a limited number and quantities of drug plants from all around the Hilkot valley during summer month. They at first dry it near home-yard and later sell them to local traders/shopkeepers. The seasonal traders purchase dried herbal drugs after grading from local shopkeepers, who then packed in gunny bags and forwarded to Mingora Market; the main trading centre in Swat where these commodities accumulate and ultimately find their way to down markets of the country for consumption and export. Different crude drug items sold by local dealers of Batal and Chatter-plain areas in the recent year.

Medicinal plant is a small component of Agriculture sector and contributes its share in economic development. The sustainable harvesting of plants having both medicinal and economic value has great potential. In fact, there is no local awareness about the proper collection of various species. Thus there is a need, therefore, to create awareness among local people of the importance of these plants and to provide them guidance and training in collection and processing to enhance their income.

TRADITIONAL KNOWLEDGE OF MEDICINAL AND OTHER ECONOMIC PLANTS

A questionnaire was designed to document traditional knowledge of medicinal and other economic plants. Field studies were conducted in 3 hamlets and information obtained from Hakim and local people who had knowledge of therapeutic value of plants. These professionals belonged to different ethnic groups.

Discussion of the properties of the plants were conducted with them with the help of informants. The number of peoples with whom the information were collected varied from 3 to 5 depending upon availability. Majority of peoples illiterate and about 15% of respondent were Primary, Matric and college education. More than 10 informants interviewed were active, cooperative and aged varied from 45 to 65 years. The average number of house holds in the hamlet were 52 with a population of 570 heads, where people lived with their own way of life, believe and cultural heritage. The number of dependent per family heads were 10 but the average number of children were 6. Majority of the residents (60 to 90%) depend on farming.

Per capita land holding varied from 0.37 to 1.20 ha, which was not sufficient to fulfil the basic needs. They were doing other jobs in addition to farming. The annual income varied from 12,000 to 25,000 with an average of 18,500. Respondent benefitted from natural resources other than firewood like collection of medicinal plants, morel, grazing and grass cutting. They enhanced their income from the sale of non-timber forest products. Majority of the respondent reluctant to tell the exact quantity of medicinal plants and morel extracted in a season.

However, some of them (10%) told that 1 to 1.5 quintal (fresh wt.) of medicinal plants and morel were collected per family for sale and local uses in a season. The plant remedies usually employed in common ailments like cough, asthma, dyspepsia, skin diseases, typhoid, malaria, eye-trouble, body pain, cuts and wounds. Thus people saved handsome amount instead of purchasing costly allopathic medicines for the treatment of these diseases. The inhabitants only preferred to visit hospital/Doctors in serious cases. The information collected on traditional uses of medicinal and economic plants.

The use of plants is indicative of intimate dependence and relationship of the peoples of hilly areas with the vegetation in their vicinity. However, there is an ample traditional knowledge of medicinal plants which need to be fully documented for restoration of disappearing knowledge as cultural heritage can be used as a source of new medicine.

PERSPECTIVE OF MEDICINAL PLANTS

ACANTHUS ILICIFOLIUS L. (ACANTHACEAE)

- *Syn:* Acanthus doloarius Blanco, Dilivaria ilicifolia Nees
- *Sanskrit name:* Harikasa.
- *Vernacular names:* Ben: Hargoza, Harkachkanta; Kan: Holeculli; Mal: Payinaculli; Mar: Maranda, Maraneli; Ori: Harkamcli; Tam: Kalutai mulli; Tel: Alei.
- *Trade name:* Harkasa.
- *Traditional Use:* Tribes of Sundarbans: Root (boiled in mustard oil): in paralysis of limbs; Folks of Goa: Leaf: as fomentation in rheumatism and neuralgia.
- *Modern Use:* Plant: In asthma; Decoction of plant: in dyspepsia; Leaf and tender shoot: in snake bite; Root: in asthma, paralysis, leucorrhoea and debility; Leaf: as fomentation in rheumatism, neuralgia and in snake bite.

- *Phytography:* Erect herb; stems up to 1.5 m, in clumps, little divided, glabrous; leaves shortly petioled, oblong or elliptic, base usually spinous, toothed or, pinnatifid,rigid, glabrous; spikes 10-40 cm, terminal, commonly solitary; flowers mostly opposite, bract and bracteoles present, sepals 4, outer 2 elliptic rounded, inner 2 broadly lanceolate, subacute, petals 5, blue, united, 2-lipped, corolla tube short, pubescent within, stamens 4, didynamous, shorter than coroll lip, filaments stout, anthers 1-lobed, bearded, carpels 2, united, ovary 2-chambered having 2 ovules in chamber, style short, bifid; capsules shining chestnut-brown, ellipsoid, compressed, 0.6-0.8 cm long; testa white, very lax.
- *Phenology:* Flowering and Fruiting: almost throughout the year.
- *Distribution:* Mangroves of Indian peninsula; Sri Lanka, Bangladesh, Pakistan and the adjoining areas.
- *Ecology and Cultivation:* Commonly grown on the river banks, tidal canal sides, low swampy areas in the mangrove forests and its vicinity; wild.
- *Chemical Contents:* Plant: Acanthicifoline, oleanolic acid, b-sitosterol, lupeol, quercetin and its glucopyranoside, trigonellin; Root: saponin, glycoside.

ACORUS CALAMUS L. (ARACEAE)

- *Syn:* Acorus griffithii Schott., A. belangeii Schott, A. casia Bertol.
- *English name:* The sweet flag.
- *Sanskrit name:* Vacha.
- *Vernacular names:* Asm, Ben and Hin: Boch; Gui: Godavaj, Vekhand; Kan: Baje, Baje gida; Kon: Waikhand; Mal: Vayambu; Mar: Vekhand; Ori: Bacha; Pun: Bari, Boj, Warch; Tam: Vasamboo; Tel: Vasa.
- *Trade name:* Boch.
- *Traditional use:* santal: use the plant in the following ways:
- They mix and grind black pepper, cloves, root of Carissa carandus lo along with little of the rootstock of A. calamus lo, then stir the same in pure mustard oil-the emulsion, thus prepared is anointed daily over the whole body of the patient suffering form epilepsy with foaming and groaning, as soon as the fit comes on; a few drops of this emulsion should be poured into the nose of the patient;
- For the treatment of indigestion, they take pills made by grinding 100 black peppers, little amount of ginger and the root of A. calamus together;
- Also use in the treatment of asthma, bronchitis, cold and cough, dry cough, epilepsy, haemopty-sis, indigestion, phthisis; Birhor: Rhizome in alopecia, Root as massage, in fever, hysteria, pain in neck, teething trouble of children, malaria and cancer.

Agni Purana: This plant is of great medicinal value; it recommends the following uses:

- For treatment of epilepsy, this plant should be boiled with Costus speciosus, shankhapushpi, along with the juice of Bacopa monnieri; the substance thus obtained should be administered to the patient;
- Drinking the decoction of this plant, Piper peepuloides, Staphyles emodi Wall., and Cyperus parviflorus Heyne and pippalimula is good for the patient of rheumatic arthritis;
- The powder or decoction of this plant helps curing chronic enlargement of spleen;
- Decoction of the plant is beneficial for the patient of dropsy; Ayurveda: Rhizome: bitter, healing, emetic, laxative, diuretic, carminative; improves voice and appetite; good for oral diseases, abdominal pain, epilepsy, bronchitis, hysteria, loss of memory, rat bite and worms in ear.
- *Siddha System:* Fresh root for bronchial asthma.
- *Unani:* An ingredient of the medicine called 'Waje-Turki'; useful in flatulent colic, chronic dyspepsia, catarrhal, in burn wounds, carminative, anthelmintic and as bitter tonic.
- *Modern use:* Rhizome: aromatic, bitter, carminative, emetic, stimulant, stomachic, useful in dyspepsia, colic, remittent fevers, nerve tonic, in bronchitis, dysentery, epilepsy and other mental ailments, glandular and abdominal tumours and in snake bite.
- *Phytography:* Perennial, erect, aromatic herb, common on river banks and marshes, ascending to 3000 m; rhizome cylindrical or slightly compressed, about 2.5 cm in diameter, much-branched, externally light brown or pinkish brown but white and spongy within; leaves distichous, large, 1-2 m in length, base equitant, margin waved; spadix sessile, cylindric, densely flowered, not completely enclosed by spathe, spathe 15-75 cm in length, narrow, leaf-like; flowers small, bisexual; berries few-seeded; seeds oblong, albuminous.
- *Phenology:* Flowering and Fruiting: July-August; fruiting very rare.
- *Distribution:* Throughout India; ascending the Himalaya up to 2000 m; Sri Lanka, Pakistan and Bangladesh.
- *Ecology and Cultivation:* Probably introduced; found from the coast to 1200 m; often near village wells and along watercourses; confined to marshy areas; gregarious herb from a stout horizontal rhizome; wild and cultivated.
- *Chemical Contents:* Dry rhizome:1.5-3.5 per cent of a yellow aromatic volatile oil-calamus oil; the oil contains b-asarone, small quantities of sesquiterpenes and sesquiterpenes alcohols; Rhizome: also contains choline (0.26 per cent), flavone, acoradin, 2,4,5-tri-MeO-benzaldehyde,

2,5-di-MeO-benzoquinone, galangin, calameone, acolamone, isoacolamone, epoxyisoacoragermacrone; Aerial parts: lutcolin-6,8-c-diglucoside; chemical constituents vary in ecotypes and polyploides.

- *Adulterants:* The powdered drug has been adulterated with siliceous earth, ground marsh mallow root and cereal flowers.
- *Remark:* Rhizomes are valued for indigenous medicine.

ALOE BARBADENSIS MILL. (LILIACEAE)

- *Syn:* Aloe indica Royle, A. littoralis Koening., A. vera Tourn. ex Linn.
- *English names:* Barbados aloe, Curacas aloe, Indian aloe, Jafarabad aloe.
- *Sanskrit name:* Ghritakumari.
- *Vernacular names:* Asm: Chalkunwari; Ben: Ghritakumari; Guj: Kumarpathu, Kunvar; Hin: Ghee kunvar; Kan: Lolesara; Kon: Kantikkor, Katkunvor; Mal: Kattarvazha kumari; Mar: Korphad; Ori: Gheokunri; Pun: Ghikur, Kawargandal; Tam: Alagai, Chirukuttali, Kuttilai; Tel: Chinnakata banda, Kala banda, Kittanara.
- *Trade names:* Ghritakumari, Ghee kunvar.
- *Traditional use:* Tribal: Leaf-pulp: in liver troubles, jaundice, fever, gonorrhoea, spleen disorder, rheumatism, piles, dysmenorrhoea, sterility in women; Leaf-mucilage: mild laxative, to cure hardening of breast tissues, in insect stings.
- *Ayurveda:* alternative, bitter, cooling, purgative, sweet, tonic, anthelmintic, useful in eye diseases, tumours, enlargement of spleen, liver troubles, vomiting, skin diseases, bilious-ness, asthma, leprosy, jaundice, strangury, ulcer; Flowers: anthelmintic.
- *Unani:* Gheekawar is useful in inflammation of spleen, lumbago, muscular pain, ophthal-mia, digestive, purgative; Leaves good for piles and biliousness.
- *Modern use:* Aloe: in menstrual diseases, stomach pain, tonic after pregnancy, uterine disorders, high fever; Pulp: menstrual suppressions, nervous imbalance; Aloe com-pound: in treatment of women sterility; Mucilage: painful inflammation; Root: colic pain; Aloe mixture with other plant extracts: for treating obstruction of lymphatic system.
- *Phytography:* A coarse-looking plant with a short (30-60 cm high) stem; leaves succulent, green, large (37 cm long, 10 cm broad, 2 cm thick), densely crowded; flowers in racemes, bright yellow, tubular, stamens frequently projected beyond the perianth tube.
- *Phenology:* Flowering: September-December; Fruiting: scarce.
- *Distribution:* A native of North Africa, Canary Islands and Spain;

naturalised in India; many varieties are found in a semi-wild state in all parts of India; also cultivated in pots and gardens.

- *Ecology and Cultivation:* Xerophyte; propagated by suckers.
- *Chemical Contents:* Plant: aloin, aloe-emodin and resins.
- *Adulterant:* Aloe candelabrum Berger is used as substitute for Aloe barbadensis Miller.

ANDROGRAPHIS PANICULATA (BURM. F.)WALL. EX NEES (ACANTHACEAE)

- *Syn:* Justicia paniculata Burm. f.
- *English names:* The great king of bitters, the creat. Sanskrit names: Bhunimba, Kirata.
- *Vernacular names:* Ben: Kalmegh; Guj: Kariyatu; Hin: Kirayat; Kan: Nelabaru; Mar: Olikiryata; Tam and Tel: Nelavemu.
- *Trade names:* Kalmegh, Kirayat.
- *Traditional use:* Plant:. febrifuge, alterative, anthelmintic, anodyne, useful in debility, diabetes, consumption, influenza, bronchitis, itches and piles; in Bengal, household medicine known as 'Kalmegh', made from leaves, is given to the children suffering from stomach complaints.
- *Homoeopathy:* Used for treatment of different ailments of head, mind, eyes, nose, mouth, tongue, throat, abdomen, stool, urine, fever and other modalities.
- *Modern use:* Drug constitute stem, leaf and inflorescence: as a tonic and in the treatment of fevers, worms, dysentery and also beneficial to liver and digestive ailments; it is reported that it has some antityphoid and antibiotic activity; Decoction: used for sluggishness of liver and in jaundice.
- *Phytography:* An erect herb with square stem, glabrous below, glandular hairy above; leaves linear, lanceolate, glabrous and distinctly pedicelled; flowers white or pale purple; capsules compressed transversely; seeds bony.
- *Phenology:* Flowering and Fruiting: September-May.
- *Distribution:* Throughout India in the plains and hills; Bangladesh, Pakistan, all South- East Asian and SAARC countries.
- *Ecology and Cultivation:* Common in stony lines in forests and in wastelands. Culti-vated as an ornamental.
- *Chemical Contents:* Plant: kalmeghin, bitter principle andrographolide; bitterness is due to nonbasic principle.
- *Adulterants:* It is used as adulterants for Chirata, and is a substitute for quinine.
- *Remark:* Whole plant is bitter.

- *English names:* Areca palm, Areca nut, Betel nut, Pinang palm.
- *Sanskrit names:* Gubak, Phalam, Poag, Pooga, Poogi.
- *Vernacular names:* Asm: Tambul; Ben: Supari, Gua; Guj: Supaari; Hin: Kasaili,
- *Supari; Kan*: Adike, Bette; Kon: Maddi; Mal: Adakka, Pugam, Pakka; Mar: Supari Ori: Gua; Tam: Kamubu, Pakku; Tel: Poke, Vakka.
- *Trade names:* Areca nut, Betel nut, Supari. There are over 150 trade types.
- *Traditional use:* Santal:
  - i. A patient of small pox is given to eat the areca nut when the pustules subside;
  - ii. A mixture for biliary colic is prepared with areca nut as a constituent;
  - iii. An ointment for chancre and syphilis is made by pestling areca nut with the root of Gymnema hirsutus, leaf of Piper betel and then cooking the same in mustard oil or butter; Tribals also use this plant in rhagadas, venereal sores, syphilis, dysentery, cholera, small pox and for fractured bones.

References to this plant are found in the Bhagva Ta along with the plants of Musa paradisica and Borassus flabellifer. Charaka Samhita: Fruit: useful in the diseases caused by bile; Sushruta Samhita: Fruit: beneficial in the diseases caused by phlegm; but overuse of this may distort voice of a man; Chacradatta: Paste of unripe fruit: may be used as liniment; Extract of unripe fruit: useful in small pox; Harita Samhita: sesame oil in which extract of unripe fruit has been boiled should be used; Ayurveda: various preparations of unripe and ripe nuts are useful in toothache, pyorrhea, gum diseases, in treatment of worms, while extract of young leaf mixed with mustard oil is useful as liniment in rheumatism; Brahmavaivarta Purana: brushing the teeth with twig of this plant is beneficial;

Agni Purana:

- Immortality can be attained by consuming decoction of this plant along with the powder of root, bark, leaf and fruit of margosa and juice of Wedelia calendulacea;
- Alkaloids of this plant are beneficial medicine.
- *Unani:* Ingradient of 'Futal (Chalia)'.
- *Modern use:* Nut: chewing facilitates salivation, it being a good source of fluoride prevents tooth decay, but constant use might cause oral carcinoma; shows antimicrobial activities; Aqueous extract of nut: exhibits vascoconstriction and adrenalin p.Qtentiation in rats; Extract of leaf and fruit: spasmogenic.
- *Phytography*: Tall, slender, unbranched palm with a crown of leaves; stem annulate; leaves pinnate with a conspicuous sheet; flowers in spadix, male many at the upper portion, female much longer and a

few at the base; fruits are single-seeded berries with flesh and fibrous pericarp and a stony seed, 3.8-5 em long, smooth, orange or scarlet when ripe.

- *Phenology*: Flowering: August-January; Fruiting: about a year later.
- *Distribution:* Cultivated in the coastal regions of India, Bangladesh, Pakistan, Sri Lanka, Myanmar and other tropical and subtropical countries.
- *Ecology and Cultivation:* This palm requires a moist tropical climate with heavy (500 cm/year) rainfall provided with good drainage. It can be grown in drier areas (rainfall 50 cm/year), if properly irrigated. It is a shade-loving plant, especially in the earlier stages and is very sensitive to drought. It grows on a variety of soils, but saline or alkaline soil, light and sandy soil are not suitable for it, but slightly saline sandy soil is good.

  It is generally cultivated as a mixed crop with coconut and plantain or along with Erythrina indica. The betel nuts are sown in October/ November with a distance of 10-15 em between two nuts. Transplanting is normally done after two years, occasionally after 3 or 4 years. Transplantation is done in July in the highlands and from February to April in lowlands. The second transplantation takes place when the first have come into bearing. In a fully planted grove, a distance of about 2 m each way is kept between the betel nut tree.
- *Chemical Contents:* Nut: alkaloids-arecoline, arecaidine, guvacine and isoguvacine.
- *Adulterants:* Fruits of Areca triandra Roxb. and Areca nagensis Griff. are substitutes for Areca catechu L.
- *Remark:* Stem and leaves are used in various ways. vascoconstriction and adrenalin p.Qtentiation in rats; Extract of *leaf and fruit*: spasmogenic.

ARISTOLOCHIA INDICA L. (ARISTOLOCHIACEAE)

- *English name*: Indian birthwort.
- *Sanskrit name*: Ishvari.
- *Vernacular names*: Ben and Hin: Isharmul; Mal: Isvaramuli; Mar: Sapasan; Tel: Eswaramuli.
- *Trade name*: Iswarmul.
- *Traditional use*: Root: Tonic, stimulant, emetic, emmenagogue, in fever, in powder form is given with honey for leucoderma; Root-decoction: in impotency; Crushed root: applied on itching; Juice of leaf: in snake bite, used for cough; Seed: inflammations, biliousness and dry cough.

- *Unani*: A constituent of 'Majnoon-e-Flasfa'.
- *Modern use*: Plant: used as abortifacient; EtOH (50 per cent) extract: diuretic and anti-inflammatory; Dried stem and root: used as drug, which should be used in minimal doses; the drug promotes digestion and controls menstruation; in higher doses, it may prove lethal, it is used as a stimulant, tonic and for fevers; in moderate doses, it is used as a gastric stimulant and in dyspepsia; Root: considered as a stimulant, tonic and emmenagogue and also used in intermittent fever and in bowl troubles of children; shows antifertility activity in experimental animals.
- *Phytography*: Twining herb, semiwoody, having more or less swollen nodes; leaves cordate or ovate, exstipulate; flowers irregular, often offensively smelling, perianth globose with a purple dilated and trumpet-shaped mouth with a strap-shaped brown purple appendage or lip behind; fruit a subglobose capsule.
- *Phenology*: Flowering: June to October; Fruiting: November to March.
- *Distribution*: Found throughout the subcontinent, mainly in the plains and lower hilly regions from Nepal to Bangladesh.
- *Ecology and Cultivation:* Found in open scrub jungles; wild.
- *Chemical contents*: Root: a crystalline substance-probably a glucoside, a micro-crys-talline principle glucosidic in nature named isoaristolochic acid, allantoin, 0.05 per cent carbonyl compounds and a small amount of an oil, with the odour of isovanillin, ishwarone, ishwarane, aristolochene.

5

Social Values in Commercial Forest Management

Apart from the policy, legal and ethical reasons noted above, there are good commercial reasons to consider social values. Forest managers are increasingly subject to pressures from other interest groups, frequently concerning social values.

- Demands from forest peoples' groups may include greater respect for local populations' rights, carrying out or desisting from specific management practices, and support for their own environmental/social projects.
- Demands from local groups to contribute to social and economic development may include support for local enterprise, employment opportunities, excision of specific areas from management, and use of company infrastructure.
- Demands from trades unions and their initiatives may include greater respect for workers' rights to organize and negotiate, fair wages and benefits, health and safety at work, and the right to skills development throughout the organization.
- Demands to recognize other forest actors' rights to monitor, control and negotiate may include the development of agreements, and procedures to manage conflicts and make compensation.

Unless an active, organized approach is taken to respond to such pressures, forest managers may find themselves facing:

- Slow-downs, strikes, blockades, boycotts, legal battles;
- Damage to forest stock;
- Arson, sabotage or vandalism to equipment and infrastructure;
- Reappropriation of forest lands for cultivation, or migration;
- Development of 'cultures of resistance' among forest-dependent people and their supporters (such as some consumers).

Considerable management skill and time may need to be invested in dealing with disputes, legal challenges and compensation claims, stalled negotiations, 'bad press' and political backlashes and general hostility towards forest managers and companies.

In contrast, participatory approaches that develop people's potential contributions can benefit forest managers, by:

- Improving the reputation of forest managers and companies;
- Uncovering and sharing useful local information;
- Broadening the base of ideas, skills and inputs applied to forestry;
- Efficient apportioning of responsibility, *e.g.* local groups may be better suited to managing recreation and harvesting of non-timber forest products;
- Better understanding of broader social, and thereby market, trends;
- Improving transparency, accountability and therefore trust between all parties;
- Longer-run cost savings and risk reduction.

By taking an active approach to people as well as to trees, forest managers greatly increase the potential social benefits from forest management and their chances of support from others. Such experience should also increase their capacity to anticipate future developments regarding social values, for example in legislation or the market, and thus to gain 'first-mover' advantage from the situation. If some social values are indicators of market trends (and they frequently are), then it behoves forestry organizations to keep close track of them. Many companies have made good business ventures by diversifying into recreation provision in particular. And it is increasingly clear that there is considerable financial value attached to brand names of certain leading companies which are known to produce social and environmental benefits alongside fibre. For example, the Greenpeace name has been estimated to be worth hundreds of millions of dollars.

SOCIAL FORESTRY DEVELOPMENT

The continuing degradation of village forests and protected forests resulted in increased pressure of the rural people on the reserved forests. The topography in Orissa is also highly dissected with many areas severely degraded. According to a recent estimate the extent of such degraded forestland in Orissa is around 12 lakh hectares. Such degradation has set in on account of over use of the forests, and ever increasing pressure of human and animal population on the forests. The National Commission on Agriculture (NCA) 1976 observes that free supply of forest produce to the rural population, and so also their rights and privileges have brought destruction to the forests. Such needs should be met by farm forestry, extension forestry and by rehabilitating scrub forest and degraded forests on priority. Therefore, in order to reduce pressure on forestlands (R.F) used for producing timber and pulpwood, peoples' participation on such lands was not at all encouraged.

Instead, to keep the people away, it was necessary to make them produce what they consumed free of charge (using community and private lands) to draw off the pressure on forestlands.

The first phase of Social Forestry Project (SFP) was initiated in Orissa in 1983-84 covering nine districts, and was extended to all 13 districts at a later stage. The major objectives of SFP were to create sustainable forest resources for the people to meet the fuelwood, fodder, minor forest produce and small timber requirements with the active involvement of the people as individuals and as members of local communities with government support, and to establish/reintroduce tree cover on degraded forest land. SFP categorically intended to involve women and economically and social weaker sections of the population (specifically those belonging to SC, ST, SF and MF) who continue to be the special interest groups of the project. In the second phase however, the following were explicitly spelt out:

- Market orientation through creation of skill of the community for ensuring common property management with intention of generating cash income from the forestry sector
- Equitable distribution of output/usufruct from the project activity
- Long term interest of environmental orientation through rehabilitation/ regeneration of degraded, but potential renewable resources.

The operational components of the SFP were:

- Creation of village woodlots over common surplus revenue land, degraded barren hills and institutional plantations.
- Reforestation and rehabilitation of degraded protected 'B' class R.F land.
- To assist landless poor families to plant fuel, fodder and fruit bearing species.
- To assist individual small/marginal farmers to plant fuel fodder and fruit bearing trees on individual owned or leased land.

A cursory review of the operational functioning of SFP in Orissa over the years suggests: (Mid-term Evaluation of Orissa Social Forestry Project 1991, Volume –I PCCF Office, Bhubaneswar).

- Awareness regarding community's role in protecting plantation in lieu of meeting household level fuelwood and small timber needs is quite high.
- Village Forest Committees (VFCs) are yet to establish themselves as major decision – making units. Though VFCs have been involved in distributing interim harvests, equity in many cases has been overlooked.
- The involvement of women in formation of VFC is not only poor, but also their awareness is unsatisfactory.

- Participation of the people in decision-making on issues like selection of land and species is limited.
- Protection to plantation is more successful where community participation is voluntary.
- Lack of adequate communication/dissemination regarding the rights on community plantations and so also with regard to the arrangements of distribution.
- The response to Farm Forestry is excellent, where strong preference is for high value timber species compared to fodder and fruit - bearing species.

The SFP in Orissa in its first phase was introduced in 1983-84, and the second phase from 1988-89, which was extended to 1995-96 (beyond 1992-93) with assistance from SIDA. During all these years (1983-84 to 1995-96) though 148.35 crores of rupees were spent, only 22.80 crores of seedlings were distributed with coverage of 1.66 lakh hectares of land area. Plantation activities were carried out in all 13 districts of the State through development of nurseries, village woodlots, plantation in barren hills and strip plantations, reforestation of degraded forests and depleted forest, social and institutional plantations, Farm Forestry, FFRP, participatory protection etc. The plantation activities of the State have been funded from the State Plan resource after 1995-96. With such resources, while 3.8 crores of seedlings have been distributed with an investment of 54.65 crores, only 7943 ha. of land have been covered during 1995-96 to 2000-01. However, plantation raised by different wings of FD by 1999-00.

In the mean time, an agreement has been signed by the State Government with the Government of Sweden to start the proposed project "Capacity Building for Participatory and Sustainable Management of Degraded Forests" in the State. The project is proposed to be implemented in two stages: Stage –I was launched in December 1997 to start with the preliminary preparations of village level organisations, demarcation of degraded forests for handing over to VSSs, trained forest personnel. Selection of 1514 villages encompassing successful JFM areas has been completed, in which 1.28 crores have already been spent (Economic Survey 2000-01, Government Orissa). A project report for Stage-II has been submitted to SIDA with an estimated cost of ₹.70.00 crores. The Government is at present actively negotiating with SIDA for an agreement in terms of MOU, though the conditionalities of restructuring of various wings of the F.D and Capacity Building Training Programmes are yet to be agreed upon.

CODES OF PRACTICE AND CERTIFICATION STANDARDS ON SOCIAL ISSUES

All initiatives to define SFM principles and criteria cover social values. Some of these are becoming enshrined in legislation, while others face forest enterprises through market relations.

Current systems of forest certification specify various social requirements at the level of the forest management unit. Even so, social issues remain perhaps the most contentious of certification standards, and there are differences between standards, particularly regarding the required degree of involvement of different interest groups in forestry and treatment of peoples' rights. There are also differences in interpretation of the standards by certifiers/assessors. Whilst some confine themselves to assessing the local social outcomes of forest management, others assess the roles of local stakeholders in the management of the forest and indeed the enterprise, and call for changes that appear to reflect their own biases. Whilst it is increasingly clear that forestry should not be a principal means of social engineering, and less still should forest certification, it is generally agreed that social standards for forestry will become more stringent in future. Note that some require precise performance thresholds to be met, while others require only that the issue shall be measured. Still others consider that the social issue is a policy concern and require it to be covered in policies only.

PARTICIPATORY FOREST MANAGEMENT

With the Pace of Population booming, increased energy consumption, over exploitation of the natural resources and rapid depletion of the forest reserves accelerated natural disaster like flood, drought and cyclones in Bangladesh.

Once Bangladesh was famous for its evergreen/ semi evergreen tropical and world famous mangrove forest. But over the years due to over exploitation of forests and its non-participatory management, more than 50% of the forest resources has been depleted. Realising the grim effect of destruction of forests and to repair the lapidated environmental condition, both the government and nongovernment organization have taken up afforestation programme. The NGOs have added a new dimension in the forest management, which has ensured participation of the community people and protection of the vegetation. Although, the government has also adopted participatory forest management but due to bureaucratic attitude easy access of the poor habitants are restricted in many cases. To overcome these situations, the existing government forestry policy, which was formulated in 1994, needs radical modification. There should be room to accommodate the NGOs, grass root organisations and general people in policy formulation, execution and evaluation of the programme.

Bangladesh lies in the North-Eastern part of South Asia between 20°34' and 26°38' North in latitude and between 88°1' and 92°41' East in longitude. The total area or the country is 144,000 sq. km with a population of about 120 million, density of population is 800 person per square kilometer. The most densely populated country in the world, Bangladesh is mainly a floodplain delta, which is formed at the confluence of the Ganges, the Brahmaputra and the Meglina rivers. Natural forest represents only 6 percent of the total land area of the country and is managed and controlled by the government. Village forest which contains annual and perennial trees and still provides a major source of food and income for majority of people, is managed by private individuals.

A rapidly increasing population is placing growing demand on natural resources, especially forest sector is under pressure to become more productive and efficient to keep pace with increasing demand. At present forest in Bangladesh is in unfavourable situation in terms of meeting increasing demand and also not adequate for maintaining ecological balance. This is primarily due to heavy population pressure and limited resource base, secondly, lack of integrated planning for development of multiple resource base with active participation of people resulting in high degree of environmental degradation, as illustrated mostly by deforestation and destruction of Natural resources.

In the phase of rapid depletion of forest aggravated by increasing demand for forest resources, and considering the prevailing socio-economic condition of the country, Government has put emphasis on participatory approach in development of forest resources of the country.

FOREST SITUATION IN BANGLADESH

Bangladesh has lost over 50% of its forest resource over the period of about 25 years. Actual forest coverage is only 6 percent of the total area and the situation is worsening despite of an attempt to preserve it. At approximately 0.02 ha per person of forest, Bangladesh currently has one of the lowest per capita forest ratio in the world. In Bangladesh, government-owned forest area covers 2.19 million ha, with the remaining 0.27 million ha being privately controlled homestead forests. Of the government owned forest land, 1.49 million ha are national forests under the control of the Department of Forest, with the rest being under control of local governments. Of the state owned forests, over 90% is concentrated in 12 districts in the Eastern and South-Western region of the country. However, due to over exploitation these forests have become seriously degraded. The natural forests of the country are classified into three categories: 1) Tropical evergreen/ semi-evergreen forest in the eastern districts of Sylhet, Chittagong, Chittagong Hill Tracts, and Cox's Bazaar: 2) Moist/dry deciduous forest also known as Sal forests in the central and the northwest region and 3) Tidal mangrove forest along the coast, known as the sundarban, the largest mangrove ecosystem in the world. These forests are official reserves and placed under the jurisdiction of the Forest Department. Unfortunately, recent inventories indicate a continuing depletion of all major forests.

Forest management in Bangladesh

In Bangladesh management of government forest is the responsibility of the Forest Department under the Ministry of Environment and Forest. In this process the department is managing, protecting, developing the forest resources, forest land and also collecting the revenues. People have never been consulted nor involved in forestry activities. From the management point of view, forest of Bangladesh are being divided into three categories such as:

- State owned forest under the administrative control of Forest Department.
- State owned forest under the administrative control of Ministry of Land through District administration.
- Private village forest managed by private individuals. Forest under Forest Department control and management again divided into three major types viz; (a) Hill Forests; (b) Plain land Sal Forests, (c) Mangrove Forests.

Hill Forests: The tropical evergreen/semi evergreen forest cover as approximately 1.32 million ha of which 0.67 million ha is controlled by the forest department and rest is under the control of hill district council. Clear felling followed by replanting with suitable species (both long and short rotation) is the method of management in hill forest. Because of increased demand for timber and fuel wood and prevailing socio-economic condition of the country this forest has greatly affected and rate of denudation is considerably high. The forest department is mainly confined in raising of single species plantation. Inventory shows that most of these plantations would not give the desirable output. This programme suffers from technical, social and administrative soundness. Another problem is most of the high forest are subjected to shifting cultivation by the hill tribes. The tribes are entitled to shifting cultivation in forest land under administrative control of district administration which has resulted in the total destruction of these tropical evergreen forest. The growing stock has depleted from 23.8 million m^3 in 1964 to less than 20.7 million m^3 in 1998.

Mangrove Forests: Known as Sundarbans, the largest mangrove ecosystem in the world. Sundarban forests are being managed by selection felling method followed by natural regeneration. Beside Sundarbans, plantations are being raised with mangrove species in the newly accreted char land all along the Coast of the Bay of Bengal. Sundarban forest is an official reserve forest, unfortunately recent inventory shows a continuous depletion due to over-cutting, illegal felling. It is estimated that in less then 25 years, the volume of commercial species Sundari, Gewa, has declined by 40 to 50% respectively.

Plain land Sal Forests: Silvicultural system applied for Sal forest was coppice with standard system. In this system matured trees were felled and the areas were protected for coppice regeneration. The typical nature of Sal forest is that this forest is scattered. In the forest areas there are agricultural lands owned by the adjacent people. Frequently these land owners are extending their lands and encroaching to forest and in the process they are destroying the forest and subsequently converting the area to agricultural land. In this process forest lands are being marginalised day by day. FAO estimated that only 36% of the Sal forest cover remained in 1985; more recent estimates that only 10% of the forest cover remains due to over exploitation and illicit felling through there is an official base on logging since 1972. Most of the Sal forest are now substantially degraded and poorly stocked. The situation calls by for involvement of community people in the forest management.

Inventories how that there has been overall depletion in forest resources in all major state owned forest. The growing stock in Sundarban has been depleted from 20.3 million m^3 in 1960 to 10.9 million m^3 in 1998. In the Hill forest of hill districts, the growing stock has depleted from 23.8 million m^3 in 1964 to less then 20.7 million m^3 in 1998. Over-cutting by timber merchants, increased consumption linked to population growth, shifting cultivation, encroachment, illegal felling and land clearing for agriculture, lack of participatory management have been the principal causes of deforestation and shrinking of forest land in the country.

Since 1960 two major approaches regarding the role of forestry in development have been reflected in the forestry sector of Bangladesh. In the 1960's, Bangladesh as a part of Pakistan and then as an independent nation has followed 'An Industrialisation Approach' consonant with the international conventional wisdom at that time. As a result, Department of Forest raised large-scale Industrial plantation which were seen as conversion of low-yielding natural forest into artificial plantation of species (mostly teak) of great economic importance. This conversion of semi-evergreen and evergreen forest into deciduous teak plantation was largely concentrated in hill forest areas. During the plantation raising local people were not consulted and often they did not drive any benefits from these plantations. The lack of support by the local people/ communities in combination with lack of silvicultural knowledge and lack of proper maintenance contributed to raise low quality plantations and these plantations were also lost due to illegal felling. In the name of plantation the genetic resource of the ever-green/ semi-evergreen forest was lost. Forest Department was considered as revenue earning department. The main activities of Forest Department were concentrated in extraction of trees from the forest and replanting of those felled areas where applicable, Forest Department has not considered the people and their participation in managing forest of the country.

In the 1980s following a change in thinking about the role of forestry in development, and peoples participation in forestry activity was encouraged. People participation with the forestry sector realised the need of people oriented forestry programme to replenish the degraded forest resources of the country. Accordingly, in 1994 Government formulated a forest policy replacing earlier one enunciated in 1979 with a due emphasis to the need for people's participation in forest management.

POLITICAL ECONOMY AND THE NEW SOCIOLOGY OF AGRICULTURE

The most distinctive aspect of the new sociology of agriculture in the United States has been a strong representation of and legitimacy accorded to Marxist and neo-Marxist perspectives. This has been unprecedented in U.S. rural sociology (despite the fact that Galeski, 1972, and others had developed comprehensive neo-Marxist treatments of Western agriculture well before the rise of the "new sociology of agriculture" in North America). Perhaps Steeves' article in *Rural Sociology* was the first instance in which RSS' official journal published a paper based largely on Marxist theory. It was not, however, until the late 1970s that there began to be elaborated systematic Marxist explanations of the dynamics of American agriculture by U.S. scholars.

Pioneering papers in this tradition were prepared by Mann and Dickinson, Friedmann, and Newby. The Mann-Dickinson paper and one of the Friedmann papers were published in the *Journal of Peasant Studies*, a British journal that had been the publishing vanguard of a revitalized political economy of peasant studies and agrarian history in Europe. The third major contribution to the development of a Marxist political economy of agriculture, that by Newby, was somewhat idiosyncratic in the sense that Newby was and still is one of the most influential "neo-Weberians" in the United Kingdom.

In Newby's 1978 paper he nonetheless made a strong case that the work of the German Social Democratic Party theorist of the turn of the century, Karl Kautsky, especially his book *Die Agrarfrage*, had palpable relevance for understanding the structural dynamics of American agriculture. Newby has elaborated this argument in a further paper in which he has suggested that a fruitful sociology of agriculture must be based upon an integration of the perspectives of Kautsky, Marx, and Weber.

What is, in retrospect, remarkable about this early phase in the development of a Marxist political economy of agriculture is that the earliest contributors to this line of scholarship had to stray very little from the classics in political economy. The Mann and Dickinson paper, for example, drew fairly directly from Marx *Capital and Grundrisse* and secondarily on Lenin's work. Friedmann likewise drew on the work of Mandel, especially his *Marxist Economic Theory*. Newby, focused largely on Kautsky's work. One should not ignore the creativity of their reformulations of these classical ideas, but there had nonetheless been a long classical tradition in the Marxist political economy of Western agriculture.

It is useful to begin this chapter by recalling why, aside from questions of scholarly acceptability, Marx had been almost totally ignored in analyses of changing agricultural structures by North American rural sociologists until the late 1970s. In addition to the unpopularity of Marxian ideas in the land-grant system, the key reason for the neglect of his work in the study of agriculture probably has been that Marx's stylized model of the polarization of economic enterprises (according to the laws of the centralization and concentration of capital and of proletarianization) into the antagonistic classes of capital and labour seemed to be negated by the very persistence of the family farm.

Marxist sociologists of agriculture, however, came to question this dismissal of Marx in two different ways, which continue to represent the major axis of debate and orientations toward research within this emergent Marxist tradition. On one hand, Mann-Dickinson, Friedmann, and others have rooted their analyses in elaborations of Marx's own arguments about why one might predict that the particularities of agriculture as a production sector would cause agriculture to experience far slower and more uneven capitalist development than would other branches of industry. Newby and, more recently, de Janvry, Goss *et al.*, Friedland *et al.*, and others have, on the other hand, raised arguments that there has been and will continue to be demonstrable capitalist development in Western agriculture, as typified by industrial agriculture in the U.S. Sunbelt and in large-scale farming in eastern England.

CAPITALIST TRANSFORMATION OF AGRICULTURE

Mann and Dickinson's pathbreaking article begins by identifying the weaknesses of prevailing subjectivist arguments as to why family farming has persisted in advanced capitalist societies (though the degree to which Chayanov eschewed structural analysis has often been exaggerated). They suggest, instead, that there are within Marx's work the major elements of a nonsubjectivist or nonvoluntarist explanation of why capitalist development, which they largely define in terms of proletarianization and the establishment of the capital-labour relation at the point of agricultural production, should proceed more slowly in agriculture than nonfarm industry.

They emphasize how agriculture, because of its seasonality, tends to involve a disjuncture (or "nonidentity") between "production time" and "labour time," which creates a barrier to the routinization of the labour process around the calendar and makes agriculture less profitable than other branches of industry. Mann and Dickinson make the case that agriculture is a unique industry in that the seasonal cycle results in interruptions in the use of labour in the production process while the growing commodity is left to natural vagaries.

Thus labour by those working in agriculture ("living labour") is both discontinuous and makes only a modest contribution to the overall production process. Since, in Marxist terms, only living labour creates surplus value, value is neither created nor transferred during these interruptions, thereby creating the nonidentity between production time and labour time. Hence, agriculture tends to be unprofitable and therefore relegated to family labour (or petty commodity) producers. Mann and Dickinson also suggest that agricultural commodities involve longer turnover times (production time plus circulation time [the time required to sell the commodity]) than do other industries, further reinforcing the relegation of farming to noncapitalist producers. Finally, Mann and Dickinson note that agriculture tends to involve producing perishable commodities, which increases the risk of production and therefore makes it even more unattractive to capitalists.

Mann and Dickinson, however, do not claim that capitalist development is precluded in agriculture. They emphasize, in particular, that agricultural research may have the effect of reducing or eliminating the nonidentity of production time and labour time, reducing turnover time, and minimizing the perishability of agricultural commodities. They point out that there are instances of capitalist agriculture in commodities in which a combination of research advances and favorable agroclimatic circumstances have permitted the establishment of capitalist relations of production.

Friedmann's work, although it has taken much the same approach as Mann and Dickinson's, has proceeded along somewhat different explanatory lines. Friedmann has drawn on the Marxist theoretical tradition, but her explanation of the persistence of household forms of agricultural production (which she terms simple commodity production) rests largely on how family farms can meet the competition of — and often outcompete — capitalist farms in the hostile context of competitive markets in means of production and agricultural commodities. Friedmann begins in much the same way as Mann and Dickinson, pointing toward the high degree of risk and the cyclical demand for labour in most agricultural commodity systems. She argues, however, that the crucial aspect of household forms of agricultural production is that simple commodity producers, unlike capitalists, do not have to earn a profit in order to reproduce their enterprises, *i.e.*, remain in business. Simple commodity producers need only accomplish "simple reproduction." Capitalists, on the other hand, are forced by the logic of competition to strive to earn the average rate of profit, lest their firms become marginalized and eventually be forced out of business.

Moreover, Friedmann has maintained that simple commodity producers in agriculture have a far greater flexibility than do capitalists in reducing their consumption to the subsistence level in order to survive severe market downturns. Capitalist farmers will typically tend to liquidate their assets if agricultural production is no longer able to generate the average rate of profit. Friedmann tested this proposition empirically with historical data which show that the world-market downturn in the price of wheat in the late 1800s led to family producers in the United States and other white settler colonies being able to out compete capitalist producers in England, Prussia, and the United States.

Finally, Friedmann has noted, much as did Mann and Dickinson, that there are "transformational tendencies" in simple commodity production, among them the subordination of independent producers by nonfarm capital. Thus, whereas Friedmann emphasizes the particularities of agriculture that lead to the persistence of simple commodity production in advanced capitalism, she recognizes that there are conditions that may lead to its transformation toward capitalist forms.

Along a similar line and influenced by the world systems school of political economy, McMichael analyzed the cotton plantation system of the Antebellum South, finding that this system was in transition during the period as its basis in mercantile capitalism became transformed into industrial capitalism with an accompanying need for specialized raw materials (cotton).

The credit system that developed concomitantly transformed the southern plantation into a system of fully commercialized relations with all the preconditions of industrial agriculture, save for the presence of slave labour. The lack of "free" wage labour — that is, the reliance of plantations on slavery and later on sharecropping as means of labour recruitment and control — proved to be extremely significant, especially by inhibiting the technological transformation of production. McMichael concluded that understanding the transformation of the relations of agricultural production requires attending to the emerging forms of the capitalist economy, "including political relations, competitive market structures, and the organization of credit institutions". Related work by Gary Green and Zey-Ferrell and McIntosh also suggests that the structural organization of the banking industry affects access to credit by farmers with farms of different sizes, and that this has implications for change in the structure and character of farms. Simultaneously with the publication of the work of Mann-Dickinson and Friedmann, there emerged a very different neo-Marxist tradition, which stressed that U.S. and Western agriculture was rapidly going down the road of capitalist development and proletarianization — a theme to which Marx had given considerable emphasis in major portions of his work. De Janvry, an agricultural economist by training and vocation but a scholar with strong ties to the sociological community, has been among the most outspoken on the issue of the demise of the family farm in advanced capitalism.

Following Kautsky *Die Agrarfrage* and Lenin and building on his own previous work on Latin American agriculture, de Janvry argued that the development of late capitalism has witnessed a startling rate of destruction of family farms and that the forces that now affect agricultural producers — rapid technological change, state subsidies of research and capital investment, and state commodity programmes — make it quite implausible that the family farm can survive.

De Janvry has argued that whereas agriculture tends to experience capitalist development less rapidly than other branches of industry, it is quite likely that the forces of proletarianization and state-subsidized capital accumulation in agriculture will continue to slowly but surely erode the position of the family farm and lead to its differentiation into antagonistic social classes. Thus, in de Janvry's view, independent producers are a transitional class in advanced capitalism; capitalist relations must inevitably and irreversibly penetrate family farming and lead to its demise, much as has occurred in other branches of industry in advanced capitalist societies. Newby, largely writing on behalf of the neglected works of Kautsky, made many of the same points as did de Janvry. It is useful to note in this regard, however, that Kautsky *Die Agrarfrage* contained a series of sophisticated arguments about why there would be a *slow* pace of capitalist penetration of agriculture.

Kautsky argued that capitalist penetration of agriculture, despite its slowness and unevenness, would ultimately proceed and would result in the decomposition of the German peasantry. Kautsky's work can be seen to at once recognize reasons for persistence of the peasantry, yet deny that the peasantry would survive over the long term in advanced capitalism.

The work of Friedland *et al.* has also been a highly visible contribution to the Kautsky and Lenin tradition, which emphasizes the primacy of analyzing emerging capital-labour relations in agriculture and the ultimate separation of independent producers from their means of production. Drawing on Marxist scholarship in the sociology of work and industry as well as on Kautsky and Lenin, Friedland *et al.* developed a comprehensive theoretical position on agricultural development and the selective industrialization of particular agricultural commodity sectors.

While their *Manufacturing Green Gold* book was based on the California lettuce industry, Friedland and colleagues have explored several other commodity sectors in California agriculture, including tomatoes and grapes-raisins. They have given particular emphasis to the penetration of capitalist relations of production into agriculture, but have also stressed that the nature and pace of this penetration vary widely depending upon the commodity system in question. Nonetheless, they take a posture similar to that of de Janvry — that while agriculture in general and particular commodity sectors exhibit a slow pace of capitalist penetration, capitalist relations do appear increasingly and bear many similarities to production relations in other branches of industry.

Agricultural Production Forms into the Capitalist Political Economy

Another thrust in the neo-Marxian political economy literature, and one that is somewhat contrary to those discussed above, has been the argument that the differentiation of agriculturalists into the capitalist and working classes may be incomplete in the foreseeable future as farm and nonfarm production become integrated into a single system incorporating different organizational forms of production. An early statement of this line of thought was that of the

German Social Democrat and Marxist theoretician, Karl Kautsky. Kautsky argued that what was crucial to understanding the evolution of agriculture in advanced industrial societies was not simply the dominant form of ownership of agricultural enterprises, but rather the functions that were served by the emerging organizational formsof agricultural production.

This approach was developed further by Mottura and Pugliesi in an historical analysis of small holdings farmed part-time in southern Italy and the functions of smallholder agriculture in contemporary decentralized economic development. The thrust of their argument was that while most agricultural production took place on farms organized along capitalistic lines, part-time farming served as a backup alternative for the workers in industrial plants located in rural areas. In times of industrial contraction and high unemployment, displaced workers with small farms could turn temporarily to subsistence production until industrial conditions improved, thus forming a reserve labour force.

This integration of agricultural and nonagricultural production spheres has been further elaborated by Bonanno, who examined the role of the state in fostering small farms as one strategy to mediate the interests of the conflicting social classes in the emerging social orders of the advanced societies, particularly Italy and the United States. In this light, various farm programmes to deal with problems in the agricultural sector can be seen in part as rooted in the legitimation function served by the continuation of small farms.

Small farms are also important in the decentralizing industrial system fostered by state policy. In this system, industrial firms move to rural areas where labour is not unionized and where wages are low because many potential workers have small farms producing inadequate incomes and few alternative opportunities. Work is also increasingly "informalized" in cottage industry, piecework arrangements. In such contexts, small farms serve the function as "keeper of surplus labour" — providing, at the same time, a source of low-cost labour for industry and, in the face of the tenuous employment, a source of security for the members of households with small farms.

Wenger and Buck, building on this line of thought but especially on the earlier work of Andre Gunder Frank, take this argument another step by examining how exploitation and superexploitation (extracting more value from workers' labour than permits reproduction of that labour) from members of farm households are necessary and dynamic features of both advanced capitalist societies and developing societies. Production organized according to obligations of kinship ("domestic relations of production") link ("articulate") in various ways with production organized along capitalist lines so that value is transferred from the domestic sphere of production to the capitalist sphere of production.

This takes place in such a way as to make the domestic sphere an "interstitial domestic reserve of labour" that subsidizes the capitalist sphere either directly or indirectly through various mechanisms. For example, unpaid household labour reduces both the wages necessary for workers employed in industry and the prices of agricultural commodities required by farm families. Off-farm income from wage work helps to pay the costs of agricultural production and thus lowers the price of food for other working class families.

Farmers as Actors in a Capitalist Political Economy

Whereas the perspectives of Mann-Dickinson and Friedmann on one hand, and of de Janvry, Friedland *et al.*, and others working in the Lenin (and, to a lesser extent, the Kautsky) traditions on the other, are, in a sense, in diametrical opposition, much of the most provocative work in the Marxist tradition in the "new sociology of agriculture" has revolved around formulations that explicitly or implicitly are attempts at synthesis. One of the most noteworthy attempts has been by Mooney.

Mooney's principal contribution has been to cast doubt as to whether the existence of conventional capital-labour relations on farms is an adequate benchmark for gauging the existence of capitalist penetration of agriculture. Following Wright, Mooney has developed a model of agrarian class structure involving "contradictory class locations" such that class positions other than family labour farmer (unity of capital and labour in the farm household), capitalist farmer, and agricultural wage labour are seen to exist. In particular, Mooney sees that there are several "detours" that can be taken by farmers in order to avoid proletarianization.

These detours involve tenancy, contract farming, part-time farming, and debt. In each, whereas there is no capital-labour relation at the point of agricultural production, farmers are exploited by some fraction of nonagricultural capital (in tenancy, by landlords; in contract farming, by agribusiness; in part-time farming, by off farm capitalists; and in debt, by finance capital). Thus, Mooney argues that the exploitation of farm wage workers by agrarian capitalists is only one form that capitalist penetration of agriculture can take.

Moreover, Mooney sees that these detours — that is, the alternative ways in which capital acts to "strip simple commodity producers of... surplus value other than through the extension of wage labour" — may be more significant than full-blown capital-labour relations at the point of agricultural production. It is significant, however, that Mooney's explanation of why these contradictory class locations in agriculture tend to emerge has a subjectivist component, based on Weber's distinction between formal and substantive rationality. Mooney sees that many farmers are motivated more by forms of substantive rationality than they are by formal capitalist rationality. Accordingly, these farmers tend to be tenacious in holding onto their farms and farm lifestyles and will often tend to take one of the four "detours" to capitalist development in order to remain in agriculture.

Mann and Dickinson, however, replied vigorously to Mooney's neo-Weberianism with two major arguments: first, that so-called contradictory class locations are really based on the same social relations of production grounds that Mann and Dickson use and, second, that Mooney has misconstrued their notion of "obstacles to capitalist development" in agriculture to be immutable barriers, so that Mooney was unable to recognize that his notion of "detours" to capitalist penetration of agriculture is similar to their own views.

Mann and Dickinson thus argue that subjectivism, and the explanatory ambiguities it involves, does not yield insights beyond those afforded by a structural, neo-Marxist theory. They were also critical of Mooney's project of synthesizing Marxian and Weberian approaches on the ground that these approaches are incompatible, except on an ad hoc, eclectic basis. Mooney added further to the debate by arguing that Mann and Dickinson have exaggerated his departure from a neo-Marxist framework-that his perspective retains Marxist insights by incorporating key Marxian categories as ideal-types within a Weberian framework.

He argued that this approach overcomes the incompatibilities of the Marxian and Weberian frameworks — unless, of course, one adopts a mechanistic Marxist or Leninist perspective. His key position was that the presumption of a predictably patterned and necessary differentiation of farmers into the capitalist class and proletariat is erroneous and that subjectively meaningful human action affects the process of differentiation substantially.

With the 1980s farm crisis coming under increasing scrutiny by rural sociologists, Mooney has extended his analytical framework to an historical examination of the state-sponsored farm credit system (Farmers Home Administration [FMHA], Commodity Credit Corporation [CCC], and the Farm Credit System [FCS]) and tax policy incentives for increasing the capitalization of agriculture. Mooney conceptualizes credit and tax policies as means of dealing with the crisis of legitimacy posed by the increasing prevalence of tenant farming produced by the Great Depression.

Mooney argues that this credit and policy system created more indebted farmers who ultimately became vulnerable to financial crises in the form of rising real interest rates and declining agricultural commodity prices, a situation such as that which occurred in the 1980s. Financial crises expose to perceptive actors the role of the state in creating the crisis, thus creating another crisis of legitimacy and providing a basis for affected farmers to mobilize against the state.

Pfeffer has taken a considerably different tack than Mooney, though Pfeffer's work has some similarities to that of Mooney in that he stakes out middle ground on the question of whether the predominant feature of agriculture in advanced capitalism is the persistence of the family labour farm on one hand, or its demise into capitalist relations of production on the other.

Pfeffer conducted an historical analysis of three systems of agricultural production in the United States (industrial agriculture in California, family farming in the Great Plains, and the sharecropping system in the South prior to World War II) and demonstrated that recruitment and maintenance of access to a suitable labour force was a crucial factor shaping the disparate organizational structures of these three systems. Only in California, largely because of preexisting land concentration and of state actions to recruit and restrict the residential, educational, and occupational mobility of ethnic minority farm workers, was capitalist agriculture able to set root prior to World War II. Noting that the U.S. South had a high degree of land concentration during the entirety of the nineteenth century, Pfeffer goes on to explain why southern planters were unable to recruit a wage labour force after the Civil War and why the tying of sharecroppers to plots on the landlord's plantation through the crop-lien system was the only possible route to recruiting the labour necessary to operate a large plantation.

Finally, Pfeffer demonstrates that a combination of labour scarcity, the unwillingness of immigrants to work for wages on farms, and severe declines in the price of wheat in the late nineteenth century led to the establishment and persistence of family farming in the Great Plains. Pfeffer thus suggests that while capitalist agriculture can emerge under particular circumstances, there have been several alternative forms of agricultural organization — sharecropping and family farming, in particular — that have become established due to regional and commodity variations in the ability of farmers to recruit a dependable labour force.

Still a different approach was taken by Whatmore *et al.*, who have developed a theoretically based typology of farms in Britain. Their goal was to understand the effects of external pressures by nonfamily and nonfarm capitals to penetrate agriculture and how these pressures articulated with internal processes on farms. By cross-classifying levels or degrees of subsumption of internal and external relations, they developed a typology with four main categories of farm types, ranging from relatively unsubsumed ("marginal closed unit") to the "subsumed unit." The internal relations variable pertained to ownership and control of farm capital and land, control over management, and the balance of family and hired labour.

The external relations variable pertained to level of dependence on industrial capitals for production inputs and purchase of farm outputs and to the degree of involvement in credit relations, especially with finance capitals. Applying this theoretically based typology to the data from three areas in southern England — an urban fringe area, an agricultural area undergoing commercial and industrial development, and a primarily agricultural area — they found that the process of subsumption of farm production relations, and thus their integration into the "wider circuits of capital," varied over time and space. Whatmore *et al.* concluded that farm families need to be understood as actors in the process of subsumption rather than its passive victims. The neo-Marxian theoretical enterprise (and that of the modernization school as well) on the conversion of traditional peasant economic relations to commodity relations under capitalism has also been scrutinized by Vandergeest.

Among his major criticisms were that neo-Marxist approaches tend to be too unilinear, too macro-structural, too denying of human agency, too inattentive to the role of the state in the process, and too unconnected with practice. He has argued, from a neo-Weberian position rooted in the work of Pierre Bourdieu, that all categories and theories are in the last analysis historically contingent, ideological, and interpretive social products.

The world is a complex whole which can only be investigated empirically and understood through theory. It cannot be reduced to the simple working out of a model derived through deductive theory — whether that of "simple commodity production" or of "capitalism". There is not a single deductive logic (such as the logic of exchange-value or accumulation) underlying or determining all relations in a capitalist formation, but there are different, historically contingent principles which we can only investigate through empirical research.

There has recently been a tendency in the neo-Marxist and neo-Weberian literatures toward a deemphasis on "deductivist"-functionalist theoretical postures. Subjectivist perspectives such as those of Vandergeest and Mooney have been influential in leading to this reorientation, though this tendency is by no means limited to those persuaded by neo-Weberianism. The three postures in the Marxist political economy of agricultural tradition — those emphasizing the persistence of petty commodity production, those emphasizing the inevitable differentiation of petty commodity producers into antagonistic social classes, and those seeking synthetic positions — have yielded a continuing, lively debate in the rural sociology literature. Particularly instructive is the debate over the Mann-Dickinson hypothesis.

Also of importance is Goodman and Redclift's commentary on the work of Friedmann in which Goodman and Redclift critique Friedmann for taking an overly deductive approach to petty commodity production that ignores the role of historical conjuncture and ideology. Bernstein has made a comparable argument — that generic theories of simple commodity production under advanced capitalism tend to overemphasize its "functional" aspects and downplay contradictions and the diversity of household forms of production. It should be emphasized that theoretical and empirical treatments of the political economy of North American agriculture have not been made only by rural sociologists. Many of the pioneers in this tradition of scholarship have been nonsociologists or sociologists who have had little or no connection with the Rural Sociological Society or the institutionalized form of rural sociology in U.S. land-grant universities. Nonetheless, rural sociologists have made influential contributions to this literature.

The emerging political economy tradition in the sociology of agriculture has led to a provocative and stimulating literature. It should be mentioned, however, that those working from this perspective are just beginning to establish a distinctive research programme; much of the existing literature, in fact, often tends to involve superimposing a new vocabulary on already-established data, such as Goss *et al.* set out to do. Establishment of a distinctive research tradition will probably occur slowly since conventional data sources such as censuses and sample surveys are often inapplicable to theoretical issues in the political economy of agriculture. There have, nonetheless, been several research papers in the political economy tradition that have utilized innovative new methodologies to generate research findings that bear directly on specific hypotheses.

Subculture and Agricultural Structure

It is useful to note that the growing interest in subjectivist approaches in the new sociology of agriculture has not been confined to those who work within the neo-Marxist and neoWeberian traditions. Anthropologically-oriented researchers have also contributed to this literature through the examination of the effects of ethnic background on state and local level farm structure.

Salamon and associates have done the pathbreaking studies in the anthropological tradition in Illinois communities, though recently this work has been taken up by others.

While their work was not intended to contribute to the "structure versus agency" debate that has raged between Mann and Dickinson on one hand, and Mooney on the other, and actually predated much of this debate, it is clearly relevant to the debate. In particular, the work of Salamon and associates pertains to the role of subjective motivations in farm decision making, especially motivations conditioned by persisting subcultural variations based in differences in ethnic origins of farm families. The key finding of this line of research has been that farm families with German ethnic backgrounds tend to view farming as a way of life and hold a strong value for keeping the family farm intact. These Salamon has labeled "yeoman" farmers.

In contrast, farm families with British ethnic backgrounds tend to be more entrepreneurially oriented, viewing farming as a way to make profits and having little attachment to farming or to particular farms. These Yankee farmers are more likely to seek growth in scale and less likely to support their local communities. This research has led to understanding differentials in farm size as a partial function of differences between these subcultural variants. Flora and Stitz found that yeoman farmers in a Kansas county generally expanded less than did Yankee farmers. Foster *et al.* also found support for the Salamon hypothesis in a study of a sample of Illinois farms that had been in the same families for 100 years or more.

Several other anthropological studies in the tradition of Salamon and colleagues have been reported in Chibnik. Of particular importance is Barlett's article in which she criticizes notions of the demise of the family farm and of the "disappearing middle" from an anthropological perspective.

BENEFICIAL ECONOMIC PRODUCTION IN COMMERCIAL FOREST MANAGEMENT

In order to get the most beneficial economic production out of our local forests, the practices and techniques of forest management need to be applied. As of 1924, Wicomico County was roughly 46% wooded with the other 54% covered by agricultural, commercial, and residential land. Most of the 46% wooded land was and has been privately owned. In Wicomico County, the majority of wooded areas are privately owned and are mostly idle lands on a landowner's property. As a landowner, especially a farmer, the more economic profits you can get for your land the better. During the late 19th century and early to mid 20th century farmers and landowners were managing their idle lots into pine plantations. The February 17th, 1948 edition of the *Salisbury Times* even had an article entitled "Farmers Discover Timber is a Crop, Shore Benefits Too" and in this article it explains how modern day forestry practices are encouraging the re-growth of loblolly pine plantations in active timber lots. The dominant forestry management practices during the 20th Century were commercially based, meaning most of our forests were used to support timber and a very small portion of Wicomico's forests were being conserved to support diversity. Through different forestry management practices to promote commercial forests there has been a major loss of ecological diversity in Wicomico County.

PRESCRIBED FIRES IN FORESTRY MANAGEMENT

One forestry management practice was borrowed from the local Native Americans and used to protect the commercial loblolly dominated forests. During the 1920's through the 1930's the United States and especially Maryland went through a dry era. This was also around the Great Depression and the famous Dust Bowl in the Mid-West. The pine industry in Wicomico County was not only an important industry it was an economic resource that affected most of the citizens in the county.

Devastating forest fires became a threat to dry pine plantations and the fires would consume thousands of dollars in timber. The reason why these fires were so devastating is because dead vegetative matter including layers of dead pine needles and cones as well as other dead vegetation was allowed to accumulate on the forest floor. This built up matter that would naturally dissipate due to natural forest fires was not allowed to because fire was viewed as a costly event and forests were highly protected.

In the 1950's foresters figured out that fire could be the best tool to prevent more fires and to help promote the loblolly. Like thousands of years of fire forest management practices used by Native Americans, prescribed burns were used in Wicomico to prevent large costly fires from happening. Prescribed burns are man-made controlled fires applied to pine plantations used to burn up extra forest floor material and to eliminate unwanted plants, trees and future fires. Another positive of a prescribed burn is that the burnt material gives the soil back vital nutrients that help promote the growth of more trees.

Environmentally the prescribed fires of the 20th Century took its toll on diversity. The Natives used fire to control the forests to be diverse to support hunting. The fires during the 20th Century were being used to not only burn excess forest floor matter but to also eliminate competing vegetation of the loblolly pine. These fires eliminated young hardwood saplings from maturing as well as other shrubs that many species depend on. Also the smoke from prescribed fires was not too pleasing to the local communities. With the right winds the smoke would drift to people's homes, along highways and into towns making many people unhappy. One of the last things a person would like to smell on a nice spring day is smoke.

Clear-Cut/Regeneration Harvests

Clear-cutting, also know as the regeneration cut, has become the most economically beneficial harvesting management technique for the loblolly pine. Before forestry management existed, clear-cutting was used to open up the land for agricultural uses and to make settlements for the early settlers. Many years after these fields were abandoned the first trees to reemerge were the loblolly pines because they grow well in direct sunlight. Loblolly forests then began to make up most of the county while the diverse mixed hardwood/ softwoods stayed in the low-lying, wet, untouched areas. While this nation was growing, it needed a timber supply to help construct cities, boats, and crates and to fulfill other construction requirements. Wicomico County and the timber industry, were extremely important because of its fast renewable timber resource and accessibility to major cities on the eastern sea board. Clear-cutting was one of the first management practices used. It was used because it allowed the industry to get as much timber as possible in a short period of time. Clear-cutting is selecting a wooded lot and cutting down all the trees and clearing away the brush. This method of forest management works well with the loblolly because its' seed cones can naturally regenerate new trees and the open sun is great for their growth. As Wicomico County and the rest of the country found out, clear-cuts could not be the only method of forest management. If everything became clear-cut then the industry would have to wait many years for the next generation to reach full maturity. Therefore, the practice of a rotating clear-cut was needed to support the timber industry. Different tracts of land had different aged stands of loblollies so that there would be a continual timber crop. Environmentally it is not a good method because it decreases the diversity of the stand because all the trees will be of the same age and a healthy forest needs a mixed forest of trees of varying ages.

In a study done by Wayne C. Zipperer of the USDA Forest Service, deforestation in Wicomico County caused by clear-cutting creates patterns in the forest cover and affects the diversity of species. According to Zipperer's study, there are five distinguishable patterns of deforestation: internal, indentation, cropping, fragmentation, removal. Each one of these patterns has a direct impact on the habitat quality of the forest patches. The interior, or the middle, of forests is important to many species for protective nesting grounds and refuge. Between the years of 1973 and 1981 the forest interior declined in Wicomico County by 3.2 square miles. This means species of birds and other animals have been forced to find other forest interiors to nest and seek refuge, thus lowering the diversity in this county. One bird that has been affected is the Red-Eyed Vireo, a Neotropical bird that breeds and nests in the mid-latitudes (Wicomico) and spends its winters in the Amazon basin of South America. In order to breed it needs deep groves of shade-trees. Wildlife also needs connected forests and habitat fragmentation is the most serious threat to having a fully biological diverse forest. The pattern of indentation is the most prevalent pattern in Wicomico County. Indentation occurs when clear-cuts are intruding into the forest interiors creating peninsulas of the forest cover. This practice promotes the loss of interior habitat and promotes forest edge habitat. Forest edge habitat is mostly used as a resting point for migrating creatures and a hunting ground for predators giving the prey less cover in which to hide.

Forests Were First Managed

For thousands of years Native Americans have been managing forests in the Northeastern United States including Wicomico County and the rest of the Eastern Shore. According to Stephen Pyne, a fire historian, Native Americans in the northeast would set fires off in forests in order to make hunting easier. According to the Native American tribes of the eastern United States fire was known as Our Grandfather Fire. Native American "economies were dependent on fire" and without fire their "economies would have collapsed". Besides burning forests to clear the way for hunting, Native Americans also used fire in the forests to obtain firewood. Although forests provided the first Europeans with timber fuel and game their views of the forest were "an obstacle to agriculture". This European ideology of the forest led to widespread deforestation during the 18th Century. While trees were being cut down to make room for farm fields, the timber cut was being sent down to the islands of Barbados and Antigua who no longer had enough timber because they used up all of their resources. During these times someone would go out into the forest with an ox-drawn cart and then load the timber onto that. Forests were slashed and burned, meaning people would girdle a tree (removing its bark) in order for the tree to die and dry. After many months once the large trees were dead and dry fire was used to clear large portions of the forests. There is actually a small town in Worcester County called Girdletree which took its name from this slash and burn technique of clearing the forests. According to Jack Wennersten an Environmental Historian, early "Chesapeake farmers and planters had little use for the forest as an aesthetic end in itself. Trees on the horizon irritated their eyes and they wanted to see bare ground".

The forest management techniques of the Native Americans and European settlers were different. The Natives used the forest to benefit themselves however left a minimum impact on the surrounding environment. The settlers viewed the forest as a both an obstacle and resource. Their views exploited the forest to fit their needs and left major impacts to the surrounding environment. Clear-cuts are also dangerous environmentally through nutrient run-off. When clear-cuts take place around bodies of water, excess nutrients in the soil runoff by erosion and into the water. The nutrients promote extra unwanted growth of aquatic vegetation that clouds the water and chokes out fish. The nutrients are allowed to run-off because the root systems of the trees that once held the soil together are no longer present and cannot prevent erosion. The extra nutrients in the water mean excess grow in aquatic vegetation that chokes out fish and other aquatic organisms.

Herbicides

With recent advances in herbicides and fertilizers forest management has turned to some fairly newer practices. Thinning and clear-cutting are still the most widely used management practices however; the use of herbicides has taken over some of the duties of prescribed burns. Although prescribed burns are still useful to eliminate forest fire fuel on the forest floor they are not needed to eliminate unwanted brush and trees. Herbicides have been used in Wicomico Country in order to allow purely loblolly pines to grow on certain areas and not allow other vegetation. In 1984 the herbicide Imazapyr, commonly know as Arsenal, was registered in the United States and in 1986 was first used in Wicomico County on pine stands after a clear-cut to promote the loblolly pine.

The first application method used with Arsenal in Wicomico County was when a tank of Arsenal was dragged around a clear cut by a skidder in an arc fashion; however this method did not last because it was not cost effective. According to Metzger, since the skidder was too expensive, local foresters contracted helicopter companies to spray sites; this method was more time efficient and less expensive. Arsenal is applied to clear-cut areas because it stops the growth of unwanted vegetation without harming the commercially important loblolly pine. Herbicides were introduced into the United States in the mid 20th Century and their first uses were for agricultural fields. Prior to Arsenal, the herbicides Velpar and Tordon were used in forestry. Metzger stated that these two herbicides were not always consistent. Tordon and Velpar were not consistent because if it rained after an application it would run-off the desired tract. According to Anthony F. Maciorowski, Branch Chief of Ecological Effects Branch Environmental Fate and Effects Division, "Due to the extreme phytotoxicity, its (Tordon) persistence under typical environmental conditions, and its extreme propensity to leach into groundwater in all soil types, the EEB is strongly recommending against the reregistration of all active ingredients of Picloram. This conclusion is based on the extreme exceedance of the acute levels of concern for non-endangered and endangered terrestrial plants."

Arsenal has been used because it does not run-off if it rains soon after an application and it consistently kills unwanted vegetation. It has both an effect on the diversity of trees and vegetation in the forest and harms forest animals. Arsenal is considered as a non-selective broad-spectrum systematic herbicide that attacks plants stems and root systems. This means Arsenal does not differentiate which plants it kills, however it does not have any effect on the loblolly. This means endangered and threatened plant species are killed if they come in contact with Arsenal. Maryland currently has ten plants listed as threatened or endangered by the United States Fish & Wildlife Service. These plants include four threatened species: Seabeach Amaranth, Joint-Vetch, Swamp Pink, and the Small Whorled Pogonia. The six endangered species include: The Northeastern Bulrush, American Chaffseed, Smooth Coneflower, Canby's Dropwort, Sandplain Gerardia, and the Harperella. The Canby's Dropwort endangerment is directly due to pine plantations. Canby's Dropwort is native to Wicomico County and was once abundant in the area. It first became threatened when its needed wetland habitat was being lost to the construction of pine plantations. Bulldozers were used to fill in Wicomico's low-lying wetlands and converted them into working pine plantations. Since the Canby's Dropwort needs a wetland habitat in order to survive, the destruction of Wicomico's low-lying wetlands are the reason why this plant is now endangered. Now there is an endangered plant where the application of Arsenal on clear-cut sites can make it even more endangered.

Local foresters claim that the amount of Arsenal required to kill a mammal is rather large. This statement is true, large quantities of Arsenal exposed through animals by oral ingestion, exposure through skin or inhalation is needed for an animal to die. However, animals never take in enough of Arsenal to kill them. Thus it is deemed safe to wildlife, which is false. Just because death is not directly related to the herbicide does not mean it does not have other negative effects on the local wildlife. According to tests performed by Caroline Cox of the *Journal of Pesticide Reform*, Arsenal's acute toxicity has been observed as the cause of many problems with animals. Arsenal causes bleeding and congested lungs in rabbits (the tested animal); congestion was also found in the kidneys, liver and intestines of rabbits as well. Arsenal is also corrosive to the eyes and can cause irreversible damage. When Arsenal is exposed to the skin of animals it has been observed to cause reddening, scaling and crusting and also cause stomach ulcers and intestinal lesions on rabbits. Arsenal also stays persistent in the soil between 60 to 436 days depending on its application and run-off. The foresters are correct, Arsenal does not directly kill animals, however Arsenal does harm animals in a way that may lead to death in another manner.

Thinning

Often, before a clear-cut harvest another technique in forestry management is used to lessen the competition for the loblollies. According to some experts, thinning is the single most important management practice a pine plantation could receive.

The goal in a clear-cut it to get the maximum income from a particular stand in one cut, however, this is not the primary goal of thinning. The goal of thinning is to get the softwood loblolly pine stands ready to provide high value timber in the future.

Thinning is when certain trees are removed in order to encourage the growth of future trees by having them somewhat evenly distributed throughout the stand. In some cases the trees that are removed could be still used commercially and thus the thinning is known as a commercial thinning. In those cases where there is not a market for the removed trees the thinning is known as a precommercial thinning. Thinning is used because if a wooded lot is going to be used commercially the amount of trees on that land needs to be regulated. If there are too many trees growing on the lot it could affect the growth of the rest of the lot produce less desirable timber.

By thinning trees out, it benefits the remaining trees' growth rate, strength and market value. There are three distinct benefits to the tree farmer through thinning. The growth is concentrated on fewer trees allowing them to reach maturity faster meaning more value for the trees that are left. The low value timber does not take up unwanted room allowing only high value timber to continue to grow. Trees that would have died before the final harvest can be marketable and worth money. Thinning is a process that would take place before a final harvest which is often times a clear-cut. An unthinned forest has benefits for some timber manufacturers as well. When the loblolly is cut to be made into poles denser wood is more important and thinning would not be used to keep the trees tall and dense. On a biological stance, thinning has great economic benefits for the tree farmer as well. The loblolly trees, along with other trees, are in a constant battle between each other for vital nutrients, sunlight, and water to survive. If the stand was just left alone without thinning, the trees would not grow as well because they have to battle for the water and nutrients. With a thinned forest, competition for the nutrients, sunlight and water is much less allowing each tree a better chance at growing into a mature and valuable tree. If natural thinning occurs most trees are too crowded and do not receive enough sunlight, and they just die. According to a North Carolina State University study, a stand that would have had 600 to 1,000 trees could be reduced only to a few hundred by the time maturity is reached at age forty. This displays that if a forest is thinned there would be less competition and more desired trees reach full maturity. One negative effect of thinning economically is that it is more expensive then clear-cutting. Since thinning is more expense the farmer would receive less money rather than if he just had a clear cut. However, with clear-cutting a farmer needs to wait 50-60 years before receiving any kind of money; with thinning some thinned trees are worth money and would give the farmer a money source between final harvests.

The management practice of thinning has been practiced for a long time in Wicomico's timber industry. During the early part of the 20th century state experts in forestry would come to Wicomico County to have lectures to teach farmers and lot owners how to manage their loblolly pine stands so that they could get the most value for their timber. In November of 1924 Fred B. Trenk, an Extension Forester of the University Maryland, gave demonstrations on thinning to local farmers. On April 22, 1926 Dr. F. B. Arenk of the University of Maryland gave a lecture on forestry and handling woodlots to local woodlot owners at the Salisbury Court House. During this lecture Dr. Arenk discussed the shortest possible time in which a loblolly's could be grown and what could be done to help the process. During this same period of time there were also demonstrations given by foresters to farmers on how to thin their forests. These demonstrations and lectures made an impact in the Wicomico area because it gave people economic benefits to their wooded lots. It was also important because it puts more land into active timber production, meaning the dominate forestry management was commercially related.

Prior to the 1980's thinning was an expensive and time consuming practice because it was done manually. Ron Metzger, Wicomico County forester for the State of Maryland, said the biggest change in thinning since he arrived here in the 1980's is the advancement in technology. Thinning is now done with specialized mechanical equipment that cuts down manual labour expenses and also speeds up the process. Now since thinning is a quicker process, more tracts can get thinned in a shorter amount of time creating more productive timber lands. This practice does damage to forest diversity because any competing trees or vegetation are thinned out to allow excess growth to the loblolly pine. Thinning promotes the growth of one species of tree at an even age. A forest with an even-aged single tree specie promotes a balanced habitat to very few organisms.

ENVIRONMENTAL ALTERNATIVE MANAGEMENT

It is extremely important to manage land for commercial timber purposes. Wicomico has historically been one of the leading counties for the timber industry in Maryland and it provides jobs and a way of life for some of our local citizens. Just as their views of how the forest should be used is important, so are the views of people who moved here from across the Chesapeake Bay and other locals who would like to preserve the forests and use the land for a variety of other uses.

Wildlife Management

In the early 1990's the Wicomico Demonstration Forest had extra funds which they used to hire a biologist to work with Ron Metzger, the county forester. Starting in 1992, Brenda Belensky worked at the Demonstration Forest and helped local woodland owners make plans on managing their forest land to support wildlife habitat rather than just managing the land for just timber. One land owner in 1992 who was interested in managing his land for wildlife habitat was Edward Beitschwerdt of East New Market who owned land three miles west of Quantico along Nutter's Neck Road. On his 149 acre forested lot, Mr. Beitschwerdt was interested in improving the wildlife habitat and contacted Belensky for her advice.

Belensky went to Beitschwerdt's forest and then wrote up a report of what needed to be done in order to improve the wildlife habitat. In her assessment she stated "Wildlife need food, water, cover, and space in order to survive; Cover for nesting or concealment and space are usually the most critical, all of these factors must be present throughout the year, be available in variety and be interspersed throughout the habitat". Another factor according to Belensky needed to manage a forest for wildlife is managing for diversity of vegetation types, this is important because different wildlife species have different habitat requirements. The rest of her report discusses how Mr. Beitschwerdt could improve the diversity of his forest to provide a working habitat for many different wildlife species.

This report proves that some local woodland owners are concerned at preserving vital habitat for wildlife; they would even go as far as seeking advice from a biologist in order to accomplish their goals. Unfortunately, due to a lack of funding, Brenda Belensky's position as county biologist had to be cut three years after it began. This means people who are interested in improving wildlife habitat on their land do not have a county biologist to get advice and suggestions from. This indicates that the state is more interested in keeping lands in timber production than promoting vital habitat. The state should provide both a county forester and a county biologist to allow local landowners a variety of options for managing their land. By just having a forester position, it only allows for timber management options for landowners and our local forests.

Oldest Pine Plantation

Mary Jester of Jesterville and her ancient loblolly forest is a perfect example of how much forests are important to the people of Wicomico County. In 1877 John F. Jester planted many loblollies on his land in Jesterville. When John F. Jester died, the land was then owned by his third wife, Mary Jester. Seventy-one years after the planting, in 1948, she owned the oldest planted pine forest not just in Wicomico County but in the entire country. This was also the same time period when a study was conducted by J.P Brown that cutting cost is cheaper on larger old growth trees. According to Brown, cutting large diameter trees saves time and money. Money is saved because older trees can provide more timber than younger trees and man hours could be saved.

Local forestry experts said Mary Jester's stand was deteriorating and that in 1922 there were 286 loblollies on her land compared to 124 in 1948. Their was a loss of about 4.5 trees a year. The foresters suggested to Mary that to get economic benefits from that stand it needed to be cut as soon as possible to salvage the remaining old growth timber. Mary Jester had other plans for her forest; she considered it to be a landmark in Jesterville and that was more important to her and the people of Jesterville than acquiring money. According to Mary "its historical and sentimental values were greater than the value that could be realized from the sale of timber". Mary Jester let the ancient pines stand and serve as a demonstration of the life history of a planted loblolly stand.

Arboretum Management

Here on Maryland's Eastern Shore there are two areas that are managed as arboretums. An arboretum is a botanical garden devoted to diverse and exotic species of trees and plants, many arboretums are used to study and observe rare plants and trees and they serve as a nice scenic place for the public to talk walks and enjoy the outdoors. In 1972 the first arboretum was founded on the Eastern Shore in Caroline County on the grounds of the Tuckahoe State Park. It was named the Adkins Arboretum after the famous timber family of Salisbury. This arboretum was funded and donated by Leon Andrus who wanted to display all of the different forest types of Maryland. After Andrus's death in 1989 he left the rest of his money for future upkeep of the Adkins Arboretum. Today the Adkins Arboretum's goal is to display all the indigenous plants of Delmarva for study and observation purposes. Another unique aspect of the Adkins Arboretum is that "it is the only arboretum or public garden in the region that focuses solely on plants native to the Mid-Atlantic Coastal Plain." Adkins Arboretum is used to promote the conservation of native plants and has an average of 14,000 visitors annually.

The Adkins Arboretum is not the only place on Delmarva managed as an Arboretum. Wicomico County has its own Arboretum which few people are aware of it is located on the entire Salisbury University Campus. In 1985

Salisbury started to collect a variety of different woody plants and trees and three years later in 1988 was declared as an arboretum. This arboretum is important to the campus's faculty and students because it provides a beautiful landscape that provides a better learning environment and is used aesthetically to help combat the many stresses of being a college student. The wide varieties of plants are used by students in a variety of different classes. Daniel Yeager, class of 2006, stated that "I have used the campus's arboretums landscaped in my Biological Drawling class; also in other art classes I have use the campus's landscape for multiple drawings and paintings". The arboretum is also used by Plant Taxonomy classes to classify different plant and tree types. The Salisbury University is a beautiful campus in part because it is a working arboretum with over 750 different species of local and exotic plants and trees that help aid learning and gives both the campus community and the local community a place to appreciate diversity.

The Delmarva Fox Squirrel

Since the majority of Wicomico's forest land today is managed to be timber productive the loss of our local diversity has taken a hit. Since less effort is being put into having a variety of different forest type management Wicomico has lost an important species that was once abundant and called this county home, the Delmarva Fox Squirrel. Mary Jester's ancient pine stand had the oldest trees in the entire Wicomico County. The word ancient is normally associated with things being extremely old like the mighty Redwoods in northern California which have been standing as long as people have inhabitant the continent. Ancient in Wicomico County refers to trees that have been standing between 70 and 80 years. The difference in meaning of the term ancient between the Redwood forest and the local forests in Wicomico County could be described as quite comical. However, it is not comical to species that depend on old growth forests in order to survive like the Delmarva Fox Squirrel which has been an endangered species since 1967 and currently does not exist anymore in Wicomico.

The Delmarva Fox Squirrel once ranged from as far north as Pennsylvania and the entire Delmarva Peninsula but now is restricted to less than 10% of its original range. Their population has dwindle so much that populations of Fox Squirrels are now only found on protected refuges like the Eastern Neck Wildlife Refuge, Blackwater National Refuge, Chincoteague National Refuge, Maryland's Wye Island National Resource Areas and LeCompte Wildlife Management Area. The Delmarva Fox Squirrel, which is the largest tree squirrel in the Western Hemisphere, has been ousted from Wicomico County due to loss and fragmentation of their natural habitat due to timber harvesting and converting forest land into farms, neighborhoods and other development. Listed in 1967 as a federally endangered species, the Delmarva Fox Squirrel needs to have mature old growth forests made of both hardwoods and softwoods. Old growth forests are extremely important to the Delmarva Fox Squirrel because old, dead, hollowed out trees provide crucial nesting areas. Without old growth forests this squirrel cannot breed. Wicomico County's forests are primarily managed pine plantations and once these trees reach the age of maturity they are cut.

Dying or dead trees that could provide a nest for this squirrel are thinned out of the forests to promote better quality timber. The nuts and seeds from oak, hickory, sweetgum, walnut and loblolly are also needed in the diet of the Delmarva Fox Squirrel. Since Wicomico's forest a primarily managed for loblolly there is a limited food source, a mixed forest provides a better habitat than just a pine dominated forest.

Who cares about the Delmarva Fox Squirrel? The Delmarva Fox Squirrel is important and special because it is native and only found on the Eastern Shore. It is a symbol to the region and many people find it interesting to observe and study because it is only located here. Without the presence of the Delmarva Fox Squirrel Wicomico County becomes less unique because it does not have this rare animal and more diversity is lost.

6

Forests and their Products

FORESTS AND THEIR CHIEF PRODUCTS

In trying to see what lies ahead for world forestry it is first necessary to take cognizance of the dimensions and the complexities of the forest problem. It is also important to keep in mind the limitations of the forecasters, for the outlook depends very much on the lookout. In varying combinations, all men have hopes and fears, tendencies to look on the bright or the dark side, inclinations to hasty or slow judgement; some are dewy-eyed about the future and for that reason cannot see clearly, while others suffer from cataracts of vested prejudice that impair the vision. Furthermore, the lookouts are not all looking in the same direction.

Some can see only the truly remarkable achievements in technology and overlook the fact that for a long time to come the main wood problem of most of mankind will not be how to obtain rayon fabrics, cellophane wrappers, or molded monocoque airplane seats, but how to secure enough firewood for cooking purposes.

Others are attracted by the improved methods of silviculture, developed particularly in northwestern Europe, but fail to keep in view the hard fact that much of what can be done in Europe cannot, for economic reasons, be done in North America and probably cannot, because of different physical conditions, be done in the tropical forests.

This personal factor is no doubt the main reason for the greatly varying reports of the prospect in view, whether they deal with trends in agriculture, forestry, or any other aspect of the man-earth relationship. Some say that a wood famine is inevitable, others assure us that no world shortage of timber is in sight and the reason for the difference in opinion obviously lies in men, not in the forest.

THE PROBLEM DEFINED

Forecasting in this field is not an exact science, partly because of personal factors that cannot be eliminated and partly because the information on which the forecast must be based is neither complete nor altogether accurate. Forest mensuration is excellent in a few countries, but the available data on forest area, volume of stand, annual growth and even yearly consumption of wood in the world as a whole are at best only rough estimates. These estimates are nevertheless important. They are, in the first place, the only quantitative data we have and they reveal the dimensions of the problem before us.

The forest inventory published in 1954 by the Food and Agriculture Organization of the United Nations (FAO) shows that the annual world consumption of wood for all purposes in recent years has been over 50 billion cubic feet and that the total area of the forests on the earth is estimated to be about 9½ billion acres.

It is not easy, indeed perhaps not possible, for the human mind to comprehend such large quantities. Many have seen the forests of Washington and Oregon and been impressed by their vastness, yet in area they constitute less than half of one per cent of the world's forests. It is not easy to envisage 9½ billion acres of forest land under management on a sustainedyield basis, but that seems to be the future goal implied by the statement in Unasylva.

"The inventory shows that the world's forests are potentially capable of furnishing a plentiful flow of forest products for a world population much higher than that of today" It is not possible to say exactly how much forest land is managed on a sustained-yield basis at the present time, because data are lacking and because good practices have been initiated so recently in many regions that we do not yet know whether yield will actually be sustained. Management of a type is practiced on some of the forests in India, Ceylon, Burma, Australia, New Zealand, in other countries and in some parts of Africa. In 1949, according to the American Forestry Association, about 55 million acres of public and private forest land in the United States were classed as under "intensive management," which is defined by the words: "high order of cutting and good fire protection" As of January 1955 nearly 34 million acres of private forests in the United States were in certified tree farms.

However, not all of these forests are truly managed as the term is understood in northwestern Europe. It is perhaps safe to say that, after more than a century of research in silviculture and experiments with forestry practices, some 160 to 180 million acres of forest land are now under management in northwestern Europe and, with an optimistic view, possibly an equal amount outside of Europe, making a total of about 350 million acres. That is, it may be conjectured that 4 or 5 per cent of the world's forest lands are at the present time under reasonably good management and 95 per cent are not. The sheer size of the task that remains to be done if the goal is to be achieved looms very large in the outlook.

The task is not only large but complex. The ultimate goal might be defined as the utilization of the world's forest lands in such a manner that they will permanently yield sufficient wood for all mankind at a price people can pay, while at the same time some of the forests will provide watershed, soil and wildlife protection, grazing opportunity and facilities for study and recreation. None of the terms in this definition can well be omitted.

The term "forest land" must be used, for in the long run it is the land that constitutes the resource and not the generation of trees that happens to occupy the land at a given time. Forestry is only one type of land use. In many regions it competes for site with other forms of land utilization: the demands of agriculture, for example, will have a decisive effect and the effect will be fatal to some of the forests. The term "permanently" must be included, for the problem is not merely to balance forest drain and growth in the immediate future, but to maintain the balance in perpetuity by increasing the growth to meet the rising demand of an increasing population.

The phrase "all mankind" is required, for the goal cannot be regarded as having been reached so long as some forest lands produce species of trees that are considered useless because there is no market for them, while other regions are so short of wood that cow dung must be used for fuel.

"Price" is perhaps the most critical term. In one way or another and regardless of type of prevailing economic theory, every forestry operation and every forest product must be paid for, whether in energy, money, or barter. Good forestry practices are simply not possible unless they are economically feasible; for all we know, some of the forests may remain inaccessible forever because access may be too costly; and technological achievement, no matter how brilliant, will be of little use if people cannot pay for the products. The terms in the last part of the definition pertain to the concept of multiple use, an idea that may or may not turn out to be practicable in the long run.

In many parts of the world problems of soil and water are far more critical than those of timber supply and large sections of the forest, probably much larger than we commonly think, will have to be reserved for the primary function of watershed protection and will serve only secondarily, or perhaps not at all, as a source of wood. Other forest lands are withdrawn from ordinary economic utilization and reserved for recreation, study, wildlife sanctuaries, or for the purpose of saving some of the undisturbed forest for future generations. An example is found in the National Parks of the United States, which contain almost half as much timber land as there is in all of West Germany.

We may not always be able to afford this luxury, but as long as the world can keep its parks and wildlife reserves they will add up to a significantly large area which, like the protection forests, cannot be included in the area of the wood-yielding forest land. There are other complicating factors. The difficulties of silviculture and management are multiplied by the many different physical characteristics of the world's forests; people have different and deeply rooted attitudes towards trees; and the problem is not made easier by the fact that the forests are under about one hundred national jurisdictions. It is not a mere matter of balancing numbers. Unasylva suggests that the wood needed for a moderately good standard of living would be an annual per capita consumption of about 35 cubic feet, basing the suggestion on prewar European experience; and makes the assumption, which seems plausible enough, that with reasonably good management the forests of the world can produce an annual yield of 30 cubic feet per average acre.

But it would be very misleading to conclude that the balance is favourable, or that no particular problem exists because there are only 2½ billion people in the world and 9½ billion acres of forest, or almost 4 acres per person.

Expected Demands for Forest Products in 1975

The outlook for the distant future depends largely on what will happen in the near future, which may be defined conveniently as the next two decades, since 1975 is the common target year in several recently published forecasts. 1 Only the major conclusions of these reports need to be considered here.

The Paley Report (1952) expects that the cubic-foot requirement of wood for all purposes in the United States will increase by 17 per cent between 1950 and 1975 and the Stanford Report (1954) foresees an increase of 14 per cent between 1952 and 1975.

These forecasts are thus not very different from earlier estimates: for example, in 1948 the Forest Service looked forward to a rise in the over-all requirement of about 50 per cent between 1945 and the year 2020, or an increase of nearly 15 per cent for each 25 years of that period. The reports are in substantial agreement in predicting a decline in the demand of wood for pilings, railroad ties, shingles and cooperage and a very marked decrease in the use of fuel wood, but they differ on some items.

The Paley Report expects that the need of pulpwood will increase by 50 per cent; the Stanford Report, by 60 per cent. The demand for peeler logs, mostly for plywood, will rise by 40 per cent according to the Paley study; by 90 per cent in the Stanford forecast. The most notable difference is in the expected board-foot requirement of saw timber for lumber, which is by far the bulkiest item in the over-all demand: the Paley Report foresees an increase of 10 per cent; the Stanford Report, one of only 3.4 per cent.

The principal reason for this difference is no doubt the fact that the Paley Report is based on the assumption of no significant change in price relationships, whereas the Stanford Report assumes that the price of lumber relative to competing materials will increase and that lumber will lose some of its markets. The Stanford assumption is well worth noting. High wood prices, causing people to prefer other materials, might have the effect of alleviating to some extent the coming pressure on the forest. A world pulp survey of the same type as the Paley and Stanford studies is reported to be in preparation by the FAO, but, to my knowledge, projections of the future world demand for all wood are not yet available. A partial world forecast, which does not include the countries in the Soviet zone, is made in the Paley Report.

The average total output and requirement of industrial wood during the years from 1947 to 1949 are compared with the average prospective output and requirement during the decade of the 1970's. Fuel wood and charcoal are not included.

The conclusion is that the total output will probably increase by 4 per cent and the total requirement by 40 per cent. It is very likely that the demand will rise, but the 4 per cent increase in output may be an overestimate. According to Egon Glesinger of the FAO, as reported in American Forests, the inventories have shown that the output of the world's forests is not rising, despite increasing demands.

The type of forest products demanded and regional differences between the United States and Latin America in the use of wood. The products are shown as percentages of the total cut of all timber, as measured in cubic feet.

	United States		Latin America
	1952	1975	1952
Lumber	58%	59%	9%
Pulpwood	17	24	2
Fuel wood	13	3	80
Other products	12	14	9
	100	100	100

An indication of regional differences in the demand and use of wood on a world-wide basis is presented in Unasylva, December 1954. Expressed in approximate percentages of world forest area, population and total production in cubic feet of roundwood in 1953, the data reveal the differences between the highly industrialized countries of the northern hemisphere and the rest of the world. By "North America" is meant Canada and the United States and "Europe" includes the Soviet Union.

	Forest Area	Population	Total Wood	Fuel Wood	Industrial Wood
North America and Europe	40%	30%	70%	50%	88%
Rest of the world	60%	70%	30%	50%	12%

The heaviest production and consumption of industrial wood products, such as lumber, plywood, pulp and paper, are clearly concentrated in North America and Europe and the demand for these products is steadily rising. Furthermore, a large part of the industrial timber cut elsewhere, chiefly in the tropical forests, is exported to Europe and North America. The industrial demand is preponderantly for lumber and pulp, but the most widespread and still the largest single requirement is fuel wood.

Almost half of the total output of some 50 billion cubic feet in 1953 was fuel wood; even in Europe this requirement accounted for slightly more than one third of the total cut; and in many countries besides Latin America 80 per cent or more of the entire production was for firewood. At the present time, then, the demand on the world's forests is mainly for fuel wood, lumber and pulp, in that order and this is likely to continue at least in the near future. Whether or not the forecasts will come true naturally depends on how valid the underlying premises turn out to be. The Stanford Report is based on the general assumptions that:

- No major war will occur.
- No radical advance in technology will increase production at a Tate faster than in the past,
- Business cycles will become more stable, accompanied by high employment. Another assumption, based on data of the Bureau of Census, is that the population of the United States will increase by 35 per cent to reach 212 million in 1975. The premises of the Paley Report are generally similar; for example, the expectation of a 40 per cent rise in the world requirement of wood rests on the assumptions of a population increase of 47 per cent, continued high demand in the industrial countries and rising consumption in others.

The safest of the assumptions is that population will increase and this alone would mean a rising demand for forest products. If a major war should come, the drain on the forest would surely increase drastically, as it has in past ways and the over-all requirement might become much larger than the forecasts indicate. If peace lasts but good economic conditions do not, the demand for industrial forest products would probably be less, but the world requirement of fuel wood might remain unaffected.

The second assumption of the Stanford Report has already been questioned by some forestry people, who believe that the large sums of money currently invested in research will result in technological improvements which will have a marked effect not only on efficiency in production but will help the industry to hold and even expand its markets.

An editor of House Beautiful magazine, speaking before the annual convention of the National Lumber Manufacturers Association in November 1954, challenged some of the Stanford predictions, declaring that the concept of abundant living demanded more lumber for dwelling units and urged the manufacturers to gear their thinking to an expanding market and an expanding American home.

It may well be that a 15 per cent increase in the over-all requirement of wood is about what can be expected in the next quarter century. But thereafter will come other quarter centuries and no evidence is at hand showing that this or any other country intends to stop growing in 1975. On the contrary, like the editor who spoke to the lumber manufacturers, most people hope for a steadily expanding economy, which of necessity means a steadily increasing demand on the natural resources, including the forests. If the hope is fulfilled, the outlook is that before very long the requirement will increase not by a mere 15 per cent, but by 100 or 200 per cent and perhaps more.

The question is how the forest will stand up under the rising pressure. The forecasters do not provide clear answers, only clear affirmations of their faith that the demand can be met. The conclusion of most of the reports, whether they deal with the United States or the world, is that the area of the forest is large enough to provide the wood needed in the future, even if the need should become twice or three times as large as today, but only on two conditions: much of the now inaccessible forests must be opened to utilization and all forests must be placed under greatly improved sustained-yield management. These are not small conditions and in them, it might be said, lies the whole forest problem.

The problem can be resolved into three major parts. The first is the question of supply: of forest area, forest soil, stand, annual growth and natural factors affecting the trees, such as fire, insects and diseases. The second is the problem of how best to utilize the supply: of silviculture, forest genetics, methods of cutting, logging, manufacturing-in short, technological knowledge. The third can be called cultural or institutional in nature; it is the question of our social-economic-political ability to apply the technological skill to best advantage.

More particularly, then, the outlook depends on trends of development in all of these fields; and the direction of the trends cannot be determined by looking only towards the future: we must also be guided by the past. Perhaps the most important thing to grasp is that in nearly all of these fields we are dealing with processes that have the tremendous momentum of history behind them.

WOOD PRODUCTS

Wood may be converted into other useful products by mechanical, chemical, or biological methods, or combinations of methods. Some wood pulp is made mechanically, some chemically and some by a combination of the two. Sugar and some other chemicals are made from wood by chemical methods, yeast and alcohol by chemical conversion followed by biological action. Other organic products can also be made by fermentation of wood sugar.

Charcoal and other wood-distillation products are the result of chemical change brought about by heating without the use of additional chemicals. Lactic, butyric and acetic acids have been made experimentally in substantial yields by direct fermentation of sawdust without intervening chemical treatment, although this conversion method is not known to be in commercial use.

From the standpoint of volume of wood used, number of employees, value of products and influence upon the world's economy, the most important of the wood-conversion industries is the pulp and paper industry..

The pulp and paper industry is really two industries which overlap to such a degree that neither one is entirely distinct from the other. In addition, the fibreboard or building-board industry is closely related to the pulp industry. Some mills produce pulp only and sell it to other manufacturers. Some produce pulp for their own use only, in the manufacture of paper or other pulp products. Other mills produce pulp that they convert into building boards. Many mills produce paper only, from purchased pulp. Paper, in turn, is produced in a multitude of grades and qualities and converted into an almost unlimited number of end products.

THE WOOD-PULP INDUSTRY

Wood pulp may be made by strictly mechanical means, by cooking wood with chemicals, or by combinations of chemical and mechanical methods.

Mechanical Pulp. This is made almost entirely by pressing blocks of wood against huge grindstones revolving in the presence of hot water. This is the cheapest method of producing pulp and gives yields of 90 per cent or more, based on the dry weight of the wood. Approximately one third of the world's pulp is made in this manner. Most of it is used in the manufacture of newspapers, but substantial amounts go into other kinds of paper. Cheap power is a basic requirement in the profitable manufacture of mechanical or "groundwood" pulp, for power is the major product consumed, in addition to the wood itself. Groundwood pulp mills are usually located, therefore, where both wood and water power are abundant and relatively cheap.

The amount of power used per ton of pulp and the quality of the pulp produced are influenced by the species of wood used, the condition of the grindstone surface and the operating conditions. Since paper made from groundwood pulp alone is too weak for most uses, stronger pulp must be added. Newsprint paper, for example, commonly contains between 15 and 20 per cent chemical pulp and the rest groundwood pulp.

Chemical Pulp. This is made by cooking wood chips under pressure in solutions of chemicals which dissolve out the lignin and some of the other soluble materials in the wood, leaving the cellulose fibres in a more or less pure state. The yield of pulp is less than half of the original weight of the wood. The quality and usefulness of the pulp depend upon the species of wood, the cooking chemical used and other cooking and processing details. In the *sulfite* process, the cooking liquor consists of a solution of calcium, magnesium, ammonium, or sodium bisulfite plus sulfurous acid. This results in a strong, relatively light-coloured pulp, which is adaptable to the widest variety of uses of any of the commercial wood pulps. One of its important uses is in mixture with groundwood pulp for the manufacture of newsprint paper.

When especially purified, sulfite pulp is used in the manufacture of viscose rayon and other cellulose derivatives. The sulfite process is used mainly with light-coloured, long-fibreed, non-resinous softwoods like spruce, hemlock and balsam, but some birch, aspen and southern yellow pine are also employed. The *sulfate* process uses an alkaline cooking liquor containing sodium sulfide and sodium hydroxide. It is adaptable to both resinous and non-resinous species and, in fact, can be used with almost any wood.

In the United States the sulfate process is used principally in the manufacture of pulp from pine, but its use for other species is growing. Most grades of sulfate pulp are used for wrapping paper, bags, fibre shipping containers and other purposes where high strength is important. The pulp can also be bleached and used for the manufacture of high-grade papers for many purposes.

In the *soda* process, also, an alkaline cooking liquor is employed, consisting of a solution of caustic soda. This method is used mainly for hardwoods and the pulp produces a bulky paper with low strength but good opacity, when used alone. Mixed with longer-fibreed pulps added for strength, soda pulp is used extensively for high-quality printing papers. Semichemical Pulps. These are newer than the others and differ from them in being produced partly by chemical and partly by mechanical means. The wood chips are softened by partial cooking in chemical solution and then pulped by passing them between revolving discs or plates. The chief cooking chemical used is neutral sodium sulfite solution, but both alkaline sulfate and acid sulfite solutions may also be used.

The yield of pulp depends upon the extent of the cooking and the severity of the processing, but is usually within the range of 70 to 80 per cent because much of the lignin is left with the fibres, in contrast with the strictly chemical processes that take out practically all of the lignin and, as pointed out, yield less than 50 per cent.

The principal use for semichemical pulps is in the production of corrugating board for fibre boxes. Bleached semichemical pulps are being used also for high-quality white papers, including glassine, bond, book, magazine and other grades. The semichemical process is especially suitable for pulping miscellaneous hardwoods, a characteristic which, together with the high yield and wide utility of the pulp, favours its increasing use.

A variation of the semichemical process consists in heating the wood in steam or water, followed by mechanical fibreization. These methods produce, with yields of 85 to 95 per cent, coarse pulps used mainly in the production of fibreboards, roofing felts and similar products. Dissolving Pulp Products. A relatively small but growing use for chemical wood pulps is for the production of highly purified pulps called dissolving pulps or high alpha-cellulose pulps. These are used in the manufacture of such products as rayon fabrics and tire cord, cellophane, absorbent tissue, lacquers, smokeless powder, photographic film, plastics and a variety of cellulose chemicals. It is estimated that more than 700 thousand tons of dissolving wood pulp were produced in the United States in 1952 and more than 420 thousand tons in Canada. Other important producers are Sweden, Norway, Finland, Western Germany, Austria, Italy and Japan.

Production and Consumption

The world production of wood pulp in 1952 was estimated by FAO at 37.7 million metric tons. Of the world production reported to FAO (not including U.S.S.R.), about 35 per cent was mechanical, 29 per cent sulfite and 36 per cent all others. The relative production of the principal pulp-producing countries and an indication of the growth of the industry are evidenced. From year to year pulp production is strongly influenced by world economic conditions; hence the relative proportions of the total contributed by different countries as well as the proportions of the different kinds of pulp vary considerably. The United States is not only the greatest producer but also the greatest consumer of wood pulp, for its pulp imports greatly exceed its exports. Canada and the Scandinavian countries produce much more pulp than they consume and depend heavily on the export markets. The United States consumes about one half of the total world production of pulp.

BUILDING BOARD OR FIBREBOARD

This classification includes coarse fibre products such as hardboards, insulation boards and similar products, largely used in building construction but also to an increasing extent for industrial products of various kinds. The estimated world production in 1953 was 2.62 million metric tons, of which hardboards, including semihardboards, constituted 48 per cent. In Europe the production of hardboards was twice as great as that of insulation boards.

The reverse was true in the United States and Canada, where insulationboard production was more than twice that of hardboards. About one third of the reported production of hardboard and two thirds of the insulation board were manufactured in the United States.

Hardboards are made in large dense sheets from various kinds of wood pulp by the use of high temperatures and pressures in hot-plate presses. Insulation boards are much lighter in weight and less dense and are dried with hot air in tunnel dryers, without pressure.

CHARCOAL AND WOOD-DISTILLATION INDUSTRY

When wood is heated to high temperatures in air it burns, but in the absence of air it turns to charcoal, giving off much gas in the process. The gas consists mostly of water, but it includes acetic acid, methyl alcohol, various light oils and tars, the proportions varying with the species of wood used and the temperatures maintained. Methyl alcohol and acetic acid made in other ways compete strongly with the wood products and the commercial value of wood tars and other distillation products is limited. As a result, most of the value of the products of wood distillation lies in the charcoal and most of the world's charcoal is produced without saving the by-products.

When the gaseous by-products are not to be saved, charcoal can be produced very simply by stacking the wood together, covering it with earth, igniting it in one or two places and maintaining a slow heat by controlling the admission of air. After the wood reaches a temperature of about 500° F. an exothermic chemical reaction begins, which furnishes much heat and reduces the amount of air required to finish the carbonization.

The time required to complete the charring process and cool the charge subsequently so that the charcoal may be removed without igniting when exposed to the air varies from three or four days to two or three weeks, according to the size of the charge and the character of the pit. Simple kilns made of brick, concrete blocks, or even metal, are often used instead of the earth covering. An ordinary five-cord concrete-block kiln can complete a charge in about eight days.

When the gases are to be condensed and saved, much more expensive equipment is required, such as steel ovens, tram cars, condensers, water pumps and refining apparatus, which make the investment much higher than when the gases are wasted.

Ovens of this kind in common use can carbonize a charge in about one day, but generally the preheating requires three days and the cooling three days in addition, making a total of seven days. Statistics on charcoal production are incomplete and inadequate. Wood used for charcoal is sometimes reported with that used for fuel and the amounts of charcoal produced are seldom reported. India is also a heavy producer, but no data on Indian production are available. Italy used about an eighth as much wood for charcoal as did Argentina.

The U.S. charcoal production is estimated at about 335,000 tons. Charcoal is used mainly for domestic fuel and carbon disulfide manufacture. In Japan and certain other countries it is used to some extent for truck and bus fuel. In the United States much charcoal is used for recreational cooking at picnics and barbecues and on similar occasions. There are, of course, innumerable industrial uses for charcoal in metallurgical, chemical and other manufacturing operations.

WOOD-HYDROLYSIS INDUSTRY

When wood is heated with acid under properly controlled conditions the celluloses and hemicelluloses are converted into sugars which can be separated and purified to produce glucose and xylose; or else the solution can be neutralized and fermented to produce alcohol, glycerine, yeast, citric acid and a number of other products.

The production of sugars from wood has been experimented with extensively in the United States and high yields have been obtained, but the process is not yet commercially successful in this country. It has found commercial use in Europe for the production of sugars, alcohol and yeast — especially in Germany, France and Switzerland. Production statistics, however, are not available.

Other Forest-Products Industries

A multitude of products other than wood comes from the forests, including naval stores, tannins and cork, which are important articles of world commerce. Rubber could be included as a forest product of great economic importance, but most of the natural rubber is now being produced from plantations instead of from wild trees in the forest. Oils, gums, waxes and resins in great variety are obtained from the forests of the world.

Many fruits, nuts, spices and other edible products originally obtained from wild trees are now produced from plantation trees of improved varieties and thus have become agricultural rather than forest products, but others are still wild-forest crops.

Christmas trees have become an important wild-forest product in the United States and Canada although gradually coming in larger quantities from plantations. In parts of the United States and Canada where hard maple is plentiful, maple syrup and maple sugar are products of local importance and esteem. The list could be extended to include hundreds of products, although many of them have local rather than international importance.

THE NAVAL-STORES INDUSTRY

Turpentine and rosin are the two principal products now included in the term "naval stores," a term that dates from the time when all ships were made of wood. Turpentine and rosin are obtained by the distillation of the oleoresin or "pitch" that exudes from living pine trees when they are "tapped" or scarified. At present these products are also obtained by steam distillation and solvent extraction from chips of resinous wood, mainly pine stumps, that have been left in the ground until the non-resinous portions have rotted away.

Substantial amounts of turpentine are also produced as a by-product in the sulfate pulping of pine chips and a much smaller amount as a by-product from the destructive distillation of pine wood.

Of the 1951 production of turpentine in the United States, it was estimated that 36 per cent was "gum" turpentine, 33.6 per cent wood turpentine (from stumps), 29.7 per cent from sulfate pulping and 0.7 per cent from destructive distillation.

Ten years earlier the percentages were 52.0, 34.6, 11.8 and 1.6. Of the 1951 U.S. rosin production, 39.4 per cent was from gum and 60.6 per cent mainly from solvent extraction. World statistics on turpentine and rosin production, which, however, does not include data from the U.S.S.R. and a number of other turpentine-producing countries.

Of the total production, the United States produced more than did the rest of the world combined. A large percentage of the production of each major producing country is exported. In addition to turpentine and rosin, pine oil, pine tar and other navalstores items are produced and an increasing number of chemicals are being synthesized from the primary naval-stores products.

Table. World Production of Turpentine and Rosin

Country	Turpentine (Thousand U.S. gal.)	Rosin (Thousand lb.)
World	53,309	1,511,797
United States	34,856	1,086,888
Other countries	18,453	424,909
France	4,685	123,457
Portugal	5,122	147,691
Sweden	3,000	6,000
Spain	2,410	57,143
Mexico	1,600	52,000
Greece	1,058	27,122
Japan	428	10,496
Others	150	1,000

CORK

Commercial cork is the outer bark of a species of oak that grows mainly in countries bordering the western half of the Mediterranean Sea, particularly France, Portugal, Spain and North Africa. Cork trees also grow in other countries in small quantities and have even been introduced into the United States, but are not industrially important there. Every eight or ten years the outer bark, usually one or two inches thick, is carefully stripped from the trees without damaging them or interfering with their growth or production of subsequent crops.

The bark is air-dried for a few days and then taken to market and sold for manufacture into insulation, bottle stoppers and cork compositions of various kinds. Portugal, the world's largest producer of cork, accounts for about half of the world's estimated production of 310,000 tons and cork and cork products are important items of export from that country. The United States uses almost one half of the world's cork crop.

TANNIN EXTRACTS

The production of tannin extracts for leather tanning amounts to a considerable industry throughout the world. The quebracho wood of South

America produces more tannin extract than does any other single source. This wood, which is very heavy, hard and high in tannin content, is chipped and leached to yield an extract that is highly valued by tanners. More than 250,000 tons of it were exported from Argentina and Paraguay in 1950.

On a smaller scale, chestnut wood chips are extracted for tannin in the United States, Italy and France. Commercial tannins are also derived from barks, fruits and leaves as well as from the wood of plants. Wattle bark from Australia and South and East Africa is an important source. Many of the forest species of the United States contain substantial quantities of tannin in their barks, but in general only the barks of eastern hemlock, chestnut oak and tanbark oak have found extensive commercial use in this country. Improvements in by-product utilization may in time bring into commercial use other barks that are available as waste in large amounts at sawmills, pulp mills, veneer mills and other factories.

Tannin production in the United States has been decreasing for years and importation increasing. In 1927 nearly 56 per cent of the vegetable tannins used in the United States were from domestic sources, but in 1950 domestic tannins constituted only about 15 per cent of the total and in 1952 the ratio was still lower. Most of the domestic tannin was obtained from chestnut wood, with much smaller amounts coming from oak and hemlock barks. Nearly 70 per cent of the tannins imported in 1950 were obtained from quebracho wood and about 19 per cent from wattle bark.

Waste Utilization

In the conversion of trees into wood products, on the average much less than half of the tree gets to market in the form of finished products. The waste is usually greater in countries that are heavily timbered or where labour costs are high than where the reverse is true. The U.S. Forest Service in 1946 estimated that of the wood cut in or imported into the United States in 1944, 43 per cent reached the hands of the user, 22.5 per cent was used under the boilers of mills and factories that processed the wood and 34.5 per cent found no use at all. This estimate did not include any bark, most of which finds no use or is burned as fuel. The waste in producing fuel wood, mine timbers and fence posts is relatively low in comparison with the waste in the production of lumber, hewed ties and cooperage, for which the estimated losses are from 68 to 72 per cent. In the manufacture of chemical pulp, the lignin and other constituents dissolved out by the pulp liquor and thus lost, amount to 50 to 60 per cent of the original pulpwood, although fuel values are received from a part of these liquors. Altogether, the total amount of lignin, bark and wood in the United States that finds no use may exceed 100 million tons annually.

As the Forest Service has pointed out, such waste could be considered equivalent to a neglected forest, a source of raw material of great potential value. The extent to which it can be used economically, however, is limited by its accessibility to markets and the cost at which it can be made available to prospective users. Manufacturers can be expected to use wood residues, instead of roundwood or lumber, as their raw material only where it is financially profitable to do so. The wood-waste problem is not one of wilful wastefulness but one of economics and technical developments.

Since 1944 much progress has been made in the use of logging, veneermill and sawmill wastes in the manufacture of pulp and building boards and these uses seem to be growing steadily. More and more sawmills are removing the bark from their logs before sawing, which increases the acceptability of the slabs and edgings from the logs for pulp manufacture. Matson estimated that the equivalent of nearly five million cords of logging and mill residues is being used annually in the production of pulp chips, hardboards and soft boards, chiefly in the Pacific Coast states.

There is also a newer and relatively much smaller use for sawdust, planer shavings and other fine material: they are combined with resins and then, by means of heat and pressure, the mixture is converted into hard, smooth sheets that can be used like plywood, hardboard and similar products, in the manufacture of doors, cabinets, toys and numerous other things. The production of such "particle boards" is expanding.

Sawdust, shavings and "hogged" sawmill waste are suitable for chemical processing and it is known that a great variety of useful chemicals, such as sugars, acids, alcohols, yeast and furfural can be obtained from them in good yields. Many of these products may in time be made profitably from wood residues but, for the moment, they do not offer attractive commercial possibilities in North America. Many useful products can be made from waste bark. Douglas-fir bark, for example, is being ground up and segregated into a variety of products to which proprietary names have been given and which, through aggressive merchandising, find many uses. Douglas-fir bark also yields useful tannins and waxes, but not yet in commercial production. The bark of California redwood is being processed commercially into a fibrous insulating material and a by-product dust. It is improbable, however, that more than a small fraction of all the bark available can be used in such ways.

Wood flour, of which possibly 80,000 tons are produced annually in the United States, is made by grinding sawdust or shavings from acceptable species and sifting it to the degrees of fineness needed. It is used in the manufacture of linoleum, adhesives, certain molded plastic products, dynamite and numerous other products where an absorbent filler is needed.

Small pieces of wood in standardized sizes and shapes are produced in substantial quantities from sawmill slabs and low-grade lumber and are sold to manufacturers of various products. Such material from softwoods is commonly called "cut stock," and that from hardwoods "dimension stock." Much skill and efficiency are required to produce these products from wood residues with the degree of accuracy and uniformity of dryness desired by the purchaser and at a profit to the producer. Many other potential uses exist for products that can be made from the residues of sawmills and woodworking factories. The problem for the plants producing the residues is first to find markets for which their residues or the products made from them are suitable and then to deliver the residues or the products to the user at a cost that is attractive to him and profitable to the producing plant. Although innumerable products can be made from wood residues, only a limited number can be made profitably.

Large owners of timberland who are operating on a sustained-yield basis and running their own manufacturing plants can make a variety of products and locate their plants so that the waste from one may be used conveniently as the raw material for another. In a number of notable instances, by integrating their industries in this way and by good management, large lumber manufacturers have eliminated their wood losses or reduced them to very low figures. Although the small sawmill operator is much more limited in his ability to use his residues, he can improve his machinery and methods so as to reduce the waste to the lowest practicable minimum. It may also be practicable in some localities for small, separately owned plants making different products so to integrate or group themselves that most of the residues from the primary breakdown of the log will find profitable use.

PRODUCTION FORESTRY IN INDIA

In the context of the current study, production forestry may be understood to be the raising of block plantations on private lands, leased forest lands or leased community lands with the following purposes:

- Supply of timber as raw material to wood-based industry, and
- Supply of fuelwood/small timber for mitigation of the huge demand-supply gap in energy needs in rural areas.

The size or the ownership pattern of the land in question may vary. It may be useful to consider the following additional definitions (and explanatory notes) by Food and Agriculture Organization (FAO), Rome for a better understanding of production forestry.

FOREST

Land spanning more than 0.5 hectares (ha) with trees higher than 5 metres (m) and a canopy cover of more than 10 per cent, or trees able to reach these thresholds *in situ*. It does not include land that is predominantly under agricultural or urban land use.

Explanatory notes:

- Forest is determined both by the presence of trees and the absence of other predominant land uses. The trees should be able to reach a minimum height of 5 m *in situ*. Areas under reforestation that have not yet reached but are expected to reach a canopy cover of 10 per cent and a tree height of 5 m are included, as are temporarily unstocked areas, resulting from human intervention or natural causes, which are expected to regenerate.

- Includes areas with bamboo and palms provided that the criteria of height and canopy cover are met.
- Includes forest roads, firebreaks and other small open areas; forest in national parks, nature reserves and other protected areas such as those of specific scientific, historical, cultural or spiritual interest.
- Includes windbreaks, shelterbelts and corridors of trees with an area of more than 0.5 ha and width of more than 20 m.
- Includes plantations primarily used for forestry or protection purposes, such as rubber-wood plantations and cork oak stands.
- Excludes tree stands in agricultural production systems, for example in fruit plantations and agroforestry systems. The term also excludes trees in urban parks and gardens.

Other Wooded Land

Land not classified as Forest, spanning more than 0.5 ha; with trees higher than 5 m and a canopy cover of 5-10 per cent, or trees able to reach these thresholds *in situ*; or with a combined cover of shrubs, bushes and trees above 10 per cent. It does not include land that is predominantly under agricultural or urban land use.

Production

Forest/Other wooded land designated for production and extraction of forest goods, including both wood and non-wood forest products.

Production Forest

Forest actually designated for production of forest goods *i.e.* where the extraction of forest products, usually wood and fibre, are the predominant management objective. It includes both wood and non- wood forest products.

Productive Plantation

Forest/Other wooded land of introduced species and in some cases native species, established through planting or seeding mainly for production of wood or non- wood goods.

Explanatory notes:

- Includes all stands of introduced species established for production of wood or non-wood goods.
- May include areas of native species characterized by few species, straight tree lines and/or even-aged stands.

The second set of definitions are borrowed from common technical parlance, with special reference to what is in vogue in entities in the wood-based industry, such as paper mills.

Farm Forestry

The practice of raising trees as crop, to primarily harvest and sell the timber without reference to the size of the holding(s).

Agroforestry

The practice of growing timber along with pure agricultural food and cash crop species and/or horticultural species

Finally, terms such as industrial plantations (with connotations similar to the first definition in this section) and tree farming are also to be found in the literature in this domain.

FOREST PRODUCTS TO THE HOUSEHOLD BUDGET

Few studies directly assess the contribution of forest-earned income to the household budget; however, some present data on the income earned from different forest based activities. While links are rarely made to the ways this income is spent, it can be assumed that income which supplements the household budget is important, especially in periods when other sources are not available.

For example, Asibey (1977b) relates that animal hunting and gathering provide an important source of supplemental income to some farmers. And Okafor (1979) presents data on the income earned by farmers in Anambra State from palm wine production. He shows that the income earned per day from palm wine production exceeds the Nigerian daily minimum wage (2.3 naira/day).

Kamara (1986) presents data on income earned from fuelwood sales by both rural farmers and retailers in Sierra Leone. He estimates that the returns per roan day from rice cultivation and fuelwood sales are almost equivalent, and notes that the fuelwood income is critical as it provides the first returns from land clearing and income during the agricultural slack period when few other sources of cash income are available.

For urban retailers (80 per cent of whom are women), income earned from fuelwood contributes from an average of 42 per cent of total household income in Freetown (where 80 per cent of traders work full-time), to an average of 5 per cent of the total household income in Makeni.

Cashman's (1987) study from southwestern Nigeria represents another example of the importance of trees as a source of household income. She notes that in this region, women earn the majority of the household's cash. Some of the regionally important income earning activities which employ women include:

palm oil processing, cola nut trade, parkia bean processing, soap making, maize processing and food sales.

Oil processing is especially valued for "bulk" expenses such as school fees. In some cases, communities have come to rely and specialise in the trade and production of forest products. In Bas Mungo, Cameroon, for example, some 20,000 villagers are dependent on the sales of palm wine to nearby Douala. Similarly, in Anyama, Senegal, Vérnière (1969) relates that the cola nut trade provides the main source of income for the town's 6000 residents. Finally, in Ahwia (a Ghanaian village in the Kumasi area) all the village men depend on wood carving activities. Carvers earn a good living (about 1300 cedis/month on average).

Forest Product Exploitation and Consumption

Studies which examine and estimate the extent to and frequency with which different forest products are used also shed light on the value of these resources. Food consumption studies, and housing surveys evaluate the extent of forest product use. These case-specific studies which quantitatively assess the day-to-day use of forest resources provide analytical data which allows the utility of forest resources to be compared with the utility of other resources, and production systems.

Food consumption studies that examine the consumption of wild and forest foods or assess quantities of snack foods consumed can show the importance of forest products. Although not from the West African region, Ogle and Grivetti's (1985) study on the cultural, ecological, and nutritional aspects of wild plant use in Swaziland is an excellent example of how information from different subject disciplines can be integrated to help understand the role of wild plants in people's diets. They include a quantitative analysis of the frequency with which species are consumed. They find that over 220 wild plants are commonly (more than once a month) consumed; many agriculturalists who were interviewed claim they consume more wild plants than cultivated varieties.

Dietworst's (1987) meat consumption survey in three Nigerian village communities provides an informative analysis of the frequency of bushmeat consumption. A village study in Sine, Senegal also examines household consumption of bushmeat. Although the area is known to have poor wild animal resources, the researchers found that bushmeat was regularly consumed (on average, 12.9 g./day/per son). They added that the greatest quantities of bushmeat were consumed by children.

Faure and Vivien's (1980) study of the local uses of forest resources in the Littoral region of southern Cameroon included an analysis of the extent to which they are used in house construction. They assert that approximately 300 poles are used for constructing one house. From this, they estimate that the nine study villages consume 4,200 cubic metres of wood to this end.

While few studies actually assess the extent to which plant medicines and traditional healing practices are used Abosede Akesode (1986) provide an unusual case study which examines the use of a traditional plant cure Nigeria. Studies which examine the extent to which resources are exploited also indicate how valuable they are to local people. Moby-Etia's (1982) study of palm wine tapping in southern Cameroon estimates the amount of palm wine tapped per person per day and the amount produced per season. In Ghana, Dodah (1970) estimates that farmers in the Krobo region tap between 25 and 100 trees per season. In Nigeria, Okafor (1979) provides data on the numbers of trees tapped for palm wine by farmers in Anambra state.

Distribution of Farm

Sometimes the types of trees on farm lands and on fallow lands differ, but often valued species are maintained regardless of their location. Regionally, trees such as oil palms are often protected and selectively left in clearings and on forest fallow lands. The multitude of functions associated with these farm trees demonstrates their value to local people. There are a number of studies from the region which inventory fallow and farm trees. The density of different species on farm and fallow lands can often indicate their importance (especially when compared with density of the same species in nearby forest areas).

Okafor and Fernandez (1987) conducted an inventory of farm and fallow land trees in southeastern Nigeria. They identified 171 edible tree species. The most commonly used and highly valued species were found in compound farms rather than in outlying farm and fallow land areas. These farm tree species provided food and beverages, stakes, fodder, fuelwood, medicines, fibres and housing materials. Other tree inventories of farm and fallow species reveal similar. Herren-Gemmill compares the uses and management of fallow areas by farmers in the forest and derived savannah region of southern Nigeria. She finds that farmers in the forest zone leave a broader range of forest emergents standing when crop land is cleared.

A great number and variety of trees are also allowed to germinate during cultivation. In comparison, savannah farmers preserve only economic species. There are many regional farming system studies that focus on the functions trees serve. For example, in the Ho district of Ghana, Asamoah (1985) notes that 76 per cent of the fallow species identified provide medicines, 92 per cent are valued for their soil improving qualities, 92 per cent have domestic uses, 88 per cent are used for fuelwood, 67 per cent have commercial value and 50 per cent serve in customary rites. In another Ghanaian study, Elletey (1986) examines the reasons why farmers protect (or tolerate) farm versus fallow trees. Among the Banen of southern Cameroon, Dongmo (1985) finds that most farm trees are valued for their leaves, fruit or seeds. A few species are also left in fields for protection and demarcation.

Assessing the Value of Forest Resources by their Functions

There are a multitude of household uses for forests. Some are region specific, while others are specific to a group of people, or even a household. In examining the uses of resources by individual households, and in assessing their importance at a regional level, it is more useful to focus on the functions they serve rather than the specific species exploited. People are not concerned with trees themselves; they value functions such as cooking, warmth, food, medicine and shelter. The first part of this study broadly defined important West African tree products and their functions: as foods and materials for household consumption, as support to other productive activities, as sources of cash income, and as cultural symbols.

Information on the functions of forest resources can be found in anthropological (Bahuchet 1978) and geographic household-level studies, as well as in studies evaluating the uses of farm fallow trees. In regions where the natural forests have disappeared, useful trees are often incorporated into the farming systems (Okafor 1981, Ijalana 1983). For this reason studies of on-farm trees often reveal information on the functions that forest resources once served.

This study has identified many of the common functions forest products serve in households throughout the West African forest region:

- Food (both animals and plants) to supplement the diet and meet seasonal shortages;
- *Drinks:* Palm wine and alcohol, "water";
- Dood and cash buffers or insurance in emergency hardship periods;
- Medicines and dental chewing sticks;
- Fuel, for all household and enterprise needs;
- Marketable products exploitable for cash income (*e.g.* cola nut);
- Material for house construction: poles, bark, liana, palm roof tiles and other roof leaves, wattle slats, timber;
- Material for household, agriculture, hunting and fishing equipment;
- Yam and other crop stakes;
- Materials for crop storage containers;
- Fencing and boundary markings;
- Fodder;
- Shade;
- Inputs for processing enterprises (*e.g.* fuelwood);
- Locations for social, religious and healing ceremonies;
- Symbols of cultural and religious identity and importance.

By focusing on the functions of forest products the role of these products can be examined and information from different areas of the region can be compared. In addition, this focus allows one to examine how uses change over time and by setting. For example, in examining the function of foods gathered from forest areas, similarities can be seen across the region: forest foods provide dietary staples and supplements; fill in seasonal and emergency food shortfalls; and provide specific nutrients and culturally symbolic foods. Forest leaves, nuts and wild animals are used in sauces which accompany main meal staples. Forest fruits and insects are consumed largely as snacks, especially by children and during periods when agricultural work is most time-consuming.

Mushrooms are consumed as meat substitutes, and are generally available only during the rains. Forest foods may have particular cultural value (such as the cola nut, a sign of welcome in many parts of the region). Some forest foods provide regularsupplements to the diet, others are consumed seasonally, when staple food supplies dwindle or during peak labour periods when little time is left for cooking. Still other forest foods are used only in emergencyperiods when no other foods are available. These generally differ from regularly consumed products, they are more energy-rich but require lengthy processing. What is important about the focus on function is that discussions move beyond species descriptions.

The changing uses of forest resources can also be viewed in terms of their evolving functions. For example, in some cases forest foods may no longer provide the diverse range of produce which they once did. But culturally important foods may still be widely consumed. In other instances, the growing market for some forest foods (*e.g.* Irvingia gabonensis seeds) may have changed their role in rural areas; trees may now be valued as a sources of cash income. Concomitant with these changing functions, changes in the ways in which these products are valued and managed may ensue. In southern Benin, for example, a new technology for palm alcohol distilling was introduced which changed the way the raphia palms were used and valued. Formerly they had served a great range of household functions and had been used by anyone in the community, but with the introduction of this new technology, they were rapidly overexploited because of the nearby urban market for palm alcohol.

There can be little doubt that the functions of forests will change for households in the rural regions of southern West Africa. The relative importance of different forest products may also change: this can already be seen as some products take on more of a commercial value. But, for most of the functions listed above, contemporary evidence suggests that forest products are still important for the majority of rural households. Although substitutes exist for many non-timber forest products, few people have the resources to buy them. Perhaps for this reason, of those noted above only "material for household, hunting, and fishing equipment", "foods as a buffer during emergencies", and "drinks" appear to be of declining importance throughout the region as a whole.

Seasonal Variation in the use and Importance of Forest Products

Perhaps one of the most crucial functions of forests is that they provide products for consumption and sale during seasons when other foods and sources of income are less prevalent. Although the seasonal variations may not be as pronounced in the humid zone when compared to more arid regions, forest product use still complements the seasonal agricultural cycle. Many smallscale enterprises are run seasonally, when labour is available.

In rural Sierra Leone fuelwood collection for market sale is concentrated in the off-peak agricultural season, thereby providing income in a period when food supplies are generally at their lowest. Similarly, palm oil processing takes place when cash is needed for food purchases. The palm fruit and kernels are processed as soon as they are harvested, despite the fact that returns would be higher if they were saved and processed later in the season (a result of seasonal variations in selling prices).

The income earned in forest based processing and gathering activities often plays an essential part in the agricultural cycle. In rural Sierra Leone, income from fuelwood sales (the first returns from cleared lands) is often used to purchase agricultural inputs such as seeds or equipment. Similarly in Ghana, the income that is earned from bushmeat sales is often invested in agricultural production.

Many forest products are gathered and consumed seasonally. In most cases this reflects a seasonal need for food supplements. However, in some instances forest foods are only available in specific seasons. Perhaps the most popular examples are snails and mushrooms which are both generally only available at the beginning of the rains in a review of bush foods consumed in southern Cameroon, Pélé and Berre (1967) found that plant foods gathered from wild areas (notably forests) were most valued when other food sources were unavailable - at the end of the dry season. Dongmo's more recent study (1985) in Banen, Cameroon reiterates these findings suggesting that forest foods are still roost important during the off-peak agricultural season. Okafor's study (1981) on forest foods in markets in southern Nigeria reveals that many are available in seasons when cultivated varieties are in short supply. He notes that these foods are only available in the dry season because they are gathered from the forest. In some cases forest species are cultivated (*e.g.* Gnetum sp.), but these cultivars do not produce for as long a period into the dry season as those found in forest habitats.

Throughout West Africa consumption of bushmeat is generally higher during the rainy season. In some communities, hunting is an important off-season activity. In southern Cameroon, trapping is common during the rainy season. And among the pygmies from southern Cameroon the species hunted as well as hunting techniques vary by season.

The Emergency or Buffer Role of Forest Resources

Forests have traditionally provided food and marketable products during emergency periods of food shortages, illness or death. This function is well illustrated in stories from the region in which trees are portrayed as providers during famines. Early works, such as Irvine's (1952) study on the emergency uses of forest products, also illustrate the former importance of forests as a buffer source of food supplies.

He relates that forest tubers, roots and rhizomes were the main source of energy during famine times. It is not however clear, from recent accounts, whether and how this function has changed in the last few decades. Forest resources have declined, so too has people's knowledge of their varied resources. In addition, the commercialised rural economies and food aid programmes may, in some cases, substitute for the food buffer forests once provided. It can be postulated that marketable and processed forest products provide a means for earning cash income during emergencies, although no information has been found on this issue.

Evaluating the Importance of Forest Resources

This discussion has focused largely on common forest products and their use. Little has been said about who within the rural community relies most on forest resources. While forests are exploited for a variety of products and functions, they are especially important for those with access to fewer resources, most notably the rural poor, many of whom are women. This is of particular importance as many development projects are geared towards improving the lives of the rural poor. In most communities in the region, exploitation of forests has traditionally been open to all for subsistence needs. The poor often rely to a great extent on forests for foods, medicines, and building materials, as well as other needs discussed in earlier chapters.

Forest foods are particularly important for poor households as they provide an available, accessible source of a diverse range of foods. Especially important are fish and wild animals, leaves, nuts and mushrooms. For some forest foods such as bushmeat, consumption is limited by supply. In these cases, the poor's access to these products may decline as they become scarce luxuries. In other cases, forest foods may be considered poor man's food. In these instances people may attempt to purchase substitute foods whenever possible. In both situations forest food consumption may decline. However, there is little information from the region which specifically addresses the changing dietary patterns of the rural poor, or which focuses on their changing consumption of forest foods.

Forest-based activities, such as gathering and processing NTFPs often provide important employment opportunities in rural regions. Gathering of forest products for sale is often dominated by the rural poor. In Sierra Leone, for example, it is the poorer households within the rural community who rely on sale of fuelwood (Kamara 1986). Similarly, poorer women often dominate the gathering and trade of forest leaves (Okafor 1979). While forest based activities may provide numerous opportunities for the rural poor, the earning potential varies substantially (*e.g.* basket-making versus wood-carving). Generally, activities which are dominated by the poor reap the lowest returns. In some cases income earned from forest based activities can be invested in agricultural assets (such as implements, or livestock). In these cases forests offer the poor a means of investing in their future.

Throughout the region women dominate the collection, trade and processing of the majority of non-timber forest products. In Ghana 84 per cent of both retail and wholesale traders are women (Ardayfio 1985). This is due, in part, to the central role of women in West African (southern regions) trade. In general, wholesale traders control the market for products which are transported over long distances. The majority of wholesale traders derive their capital from personal savings as banks are not supportive of women. In southern Cameroon, Kenge's (1987) study of more than 1500 markets reveals that women (commonly known as "bayam sellems") dominate the wholesale and retail trade of almost all forest products with the exception of cola nuts, which men control.

Trading activities are often conducted seasonally, when demands for agricultural (or other) labour are low. For example, Riss (1984) finds that in the Kaolack region of southern Senegal, forest product gathering is an extremely important dry season activity for most women. All women collect forest products for the market.

In addition, women generally use forest products to help meet their household's basic needs: foods, fuel, medicines and other products are frequently gathered. Women, therefore, can combine gathering forest products for subsistence needs and for the market. In addition, because of their experience in forest gathering they are knowledgeable about forest product exploitation. Visser (1975) found that among the Ando in Côte d'Ivoire, for example, women were more knowledgeable about gathering and using plant medicines than other members of the community. Forest product processing activities can also be adapted to women's other work. Often processing can be performed near the home, allowing women to combine these income earning activities with some of their household work (*e.g.* childcare).

7

Forest Policy and Management

SOCIAL PARTICIPATION AND FOREST POLICY

Decentralization in Bolivia was motivated by increasing pressure from civic committees seeking to have greater control over natural resources, the general trend towards decentralization in neighbouring countries and the prominence of decentralization in donors' agendas. Its implementation has been affected by social participation dynamics, and the new forestry regulations have had implications for democratization of forest resources access.

ANTECEDENTS OF DECENTRALIZATION

Bolivia has three levels of government: central government; departmental government or prefecture, whose main authority (the *prefecto*) is appointed by the president; and municipal government, in which democratically elected municipal councils elect the mayor. Before decentralization most decisions were made at the central level. The municipalities had limited resources and little influence in policy-related decisions, even those directly affecting the development of their municipal jurisdictions. The Bolivian lowland forest area was largely marginalized from the political centre in La Paz, where most political decisions were made. In the early 1960s that region was progressively integrated into the national economy through the expansion of natural gas extraction, agriculture and logging. Those factors fostered the growth of a regional elite, expanded the contribution of that region to the national income and increased its influence on development programmes. In the 1970s, the government took its first step towards decentralization by establishing corporations for regional development. This was closer to an administrative attempt to transfer some investment decisions to the departmental level but the central government still appointed the presidents of such entities, and most of the decisions were negotiated at higher levels. Civic committees (groups of local social organizations) had been seeking greater access to forest revenues and greater participation in the formulation of forest policies since the mid-1970s. In the 1980s, legislation was approved establishing the collection of a forest fee of 11 per cent, to be used in regional development projects. (In 1993, further legislation was passed stating that forest companies would pay 80 per cent of their taxes directly in the areas where the resources originated, but the mechanism was hard to implement in practice.) By the late 1980s, the national forestry service was deconcentrated to local branches. This move towards deconcentration, however, did not make the forestry service a more efficient and less corrupt institution. Municipal authorities, meanwhile, continued to respond to the leaders of their respective political parties rather than to their constituents.

Decentralization was prompted through approval of Popular Participation Law (No. 1551) and Administrative Decentralization Law (No. 1654), both passed by Congress in 1994. The first altered the responsibilities of the municipal governments, while the second modified the responsibilities of prefectures or departmental governments. In 1996 a new Agrarian Reform Law was issued, as well as a new Forestry Law. The Agrarian Reform Law's objective was to define the legal basis for a system of titling and land regularization, and to redefine the conditions of access to rural property. The Forestry Law attempted to redefine the conditions for obtaining and maintaining forest rights. Both affected the way in which landholders and forest users can access and maintain their rights for forest resources use.

PARTICIPATION IN INVESTMENT DECISIONS

The Popular Participation Law expanded the municipal government's jurisdiction beyond the urban centers to the whole rural area within the municipal borders. It made municipalities responsible for local schools, health facilities, roads maintenance and water systems. To finance these new responsibilities, the central government allocated 20 per cent of the national budget to the municipal governments, to be distributed among municipalities in proportion to their populations. Both rural and urban property taxes were earmarked for the municipal governments, who now administer their collection. The Popular Participation Law has strengthened municipal governments and made them more democratic. Rural populations – mainly smallholders and indigenous people – have gained the right to participate in municipal elections and run for the municipal councils. Nonetheless, national political parties still appoint individual candidates, allowing political parties to maintain their control over local political agendas, and to reproduce a system of political patronage with local leaders. Local candidates who want to run for office have to negotiate their agendas within the priorities of the political parties, and if they are elected they are accountable to those parties.

Furthermore, the law sought to introduce community control over municipal governments by local social organizations (ie local farmer organizations, neighbourhood committees and indigenous groups) and community-based vigilance committees. Nevertheless, these committees' representatives are exposed to continuous pressures from political parties.

Rules and Regulations for Forest Use

The Forestry Law of 1996 defined a set of regulations for forest use, somewhat differentiated according to forest user, under the premise that sustainable forest management is feasible under the right practices. It established a new system for monitoring forest management, enforcement and sanctions to illegal logging, as well as introducing some market-oriented regulations and taxes to discourage unsustainable forestry operations. The goal is to achieve sustainability of forest management through progressive incorporation of less valuable timber species and the application of extraction techniques that promote natural regeneration. Furthermore, the law seeks to create clear rights over forest resources, thereby encouraging investments in forest management; and to eliminate forest crime and illegal logging, as well as set technical criteria for forest management. The public institutional system of the forest sector was substantially altered. The Ministry of Sustainable Development and Planning is the ruling entity, the Forestry Superintendence is the regulation entity, and the National Forestry Development Fund is the financial entity.

Noncommercial forest uses do not require authorization, and a forest management plan is an essential requirement for all types of commercial forest activities. Hence, forest concessionaires as well as private landholders are obligated to design management plans as an instrument to regulate commercial logging activities, including forest inventories and mapping. Forest management plans have to comply with many technical requirements. Forest management, when based on selective management, must respect a minimum cycle of 20 years between logging operations on the same area, and a minimum cut diameter must be respected. Furthermore, annual operations plans are required. The regime to be applied to nontimber forest products is similar.

Democratizing Access to Forest Resources

The new forestry regulations included two provisions that have had some impact in democratizing access to forest resources. The first refers to the exclusive right of indigenous peoples to use the forest resources within their indigenous territories, recognized legally by the Agrarian Reform Law. According to this law, indigenous claims are considered titled after completion of a process of land regularization. Currently, a total of 19 million ha have been claimed for titling as indigenous territories, but it is not known how much will ultimately be effectively titled in this way. Stocks (1999) estimated 5 million ha to be the area with commercial logging potential in areas claimed as indigenous territories. A provision of the Forestry Law states that local forest user groups can benefit from forest concessions within areas declared as municipal forest reserves, which represent up to 20 per cent of public forest within each municipal jurisdiction. Local forest users can be granted a forest concession if they are recognized as a local user association by the Ministry of Sustainable Development and Planning. This mechanism was conceived as a way to formalize the access for local forest users or small-scale loggers who, because they had no legal right to access forest resources, were previously conducting forestry operations informally.

POWERS TRANSFERRED TO MUNICIPAL GOVERNMENTS

According to Ribot (2001), outcomes of decentralization depend on the type of powers that are transferred to lower levels and on who receives such powers. In Bolivia, as well as in most countries of Latin America, decentralization has followed a top-down format, and municipalities have been the main recipients of authority transferred from the central level.

A Top-Down Model of Delegation

Although the Popular Participation Law did not grant municipal governments any new explicit function related to natural resources management, it motivated some municipal governments, as a result of their larger political authority, to become involved in natural resources issues and thereby capture part of the benefits. Because mayors became relatively more powerful, the central government and the international donors began to consider them more seriously as partners in environmental projects. The increasing political power of municipalities led the government to consider them for dealing with some problematic issues, such as social monitoring of illegal logging and formalizing forest rights for small-scale loggers and other local users. These were included in the Forestry Law of 1996.

The current powers and functions are divided as follows:

- Formulate forest policies, strategies and norms;
- Determine land classification and evaluate forest potential;
- Prepare demarcation of concession areas for timber companies and local groups;
- Set prices for concession fees and volume-based taxes;
- Promote research, extension and education; and
- Solicit technical assistance and funding for forestry projects.

Forest superintendence (SF):

- Supervise technical compliance with the forestry regime;
- Grant management rights to eligible forest users;
- Approve forest management plans for different forest rights;
- Enforce forest regulations and sanction illegal forest users;
- Issue concessions, authorizations and logging permits;

- Request external forest audits of forest operations; and
- Collect concession fees and volume-based taxes and distribute them.

Prefectures:

- Formulate forest development departmental plans;
- Develop forest research and extension programmes;
- Promote programmes of rehabilitation of degraded forest systems; and
- Develop programmes for strengthening municipal forestry units' institutional capacities.

Municipal governments:

- Propose the delimitation of municipal forest reserves up to 20% of available public forest;
- Protect and conserve the reserve areas until they are conceded to local user associations;
- Inspect and control all forest activities within their territorial jurisdiction;
- Report violations of forest regulations to the Forestry Superintendence;
- Provide support to local forest users in implementing their management plans;
- Establish the registry of forest resources in their jurisdiction;
- Develop soil use plans corresponding to the departmental use plans;
- Organize training events for local forest users; and
- Facilitate and promote social participation in local forest development.

To carry out their new responsibilities, municipal governments are expected to create municipal forestry units. Municipalities can form consortiums with other municipalities to create such units. In theory, the entire system should be entirely financed with the revenues coming from both concession and clearcutting fees.

Prefectures receive 35 per cent of the concession fees and 25 per cent of the fees charged for clearcutting operations. Municipal governments get 25 per cent of both types of fees. The National Forestry Development Fund receives 10 per cent of the concession fees and 50 per cent of the clearcutting fees. SF gets 30 per cent of the concession fees. A reduction of forest concession fees in March 2003 has diminished the financial resources going to prefectures and municipalities.

Restricted Powers for Municipalities

Municipal governments must comply with national regulations regarding property regimes and forest regulations. Hence, their autonomy to make decisions about natural resources depends largely on decisions made at the central level. The legislation thus regards municipal officials as rule followers rather than rule makers, and as implementing agencies for policies defined at the central level. In short, the new institutional forest system has not delegated important responsibilities to municipalities and has therefore not led to dramatic changes. The central level reserves for itself major decisions regarding allocation of forest resources rights, granting forest concessions, approving forest use regulations, and collecting taxes from forest resources use. Municipalities have little to say in these areas, and all informal actions of municipalities for collecting forest taxes and controlling timber transit are considered illegal.

Although municipal governments are empowered to control forest crime, promote community forestry and take other forest-related actions, their power to make autonomous decisions regarding the allocation and use of forest resources is restricted. For instance, they can decide how to allocate the forest resources within the municipal reserves but cannot decide about the size of such reserves. This reflects the tension between the central level, which defends the strong role of the national forestry service, and those who support a more active and autonomous role for municipal governments.

Limited Autonomy for Local Forest Users

The situation of indigenous groups has improved. Indigenous communities whose forest resources were subject to encroachment from illegal loggers now have exclusive access to resources within their territories, though problems persist. However, before indigenous people can take commercial advantage of forest resources, they have to develop forest management plans according to Forest Superintendence regulations, and they have little scope to adapt such norms to their own management practices (BOLFOR, MDSMA, and Superintendencia Forestal, 1997).

And even though specific regulations for forest management in indigenous areas have been approved, local knowledge has been ignored in much of the forest policy. Enforcement of indigenous property rights depends on some institutional arrangements made at the departmental and regional levels, over which indigenous people have little influence. This issue is linked to a more complex bureaucratic process of land use planning and titling with poor overall outcomes.

The other social actors who have benefited from access to forest resources – small-scale timber extractors and other local forest users – also have no autonomy to make decisions about the way in which they use the resources, and all of them have to comply with forestry regulations to maintain access to public forest resources through forest concession systems.

The Forest Superintendence has instituted command-and-control mechanisms to enforce the implementation of what it considers good forest management practices among local forest user groups and small landholders.

Those practices, though appropriate for large-scale forest concessionaires, act as barriers for small-scale forest users.

Implementation of Decentralization Policies

There are always failures in the implementation of policies, and decentralization is no exception. In Bolivia, transferring responsibilities to municipalities meant building local capacities in municipal governments, as well as interacting with actors who had disparate incentives and interests to use the forest within the new institutional context.

Building Institutional Capacities

Municipalities with forest resources began to receive their shares of forest taxes in 1997, when they started to set up municipal forestry units. The resources transferred to municipalities have tended to decrease because forest concessionaires did not comply with the forest fees payments. In 2002, a new system formally reduced the amount of taxes collected by the state from forest operations to almost half of what was originally expected, formalizing the reduction of transfers from the central government to municipalities. By the end of 2001, almost all municipalities with forest resources (about 109) had created their municipal forestry units, and each had at least one forest or agricultural technician. In municipalities with difficult access and little population, the forest units are the only local providers of technical services, and governments tend to value their role in local planning. The main limitations are the staffs' lack of technical skills and inadequate training in social issues, such as conflict resolution.

Building technical capacities in municipal forestry units constituted an important step forward in relation to the past. Nevertheless, progress is not uniform and varies with the financial support the units receive from the municipalities. That in turn depends on the amount collected in forest fees and what proportion of it goes to supporting operational budgets. A significant portion of municipalities consider it enough to provide minimum resources to the municipal forestry units and spend the rest, if any, on other activities. It is worth mentioning that local government priorities are providing social services and infrastructure, and they have little motivation to support productive projects, though this is changing.

Incentives for the Actors

The new institutional system resulting from both decentralization and the shift in forest policies has modified the incentives for municipalities and forest stakeholders to continue doing what they were used to doing, or to adapt their social and financial strategies to the new conditions. The main incentive for municipalities to engage with the new decentralized order of things was the likelihood of getting a share of the forest taxes, as well as the possibility of administering the municipal forest reserves. Municipalities also are interested in penalizing illegal clearcutting due to the fact that they get a portion of the fines, but this does not happen in relation to illegal logging. Furthermore, municipal governments have been interested in being active players on forest issues in the cases where local forest users have political influence on local decisionmaking, or in cases where forest-dependent people represent important votes to keep them in office.

The incentives of local forest users to engage in the process are diverse. Indigenous people have received important benefits from forest policy reform and decentralization. They have gained rights to make exclusive use of their forest resources within their territories, and have the chance to expand their influence to participate in municipal decision making. In this context, forest management might increase the social legitimacy of indigenous people's claims to land. In turn, local small-scale timber extractors' main incentive has been to get formal access to forest resources through the forest concession system, and to benefit more from formal markets. Furthermore, this group should benefit from the technical assistance provided by the municipal forestry units, which are receiving resources from the forest taxes to support such activities. Both groups have benefited from several forest projects (eg BOLFOR) and NGOs with an interest in supporting community forestry.

In the short run, the main losers under decentralization were absentee forest concessionaires, who must now negotiate with the forestry service. Furthermore, a forest tax has been imposed, and they have had to acknowledge indigenous people's demands. The main incentive for forest concessionaires to adapt to the new conditions was their interest in keeping their forest areas, and an implicit commitment from the central government to help them through a difficult financial situation originating in the timber crisis in regional markets. Municipal governments reacted in contradictory ways regarding forest concessions. Although some are critical of concessions' activities within their jurisdictions, others consider them sources of economic growth and employment.

Homogeneous Solutions for Heterogeneous Municipalities

The Bolivian model of decentralization does not account for regional variation, and its design assumes that all municipal governments will react uniformly to the challenges arising from the new conditions. Reality proved rather different. Implementation of decentralization has had to face three issues: uneven distribution of resources to municipalities, the minimal availability of public forest declared as municipal forest reserves, and the hetereogeneous interests of municipalities regarding forest-related activities.

Uneven distribution and allocation of financial resources. The financial resources allocated by the Forestry Superintendence to municipalities have varied. From 1997 to 1999, only 30 municipalities benefited, with more than 80 per cent of the total resources transferred to them. In the richer municipalities, not all income from forest taxes is spent on forest-related activities; some is diverted to other sectors. The poorest municipalities likewise have urgent demands that are outside the forestry sector.

Minimal municipal forest reserves. Even though the law specified that up to 20 per cent of public forest would be declared municipal forest reserves, in practice such areas were not available in all municipalities – in some cases because of the existence of overlapping claims over public forest, in others because public lands were maintained as forest concessions. In some municipalities there were no areas to declare as municipal reserves to allocate as concessions to small-scale loggers. By early 2001, from a total of 2.4 million ha demanded by municipalities as municipal reserves, only 681,000 ha had been designated.

Municipalities' priorities. Only a few municipal forestry units have accomplished the functions they have been granted. Municipalities prioritize their investment in response to social pressures or to local authorities' political motivations. The level of municipal engagement is also related to municipalities' incentives to respond to their constituents and be accountable to higher authorities. For instance, whereas some municipalities are interested in allocating resources to establish a system of forest concessions within municipal reserves, others choose to control illegal clearcutting or make forest management viable for small farmers.

Uneven Outcomes

Transferring responsibilities to municipalities has modified the political and institutional arrangements for forest management, with implications for both people and forests.

Participation in Local Politics

In many lowland municipalities, small farmers, indigenous people and small-scale loggers have been elected to office for the first time. Indigenous groups have been able to obtain political support from the municipal councils to reinforce their land claims, small-scale loggers have obtained support to negotiate temporary logging authorizations, and small farmers have obtained support favouring their efforts to modify land-use and forest regulations. Thus, municipal governments have contributed to political support for some local actors' claims on resources. This is also the case where these groups have strong organizations that can influence the municipality's decisions or where they represent the majority of voters. In these cases, municipal governments may amplify the demands of social actors. In other cases, however, transferring responsibilities and resources to municipalities has reinforced the power of preexisting local elites – elite capture, particularly in municipalities of northern Bolivia, and where cattle ranchers and timber companies are highly influential in local politics. These local elites have, in some cases, influenced municipal governments to build local alliances against indigenous land claims and strengthened their power over use of resources. The local elites of these municipalities often benefit from activities based on mining of natural resources and promote concentration of benefits in a few hands. Decentralization, in these cases, tends to produce undesired results in social equity and forest conservation.

Where the social composition of local government is more complex, local elites have to negotiate with small farmers and indigenous people. It is not unusual to find alliances built among the different social groups that support certain development agendas, such as infrastructure development and basic social services. Those social agreements are, however, difficult to arrange for natural resources management, though in some cases alliances have been established to protect conservation areas against encroachment of foreign timber and mining companies (ie municipalities of Rurrenabaque and San Ignacio de Velasco).

Much of the impact of decentralization on reconfiguring social participation in local politics depends on the local political economy and on the social capital of marginalized groups. In other words, the more democratic municipalities have traditionally had more equitable access to resources. Those in which local elites have imposed their interests are affected by the extent to which local groups have been able to build social capital.

POLICIES IN INDIA ON PRODUCTION FORESTRY

NATIONAL AGRICULTURAL POLICY

National Commission on Agriculture (NCA) recommended a change over from the conservation-oriented forestry to more dynamic programme of production forestry. According to the Commission, production of industrial wood would have to be the main reason for the existence of forests and should be project-oriented and economically feasible.

The NCA recommended against leasing forestlands to industry and instead wanted government to allocate them forest raw material through enhancing commercial forestry. For the purpose of commercial forestry, it further recommended that out of 64 million hectare (Mha) of forest lands available in India at that time 48 Mha should be brought under production forestry and remaining 16 Mha for biological diversity.

NATIONAL FOREST POLICY (NFP)

NFP, 1952 acknowledged the need for sustained supply of timber and other forest produce to meet the developmental need of various industries. The policymakers had two major objectives in mind while framing NFP 1952. First to ensure that forests were preserved and managed on a sustainable basis, and second to use them for meeting national interest as a source of timber. Since both these objectives somewhat opposed each other, NFP came up with a concept of *'treelands'*. It identified the scope for involving state governments as well as various other institutions, such as, Defence, Rail-ways, Public Works Departments, Universities and Colleges, Boards, Municipalities and other local authorities, associations and institutions in the process by converting the land at their disposal into treelands. To ensure that the needs of forest-based industries are met without putting undue pressure on forests the need to substitute tree-species of commercial importance in place of inferior tree–species was advocated. The policy also mentioned involving both the industries and individuals in a bigger manner and emphasised on considering commercial and industrial interests for establishing closer contacts and bonding between Forest Research Institutes and industries utilising timber and forest products.

Forest Conservation Act, 1980

The Act put a ban on the de-reservation of forests or use of forestland for non-forest purpose. The Act of 1980, consequently, brought the subject of forests from state list to concurrent list enabling the parliament of India to look into the matter of forests. After the Act, no state government could use forestland for non-forest purposes without prior endorsement by the central government. This put up a check not only on the conversion of forests but also brought to halt the fragmentation of the remaining forests. This ensured that a local party could not take the decision of diverting the forests for taking up any political mileage. The centre acted as an independent agency, to which the state governments and their decisions were answerable.

National Forest Policy, 1988

The NFP, 1988 looked upon forests not as a source of raw material for commercial purposes, but primarily for conserving soil, water and biodiversity besides meeting subsistence requirements of the local people. The policy clearly mentioned that the economic utilities coming from the forests would be secondary to this prime aim.

The NFP 1988 shifted the official focus from fuelwood and timber to the management of forests primarily for their services. It made it imperative to ensure that the forests are not only conserved but also their cover and productivity is increased so as to meet the demand of goods and services coming from forests. The policy, while addressing the production forestry programme, expressed its concern in plugging the increasing demand-supply gap of fuelwood and meeting the national needs. But it explicitly mentioned that no such activity should result in any sort of clear felling of already existing natural forests. It expressed the desire that such programmes should help the country meet with its objective of achieving one-third forest cover. The policy put a thrust on meeting two important concerns of utilising the wastelands and increasing tree cover by promoting major forestry programmes. To reduce the pressure on forests, it also aimed at promoting substitution of wood besides encouraging better and efficient utilisation of forest produce. Since land plays an important role in taking up plantations, it advocated that a slight modification in land laws should be taken up so that the process becomes smooth for the investors.

At the same time, it maintained that any sort of leasing should be in coherence with the existing land ceiling act. The policy discouraged the earlier trend of meeting raw material requirements of forest-based industry by operating on natural forests. It directed these industries to meet their requirements by establishing a direct relationship with individuals who had the capacity to do so. The industry was encouraged to chip in by contributing its resources and expertise at various levels during the total project duration. The policy also gives more importance to native species over the exotic species. It discourages the use of exotic species without prior scientific trials to establish that there are no adverse effect on the environment.

National Forestry Action Programme, India (NFAP), 1999

The NFAP aimed to prepare an action plan for next 20 years, in conformity with NFP 1988. It is a comprehensive strategic plan to address the issue underlying the major problems of the forestry sector and to reverse the process of degradation for sustainable development of forests. The consumption of fuel-wood in India was reported to be about five times higher than what could be sustainably removed from forests. Further, a large tract of forestland was claimed (nearly 4.3 Mha) for undertaking industrialisation and developing infrastructure necessary for meeting the development goals of the nation. The NFAP aimed at meeting the requirements of forest based industries without compromising the conservation and protection of natural forests.

The basic purpose of NFAP was to establish direct linkage between the NFP and the National Five-Year Plans (FYP). In the past, a comprehensive and constant programme structure for forestry was found missing. Every plan had its own programme structure. So it was difficult to find linkages and establish trends. Although plans had specified objectives and programmes, the main activity under most of them was tree planting. NFAP recognised the capability of plantations to help conserve the natural forests by providing an alternative source for forest products. The Programme was also optimistic regarding the capability of plantations to earn foreign exchange, besides meeting the domestic requirements of the country. The Programme admitted that despite the policy addressing direct relationship between industry and farmers, the government did not adequately support private initiatives. It raised concern on the inability of the government to provide these initiatives with relevant research, extension, technological packages, input delivery, and market information or credit facilities. It felt and remarked that it was imperative to encourage small operators, keep them interested in sustainable forestry development and understand their needs adequately.

NFAP suggested looking at these plantations as a means of raw material for industries or for meeting energy requirements. It intended to conserve and rehabilitate 31 Mha of degraded forests (less than 40 per cent crown density) in addition to bringing 29 Mha of non-forest land under plantations. It advocated the use of different strategies for both these targets. The problem of degraded forests was to be tackled by involving local communities, especially the areas near villages through Joint Forest Management (JFM). For non-forest land, market-oriented massive tree plantation drive involving multiple agencies was proposed. The NFAP came up with a strategic approach to meet its objectives. The approach had five interrelated 'strategic areas' which formed the very basis of the Programme. These approaches were:

- Protect existing forest resources
- Improve forest productivity
- Reduce total demand
- Strengthen policy and institutional framework
- Expand forest area

The state governments while preparing the State Forestry Action Programmes (SFAPs) incorporated all planned activities as part of these activities.The NFAP recommended that for the sustainability of forests, the productivity of forest plantations was to be increased at least 3 to 5 cubic meter per ha per year (m^3/ha/yr) by promoting regeneration and enrichment of plantations. Plantations to be carried out on all categories of wastelands were also suggested. Keeping in mind the fuelwood requirements of the country, emphasis was paid on taking up plantations of fuelwood species on non-forest wasteland. Strengthening the institutions for people's participation in protection and development of degraded and fringe forests was emphasised.

Regarding the financing part of the programme, the sources of funds were grouped under four broad categories, namely, domestic public financing, domestic private financing, external public financing, and external private financing.

NATIONAL ENVIRONMENT POLICY

National Environment Policy (NEP), 2004

NEP emphasised the need to develop a strategy to meet the goal of raising the forest cover of the nation to 33 per cent by 2012. It promoted the involvement of non-forestry sector as well. For increasing the forest and tree cover of the nation, multiple stakeholder partnerships have been recognised where each stakeholder would have his role clearly defined. For achieving the aforesaid target of 33 per cent forest cover, the NEP 2004 suggested that the afforestation activities should be taken up on degraded land, wastelands as well as private land holdings. Key elements of the strategy would include: (i) implementation of multi-stakeholder partnerships involving the Forest Department, local communities, and investors, with clearly defined obligations and entitlements for each partner, following good governance principles, to derive environmental, livelihood, and financial benefits; and (ii) rationalisation of restrictions on cultivation of forest species outside notified forests, to enable farmers to undertake social and farm forestry where their returns are more favourable than cropping. The policy called for development of a strategy to achieve the targets set for the eleventh five-year plan.

The problem of climate change and its underlying causes in global warming and increased usage of GHGs has been addressed in the Policy. It identifies deforestation in the country as one of the reasons for climate change expresses concern that India and other developing nations would be affected the most by climate change. The current level of emission in India is substantially lower than that of the developed nations; however, India's economic growth could result in an increase in GHG emission. However, government policies favouring renewable energy and afforestation projects as well as the growth of less energy intensive service sectors would result in a decrease in the level of emissions.

PLANNING COMMISSION REPORTS

Report on Leasing of Degraded Forest Lands, 1999

The Report was of the view that the degraded forestland should not be leased out to private entrepreneurs. In accordance with NFP 1988, it recommended that industries needing forest raw material should establish contact with farmers. The government would lease land to Forest Development Corporation (FDC) who, in turn, would enter into proper MoU with the user agency without leasing the land to them, as per the GOI guidelines of 1994. This MOU would give the user agency the right to undertake afforestation and take a fixed percentage of forest produce at the time of harvesting.

The Report recommended leasing barren land far away from habitations, available in plots of 1000 ha or more, and of no use to the villagers. These are desert or ravine or saline lands, which require huge investment before they can be made productive. The Report gives reference of Investment Promotion Scheme of Ministry of Rural Development, Government of India wherein such enterprises would be entitled to 25 per cent subsidy on their capital investment. This means that the land needed for production purposes could be mobilised for meeting the demand of industry provided the industry is ready to put in huge investment besides following the guidelines. The report estimated that 33 Mha of degraded non-forest lands and 27 Mha of degraded forests (a total of 60 Mha) would be available for tree growing.

The Report also addresses the issue of difference between barren and degraded lands. Uncultivated public land was classified under these two categories. Barren land were defined as having forest/tree cover less than 10 per cent whereas degraded land were classified as having forest/tree cover between 10 to 40 per cent.

Greening India for Livelihood Security and Sustainable Development, 2001

Greening India Programme proposes to cover 43 Mha degraded land (15 Mha of degraded forestland, 10 Mha of degraded irrigated land, and 18 Mha of degraded rainfed land). It recognises that there exist numerous problems that make the implementation of agroforestry programmes difficult:

- Cumbersome legislation with respect to tree felling, wood transportation and processing.
- Lack of market information and infrastructure
- Dearth of appropriate agroforestry models
- Absence of economic security and incentives for tree growers
- Lack of extension training and demonstration
- Non-availability of quality planting material
- Unfavourable Import and Export policy

The Report highlighted the lessons learnt from the farm forestry programme:

- Tree planting should not be undertaken in uncultivable lands, but in cultivated-field and homesteads.
- All wastelands, non-forest areas and degraded forestlands should be brought under silvi-pastoral system with suitable species for fuel and fodder production. This can be addressed through JFM.
- Coastal land through afforestation, ravines and sand dune area for land reclamation, area under mining leases, water-logged areas can be targeted for converting into forested land.

Five-Year Plans

Forestry has also been covered from the first five-year plan, though it remains neglected most of the time in the planning process. Of the total fund allocated to various sectors, funds for forestry in India hovered around 1 per cent only. The expenditure on forestry sector has increased substantially since sixth five-year plan in accordance with the increase in afforestation activities undertaken to meet the desired targets. The sixth five-year plan coincided with the FCA 1980. So the increase in spending on forestry sector can be attributed to a shift in governmental policies. In the fifth plan, the spending was a meagre ₹.107.28 crore, which increased to ₹.15964.06 crore at the end of ninth five-year plan. The area afforested under the same time period has increased from 12.21 hectares to 80.50 hectares. The comparison shows that the spending has increased at a much higher rate than the afforested area. The area afforested under seventh, eight and ninth year plan has been almost same, but the spending has almost tripled in same time period. This shows that growing trees alone will not make these afforestation activities successful. Proper care and maintenance of the area afforested needs higher allocation of money. In fact, money spent in ninth five-year plan was close to 90 per cent of what had been spent till date in the country on these activities. This sends positive signals regarding finance to the project proponents and implementers about the success of afforestation.

Tenth Five-Year Plan (2002-2007)

The current five-year plan targets to increase the forest/tree cover to 25 per cent. It agrees that no strategy would be successful unless and until the basic needs are met. Recognising the role played by JFM in regeneration of degraded forests, the plan recommends taking further steps in identifying its strengths and weaknesses, so that the area under implementation can be increased. Raising concern on high imports of round timber and other forest produce, it expresses a desire for reversing this trend. This could be achieved by utilising community land, degraded forests or private farmlands of the country.

Implementing the same would mean removal of government subsidies, regulation of tariff on imports and other such policy modifications, which will make the plantation activities more desirable among farmers and village communities. Promotion of technology, credit support, developing marketing infrastructure and providing extension and training to interested farmers has also been recommended. Policy recommendations for tackling the problems related to constraint of felling, transportation and selling of forest produce which act as disincentive for growing trees are also suggested. This asks for creating a favourable policy environment, which promotes positive interaction among various stakeholders.

Keeping up with the challenges facing the society, plan proposes to utilise the wastelands and degraded lands for taking up CDM projects. This would help in utilising the wastelands besides generating additional incentives for taking up plantations. Emphasis has been put on growing species such as *Jatropha curcas* and *Pongamia pinnata*, which also grow naturally and can be utilised for generating bio-diesel, although success of these schemes are yet to be fully realised.. These plantations are cost-effective and easily replicable. To take up the afforestation activities more seriously all programmes have been merged under a single scheme called 'National Afforestation Programme (NAP)'. It is being operated through Forest Development Agencies (FDAs). Similarly, another programme named National Action Programme to Combat Desertification under UN Convention to Combat Desertification (UNCCD) has been taken up by MoEF. A 20 years' comprehensive NAP to combat desertification in the country was prepared with the following objectives:

- Community based approach to development,
- Activities to improve the quality of life of the local communities,
- Raising awareness,
- Drought management preparedness and mitigation,
- R&D initiatives and interventions which are locally suited,
- Strengthening self-–governance leading to empowerment of local communities.

For the Tenth Five-Year Plan, it has been proposed to initiate activities that include, among others, assessment and mapping of land degradation, drought monitoring and early warning system groups, drought preparedness contingency plans, and on-farm research activities for development of indigenous technology, etc.

The growing demand of raw material from our natural resources is threatening them. Envisaging the threat to the natural resources due to growing demand of raw material,is, the plan Plan proposes to take up plantation, which would reduce pressure on the natural forests and reverse the negative impact of deforestation while meeting the increasing demand. The Plan proposes to encourage agro-forestry by promoting technology, extension, and training, credit support, marketing infrastructure, etc., and providing a policy environment, which assures the farmers of a remunerative price. It also proposes to removes the constraints of felling, transport and marketing of forest produce from private holdings in different States and to formulate a common guideline for this purpose.

The current mean annual increment (MAI) of forest plantations varies from about 2 m^3/ha/year for valuable timber species to about 5-8 m^3/ha/year for eucalyptus and other fast growing species. Generally, MAI is around 10 m^3/ha/year in good quality plantations in various countries. This poor performance of forest plantation remains a great concern in the area of policy decisions. The Plan suggests measures including appropriate site selection, site-species matching, planting of elite clones, proper maintenance and protection, timely tending, thinning, irrigation, application of manures and pesticides, etc. for improving the productivity of plantations. For improving the utilisation of plantation, the plan identifies Indian Plywood Industries Research and Training Institute (IPIRTI) to be actively involved. IPIRTI can also help develop programmes that will not only fulfill the demand, but also provide with more wood substitutes.

POLICIES GOVERNING FOREIGN TRADE IN FORESTRY PRODUCE

Timber price in India has been increasing at the rate of 15 per cent per year, making import of timber more attractive, and Tthe current import policy allows duty free import of timber and pulp. In order to help wood-based industries meet their requirements, the government removed the trade barriers and liberalised the import of timber on Open General License (OGL). For industries, it was a welcome step and had an additional benefit of growth of industries in the coastal belt. This policy change led to increased import of timber. However, the produce from the imported timber is sold mainly in domestic market and there is practically no export of products against import. Export is less than one tenth of import. India's foreign exchange reserve as well as interest of tree growers has been put under an unwanted pressure. It created a sense of insecurity among tree growers of the country who now had to be satisfied with a smaller share of the market, as global players offered attractive deals to capture a bigger share of the growing market. Despite tough competition from the forestry sector and importing agencies, farmers are still supplying 50 per cent of wood supplies from their holdings. The importance and potential of agroforestry and several other such models has not been realised.

The acceptance of timber from plantations as raw material in wood based industries has opened new avenues for these farmers. However, to give a boost to tree growing activity as a means for import substitution, certain policy initiatives were felt necessary and were recommended.

- To impose heavy import duty on such wood products, which are/can be produced within the country to meet domestic needs.
- Enhance R&D efforts to manufacture quality products from plantation grown wood and other renewable fibres for import substitution.
- Export of wood and natural fibre based products promoted through incentives and simplification of procedure.
- Evolution and implementation of minimum mandatory material and product standards.
- Mechanism for collection and dissemination of information regarding import, export, prices and trade of timber needs to be developed.

The import of various wood-based commodities has been quite high than the exports both in terms of quantity and money involved. Though the exports have increased a bit compared to import in year 1999-00 over 1998-99, huge gap still remains. Besides, the farmers would find it difficult to make a financial comeback to take up this activity again if their initial investment does not return enough profit. Moreover, import of wood reduces the option of generating additional employment opportunities in the country, which would be easily taken up by the low-income class. A general reason cited for this import has been to reduce pressure on forests. Production forestry, farm forestry, agroforestry, if utilised to their hilt can do away with this import, which as of now puts a burden of ₹. 8,000 crores annually. Moreover, this would also help achieve the goal of one-third forest cover. Now the industries are also interested in taking up these activities by building relationship with farmers. The north-western part of the country took these efforts on a large scale, and massive plantations of eucalyptus and poplar were raised. However, a lack of organised market along with government policies, which make the process of harvesting trees and their transportation cumbersome, did not allow this effort to get the optimum revenues.

Wood import under Open General License (OGL) made the proposition of importing wood raw material more attractive. Generally, this imported wood comes from natural forests outside the country. In many cases, the harvesting procedure is unsustainable. In a way, these steps save Indian forests at the cost of forests in other wood-exporting countries. In today's scenario of climate change, a phenomenon occurring at one place can have complex implications at far off distances as well. So the problem gets transferred instead of getting solved. So the solution lies in raising more trees within the country. This will provide incentive for local farmers and a disincentive for those countries indulging in these unsustainable activities by taking benefit of imperfect market conditions.

Financing Schemes

Institutional funding is very important in areas where a farmer-industry relationship is to be established. In order to promote the afforestation activities, the central government has been spending money through the five-year plans. Schemes such as Investment Promotional Scheme have been instrumental in initiating and promoting production forestry throughout the nation, though not as successfully as they were initially conceived.

The experience in the last two decades show that institutional funding has been minimal in forestry programmes. These are some important reasons:

- Dearth of technical and economic data on different farm forestry models. This limits the ability of banks to evaluate bank ability of various farm forestry projects.
- Producers and banks often find the associated risk unacceptable. There are no insurance system to guard against the loss to producers and banks arising from various natural calamities.
- The lending banks do not have adequate capability to assist in formulation and appraisal of projects for farm forestry.

Investment Promotional Scheme

The Scheme was launched in the year 1994-95 in order to stimulate involvement of the corporate sector/financial institutions, etc. to pool in resources for development of non-forest wastelands.

The principal objectives of the scheme were:

- To facilitate/attract/channelise/mobilise resources from financial institutions, banks, corporate bodies including user industries and other entrepreneurs for development of wastelands in non-forest areas belonging to Central and State Governments, panchayats, village communities, private farmers, etc.

- To promote group of farmers belonging to different categories, namely, large, small, marginal and SCs/STs for bringing wastelands under productive use.
- To facilitate production and flow of additional biomass including farm-forestry products used as raw material inputs for different types of industries.
- To facilitate employment generation through land development and other allied land based and related activities including plantations.

The Scheme was restructured to make it broad-based and circulated to all the states and other concerned in August 1998. Under this Scheme, Central Promotional Subsidy was limited to ₹. 25 lakhs or 25 per cent of the project cost for on-farm development activities, whichever was less, subject to condition that the promoter's contribution in the project shall not be less than 25 per cent of the project cost. The projects promoted by the Scheduled Commercial Banks (SCBs), Regional Rural Banks, Land Development Banks and Cooperative Banks were eligible for promotional grant/subsidy under the Scheme. Under the Scheme, 41 projects covering an area of 1435 ha with a total cost of ₹.16.88 crores (firmed up by the bank) and subsidy of ₹. 1.09 crores have been sanctioned up to March, 2004. Because of slow progress, the Scheme was discontinued in 2003-04.

Tax Deductions

Tax deduction is an important financial incentive for production forestry. The Government of India announced tax deduction to companies for carrying out projects of softwood plantation on degraded non-forest land.

FOREST MANAGEMENT ACTIVITIES

To facilitate efficient management, the forest has been divided into three blocks which cover areas of 91, 124 and 129 hectares. The intention is to protect and provide a sustainable and equitable utilization of the forest. Users have been involved in planting of various species assisted by forest technicians and committee members. In 2052 (1992), the women's groups planted 11,000 Sissoo seedlings. The following year the users planted 8536 seedlings of bamboo, Bakaina and Sissoo. There are plans to establish a plantation for Eucalyptus, Sissoo, Khair, Botlle Brush, Gul Mahar, Asoka and other species in the near future. The group is also undertaking NTFP farming in suitable areas under the guidance of forest technicians and other organizations. In collaboration with the Agro Herbal Company, a private company promoting NTFPs which recently set-up a field office in Dipyapuri, around 100 types of NTFP have been identified. The group has also established a tree nursery. The general level of awareness about community forestry has been strengthened and the popularity of the FUG increased. While people were afraid of DFO staff in the past, these relations have now improved.

PROTECTION

The protection wing has the overall responsibility for forest protection and has put in place rules and regulations to achieve this goal. Three user-managed protection posts have been set-up at strategic locations in the forest and three forest guards employed. Their job is to protect the forest against illegal felling, the use of fire and destruction of flora and fauna through grazing, poisoning, shooting and other harmful activities.

Controls to regulate the collection of fuelwood, cutting of grass and pruning of fodder are in place and a graded penalty system where fines are calibrated according to the severity of violations is operative. There is a complete restriction on entrance into the forest from Chaitra 1st to end of Jestha as a precautionary measure to prevent forest fires. The group plans to construct a 5 m wide fire line in the north and west of the forest. Notice also that the forest is completely closed for grazing because of the high regeneration rate. The combined effect of these efforts is argued to effectively curtail illicit activities.

FOREST PRODUCT UTILISATION AND DISTRIBUTION

The Forest product distribution wing is responsible for the distribution of forest products and the process governing the allocation of timber is very similar to Dhuseri. Likewise, the forest product rates across the two groups are almost identical. Records are maintained for extracted and distributed forest products. To access timber quotas, users should submit an application along with ₹ 25 and state the reason behind the need for timber. After a recommendation (or rejection) of the application by the head of the sub committee, the committee will allocate timber as per the rules.

The role of the monitoring committee is to evaluate whether users have utilized forest products to fulfill their needs. The monitoring committee has a formal authority to penalise violations. It should be mentioned that while the mechanism for control of timber utilisation in Chautari is a replica of the process in Dhuseri, the above description provides the "official" account of the process of distribution of timber in Chautari. In contrast to Dhuseri, where we know that the control mechanism is ineffective, data limitations make it hard to establish precisely how well the mechanism operates in Chautari. While the incentive problems and scope for arbitrage are as strong as in Dhuseri, it is distinctly possible that the contrast between the official and the hidden economy is less pronounced in this case.

Branches and twigs damaged by the wind are distributed free of cost to users every year from 1st to end of Poush and in Jestha for 15 days but this is restricted to 2 people from each HH. The users can also collect the twigs and fallen small branches every Saturday during Shrawan and Bhadra. Users may also purchase fuelwood from the group for ₹ 100/quintal which exceeds the price of ₹ 75 charged by Dhuseri. Grass cutting is allowed from Bhadra 15th to Ashoj 15th and Mangsir 15th to end of Poush for the growth of the tree species. The forest is also open for fodder from Magh 1st to end of Baishak.

Special Provisions and Development Expenditure

Free membership has been granted to schools in the users' area of the CF. Timber is mainly provided to schools against a fixed price. The temple can get up to 5 cubic feet timber free of cost but have to pay for further requirements. The user group has awarded construction grants to Barchuli Junior High School Rajahar for extensions of classrooms and roof support to Saraswati Primary School in ward no. 4. A construction grant of ₹ 75.000 has also been given to the sub health post in Rajahar. Other financial and timber support has been provided to other schools, the police office, mothers groups and NGOs. Moreover, a grant for a biogas plant of ₹ 75.000, aimed at reducing fuelwood consumption has also been granted. The group has also given support in the form of disaster relief, mainly in connection with Jharahi floods.

Problems, Issues and Conflicts

Dhuseri and Chautari are undoubtedly advanced forestry user groups both in infrastructure development and in their respective approaches to community forestry. The user groups share another common feature: female leadership and participation remains very limited. Moreover, as noted, the motion for differentiation of users by socio-economic status was recently defeated in the General Assembly.

Based on a claim of being deceived by people living near the forest, *e.g.* residents in ward no 8, users from ward 5 have argued that a separate part of the forest should be allotted to them. Having much cultivated land and substantial livestock holdings, ward 5 has a high demand for forest resources to meet agriculture, domestic and livestock needs. The claim of deception was rooted in the observation that users in ward 8, adjacent to the forest, collect more forest products, legally and illegally. In 1999/2000 an interesting conflict emerged over a plan for a ward-wise division of the forest into plots. A demarcation for this purpose was undertaken on the initiative of the then Chairman X. However, users in ward 8, resisted this initiative. Having used the barren areas of the forest for grazing, a ward-wise division of the forest would effectively restrain their grazing opportunities. These users now accused the former Chairman, Mr X of being responsible for conflict claiming that he had received money from people from other wards after encouraging and backing their demands for a ward-wise division.

The committee pays field allowance of ₹ 12.-14.000 per year to DFO-staff during the utilization season. The role of the ranger during the harvesting period is to approve various steps in the harvesting process including estimates of felling, blazing and numbering of trees, to grant permissions for sawing in the sawmill as well as permissions to sell any surpluses outside the VDC. This provision of technical assistance falls within their official responsibilities and covered by regular salaries. Despite of this, the FUG is being charged for these services. There is much disagreement about the payment and the scale of payment to the forest officials. The Nepal-German Ayurvedic society was prepared to enter into a 20-year agreement with the user group with a view to promote NTFP production and sales. An almost completed agreement was, however, undermined by strong opposition from the current chairperson Mr Y, and the proposal eventually scrapped.

His official claim was that the project could jeopardise the daily needs requirements of the users, due to a leasing clause in the proposed agreement. Mr X (the then chairperson) who had been supporting the initiative felt that this resistance threatened and undermined his leadership. There is a rather strong element of personal politics in this narrative. Mr Y's hidden agenda was to undermine Mr X's position to overtake the Chairmanship himself, a goal eventually accomplished, since the Ayurvedic society project compelled Mr X to resign. Mr X now claims that he can prove that the present chairman, Mr Y has been involved in illegal activities, more specifically, that Mr Y has felled green trees in conflict with the Operational Plan. However, Mr X is reluctant to provide further details because he is concerned about the reputation of the FUG.

During the chairmanship of Mr Z in 2057/58, an allegation of financial misconduct was raised in the assembly. It was found that he had spent ₹ 11000 to buy alcohol for the DF staff and for employing laborers for the transportation of woods from the forest to the depot. ₹ 11.000 was spent on food and travelling to the DFO in order to obtain the harvesting permit. A considerable sum of money was spent to persuade the ranger to approve a larger than previously agreed quota. Another case, accusing Mr Z for misuse of ₹ 9000 by giving favour to people already privileged through other FUG-activities, related to the loading of timber. The staff was given ₹ 9000 for loading in addition to their regular payments. Poor users argued that they should have been given the loading job and Mr Z was accused of denying the poor employment opportunities.

During his tenure, Mr X provided ₹ 1500/- to a DF staff in the harvesting season, *e.g.* December 2056/57 in connection with a visit to the District Office to obtain the blazing order for felling of trees. Mr X and the then vice chairman requested the ranger to produce the blazing order. The ranger lingered and asked for money. He was given ₹ 1000/- on the spot. The ranger then requested the chairman to buy lunch and incurred further expenses of ₹ 500. Two days later the blazing order was sent.

After issuing the blazing order, DF staff marked 1700 cft for felling. While cutting it was discovered that some trees were hollow and the committee asked for permission to cut more trees to fill the allotted quota. The ranger accepted this request after extensive bargaining. Having been granted this second permission, the majority of the committee, who were aligned with the Chairman and with forest staff overstepped their mandate and felled old green trees as well. Inspecting the spot, the ranger gave the impression that the illegal felling had been reported to the district officer. He said that the committee should attend DFO for clarification without any further delays. The committee members were worried and asked the ranger to do whatever he could to minimize the offence. For this favour the ranger demanded 20 cubic feet of timber. The committee provided the timber immediately to save themselves from further trouble and embarassment.

Another interesting example concerns the sawing of timber. In July 2002, the ranger had given the committee permission to saw in Dibyapura Saw Mill at a rate of ₹ 38/cft.[3] Instead, the committee decided to process the timber at Pragatinagar saw mill (4 km west) which offered a rate of ₹ 30/cft, thereby permitting a saving of ₹ 8/cft. When informed the ranger sent a letter asking for clarification. He didn't approve of the answer thinking he had lost commission from the saw mill. The committee members involved in this incident are reluctant to provide further information about the matter.

TRADITIONAL REGIME FOREST MANAGEMENT

Forest management in the state is being carried out both in the traditional ways and according to the policies of the Forest Department.

THE TRADITIONAL REGIME

Traditional management systems have certain time-tested, practical and effective ways of managing as well as utilising natural resources. The Sarna (sacred groves) system, common in the northern districts of the State is an excellent example of sustainable management. The cutting of trees in these sacred groves is prohibited. Sanctified by belief and practice, this system has been an important factor in conserving the green cover of the State.

The Official Regime

The Forest Department of the State manages the State's forest wealth in accordance with prescribed policies and guidelines. The Joint Forest Management (JFM) system encourages people's participation in managing forest resources. Members of JFM committees receive usufruct rights, a portion of the revenue from the felling of timber and from intermediate thinning. They are also eligible for employment under afforestation and other programmes carried out by the Forest Department. The Forest Development Agency and the Chhattisgarh State Minor Forest Produce Co-operative Federation are involved in the management and development of forests and nationalised MFPs. The Village Jan Rapats have suggested solutions for managing and maintaining forests. While these suggestions are quite varied, they do reflect a sense of disquiet at the denuding forest resources and the helplessness that people feel in the circumstances.

Other Issues Related to Forests

Other forest-related issues include the depletion of forests, their legal status and control.

Depletion of Forests

A common concern cited in many reports is the degradation and depletion of forests. The causes, according to the Village Reports, are the increasing biotic pressure on forests from the increase in human and animal population. Significantly, many Village Reports state that distancing people from the management of forests has also been a contributory factor.

According to them, since people have been alienated from utilising forest produce, they have become less concerned about conserving the forests. The people say unequivocally that they want to participate in preserving their forests. They also feel that unless they are fully involved in the work of protection, forests will continue to get degraded.

The Legal and Institutional Framework

The State Forest Policy guides the legal and institutional arrangement, based on the guidelines of the National Forest Policy, 1988, provided by the Central Government. Along with this, the provisions of Scheduled V areas in the Constitution of India and the Provisions of the Panchayats (Extension to the Scheduled Areas) Act, 1996 (PESA) also determine the legal situation.

The State Forest Policy asserts that the management of the forests should be such that forests are converted from an Open Access Resource to community controlled, prioritised, protected and managed resources through Joint Forest Management (JFM), People's Protected Areas (PPAs) and other such measures. The Government, through its Forest Policy, has made an attempt to recognise the ownership and relationship of the forest dwelling communities, especially the tribals.

The Policy states, "...For sustainable forest development, livelihood security and bio-cultural diversity conservation, People's Protected Areas (PPAs) should be established. This paradigm shift of adaptive management can reconcile the dichotomy of threat perception arising out of conservation-development orthodoxy by taking into account human sensitivities, socio-cultural norms, beliefs and systems borne out of history, culture and traditions."

From the tenor and content of the Jan Rapats, it is however apparent that the people and communities feel a sense of deprivation and alienation as well as a loss of access to their valued and valuable resource – the forests. The forest laws and its regulatory regime has divided the people from the forests and led to a realignment of the age-old relationship.

Village Jan Rapats repeatedly affirm that preserving and using the forests in a sustainable manner, was, and should be a way of life for the people. The forest laws and their implementation has resulted in the alienation of the people from their resources, and turned them into mere 'users' of the forests. Most people feel that the real control and therefore, the responsibility for the forests, now lies with the Government. They no longer feel a sense of ownership.

The Extension of PESA to Chhattisgarh

The Constitution provides for special provisions for administration and control of Scheduled Areas. The provisions of the Panchayats Extension to Scheduled Areas (PESA) Act, 1996, give special powers to the Gram Sabhas in Scheduled Areas especially in the management of natural resources. Areas with pockets of substantial Scheduled Tribe populations living within the dominance of non-tribal communities have been categorised in the Constitution as Scheduled V Areas. Of the 16 districts in Chhattisgarh, seven districts (Surguja, Korea, Jashpur, Kanker, Bastar, Dakshin Bastar Dantewada and Korba) are categorised as Scheduled V Area districts and six (Bilaspur, Durg, Rajnandgaon, Raipur, Raigarh and Dhamtari) are partial Scheduled V Area districts. The objective of PESA is to enable tribal communities to safeguard their traditional rights over natural resources. The Act emphasises the rights and ownership of people's institutions and respects tradition in the control and management of resources.

It clearly states that, 'A State legislation on the Panchayats that may be made shall be in consonance with the customary law, social and religious practices and traditional management practices of community resources'. Further it states that 'A village shall ordinarily consist of a habitation or a group of habitations or hamlet or a group of hamlets comprising a community and managing its affairs in accordance with traditions and customs.' Some of the powers vested with the Gram Sabha in Schedule V Areas include:

- The ownership of minor forest produce.
- The power to prevent alienation of land in the Scheduled Areas and to take appropriate action to restore any unlawfully alienated land of a Scheduled Tribe.
- The power to exercise control over institutions and functionaries in all social sectors.

- Exercise control over local plans and the resources for such plans including tribal sub-plans.

Control, Ownership and Power Equations

Forests are a controlled natural resource. This control impacts substantially on the lives of people who depend on forests.

- For communities and households dependent on forests and for others for whom the forests sustain and supplement their livelihoods, accessing forest resources means contact with the Forest Department, the regulatory arm of the State. The unvarying threat of a powerful institution, with legal and physical resources to control this interface makes people, especially tribal communities, feel vulnerable and uncomfortable.
- Communities that have lived with the forests, managed and conserved them for generations now find that the space for participating in forest management is dependent on the benevolence of the regulatory regime. They find this difficult to comprehend. The conservation effort is no longer natural but programme driven. People from all the villages state that the experience with officials and the mechanisms for interface are neither adequate, nor conducive to the common goals of society and State.

The issue of forest management involves a series of complex relationships between the stakeholders of the forests, the revenue department, the Panchayats and people. Regulations are perceived as being arbitrarily used by the Forest Department. This, combined with the restrictions imposed by the Government, causes friction between the people and the administration.

The critical balance between resource use and the issue of rights and people's ownership, and therefore responsibility of these resources especially in relation to forests, is an idea that the Forest Department is still coming to terms with. It is imperative for the State to define a role for itself vis-à-vis forests and the people who depend on them, in order to be able to stop forest depletion and encourage afforestation.

This will help to re-establish the vital balance in the forests of Chhattisgarh owned and managed for centuries by its people.

LAND

The land area of Chhattisgarh is about 1.35 lakh square kilometres. About 36 per cent of the area is cultivated, and another 44 per cent is under forests (forest land and revenue forests). Of the total land area in the State, 4,828 thousand hectares are sown, and the net sown area 13 per head is 0.24 hectares. The gross sown area is 5,327 thousand hectares.

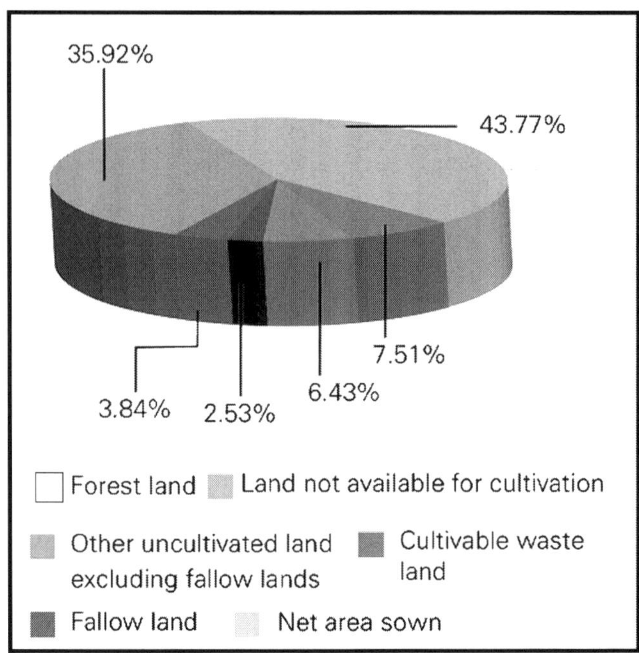

The highest percentage of land under agriculture is in Durg, Janjgir-Champa, Mahasamund (all above 50 per cent), followed by Raigarh, Bilaspur, Kabirdham, Rajnandgaon and Raipur (all above 40 per cent). The lowest percentage of net sown area to total area, is in Korea (18.7 per cent), followed by Dakshin Bastar Dantewada (19 per cent) and Bastar (21 per cent).

SOIL TYPES

Chhattisgarh has at least five different types of soil. In the districts of Bilaspur, Surguja, Durg, Raipur and Bastar red and yellow loamy soil is dominant. Both are low in nitrogen and humus content. A major part of paddy production comes from this region. In the hill ranges, the soil is sandy loam, which is also suitable for paddy. Laterite soil is good for cereal crops, while the black soil is best suited to cotton, wheat and gram. In the Jan Rapats, land has been categorised according to the traditional classification. This varies from district to district. The choice of the type of seeds, the crops that are sown and the technology that is used depends on this classification. It is a choice that has been tested and tried over generations and ensures some productivity irrespective of the quality of the land. In many villages, the quality of land is not suitable for agriculture. While the undulating terrain and rocky surface is a constraint, the setting up of coal mines and coal related industries in districts like Korea, have meant that both land and water have been contaminated by pollutants such as fly ash. Many Village Reports have highlighted the fact that indiscriminate use of chemical fertilizers has affected land quality and led to a decline in productivity.

MINING IN CHHATTISGARH

Chhattisgarh is rich in mineral resources. Vast reserves of coal, iron ore and bauxite are found here, along with limestone and dolomite. This is the only State in the country where tin ore is found. Diamonds and semi precious stones like corundum, quartz and garnet are also mined here. While mining provides employment to some people and substantial revenue to the State, the industry has an adverse impact on the environment in some districts.

Pollution is one of the major impacts of mining, according to the Jan Rapats. This results in a number of problems ranging from declining productivity to contamination of drinking water.

- Village Jan Rapats mention that mining activities have affected the productivity of land and quality of water. District reports such as that of Korea have mentioned that the coal dust from coal handling plants covers the agricultural fields and affects the yield adversely.
- Pollution of the water that drains into reservoirs and rivers is another major problem. Several villages depend on surface water for domestic purposes, nistaari and irrigation. Polluted water has adversely affected both health and crops.
- Some reports have pointed out that illnesses related to breathing and respiration, falling levels of immunity, weakness and ill health are all outcomes of pollution. In some cases, people have been forced to migrate due the adverse impact of pollution on their health.
- Forest degradation due to mining activities has also been detailed in the Jan Rapats.

LAND DISTRIBUTION AND FRAGMENTATION

Land ownership and distribution are other important issues. The land distribution pattern is skewed, by the presence of a number of large farmers, due to benami land records and old malgujars (landlords who were earlier responsible for collecting rent on behalf of the State), who continue to operate in the central belt of the State. Increasing population and subdivision of holdings has led to tiny and unviable plots of land for small and marginal farmers.

LAND – AN ERODING RESOURCE

Soil degradation and soil erosion are increasing problems, leading to a decline in agricultural productivity. The Jan Rapats have noted this, and the following reasons have been cited:

- Pollution due to mining activities in the vicinity of agricultural fields and excessive use of chemical fertilizers.
- High cropping intensity without allowing the land to replenish the nutrient content and aerating the soil.
- Absence of good forest or vegetative cover, which leads to more soil

erosion. The lack of good vegetative cover has also reduced dry leaves and twigs that fall on the land and which add to the productivity of the land.

LAND RECORDS

Two issues find frequent mention in the Jan Rapats:

- The problem of information on land records,
- Errors in the records.

Access to land records is not easy and the role of field level revenue officials is not always that of a facilitator. In many cases the records do not reflect actual ownership, especially in the case of larger landholdings. Another problem is that a large number of forest dwellers do not have clear land titles. Many of them have officially been categorised as 'encroachers' on forestland, although they were there long before the State declared their land as State forests.

ENCROACHMENTS AND DISPLACEMENTS

The issue of encroachments has been regularly cited in the Jan Rapats. While encroachments are present in almost all categories of land (private, State owned, open access and common lands), common lands have suffered the most, especially pasture and grazing lands. This has affected the quantity of fodder available for the cattle, especially for the landless, small and marginal farmers who depend on grazing and pasture land for feeding their cattle (they are unable to produce enough crop residues to feed their cattle).

Grazing is prohibited in forest areas and the continuously degrading forest cover does not provide enough fodder to feed their cattle, for the whole year. The Village and District Reports express serious concerns over encroachment. The political and power dynamics of these encroachments are such that people believe strong State intervention is essential for stopping and removing encroachment.

There have been instances of families being displaced for the construction of dams, factories and industrial projects, and have not been fully rehabilitated.

Forest Management and Policies

Pre-british Periods

In pre-British times the forests of India enjoyed a measure of protection owing to their very inaccessibility-their lack of transport facilities, malarious nature and wild beasts -- and, above all, owing to the limited demand for timber in a country torn with strife and unrest. True, the Arabs carried on a trade in teak for building sea-going craft, but their requirements were small and easily met. Some measure of control was exercised by the rulers of the day, but with respect only to valuable species like teak and sandalwood, which were declared royal trees, for the felling of which permits had to be obtained. Otherwise, every one was free to fell what he liked, without let or hindrance.

The British Régime

As has been pointed out, destruction of the forests assumed menacing dimensions with the advent of the British and the consolidation of their power by the end of the eighteenth century. The havoc, however, proved a blessing in disguise, for the next fifty years witnessed widespread concern over the vanishing of forest resources that had been assumed to be inexhaustible. In 1805 the British government inquired of the Court of Directors of the East India Company regarding a sustained supply of teak logs for the British Navy. In 1806 a policeman was placed in charge of the Malabar teak forests, an appointment suggestive of the interest which the government of Madras took in their teak. During the first half of the nineteenth century the forests became largely the concern of the district administrative officers.

The Collector (administrator) of Malabar established the famous Nilambur Teak Plantations in 1844 and the Bombay government appointed the then Director of the Botanical Gardens as the first Conservator of Forests in 1847. The government of Madras followed suit and appointed a Conservator in 1856. About the same time, a forest officer was appointed to look after the forests of Duns and Oudh; and the Commissioner of Kumsun worked as Conservator in addition to his other duties.

Establishment of Forest Departments

The introduction of scientific forest management and the organization of forest departments in India owe their inception to Dr. Dietrich Brandis, a professor of botany from the University of Bonn, who was engaged by the East India Company in 1856 as the superintendent of teak forests in Burma. His resourcefulness, ability and consummate skill led to his appointment in 1864 as the first Inspector General of Forests for India and as a result of his initiative forest departments were constituted in the then British provinces.

A Forest Act, later replaced by the more elaborate Acts of 1878 and 1927, was passed in 1856 and in accordance with its provisions valuable timber-bearing regions were declared as either "reserved," "protected," or "unclassed" forests. In the main the difference lies in the degree of control prescribed. In especially valuable areas, declared as reserved because of the vital role they play in the national economy, only welldefined and limited private rights are recognized. In protected forests, private rights are admitted freely and restricted only in the interest of the right-holders themselves. In such forests, while the reasonable needs of the local population are met, the local people are not permitted to exercise rights and privileges in blissful disregard of the interests of the generations to come. Stated succinctly, the distinction consists in this: in a reserved forest everything is treated as an offense which is not permitted, whereas in a protected forest nothing is an offense unless it is prohibited. The "unclassed" forests, as their name signifies, are those awaiting classification as either "reserved" or "protected" While the forest departments in the former British provinces of India were highly organized, such was not generally the case in the Indian States, where forests attracted attention more for the sport that they provided than for their protective and productive functions.

Most of the states were too small and poor to afford full-fledged forest organizations and the bulk of their forests were far from valuable. The integration brought about by recent constitutional changes since the dawn of independence has now made it possible for each group of states to have its own forest department.

Private Forests

During recent years attention has been focused upon the need for protecting private forests from the short-sighted policies of their owners, as a means of conserving an essential national economic resource. With no prospect of quick annual returns, an owner is frequently tempted to sacrifice his capital for an immediate gain. The provisions of the Indian Forest Act of 1927 did not suffice to arrest the destruction of these forests and the consequent physical deterioration of the areas in which they lie. Recent legislation for the control of private forests, however, has sought to establish the following procedure:

- Designation by the government of private forest areas over which control is to be exercised;
- Issue of felling permits, pending compilation of working plans for the areas so designated;
- Affording the owners of the private forests concerned the opportunity of managing them in accordance with approved working plans;
- Vesting control of private forests in the government in cases where recalcitrant owners indulge in reckless fellings in flagrant disregard of the working plans. While the title to such "vested" forests continues unaffected at present, existing trends point to the complete abolition of the private ownership of forests.

Forest Policy

1894. Although the foundations of regular forest management were laid in the sixties of the nineteenth century, it was not until 1894 that the Government of India adopted the forest policy that constitutes the Magna Carta for the forests of India. Since then the vital role of the forests in relation to agriculture, industry, transportation and defence, has received increasing recognition. Their protective functions have also come to be better understood. The old forest policy was designed largely for the former British provinces. Its provision for the relinquishment of forest land "without hesitation" for the extension of agriculture-subject to certain conditions honored chiefly in the breach-led to undesirable consequences. In the original policy no mention was made of sustained yields, working plans, forest education, or forest research; nor was any cognizance taken of wildlife, an important and attractive feature of India's forests.

The New Policy

The recent constitutional changes have directed attention to the shaping of an over-all policy for the country. The government has revised the forest policy in relation to the progress that has been made in the physical, economic and political fields. The New Policy of 1952 provides, among other things, for the classification of forests into:

- Protection Forests, the preservation of which is directed by purely physical and climatic considerations;
- National Forests, to be maintained and managed to meet the needs of defence, industry and transportation;
- Village Forests, to be maintained for their role in the agricultural economy of the country, such as provision of firewood and of small timber for agricultural implements and dwellings;
- Treelands, or areas covered with tree growth of some sort, which, though outside the scope of regular forest management, are essential to the amelioration of the physical environment. These classes are by no means mutually exclusive, since each forest usually fulfills functions subsidiary to those specifically assigned to it.

The notion, once widely entertained, that forests as such have no inherent right to land, but may be permitted on sufferance on residual land not required for other purposes, is being effectively dispelled. In the New Policy, the protective and productive role of the forests finds recognition in a directive to the effect that a proportion of the whole land area to be determined by each state should be permanently maintained under forest. Each group of villages is to have a complement of forest, constituting a fuel, fodder and timber reserve.

Under the New Policy, moreover, attention is given to such matters as:

- Balanced land use; putting each type of land to such use that it will produce most and deteriorate least;
- State control of private forests;
- Preservation of wildlife;
- Control of grazing;
- Control of shifting cultivation;
- Provision against fluctuating budgets.

Special provision is also made for the training of forest personnel, for forest legislation and for research. The principle of sustained yield and the need of setting up an organization for dealing with working plans have both been especially stressed.

8

Changes in the Forest Natural Environment

Forests and woodlands are an important part of our landscape and provide many benefits to society. The tree species that are native to the UK have adapted to the local climate, atmosphere and soils over many years. However, human activities have resulted in changes to the natural environment, especially over the past 200 years.

It is expected that the climate of the UK will become milder and wetter in winter, and significantly hotter and drier in the summer months over the coming century. These changes to our climate are predicted to be larger and more rapid than any since the last ice-age, posing real problems for trees, woodland and forestry.

Climate changes directly and indirectly affect the growth and productivity of forests: directly due to changes in atmospheric carbon dioxide and climate and indirectly through complex interactions in forest ecosystems. Climate also affects the frequency and severity of many forest disturbances.

In the context of climate change, sustainably managed forests – and the products derived from them – play an essential mitigating role. Forests are one of the globe's greatest carbon-sequestration tools, and sustainable forestry naturally creates an endless cycle of carbon absorption and storage.

Trees and forest products play a critical role in helping to tackle climate change and reduce greenhouse gases. As trees grow, they clean the air we breathe by absorbing carbon dioxide from the atmosphere, storing the carbon in their wood, roots, leaves or needles and surrounding soil, and releasing the oxygen back into the atmosphere. Young, vigorously growing trees absorb the most carbon dioxide, with the rate slowing as they reach maturity.

When trees start to decay, or when forests succumb to wildfire, insects or disease, the stored carbon is released back into the atmosphere. In any of these cases, the carbon cycle begins again as the forest is regenerated, either naturally or by planting, and young seedlings once again begin absorbing carbon. Manufacturing wood into products requires far less energy than other materials – and very little fossil fuel energy. Most of the energy that is used comes from converting residual bark and sawdust to electrical and thermal energy, adding to wood's light carbon footprint. Climate is a strong influence on forestlands in B.C. It affects tree growth, productivity, and numerous resources derived from these lands. By maintaining biodiversity in our forests, we can help ecosystems to withstand environmental changes such as climate change.

STRENGTHEN ADAPTIVE CAPACITY OF FORESTS

Negatively affect forests and many of their plant and animal species. In addition, they may negatively affect the availability of other resources, necessary for species survival.

Current forest composition and structure are however, the result of past changes in climate and shows that forests and their species have an inherent capacity to adapt to change. The main differences of current climate change with historic changes are the increased rate of these changes and the degraded and fragmented state of the remaining forests, which reduces the capacity of the species and ecosystems to adapt. The challenge is to help species and ecosystems to adapt to climate change while at the same time ensuring that ecosystem services are maintained. This will require the identification of the changes to which the forest will need to adapt.

Locally, changes may be disastrous, unless climate, ecosystem and species changes are accompanied by adjustments in the local social and economic systems. For example, increased occurrence of severe fires will require greater collective action to prevent fires as well as improved weather and fire danger forecast services. Companies producing furniture of high value species from natural forests, whose natural regeneration under changed climate conditions has become increasingly difficult, may have to change geographic range for their inputs, or change to other species and/or other processing procedures. Communities and private landowners depending on local forests may have to change livelihoods after severe hurricane damage.

Nationally or at the landscape level, changes may be slower and less disastrous in the short term. New challenges include the identification of those species groups and ecological processes that are essential for the most important ecosystem services. This would include in most cases identification of water catchment areas (hydrogeology) and the role of forests in maintaining water quality and quantity. It will be important to increase the probability that changing ecosystems will continue to provide the important services and goods.

In particular, ecosystems in geographic locations at the extreme limits of climatically well-defined areas, such as mountainous forests, rangelands and boreal forests, are likely to be severely affected and may disappear. Some authors suggest that maintaining functional diversity and 6 composition will preserve ecosystem services, while others found that different functional groups will react differently to environmental changes, indicating that climate change may favour some functional groups over others. More research is needed however, to identify those functional groups essential for the desired ecosystem services and goods in particular areas and to understand how these can be conserved and protected.

Reduce Risk and Intensity of Pest, Disease and Fire Outbreaks

Reducing the climate induced risk of pests, diseases and fire outbreaks, in particular, in dry areas and less diverse forests will be a major environmental challenge. Breeding of more resistant or more resilient varieties is a medium to long-term solution for plantation species, although, that introduces new risks because strengthening the adaptive capacity of a species for one trait may weaken it to other traits. Identifying species for their "realized fitness" - for example, varieties of a species that survived insect attacks, diseases or fires, similar to the expected events in a particular region - and then facilitating their migration to the area of interest, may be another strategy. In both cases, identification of the traits that will increase resistance or resilience will be important as will be replicating those traits over generations and successfully introducing the species or varieties in the area of interest, without introducing new problems (such as undesired invasion).

Predicting future changes in pest and disease outbreaks and adjusting management accordingly is another option, which requires the development and validation of models that reliably predict impacts under different climate and management scenarios. A further option is the identification and implementation of forest management systems that are known or thought to reduce the risks of pests, diseases and/or fires.

While there are several well known means to protect forests and plantations, in many cases these are not applied for a variety of reasons, or are not applied to those forests most in need. The challenges are to identify and address the reasons for the lack of application of management techniques and to adjust management options to the threats in a participatory, socially and economically acceptable manner.

RISK OF MIGRATION INTO FOREST AREAS

Climate change will affect all people but in particular, rural people that depend on nature for their livelihoods, and poverty stricken communities in the urban-rural interface that are often subjected to the consequences of extreme weather events. Climate change is expected to change the aptitude of lands for specific crops, cause problems of droughts, fire and flooding and may drive many people from their lands. These people are likely to either go to cities to look for jobs, often adding to urban poverty, or to other rural areas to look for other lands where they may be able to continue their agricultural livelihoods or find employment in the agricultural sector. The surge of interest in fuels from biomass (*e.g.* corn, sugarcane and oil palm) adds another dimension to this migration. The purchasing of land, often based on speculation, in the hope of selling later for higher prices to investors interested in biofuel production, may cause migration. The expected high incomes from biofuels may also motivate landowners to convert their forests into energy plantations, oftentimes in an unsustainable manner. On the other hand, if well planned, biofuels could also help avoid or reduce migration by providing off-farm employment.

Forest use values, even in the case of the most successful enterprises, will not be able to compete with oil palm or other energy crops in those lands suitable for the crops. Legal definition of user and owner rights of forest areas and the mechanisms to defend those rights will be important elements of strategies to prevent unauthorized entrance into forests. Market mechanisms that restrict trade of products from companies that do not show social and environmental responsibility in their production and purchase policies may be another strategy. An individual forest user or owner will find it difficult to influence legislation, their implementation or the way that markets function. Collaboration with other stakeholders, neighbours, value chain members, and state administrators will be essential to the development of adequate measures to reduce the conversion and degradation of forests. Forest users and owners, however, have a longstanding tradition of independence and in the past have not shown tendencies to such collaboration. Lack of trust (often justified), has often hampered relations between different stakeholders in the forest and environmental sectors. Building sufficient trust to facilitate collaboration may be the biggest challenge of all for future forest management and needs the collaboration of all actors involved.

Environment: A Concept of Wholeness

The environment is a concept of wholeness (nature), with non-living and living components interdependent among themselves. It is aptly defined as 'the sum total of all conditions and influences that affect the development and life of organisms'. This comprehensive definition stresses totality, and every living organism from the lowest to the highest, including human being, has it own environment. The word 'nature' in the *Gita* also conveys the idea that it does not belong to anyone but everyone belongs to it, like a family does not belong to anyone but everyone belongs to the family. Like in a family, in the environment also interactions between its different constituents are expected, and these interactions sometimes might lead to hazardous situations. Interaction is leading to the faster deterioration of the environment.

Traditionally, our understanding of the environment was holistic. A *shloka* from the *Isha Upanishad* goes, 'the whole universe together with its creatures belongs to the Lord (nature). One can enjoy the bounties of nature by giving up all greed'. Implicit in this thought is that no creature is superior to any other, and human beings should not have absolute power over nature. Let no one species encroach on the rights and privileges of nature. The element of sustainability is ingrained in this, because the emphasis is on using nature without greed. Once the element of greed enters, exploitation starts and we cease to utilise nature for the good of all human beings.

Traditional cultures have always lived in harmony with their natural environments. Nature and humankind (*prakriti* and *purusha*) form inseparable parts of the life support system. This system has five elements: air, water, land, flora and fauna, which are interconnected, interrelated and interdependent. Deterioration in one element affects the others.

Traditional social ethics placed great emphasis on the values, beliefs and attitudes that helped man to live in harmony with nature. The *Bhumi Suktam* in the *Atharvaveda* is said to be the most impressive and eloquent testament of ecological values that can be found anywhere in world literature. These and similar texts from diverse cultural traditions throughout the earth express a world-view which is informed by the spirituality inherent in nature and stress the holistic and harmonious relationship between humanity and nature.

In the *Manusmriti* (5.45) it is written that 'he who injures innoxious beings from a wish to give himself pleasure, never finds happiness, whether living or dead'. Reference to ecological concerns is also found in *Charaka Samhita*, *Vimansthan*, 3.2. 'The destruction of forests is most dangerous for the nation and human beings. *Vanaspati* has a direct relation with the well-being of society. Due to the pollution of the natural environment and the destruction of forests, many diseases crop up to ruin the nation'.

During Ashoka's time (272-232 bc), perhaps for the first time in the history of the world ecological concerns became state concerns. His imperial edicts laid down rules of conduct that had to be obeyed with respect to the environment. Non-compliance was met with punishment.

T.N. Khoshoo writes, quoting Gandhiji in *Mahatma Gandhi: An apostle of applied human ecology*, that 'it is an arrogant assumption to say that human beings are lords and masters of the lower creatures. On the contrary, being endowed with greater things in life, they are the trustees of the lower animal kingdom'. The delicate and holistic balance that exists in nature has to be respected and maintained.

The Himalayas, the proverbial 'Third Pole', have always remained a source of fascination and inspiration for different people and have been deemed to be the cradle of civilisation in the subcontinent. There seems to be general agreement that the ecology of the Himalayas has been endangered. The Himalayas have exercised a great influence on the environmental conditions of northern India and the people living in the Indo-Gangetic plain. They have prevented the monsoon winds from crossing over Tibet and forced them to precipitate most of their moisture on the Indian side in the form of rain and snow. This unique ecology of the Himalayas, which has such an extensive and pervasive influence on the life of our people, needs to be preserved, conserved and qualitatively upgraded.

The developmental activities of man such as the construction of high dams, roads, exploration for minerals and mining activity and the quest for arable land have to face the challenge of intensified dynamic process, commonly referred to as geographical hazards. Natural resources are being exploited in the name of economic development. Indira Gandhi's interpretation is that the real conflict is not between environment and development but between the environment and reckless exploitation by man in the name of efficiency. We have to live a life according to the rhythm of nature. Human inference in natural environmental conditions often gives these dynamic processes catastrophic proportions, leading to disasters and irreparable damage to the natural balance of the ecosystem. It is not just concern about the extinction of the big cats, but concern for all inhabitants and non-living resources. We have to stop this undeclared war against nature. Human beings are at the crossroads. Careless application of technology is leading to eco-degradation and pollution. Gandhiji emphasised, 'The earth provides enough for every man's need but not for every man's greed'.

Sustainable development is, therefore, a concept of good and sound economic growth that can be maintained indefinitely with damage to the environment. Good environment generally begets good economics.

The words 'economics' and 'ecology' have the same root, *oikos*, which refers to a house. While economics deals with financial housekeeping, ecology deals with environmental housekeeping.

Studies have shown that the perspectives of ecology are different from those of economics in that the former stresses limits rather than continuous growth, stability rather than continuous 'development'. The ecosystem is the basic unit which has biotic and abiotic components that form an interrelated, interconnected and interdependent system. The most important characteristic of an ecosystem is that it is dynamic, evolving and auto-sustainable as long as it remains reasonably undisturbed and there is incoming sunlight. The equilibrium of an ecosystem is disturbed by external stimuli such as natural cataclysmic changes and ever-increasing human activities dictated by socio-economic growth. The basic difference is that the socio-economic system, in contrast, is hitched only to one species, human beings. In an ecosystem, different species of plants and animals including human beings and micro-organisms form an interacting system. Thus, the economic process is unidirectional and human beings can only progress forwards. Conflict between the ecosystem and the socio-economic system arises from unidirectional and unlimited human wants to meet genuine needs as also greed. This has caused ecological crisis, which in other words means human exploitation of resources at a greater rate than can be normally regenerated under natural conditions.

Central Himalayas

The central Himalayas comprise eight hill districts of Uttar Pradesh, namely Chamoli, Pauri, Tehri, Uttarkashi, Dehradoon, Almora, Nainital and Pithoragarh, spread over an area of about 52, 000 sq km. The people of the region are poor, ignorant and backward but the environment has made them simple, honest, hard-working, cheerful and courageous. The region is quite rich in religious and cultural heritage. The Hindu shrines of Badrinath, Kedarnath, Gangotri, Yamunotri and the Sikh gurudwara at Hemkund near the famous valley of flowers attracts pilgrims every year. People come not only on pilgrimage but also to escape the stresses and strains of urban life, to relax and to enjoy the beauties of nature.

Forest: A Womb

The term 'forest' applies not only to trees but also to scrub vegetation and grassland. It is aptly defined as 'a peculiar organism of unlimited kindness and extends generously the products of its life activity; it affords protection to all beings, offering shade even to the axeman, who destroys it'. Trees and forests are also important for deep psychological reasons. In returning to the forest, we are returning to the womb, not in psychoanalytical terms but in cosmological terms. We are returning to our origins. For centuries forests and the people living around have complemented each other, the latter deriving their livelihood from the farmer, who in turn maintained the ecological balance and environmental quality together with conservation of soil and water. The hill people utilise their traditional knowledge to use forest resources without destroying them. From the forest they get fuel for cooking, fodder for their cattle, fruit, timber for building their houses and medicinal herbs for curing diseases. The forest helps in maintaining the flow of perennial springs, in bringing rain, in keeping the soil and water conserved, in preventing landslides, thereby giving protection from this natural calamity. It helps regulate watershed management so as to maintain the fertility of the soil, control droughts and floods, and preserve wildlife.

Massive deforestation in the Himalayan region is the important factor in ecological degradation. Non-availability of certain species, decline of fodder and wood resources, loss of the habitat of wildlife, soil erosion, recurrent floods and drying-up springs and seasonal streams and climatic changes are the consequences of man's activity. It is obvious that there is something wrong with the management of these vital resources.

The deforestation which has taken place due to commercial exploitation of trees for timber, resin, medicinal herbs, etc., the developing of new agricultural fields, over-grazing by animals, the coming up of new habitation (*e.g.* because of the construction of the Tehri dam), the building of roads mainly after the China invasion of 1962, tourism development and other development activities, increase in the population (men as well as animals), all have had an adverse affect on the environment and have brought about ecological imbalance.

The forest has gone away from the villages. It is reported that there is a scarcity of fuel, fodder and fruit. Medicinal herbs are going to be extinct. The adverse affects noticed by us were that due to deforestation in the villages of Garhwal there is watershed failure, which has resulted in both drought and flood conditions, soil erosion, landslides, changes in the microclimate, increase in the silting rate which has caused a rise of the river beds, loss of wildlife, drying up of natural springs on which the villagers depend for drinking water.

The Chipko movement took place in April 1973 in Mandal near Gopeshwar of Chamoli district. It is a grassroots non-violent and non-political movement. It is purely an ecological movement which has brought the women of the region in the mainstream of public life, and it is guided by common rural folk and not by professional leaders. 'Chipko' means to cling to the trees to save them from being cut. It awakened among the people the need for the protection of the forests.

One aspect of the deteriorating forest ecology is the large-scale replacement of natural forests by the plantation of only commercially profitable trees. These man-made forests are not capable of working in the same way as the natural forests for maintaining the ecological balance. In some instances they may do positive harm. For example, in the Himalayan forest, the oak tree is regarded as the farmer's best friend because it absorbs water for a long time and releases it slowly. This gives rise to springs around which hill villages have been established. Its leaves are used as fodder, it has a leafy canopy and a rich undergrowth of grasses which protect the soil from being directly struck by rain, and its wood is used for making agricultural implements. Now it is being replaced by pine trees because of their commercial use. The pine tree has not the capacity to retain water, which has resulted in the drying up of springs, creating a scarcity of drinking water. It has no canopy and no undergrowth, thus leaving the mountain slopes fully exposed to erosion by rain and wind. Its leaves are not used as fodder, and they are inflammable and acidic, which makes the land infertile. But in order to extract resin from the trees the planting of pines is going on.

Highly Disturbed Environments

Where disturbances are frequent, large scale or severe, forests tend to be dominated by intolerant and fast-colonizing species. Three examples illustrate the range of circumstances.

Floodplain Forests

Floodplain forests are influenced by channel movement, which destroys mature stands but reworks the deposits into new shoals. In northern temperate regions, these are colonized mainly by *Salix, Alnus* and *Populus* species, which grow into even-aged, often monospecific stands. The sequence of channel movements is manifested as a pattern of elongated even-aged stands, whose age increases with distance from the channel. Tolerant species colonize beneath these pioneer stands and, given sufficient time, develop into mixed old-growth. In northern temperate deciduous regions the principal long-term dominants are *Ulmus, Fraxinus, Quercus, Carya, Sassafras* and, in the Pacific North-west, *Picea sitchensis* and *Pseudotsuga menziesii.* At any one time, the pioneer stands tend to predominate near the present channel, and the mixed old-growth tends to survive in elongated patches at some distance from the river.

Ice-dominated Forests

The classic type is the wave-regenerated *Abies* forests of the eastern USA and Japan. Exposed mature forest degenerates when foliage is stripped by ice and wind from trees that have already lost the vitality of youth. Death of exposed trees exposes others, leading to a 'wave' of mortality, which moves steadily through the forest in the direction of the prevailing wind. Regeneration starts within the degenerating stands and grows vigorously in the lee of slightly older stands. The forest as a whole takes the form of a series of parallel waves, which move through the forest at 1-3 m annually on a return time of 60-70 years. This perpetual recycling ensures that *Abies balsamea* remains dominant and that the longer-lived *Picea rubens* is perpetually excluded.

Fire-dominated Forests

The most widespread form of highly disturbed forest is dominated by fire. Most boreal forests are naturally fire-dominated, but so too are Mediterranean forests and the forests that fringe extensive grassland and desert regions. Each region has a suite of species that undergo a characteristic succession after fire, for example in Scandinavia *Betula-Pinus* develops into *Pinus* dominance, which is then succeeded by *Picea.*

Exceptionally, some patches remain unburned, which allows the pioneers to be completely displaced, although generally fire returns in good time to ensure that pioneer species remain a permanent feature of the forest. In fact, there is much variation in return time, associated with variation in topography, ground vegetation and the configuration of water bodies. Nevertheless, fires were frequent enough to maintain most boreal forests as young or maturing stands, not old-growth.

Similar fire-dominated regimes control other forests, such as the *Eucalyptus* forests of Australia and the *Pinus*-dominated forests of the coastal plain of the south-eastern USA. However, in western North America many tree species not only withstand fires once they have achieved a moderate size but also grow to great size and age, thus generating the monumental forests of *Sequoiadendron giganteum, Sequoia sempervirens* and *Pseudot-suga menziesii* in which old individuals may bear the scars of several fires. On the margins, the boundary between mesic- and fire-dominated forests advances and retreats according to the history of fires.

FORESTRY ENVIRONMENTAL DEVELOPMENT AND COLLABORATION

Collaborative or cooperative approaches to environmental and natural resource management provide potential solutions to the dilemma of the environment development tradeoff. These approaches rely on positive incentives and partnership arrangements.

Over the past decade the term social capital has received considerable attention from scholars in a variety of fields. Social capital is valuable because it provides resources to solve problems of coordination and cooperation, reduces transaction costs, and facilitates the flow of information between and among individuals in community or organization. Similarly, Putnam (1993) argues that social capital makes collective works easier and, ultimately, facilitates economic and community development

The concept of social capital has become increasingly popular in a wide range of social science disciplines, but there is a lack of consensus on the meaning of term. In social science research "social capital" is used in vastly different ways. Critics have characterized research examining the impacts of social capital as '"casual empiricism", because it lacks of an obvious link between theory and measurement.

In order to better understand how social capital can help state and local governments reconcile environmental and development goals, we systematically define and classify social capital based on its scope and form. This allows us to identify different "types" of social capital that can shape collaboration and partnership among actors concerned with environment and economic development.

THE FORMS OF SOCIAL CAPITAL

The Uphoff (2000) suggested two dimension of social capital—structural and cognitive. Structural forms of social capital concern the roles, rules, procedures, and networks that facilitate information sharing, and collective action and decisionmaking through established roles, social networks and other social structures supplemented by rules, procedures, and precedents. As such, it is a relatively objective and externally observable construct. Cognitive social capital refers to shared norms, values, trust, attitudes, and beliefs. It is therefore a more subjective and intangible concept (Uph off, 2000). Landry, Amara, and Lamari also classify two form of social capital: Structural and Cognitive. They measure three type of structural social capital: Network capital, Relationship capital, and Participation capital. Cognitive social capital was measured by trust capital. Krishna (2000) makes a similar distinction between institutional capital and relational capital.

The structural (Institutional) dimension of social capital includes rule of law, formal institutions and organization structures, but it also encompasses the overall pattern of relationships in an organization and its included network. This conceptualization is similar to Granovetter's (1973) notion of weak ties. The relational dimension of social capital concerns the nature of connections between individuals. It is characterized by levels of trust, shared norms and perceived obligation, and sense of mutual identification. This conceptualization of relational social capital is similar to Granovetter's (1973) notion of strong ties. Likewise, Feiock and Tao (2002) distinguish endogenous and exogenous social capital, and examine their effects on the regional economic development partnership as one form of collective action.

The Scope of Social Capital

The scope of social capital ranges from the micro to the macro level. Analysis of social capital at the micro level is usually associated with face-to face interaction between and among individuals, and those features of horizontal relationship, such as networks of indivi duals or households, and the associated norms and trust, that generat e externalities for the community as a whole. James C oleman (1990) includes vertical as well as horizontal associations and behavior within and among organizations by expanding the unit of ob servation and introducing a vertical component to social capital.

A macro-view of social capital includes the social and political environment that shapes social structure and enables norms to develop. This view includes the most formalized institutional relationships and structures, such as the rule of law, the political regime, the court system, and civil and political liberties. This focus on institutions draws on the work of Mancur Olson (1982) and Douglas North (1990), who have argued that such institutions have a significant effect on the pattern and rate of economic development. The phenomena related with the micro and macro level conceptualizations are complementary and their coexistence maximizes the waves of social capital on economic and social outcomes. For example, macro institutions can provide an enabling environment in which local associations can develop and flourish; local associations can sustain regional and national institutions and add a measure of stability to them.

A Typology of Social Capital

Whether at the micro or macro level, social capital exerts its influence on development as a result of the interactions between two distinct types of social capital—structural and cognitive. Cooperation and coordination among neighbours can be based on a personal cognitive bond that may not be reflected in a formal structural arrangement. Similarly, the existence of a community association does not necessarily testify to strong personal connections among its members, either because participation in its activities is not voluntary or because its existence has outlasted the external factor that led to its creation. Social interaction can become capital through the persistence of its effects, which can be ensured at both the cognitive and structural level.

We craft a typology of types of social capital framework based on these two key dimensions: its scope and its form. The framework treats social capital as a genuine asset that requires investment to accumulate and that generates a stream of benefits.

Ideally empirical investigation of social capital would examine and measure all four quadrants. Empirical work had generally focused on one or at most two of these quadrants. The most extensive work has been on micro level institutions or norms. Recent work has used confirmatory factor analysis to empirically isolate these dimensions.

Social Capital, Environmental Collaboration

Differentiating the types of social capital may help us understand how some state and local governments are able to overcome tradeoffs between environmental and economic gains. Lubell and Scholz (2001) suggest that reciprocity in relationships among governmental and non-governmental actors and lengthy time horizons are necessary to achieve sustainable development and to overcome collective action problems in environmental management. By extending these arguments, we contend that overcoming tradeoffs between developmental and environmental concerns requires: 1) participation in democratic political institutions; 2) social mechanisms to resolve conflicts from unharmonious development; and 3) information sharing for the diffusion of innovations. Each of these is facilitated by social capital in the community.

Specific types of social capital influence collective action and economic performance. Any form of capital-material or nonmaterial-represents an asset or a class of assets that produces a stream of benefits. The stream of benefits from social capital-or the channels through which it influences development-includes several associated elements. First, Cognitive social capital at the micro level (*i.e.*, endogenous social capital) such as trust, shared norms, and informal sanction reduce transaction costs. Reputations built through trust and reciprocity reduce information, monitoring, and enforcement costs and thus facilitate cooperation and collective action.

Second, Structural social capital such as associations, networks, and institutions provide an informal and formal framework to organize information sharing, coordination of activities, and collective decision-making. Participation by individuals in social networks increases the availability of information and lowers its cost. This information, especially if it relates to such things as new "green" technologies can play a critical role in increasing the returns from economic production while mitigating adverse environmental consequences.

Participation in local networks and attitudes of mutual trust make it easier for a group to reach collective decisions and implement collective action. Since property rights are often imperfectly developed and applied, collective decisions on how to manage common resources are critical to maximizing their use and yield. Finally, networks and attitudes reduce opportunistic behavior by community members. In settings where a certain behavior is expected from individuals for the benefit of the group, social pressures and fear of exclusion can induce these individuals to provide the expected behavior by reducing transaction costs and encouraging innovation.

Social capital contributes to sustainable economic development and growth by reducing conflict and the transaction costs of environmental management and by facilitating information sharing and the diffusion of innovation. Environmental governance systems based on partnership provide one mechanism to exploit existing social capital in its various forms and generate additional social capital resources.

FOREST COMPOSITION AND ENVIRONMENTS

Interactions between tree species and between them and disturbance regimes generate distinctive assemblages of species, forest dynamics and landscape patchworks. These are best illustrated by examples at the ends of the range of disturbance frequency.

RELATIVELY UNDISTURBED ENVIRONMENTS

At the other end of the range are mesic forests growing in relatively undisturbed environments. These are not disturbance-free; instead, catastrophic disturbances are rare enough to allow most of the forest to develop into old-growth, where disturbances are small-scale events.

Over much of the north temperate zone, a distinction can be drawn between *Fagus* forests and mixed deciduous forests. *Fagus*-dominated forests are found mainly in northern latitudes and submontane elevations, where *Fagus* spp. often share dominance with conifers, for example *Tsuga canadensis* in the eastern USA, *Abies alba* and *Picea abies* in central Europe.

European beech, *Fagus sylvatica,* is not long-lived, but casts dense shade, is capable of regenerating in the small transient gaps generated in beech forests and is almost fireproof, so that it is able to both dominate the site and perpetuate this dominance.

However, it is prone to disaster, in the sense that mature stands are vulnerable to drought and high winds. A few intolerant species, such as *Salix caprea,* maintain a foothold in large gaps, while the shade-tolerant *Acer pseudoplatanus,* like *Acer saccha-rum* in the eastern USA, fills gaps, competes in advance regeneration and can grow into mature stands. Diversity is maintained partly by the tendency of species not to regenerate under themselves. Thus, *Fagus grandifolia* and *Acer saccharum* in the USA and *Fagus syl-vatica* and *Abies alba* in Europe have been reported to alternate, thereby maintaining a small-scale mosaic of different dominance, though in the former case coexistence has been ascribed to different responses to light intensity. Occasionally, such stands are destroyed by storms, whereupon pioneer species dominate the regrowth, although beech thrives in the underwood and eventually restores its position.

Mixed deciduous forests are those which lack the dominating influence of beech. At their greatest development, for example in the southern Appalachians, they comprise a mixture of several dozen species, each with the capacity to occupy the canopy or subcanopy. A wide range of genera are represented, notably *Acer, Quercus, Fraxinus, Carya, Aescu-lus, Betula, Castanea, Tilia, Magnolia, Carpinus* and *Halesia,* forming rich mixtures in which no single species becomes absolutely dominant. Such forests are rarely devastated by any single disturbance and for most of the time are renewed by gap-phase regeneration on a small scale. Pioneer species regenerate in the larger gaps and may dominate the canopy after periods of enhanced gap creation. An example is *Lirioden-dron tulipifera,* which not only forms the tallest trees in the Appalachian forests but can also live for 500 years, enabling it to perpetuate itself through long periods lacking disturbance.

Within these complex mixtures, each species has a distinctive pattern of growth, longevity and regeneration. Furthermore, there is a tendency for individuals of one species to be replaced by another species. The forests comprise a small-scale mosaic of groups of different canopy and underwood species, each with its particular successional trend. The trends in one patch are countered by opposite trends in other patches, thereby retaining the mixture. Recruitment of particular species tends to be irregular, depending on particular combinations of mast-years and disturbances. Composition remains fairly constant overall but at a small scale changes perpetually, except where individual trees replace themselves vegetatively, *e.g. Tilia* spp.

Single-species groups are common in mixed forests. These may develop in response to small differences in site conditions and/or the chance coincidence of an episode of gap creation with heavy seed production by a particular species. Simulations have recently shown that neighbourhood effects may also play a part. Where there is a high probability that canopy trees will be replaced by individuals of the same species, 10 generations is enough for this feedback to generate small-scale single-species patches. The scale of the patches increases substantially where minor environmental differences result in 5 per cent alterations in recruitment probabilities.

9

Urban Forestry Development and Management

The urban forest is all of the woody vegetation growing in an urban area, including trees, shrubs, and vines found along city streets, public parks and private property. The City is responsible for managing an urban forest that contains over 40,000 street trees and 6,600 park trees (mowed areas).

There are several policies, programmes and projects issued and implemented for the past several decades which is an indication of continuing concern on the deterioration of urban environment. It is noticeable that new policies and programmes evolve whenever there is a change in administration (a common phenomenon in the Philippines) indicative of lack of continuity of previous initiatives. The major policies and programmes related to urban forestry are chronologically listed below:

- PD 1153 of Pres. Marcos dated 1976 (Tree Planting Decree to support PROFEM)
  - Requires all able-bodied Filipinos 10 years old and above to plant a tree per month for 5 consecutive years.
  - Certificates of planting and survival— requirement for graduation from school, renewal of job appointment and business permit and approval of retirement from service.
  - "Halamanan ng Bayan" launched by MHS to support this programme. It required each city or municipality to put up a nursery, garden and park.
  - Repealed by EO 287 dated July 25, 1987 because of dictatorial provisions and harsh penalty.
- PD 953 of Pres. Marcos dated July 6, 1976 (Greening of Private Lands Including Residential Subdivisions)
  - Requires private landowners to plant trees extending at least 5 m on each side of the rivers/ creeks.
  - Developers or owners of residential subdivisions and commercial/

industrial lots to set aside 30% of total area as open spaces for parks and recreational areas.
  - Penalizes unauthorized cutting, destruction or injury inflicted on naturally-growing or planted trees or vegetations in any public places.
- LOI 1312 of Pres. Marcos dated April 23,1983 (Establishment and Development of Local Government Forest or Tree Parks Throughout the Philippines).
  - Requires each barangay, municipality or city to establish and maintain at least one forest or tree park of considerable size.
  - MNR (now DENR) to allocate public lands for this purpose and to provide technical assistance and seedlings needed.
  - MHS to ensure that establishment of forest or tree parks is included in the land use plan of each barangay, municipality or city.
  - MILG (now DILG) to appropriate funds and implement establishment and maintenance activities.
- Memo Order Nos. 198 and 199 of Pres. Aquino dated November 9, 1988 (Luntiang Kamaynilaan Programme (LKP)/ Hardin ng Bayan Programme).
  - Issued to help insure healthy environment in Metro Manila (MM) and to serve as model programme for other cities/municipalities.
  - Anchored on the "Hardin ng Bayan" concept wherein each city or municipality should have gardens or parks of their own, transforming MM into a garden metropolis with lush vegetations, cool and fresh air like the countryside.
  - Objective- to plant 2 million trees in 2-3 years and achieve a desired 1:4 tree-man ratio.
  - For efficient, effective coordinated implementation, an Inter-Agency Committee (IAC) was formed: Co-chair- DENR and MMA (now MMDA); members- DPWH, DOTC, Metro Police Force, DOT, OPS and PMS.
- Memo Cir. No. 5 of Pres. Ramos dated August 27, 1992 (Clean and Green Programme).
  - Similar to LKP (same IAC composition except MMDA as chair/ lead agency) but wider in scope (not only greening but also cleaning activities)
  - Objective- massive planting (0.5 million trees/year or 2.5 million trees in 5 years from 1993-1997) to achieve the ratio of one tree for every 4 persons.
  - Although focused in MM, CGP has nationwide coverage and encouraging cities and municipalities to join nationwide contest for cleanest and greenest city or town.

- EO No. 113 of Pres. Ramos dated July 22, 1993 (Multi-sectoral Tree Planting Activities in Support of ENR Programmes/ECOREV).
  - Scope/ Objective – regreening and rehabilitation of all open and denuded lands of public domain, idle lands, private lands and other suitable areas (both urban and rural) including rehabilitations of coastal and marine areas.
  - DENR to identify, assess and designate suitable area for planting and management and to provide technical assistance to participating agencies.
  - LGUs implement the programme in their respective level and set up counterpart funds.
  - Private sector participation encouraged via MOA or other appropriate arrangements with DENR.
- EO No. 118 of Pres. Ramos dated August 12, 1993 (Mandating the active participation of all government agencies nationwide in urban greening through an Adopt-A-Street/Park Programme)
  - Objective – greening of streets and parks in urban centers.
  - Requires all government offices and government owned/controlled corporations to adopt a street or park in coordination with concerned LGUs, NGOs and private sector by planting appropriate species and maintaining them for at least 5 years using their own funds/resources. and other resources.
  - DENR to manage and coordinate the programme through a designated National Coordinator.
  - Project to be turned over to concerned LGU for maintenance and protection.
- DENR-DILG-DPWH-CSC Joint Memorandum Circular No. 1 dated December 17,1993 (Implementing Guidelines for EO 118-Adopt-A-Stree/Park Programme)
  - Described the roles of each participating agency and outlined the schemes in the identification, selection and adoption of a street or park to be developed.
  - DENR to provide assistance to "adopters" in selecting suitable streets or park sites, in providing necessary planting materials and in monitoring performance.
- OPLAN SAGIP PUNO Programme of FMS-NCR/DENR launched on June 5, 2000.
  - Conceived as a component of "Lets Go Green Programme" of former DENR Secretary Antonio Cerilles.
  - Application of appropriate silvicultural treatments (*e.g.* removal of nails, wires/cables, water sprouts; surgical treatment of injured stem or root) to prolong life span and promote good health and

vigor of trees planted in parks and along thoroughfares and streets in MM.
  - Supplemented by public awareness campaign.
  - DENR enters into MOA with participating agencies (*e.g.* subdivision homeowners association, city/ municipal government, NGOs, etc.)
  - DENR's role — conduct inventory and assessment of damaged/ injured trees; undertake appropriate silvicultural treatments; conduct information dissemination and training on tree care and maintenance; provide technical assistance and planting materials to sustain the project.
  - LGU's role — provide tree care and maintenance crews to sustain the project; assist DENR in information dissemination on maintenance and protection of trees.
- Proclamation No. 396 of Pres. Arroyo dated June 2, 2003 (Enjoining the active participation of all government agencies including government-owned or controlled corporations, private sector, schools, civil society and citizenry in tree planting activity and declaring June 25,2003 as Philippine Arbor Day).
  - Objectives- to promote multi-sectoral participation in tree planting nationwide; to develop greater awareness on the importance of trees in environment, health and human life.
  - Participating agencies, LGUs, schools, etc. to identify areas to be planted in coordination with agencies which have jurisdiction over such areas *e.g.* DENR in case of public lands, LGUs in areas within their jurisdiction, DND for military lands reservation, DOT for ecotourism areas, etc.
  - DENR, LGUs and schools — to establish and maintain nurseries.
  - Respective participating agency/ instrumentality — to maintain and protect the planted seedlings.
  - DENR — to provide technical assistance to all participants.

In general, the following goals and objectives are common to the Urban Forestry (UF) policies and programmes described above:

- to provide/maintain green, clean and beautiful environment;
- to promote public awareness on the importance of trees (promote environmental consciousness);
- enhance people's participation in the programme;
- promote multi-sectoral collaboration, cooperation and support; and
- in the case of LKP and CGP, the specific objective is to attain a 1:4 tree to person ratio to sustain ecological balance. As strategy to enhance successful implementation of the project, DENR is usually tasked to provide technical assistance in planting, site and species

selection, and maintenance operations, including provision of the planting stocks. Understandably, the DENR is also looked up to as the lead agency when inter-agency collaboration is involved in the programme. On the other hand, the city, municipal and barangay governments, which have jurisdiction over the project site, are usually tasked to maintain and protect the tree parks established and streets planted. They are also required to provide counterpart funds and other resources needed for these projects.

At the end of each programme, there seems to be no serious post – project accounting or evaluation of outputs and accomplishments, including evaluation of success and failures. This may be attributed to the fast rate of turn – over of urban forestry/greening programmes being implemented. Another reason maybe lack of manpower and resources to monitor all the projects. For instance, in the case of Metro Manila, the Urban Forestry and Law Enforcement Division Office of FMS – NCR/DENR only has a small unit (Cooperative Planting Unit) under the Urban Forestry Section which is tasked to do the monitoring activities. Needless to say, the synthesis of lessons learned is an important input for planning and formulation of new programmes (*i.e.* we do not have to " reinvent the wheel" so to speak).

Urban Growing Conditions

Urban growing conditions differ significantly from those in the rural landscape, and produce difficulties as a result of both above- and below-ground influences.

Stress Factors

The harsh soil and air conditions that exist in urban planting are problems that do not play the same role in landscape planting. Growing conditions may also be difficult due to shading effects, recreational users, etc.. The modified urban mesoclimate affects the quantity of contaminants in urban areas, which is raised by a factor of around 25. In general, the average lifespan of a newly planted street tree may be as low as 10-15 years.

During the last 30-40 years, the vitality of street trees has fallen drastically. Heavier traffic patterns have increased demands for road construction, which consequently has changed the growing conditions of many roadside trees. Also, pollution from traffic has a highly detrimental impact on street trees. The fact that 50% of the trees planted in an urban environment die within the first year emphasizes this point. Nowak *et al.* (1990) found that 34% of 480 trees died within 2 years of planting, while Miller and Miller (1991) found that the mortality rate was 25-50% for a number of species planted in Wisconsin, USA. Temperature extremes can occur, especially where trees are widely spaced and where heat is reflected from hard surfaces. Harris (1992) described that, occasionally, tree limbs up to 0.6 m and trunks up to 1.2 m in diameter break and fall during hot calm summer and autumn afternoons and subsequent evenings. Roots are more sensitive to temperature extremes than the tops of plants.

Wind speed will vary according to the shape and height of buildings. Areas with tall buildings will usually be relatively cool in summer due to shading effects, and warmer in winter due to wind-protection effects. On the other hand, winds are more variable and more extreme at exposed corners of tall isolated buildings. Buildings deflect strong winds downwards and concentrate their force at the base and corners of buildings, forming 'wind tunnels'. Trees planted in these exposed gaps may suffer scorched leaves and shoots, which lead to a stunted canopy, especially on the windward side. Newly planted trees will transpire more rapidly in windy situations, which can lead to the death of a tree already severely stressed by drought. The wind stability of trees is determined by tree species, stand structure, spacing, thinning regimes, soil classes, breeding and tree age at the time of anchorage.

The presence of airborne pollutants in the atmosphere has been a characteristic feature of the urban environment since the beginning of the Industrial Revolution. Air pollution can occur in a variety of forms but the principal ones are dust, SO_2 and NO_x. Leaves are the plant parts most likely to show symptoms of air pollution injury. On broadleaved plants, leaves may develop interveinal necrotic areas, marginal or tip necrosis, stippling of the upper surface, or silvering of the lower surface. However, trees in the urban environment also play a role in the quest for cleaner air in the cities. Scott *et al.* (1998) showed that daily uptake of NO_2 and particulate matter represented 1-2% of anthropogenic emissions for the county of Sacramento, California.

In areas with winter temperatures below 0°C, the use of de-icing salt is a well-known problem. De-icing salt is applied to the surrounding environment by surface run-off, wet spraying and airborne drifting.

The initial and most common symptom of de-icing salt damage on trees and shrubs is reduced growth. This is often difficult to recognize or may be confused with other stress factors. Reduced growth is usually followed by early autumn colours and premature leaf fall. De-icing salt is usually accumulated on the windward side of trees. The damage is easily recognized because it faces the road and is normally regarded as the best indication of de-icing spray damage. The majority of trees and shrubs subjected to either soil salt or salt spray typically show necroses at the edges of the leaves or needles. Wounds, often related to pruning, are a common place for spray salt to infect the plants. The damage may cause lack of sprouting and eventually dieback. Conifers are very susceptible to de-icing salt spray damage because they are green all through the winter maintenance season. Trees and shrubs damaged by de-icing salt and showing dieback are difficult to cure.

Characteristics and Restriction of Rooting in the Built Environment

Urban soils as a growing medium are poorly understood and often misunderstood. Therefore plantings are carried out with little appreciation or attention to the character and quality of the material that lies beneath the surface. One major problem in relation to planting in the urban situation is soil compaction, which may occur in small as well as large urban sites.

Soil compaction can be divided into two types: (i) intentional soil compaction, which occurs when soil is deliberately compacted for site stabilization under roads, houses, etc. and (ii) unintentional soil compaction, which occurs when traffic uses areas intended for planting (Randrup 1997). In the urban situation, unintentional soil compaction is primarily found along roadsides and on construction sites.

When soil is compacted, its bulk density increases and its porosity decreases. These effects inhibit plant growth because the soil becomes impenetrable to root growth and, furthermore, restricts the water and oxygen available to the roots. For example, root growth of most plants is impeded once soil bulk density rises above 1.6. One consequence of compacted soil is waterlogging, which can kill roots around existing trees. Soil loosening has proved to be effective in alleviating compacted soil.

However, there is no doubt that the best treatment for compacted soil is to protect the soil from being compacted in the first place. Florgård (1987) suggested protecting trees growing on construction sites by dividing the site into zones in which different types of construction traffic are permitted. The principle of construction site zoning was adapted by Randrup and Dralle (1997) to protect the soil from being compacted. They suggested that the entire construction site be divided into a building zone, a working zone and a protection zone.

DECENTRALIZATION OF FOREST MANAGEMENT

Although a majority of forests continue to be owned formally by government, the effectiveness of forest governance is increasingly independent of formal ownership. Since neo-liberal ideology in the 1980s and the emanation of the climate change challenges, evidence that the state is failing to effectively manage environmental resources has emerged. Under neo-liberal regimes in the developing countries, the role of the state has diminished and the market forces have increasingly taken over the dominant socio-economic role. Though the critiques of neo-liberal policies have maintained that market forces are not only inappropriate for sustaining the environment, but are in fact a major cause of environmental destruction. Hardin's tragedy of the common (1968) has shown that the people cannot be left to do as they wish with land or environmental resources. Thus, decentralization of management offers an alternative solution to forest governance.

The shifting of natural resource management responsibilities from central to state and local governments, where this is occurring, is usually a part of broader decentralization process. According to Rondinelli and cheema (1983), there are four distinct decentralization options: these are: (i) Privatization – the transfer of authority from the central government to non-governmental sectors otherwise known as market-based service provision, (ii) Delegation – centrally nominated local authority, (iii) Devolution – transfer of power to locally acceptable authority and (iv) Deconcentration – the redistribution of authority from the central government to field delegations of the central government. The major key to effective decentralization is increased broad-based participation in local-public decision making. In 2000, the World Bank report reveals that local government knows the needs and desires of their constituents better than the national government, while at the same time, it is easier to hold local leaders accountable. From the study of West African tropical forest, it is argued that the downwardly accountable and/or representative authorities with meaningful discretional powers are the basic institutional element of decentralization that should lead to efficiency, development and equity. This collaborates with the World Bank report in 2000 which says that decentralization should improve resource allocation, efficiency, accountability and equity "by linking the cost and benefit of local services more closely".

Many reasons point to the advocacy of decentralization of forest. (i) Integrated rural development projects often fail because they are top-down project that did not take local people's needs and desire into account. (ii) National government sometimes have legal authority over vast forest area that they cannot control, thus, many protected area project result in increased biodiversity loss and greater social conflict.

Within the sphere of forest management, as state earlier, the most effective option of decentralization is "devolution"-the transfer of power to locally accountable authority. However, apprehension about local governments is not unfounded. They are often short of resources, may be staffed by people with low education and are sometimes captured by local elites who promote clientelist relation rather than democratic participation. Enters and Anderson (1999) point that the result of community-based projects intended to reverse the problems of past central approaches to conservation and development have also been discouraging.

Broadly speaking, the goal of forest conservation has historically not been met when, in contrast with land use changes; driven by demand for food, fuel and profit. It is necessary to recognized and advocate for better forest governance more strongly given the importance of forest in meeting basic human needs in the future and maintaining ecosystem and biodiversity as well as addressing climate change mitigation and adaptation goal. Such advocacy must be coupled with financial incentives for government of developing countries and greater governance role for local government, civil society, private sector and NGOs on behalf of the "communities".

SOCIAL FORESTRY DEVELOPMENT

Social forestry means the management and protection of forests and afforestation on barren lands with the purpose of helping in the environmental, social and rural development. The term, social forestry, was first used in India in 1976 by The National Commission on Agriculture, Government of India. It was then that India embarked upon a social forestry project with the aim of taking the pressure off currently existing forests by planting trees on all unused and fallow land.

THE SOCIO-ECONOMIC UPLIFTMENT OF THE TRIBALS

There is no tangible impact of the industrial units on the socio-economic upliftment of the tribals, since they are based neither locally nor at the household level. The limited knowledge of the tribal community with respect to scientific method of extraction, processing, marketing, value addition etc. has never helped them in any way. Further, their poverty, illiteracy, ignorance and impoverishment have accentuated their weak bargaining strength resulting in disproportionately low returns to their labour. In spite of their processing skills and experience in processing of bamboo, sabai grass, broom sticks etc they are prevented from their legitimate dues partly due to localised markets and weak bargaining power, but mostly due to the restrictions imposed on them by the Forest Department (based on provisions in the Forest Acts). Instances of such cases; kendu leaves grown in private lands, value added products like neem, tooth sticks, brooms, sal and siali leaves are not uncommon. The continuing restrictions on the household economic activities of forest dwelling communities put a great deal of difficulties as far as local processing is concerned.

IMPEDIMENTS

- Lack of financial support and incentives to the entrepreneurs
- Lack of dissemination of information about the socio-economic benefits of processing
- Uncertain supply of raw materials not only due to market fluctuations, but also due to natural disaster
- Inefficient processing techniques leading to low yields, and poor quality products.
- Poor harvesting and post harvest practices
- Lack of R & D on product and process development
- Constraints of local markets for primary processed products
- Lack of down-stream processing facilities
- Lack of trained personnel and equipment.

- Lack of access to latest technological and market information.
- Lack of capacity building activities at the grassroots level.

PROSPECTS OF VALUE ADDITION

- Lifting restrictions on setting up processing units at the village/ Panchayat level
- Relaxing controls over marketing of finished products
- Undertaking skill development programmes for the primary gatherers at the village level to impart training in simple processing techniques
- Involving women groups to learn processing and value addition to secure self-employment on sustainable basis
- Allowing local forest resource user groups to set up processing units on a co-operative basis or under the aegis of JFM, where the F.D may act exclusively as facilitator rather than regulator
- Permitting primary collectors to sell a major part of their finished forest products to Orissa Rural Development and Marketing Agency Society (ORMAS), created in 1989 for marketing of rural products.

The processing unit could organise the pooling of the resource either at the level of pre-processing or processing or marketing, depending on the nature of the products and the processing techniques in order to reap the benefits of scale of operation. Products like wild fruits need to be graded before primary processing. Hence, pooling of the products is essential. Products like honey could be processed at the village level due to the capital costs of the machinery involved. In such cases of complicated processing pooling at the primary processing is necessary. Making leaf-plates, baskets, etc. could be taken up at the household level. Hence, pooling of such products would be at the stage of marketing. Processing unit can move the products forward to marketing bodies such as State marketing agencies, open markets, national international markets with the involvement of the resource user groups and other stakeholders. It should work in close collaboration with the State agencies in all the functions. The product could move to the external markets directly or through the State agencies depending on the nature of the end product.

The unit should have specific tasks for resource management to ensure sustainable use of the forests, processing-cum-marketing and community organisation for sustainability of involvement of the resource user groups and other stakeholders. It should work in close collaboration with the state agencies in all the functions. The product could move to the external markets directly or through the state agencies depending on the nature of the end product.

ACHIEVE SUSTAINABLE FOREST MANAGEMENT IN INDIA

Historically, Indian forest policies have alienated people from the forests, thereby, exacerbating the rates of deforestation. Post-independence forest policies contributed to an expansion in agricultural production, met industrial demand for raw materials, and tightened control of forest lands through restricted access to forests and forest products. Protection policies increased the hardships of vulnerable social groups by denying them access to forests. While the state took responsibility for managing forest resources, it did not have the commensurate resources to effectively manage and police the forests from traditional users. Before state intervention, forests were managed as communal property; the crucial role of forests in the economic subsistence of individuals, families and community was the basis for managing them as communal resources. A failure to recognize community control of forests led to a collapse in institutional norms that were instrumental in protecting and managing forest resources for local use. A shift in property rights to the state steadily undermined the rights of tribals to use and extract forest resources.

Involvement of rural communities living close to forests in protection and management of forest resources is enshrined in the National Forest Policy 1988.Translation of policy found expression in the resolution of Government of India, Ministry of Environment and Forests issued in June 1990.It envisaged that in lieu of the participation, the local communities will be entitled to sharing of usufructs in a manner specified by the concerned State Forest Departments. This led to the initiation of Joint Forest Management (JFM) programme. Importance of the programme is evident from the fact that the Government of India has constituted a "JFM Network" with the Inspector General of Forests, Government of India as the Chairman.

The objectives of the network are (i) to act as a regular mechanism of consultation between various agencies engaged in JFM work in the country and (ii)To obtain constant feedback from various stakeholders on the JFM programme for proper policy formulation and suitable direction to States. World leaders adopted the Millennium Declaration at the Millennium Summit in September 2000. The proportion of land area covered by forest globally is one of the indicators for the seventh MDG i.e to ensure environmental sustainability.

In addition to quantitative, time-bound targets, the Millennium Declaration calls for other actions, including intensified efforts for "the management, conservation and sustainable development of all types of forests", an international commitment to sustainable forest management made in 1992 at the United Nations Conference on Environment and Development (UNCED) and embodied in the Forest Principles. Subsequent intergovernmental deliberations to promote progress towards sustainable forest management took place in the Intergovernmental Panel on Forests (IPF) and Intergovernmental Forum on Forests (IFF) from 1995 to 2000, and continue in the United Nations Forum on Forests (UNFF) as well as in other fora.

SOCIAL FORESTRY IN INDIA

Social forestry means the management and protection of forests and afforestation on barren lands with the purpose of helping in the environmental, social and rural development.

The term, social forestry, was first used in India in 1976 by The National Commission on Agriculture, Government of India. It was then that India embarked upon a social forestry project with the aim of taking the pressure off currently existing forests by planting trees on all *unused and fallow land.*

SOCIAL FORESTRY PROGRAMME

Government forest areas that are close to human settlement and have been degraded over the years due to human activities needed to be afforested. Trees were to be planted in and around agricultural fields. Plantation of trees along railway lines and roadsides, and river and canal banks were carried out. They were planted in village common land, government wasteland, andPanchayat land.

Involvement of Common People

Social forestry also aims at raising plantations by the common man so as to meet the growing demand for timber, fuel wood, fodder, etc., thereby reducing the pressure on the traditional forest area. This concept of village forests to meet the needs of the rural people is not new. It has existed through the centuries all over the country but it was now given a new character.

With the introduction of this scheme the government formally recognised the local communities' rights to forest resources, and is now encouraging rural participation in the management of natural resources. Through the social forestry scheme, the government has involved community participation, as part of a drive towards afforestation, and rehabilitating the degraded forest and common lands.

Need of Social Forestry

This need for a social forestry scheme was felt as India has a dominant rural population that still depends largely on fuelwood and other biomass for their cooking and heating. This demand for fuel wood will not come down but the area under forest will reduce further due to the growing population and increasing human activities. Yet the government managed the projects for five years then gave them over to the village panchayats (village council) to manage for themselves and generate products or revenue as they saw fit.

Types

Social forestry scheme can be categorized into groups; farm forestry, community forestry, extension forestry and agroforestry.

Farm Forestry

At present in almost all the countries where social forestry programmes have been taken up, both commercial and non commercial farm forestry is being promoted in one form or the other. Individual farmers are being encouraged to plant trees on their own farmland to meet the domestic needs of the family. In many areas this tradition of growing trees on the farmland already exists. Non-commercial farm forestry is the main thrust of most of the social forestry projects in the country today. It is not always necessary that the farmer grows trees for fuelwood, but very often they are interested in growing trees without any economic motive. They may want it to provide shade for the agricultural crops; as wind shelters; soil conservation or to use wasteland. Farm Forestry is another name for Agroforestry; a part of Social Forestry.

Community Forestry

Another scheme taken up under the social forestry programme, is the raising of trees on community land and not on private land as in farm forestry. All these programmes aim to provide for the entire community and not for any individual. The government has the responsibility of providing seedlings, fertilizer but the community has to take responsibility of protecting the trees. Some communities manage the plantations sensibly and in a sustainable manner so that the village continues to benefit. Some others took advantage and sold the timber for a short-term individual profit. Common land being everyone's land is very easy to exploit. Over the last 20 years, large-scale planting of Eucalyptus, as a fast growing exotic, has occurred in India, making it a part of the drive to reforest the subcontinent, and create an adequate supply of timber for rural communities under the augur of 'social forestry'.

Extension Forestry

Planting of trees on the sides of roads, canals and railways, along with planting on wastelands is known as 'extension' forestry, increasing the boundaries of forests. Under this project there has been creation of wood lots in the village common lands, government wastelands and Panchayat lands.

Schemes for afforesting the degraded government forests that are close to villages are being carried out all over the country.

Agroforestry

In agroforestry, silvicultural practices are combined with agricultural crops like leguminous crop, along with orchard farming and live stock ranching on the same piece of land. In lay man language agroforestry could be understood as growing of forest tree along with agriculture crop on the same piece of land.

In a more scientific way agroforestry may be defined as a sustainable land use system that maintains or increases the total yield by combing food crop together with forest tree and live stock ranching on the same unit of land, using management practices that takes care of the social and culture characteristic of the local people and the economic and ecological condition of the local area.

FORESTS AND THE MILLENNIUM DEVELOPMENT GOALS

The MDGs call for the integration of the principles of sustainable development into environmental policies. Environmental sustainability is being mainstreamed in forest policies around the world, particularly since UNCED, while the integration of the goals of poverty and hunger reduction in forest policies and plans is less widespread.

Community-based forestry, or participatory forestry, is particularly well placed to address poverty reduction. Community-based forestry is now well accepted and established in various countries in all regions, and programmes are beginning to generate financial and other benefits. Improving local peoples' rights and access to forest resources is a tool to the success of community-based forestry programmes. However, much still remains to be done to clarify and secure access rights. Many countries are working to strengthen forest governance, some through decentralization processes that allow the poor to derive more benefits from forests and be more involved in decision-making and forest management itself.

Although improving rights and access to forest resources and developing small-holder forest-based enterprises (including through community-private sector partnerships) show particular promise for poverty reduction, local political and economic realities, opportunity costs for the use of local resources, and other factors may prevent the poor from benefiting from community-based forestry programmes to the extent intended.

Intersectoral coordination is important for the achievement of all MDGs, but is particularly critical for reducing poverty and hunger and ensuring environmental sustainability, which are highly cross-sectoral by nature. Improved intersectoral cooperation and coordination will help efforts both to integrate the principles of sustainable development into forest-related policies and to integrate forests into sustainable development plans.

Joint Forest Management

Forest-based poverty reduction efforts tend to be linked to other land uses and should form a part of rural development strategies. Conversely, the potential for forests and trees outside forests to contribute to environmental sustainability cannot be fully realized without intersectoral cooperation and coordination. Intersectoral coordination, although difficult and time consuming, is necessary for sound decisions on land use and resource allocation, particularly when there are trade-offs between national development goals. National Forest Policy in India treats forests as environmental and social resource. With the initiative of assigning ownership of Non Timber forest Produce (NTFP) to the local communities including the grass root level democratic institution for enhancing their livelihood opportunities and also improving their income with the value addition.

India has shifted the approach of forest management from regulatory to participatory mode of management with the resolution promulgated in 1990. At present, more than 17 million forests is managed by almost 10,000 Joint Forest Management Committees with the benefit sharing mechanism. In addition, the Government of India is in process to frame legislation for the settlement of tenurial rights of the forest dwelling communities mainly tribal on forests. This would definitely help in reducing the poverty of forest dwelling communities. The JFM resolution was circulated by Ministry of Environment and Forest in the year 1990 and 2000. JFM is a government resolution. A government resolution is a executive order or opinion of the legislature. A resolution does not have any legal backing.JFM as the term indicates is the management of forest by more than one party. In India there are two parties: the government represented by the Forest Department and the people living in villages located within forest or on the fringes.

There are two major reasons behind introducing JFM: one that the government's management system was not succeeding in arresting growth of forest degradation and deforestation.Second a new management paradigm was evolving in which the local people's participation was found to be an appropriate and promising tool in arresting forest degradation.

However in pre-independent India the concept of JFM didn't exist. The first National Forest Policy was adopted in 1894. Following were the guide lines

- Ensure maintaneance of adequate forest cover
- Meet the needs of local people.
- Collect maximum revenue after meeting the needs of the local people.
- Give priority to permanent cultivation over forestry land

In post independent India there was a shift in policy. In1988, the new forest policy was adopted which covered all the sustainable management approaches. The new policy had a few unique features. Which were as follows;

- Maintenance of environmental stability and restoration of ecological balance, soil and water conservation
- Conservation of natural heritage and genetic resources.
- Increasing productivity to meet the local needs then the national need
- Creating massive peoples participation movement to protect forest and tree cover and achieve the objective of reducing pressure on existing forests and meeting peoples need.
- Deriving economic benefits must be subordinated to these principal aims.

This initiated a process of reform at the local policy and operational level of forest management ensuring that the Forest Department developed close collaboration for protection and sustainable management of forests.

The aim was –Involvement of village communities and voluntary agencies of degraded forest land.

Important guidelines were as follows:

- The programme should be implemented under an arrangement between a voluntary agency or beneficiaries .and the State Department.
- No ownership rights or lease should be given over the forest land.
- The beneficiaries should be entitled to share usufructs to the extent and subject to conditions prescribed by the State Government.
- Access to forest land usufructs should be available only to benefactress who get organized into a village institution especially for forest regeneration and protection. This could be through a village panchayat or a Village Forest Committee.
- The beneficiaries should be given usufructs like grass, lops and tops of branches and minor forest produce. If they successfully protect the forest they will be a portion from the sale proceeds when they mature.
- Areas selected from the programme should be free from claims from any person who is both a beneficiary under the scheme.
- The selected site should be worked in accordance of Working Scheme duly approved by the state government.Such a scheme may remain in operation for ten years and revised after that. The working scheme is prepared in consultation of with the beneficiaries
- It should ensure that there is no grazing at al on the forest land protected by the Village Forest Committee. Permission to cut and carry grass free of cost should be given so that stall feeding is promoted.
- No agriculture should be promoted on the forest land.
- Cutting of tress should not be permitted before they are ripe for harvesting. The Forest Department should not be permitted to cut to cut trees protected by the Village Forest Committee except in a manner prescribed in the working scheme. In case of emergency needs the village community should be taken into confidence.
- The Forest Department should closely supervise the work.If beneficiaries are unable to perform their assigned duties in a satisfactory manner the usufctory benefits will be withdrawn without giving any compensation.

Such set-up, however suffered from certain flaws:

- Bye- laws have not been formulated for the functioning of the JFMC though now most of the states have issued executive orders for the functioning of JFMC but these executive orders are not binding on JFMC. The aim was to decentralize the process and make JFMC.

- Minor Forest Produce (MFP) has not been defined neither by the State legislature or by the Centre.
- Central and State/UT Governments have issued guidelines for the creation and functioning of JFMC but these guidelines are not in conformity with the provisions of the Constitution
- Through the Constitution (Seventy-third Amendment) Act, 1992 and Panchayat (Extension to the Scheduled Areas) Act, 1996 ownership rights over minor forest produce (MFP) have been given to Village Panchayats. Now on the same resource base *i.e.* NTFP/MFP we have two sets of groups having ownership and while the Panchayats have a legal backing, JFMC don't have. conservation have been raised while the proponents of Panchayats have termed JFM as a parallel institution against the spirit of the Constitution.
- The JFM resolution only provides 20% of share to be given the Joint Forest Management committees, while rest of the income would go to the Forest Department. There is an obvious unequal distribution of benefit sharing between the parties. These committees would have to protect the forest for ten years,and would only receive 20% of the share.
- The national resolution provides that at least 33% of the seats shall be reserved for women in the specified committees. However states like Rajasthan are not following this provision.

Panchayati Raj System

The concept regarding Panchayati is contained in the Part IX of the 73rd amendment of The Indian Constitution.This amendment came into force in on 24th April 1993. It institutionalized the third stratum of government (Panchayats) at the local level.

Through the Constitution (Seventy-third Amendment) Act, 1992) Part IX "The Panchayats" was inserted in the Constitution which paved the way for "Village Panchayats" by making provisions for the constitution of Panchayats, their composition, election, powers, authority, responsibility, audit, etc. This Act doesn't apply to Schedule Area referred to in clause (1) and tribal areas referred to in clause (2) of Article 244 and certain other specified areas Village Panchayats have been given the responsibility of social/farm forestry, minor forest produce (MFP), and soil conservation through Eleventh Schedule.

"Panchayat" means an institution (by whatever name called) of self-government constituted under article 243B, for the rural areas. The amendment it fails to define what is 'self government'. It does not clarify whether self government means complete autonomously or extension of the state.It is left to states to derive their own interpretation regarding the nature of self government at the local level.By the word "nature" of self government it is meant reservation to be provided for the marginalized section of the society, the powers given to each level of self governing relating to administration, execution and performing the defined roles would be different in each State. Thus this will defeat the purpose of uniformity regarding the nature and concept of self government at an all India level.

The flaw again lies that the amendment has failed to assert the nature of 'Power And Authority'.This task is left to the state legislatures.Again defeating the purpose of uniformity. The consequences will be such that either the states will deny power to the panchyats instead of becoming autonomous local governing units they will basically remain in bureaucratic control.The burecratic trend can be seen most of the states.It is seen in the State of Goa power and functions have not yet been transferred to the Panchayats. As per the law there should be continuous elections every five years.However the statistics says that this status is not achieved in most of the states.None of the states except WestBengal, Tripura and Rajasthan have not been able to hold continuous elections every five years. The judgment provided by the Supreme Court states that it is mandatory for every state to hold elections to Panchayat.

Giving powers to the third stratum of government for effective management of resources at the district,intermediate and village level. Parallel institutions have come about for management of the natural resources which

Participatory Approach

According to United Nations Development Programme's report 67.7 million people belonging to "Scheduled Tribes" in India are generally considered to be 'Adivasis', literally meaning 'indigenous people' or 'original inhabitants', though the term 'Scheduled Tribes' is an administrative term used for purposes of 'administering' certain specific constitutional privileges, protection and benefits for specific sections of peoples considered historically disadvantaged and 'backward'.

Out of the 5653 distinct communities in India, 635 are considered to be 'tribes' or 'Adivasis'. With the ST population making up 8.08% (as of 1991) of the total population of India, it is the nation with the highest concentration of 'indigenous peoples' in the world. 68 million tribals who inhabit forests and wild lands throughout India, Adivasis have evolved an intricate convivial-custodial mode of living.

The Beginning of Land alienation

Introduction of the alien concept of private property began with the Permanent Settlement of the British in 1793 and the establishment of the

"Zamindari" system that conferred control over vast territories, including Adivasi territories, to designated feudal lords for the purpose of revenue collection by the British. This drastically commenced the forced restructuring of the relationship of Adivasis to their territories as well as the powe relationship between Adivasis and 'others'. The predominant external caste-based religion sanctioned and practiced a rigid and highly discriminatory hierarchical ordering with a strong cultural mooring.

After the transfer of power, the rulers of the Residency Areas signed the "Deed of Accession" on behalf of the ruled on exchange they were offered privy purse. No deed was however signed with most of the independent Adivasi states. They were assumed to have joined the Union. The government rode rough shod on independent Adivasi nations and they were merged with the Indian Union. This happened even by means of state violence as in the case of Adivasi uprising in the Nizam's State of Hyderabad and Nagalim. The Constitution of India, which came into existence on 26 January 1950, prohibits discrimination on grounds of religion, race, caste, sex or place of birth and it provides the right to equality, to freedom of religion and to culture and education. STs are supposedly addressed by as many as 209 Articles and 2 special schedules of the Constitution - Articles and special schedules which are protective and paternalistic. Article 341 and 342 provides for classification of Scheduled Castes (the untouchable lower castes) and STs, while Articles 330, 332 and 334 provides for reservation of seats in Parliament and Assemblies. For purposes of specific focus on the development of STs, the government has adopted a package of programmes, which is administered in specific geographical areas with considerable ST population, and it covers 69% of the tribal population.

10

Principles of Economics in Land-Use

URBAN PLANNING OF FOREST LAND POLICY

Since urban planning in India is largely concerned with development of land, it would be relevant to briefly consider how perceptions about land and real estate property have evolved. The Indian Constitution initially recognised 'to acquire, hold and dispose of property' as a fundamental right. Consequently when land was to be compulsorily acquired 'compensation' at market price was payable. Subsequently the term compensation was replaced by the term 'amount'. This ideology culminated in the enactment of Urban Land (Ceiling and Regulation) Act 1976 that attempted nationalisation of vacant urban land by paying nominal amount. Finally the fundamental right to property was deleted from the Constitution. The first articulation of the Urban Land Policy was proposed by the Urban Land Policy Committee (Ministry of Health) appointed by the Government of India in 1965. The Committee articulated the following Land Policy Objectives

1. To achieve optimum social use of urban land;
2. To make land available in adequate quantity, at right time and for reasonable prices to both public authorities and individuals;
3. To encourage cooperative community effort and bona fide individual builders in the field of land development, housing and construction;
4. To prevent concentration of land ownership in a few private hands and especially to safeguard the interests of the poor and under-privileged sections of the urban society.

Further the Committee observed that to realise the objectives "there is no escape from large scale public acquisition if the question of guiding urban development or the provision of adequate housing and other facilities is to be tackled effectively and large scale advance acquisition of land would really be in the interests of the society as a whole. It is by far the best and perhaps the only way to put an end to speculation in land and to capture subsequent increases in land values. These surpluses, where realised by the public authorities, should benefit the community in more ways than one." Not surprising the role models of Indian Town Planners — Delhi Master Plan, Chandigarh, Gandhinagar and Navi Mumbai were all based on public ownership of land. Whether public ownership in fact achieved the land policy objectives in such cases may be a matter of debate. But a verdict on Delhi experience was;

1. It has not been possible for DDA to provide land at affordable prices to low income beneficiaries resulting in large scale jhuggi jhopadi colonies.
2. In the absence of price signals land has been sub optimally used, resulting in over provision to powerful groups, and
3. DDA's policy to auction very few plots at a time and treating the maximum price quoted in such biding as the real market price has in fact meant artificially increasing the land price through deliberate scarcity."

However, securing large-scale public ownership of land implied compulsory acquisition of land. There was considerable discontent amongst the original landowners about the manner in which compensation was determined and paid. The Land Acquisition Act 1894 initially provided the date of declaration of intention to acquire the land as the reference date for determining the market value.

However no time limit was laid down for actual payment of compensation. 1984 amendments introduced the time limit of three years and also provided for payment of interest from the date of award to actual payment or possession of land and solatium of 30 per cent of market value. However the market value is to be reckoned at current use value at the exclusion of expected rise in value on account of future use. The proposed changes in the LA Act and the R and R Policy attempt to remove many of these lacunae. But planned urban development is not being recognised as a public purpose for which powers of eminent domain could be used and in practical terms the proposed method of deciding compensation and rehabilitation package would make recourse to compulsory acquisition of land expensive for lands that also require substantial investment in trunk infrastructure. This would compel search for new paradigm in respect of urban land. The thinkers in the first world too were enamoured by the socialistic notion of community ownership of land.

However on practical considerations they sought solutions short of nationalisation of urban land. The two extreme proposals had one thing in common. Both considered right to own land and right to develop (or build upon) as separate rights. Henry George argued that a private landowner may have right to own both land and development rights. But he has no rights on the rents accruing to land, as they are results of monopoly and not efforts of the owner. He therefore argued that the state has legitimate right to recover 100 per cent of such rents by way of taxes. He allowed the owner to retain the returns on his investments in improvements. He was also prophetic about the ills of public ownership of land. In 1879 he stated, "I do not propose to purchase or confiscate private property in land. It is not necessary to confiscate land — only to confiscate rent.

Taking rent for public use does not require that the state lease land; that would risk favouritism, collusion, and corruption." On the other hand a committee under the chairmanship of Justice Uthwatt in UK suggested that the betterment occurring on account of development of land should be balanced with the compensation to be paid for acquiring land for public purposes. To enable recovery of betterment the Committee proposed nationalisation of development rights (by paying compensation).

Development required planning permission subject to payment of betterment. Despite three attempts to recover betterment since 1947 it has still not succeeded. A cryptic comment on this reads, "The state expropriates property rights, and then charges those from whom it has taken those rights for granting permission to use them on its terms. A betterment levy is wrong in principle, and like most things that are fundamentally wrong, it will always fail in practice" The Indian urban planning thought under the pre 1991 macroeconomic framework was oblivious of property rights and resultant land and real estate market. Hernando de Sotto argued the importance of clarity of property rights and labelled poorly recorded property rights as the 'dead capital' unable to ensure finance for poor. But his arguments have evoked little debate in India. Lack of conceptual clarity about land and property rights have given rise to many expedient policy initiatives.

Instrument of Nationalising Development Rights

FAR essentially a zoning tool in US cities rationalises the intensity of development that could be permitted considering the existing level of development, accessibility and use. The FAR in US cities varies considerable from less than one to 15. However in most Indian cities such considerations are not used in defining FAR. In many states common FSI values are prescribed across all cities as part of state wide building regulations and do not form part of master plan of individual city.

There has been two-fold argument justifying this position. First, varying FSI within a city would be seen as discriminatory between different land owners and second, varying FSI across cities would lead to demand from political quarters to increase rationally defined FSI to an arbitrary level proposed in another city. The general tendency has been to prescribe low uniform FSI (around one). This has meant scarcity of development rights particularly in cities that experience faster economic and population growth and resultant increase in demand for per capita floor space. Instead of adopting measures to reduce scarcity of development rights by rationalising FSI pattern, retaining existing low FSI regime is being implicitly used as an instrument of nationalising development rights beyond prescribed FSI (without paying compensation). Armed with such nationalised development rights the state administrators could allot these rights on conditions of payment or fulfilling other obligations like providing free houses to slum dwellers. (Hyderabad Master Plan proposed a base FSI and permissible increase subject to payment. Maharashtra Government increased FSI in Mumbai subject to payment that would be equally shared between Municipal Corporation and the state government. Extra FSI is similarly allowed in Chennai. Similarly extra FSI is allowed for rehabilitating existing occupants of rent controlled buildings and slums, free of cost). In this context the objectives of raising revenue or helping a class (not necessarily poor) will succeed when base FSI is low and scarcity of development rights is created. Creating scarcity is not a healthy way of managing any market.

FINDINGS AND SUGGESTIONS OF URBAN PLANNING

Urban planning is basically concerned with the location, intensity and amount of land development required for various space using functions of city life industry, wholesaling, business, housing, recreation, education, religious and cultural activities of the people. Thus urban planning is itself neutral. But the institutionalisation of planning practice within a complex bureaucracy has contributed to the re-politicisation of urban planning. It has become a mode of intervention that is only implemented when it serves the specific interests of the interest group parties.

Thus slum demolition is a process in urban renewal, a process in urban planning, which has become a mode or tool of the ruling classes for fulfilling their own interests. In shaping the city in such a way that it conforms to the upper class notion of the city, it is its interests, which are furthered. In actuality clearance is necessary to make the centrally located areas available to the capitalists for various economic activities.

As far as Indian urban policies has been concerned it has been seen that there has been a lag between the promises made in different plans in paper and actual practical work that has been done. Though the state within its set structure of the society has tried to work for the poor through different urban planning policies and housing policies like the different slum development policies in Mumbai, urban land (ceiling and regulation) act, more peoples participation in development activities through 74th constitutional amendments, different poverty alleviation programmes but in actual reality very less has been done. The politicians, builders, businessmen, slumlords, the elite class has continuously manipulated the different policies according to there need and profit maximisation motivations and left the urban poor in constant misery.

Urban policies in general and urban planning in particular has been become an instrument in the hand of the capitalists to fulfil there needs. Thus there is need to make urban development pro-poor or to evolve an urban development framework to agree to the needs of the most vulnerable sections of the urban population.

They should not be concerned about the needs of the capital alone. This can be done through two things. One is the representation in the planning and policy-making bodies and other is the creation of mechanisms or forums for participation in policy making. Thus decentralization of decisionmaking should be done as has been done through 74th constitutional amendments.

But the decentralization should mean change in the structure or power sharing in the society and not decentralization of some convenient functions or responsibilities in a centralized society as of now where economic processes and decision making paradigms are centralized. So decentralization is not only about taking it down to the community but looking at how communities themselves can determine as stakeholders what should happen around them and whatever happens around them should be for them.

People's participation, decentralization, and Privatisation should not be taken as synonyms of each other. Role of the state and role of private sector and people's needs should be appropriately and adequately discussed so that some general understanding is arrived at, as there cannot be a single model applicable to all the urban housing and basic services and utilities. All dimensions, political as well as economic, of the 74th constitutional amendment be analysed and understood realistically and not on ideological or emotional basis. A proper understanding of urban institutions and their functioning has to be developed. The outcomes of NGO's acting as catalysts in the community actions towards development are very encouraging. The experiences and experiments have been regarding alternative institution building, where the stakeholders themselves are directly brought as actors in the development process.

But NGO's as the solution for housing struggle of the urban poor has also been questioned upon. This has been mainly because their internal limitations set to them like the financial constraints and the external limitations like the power politics and administrative constraints. Housing today is looked upon merely in real estate terms. This is what the real –estate agenda has encouraged today due to the Privatisation thrust in housing and corporatisation of the various development and construction activities. Housing projects are evaluated in terms of size, the built up area, the FSI consumed, the financial turnover, and various other business and marketing merits. The bigger the project, the better it is and the greater the attraction for developers in undertaking the scheme. A huge network is thus established between the developers, the landowners, and the financial institutions wherein the slum dwellers find no place.

Thus there is need of changing in the attitude of the government and the elite towards the slum dwellers. Programme for slum development must primarily be seen as an environmental scheme and not merely as an agenda for real estate development and construction turnover. It is the slum-like conditions *i.e.* lack of drinking water, inadequate toilet facilities, garbage, heaps, lack of sewage disposal, absence of open-spaces, inadequate and unsafe access that are of primary concern. Even with the rehabilitation programmes by the Government and the NGO's some basic element is lacking in these projects that is the people. This has been particularly the case of the rehabilitation of the evicted SGNP slum dwellers.

It is obvious from the above argument that neither the state nor the private sector alone can handle the problem of housing for the poor. So there is need for the NGO intervention. But NGO's have there own drawbacks in terms of financial and administrative constraints. So the solution to overcrowding and housing is to ensure that the socioeconomic compulsions that force mass migration towards the cities are ended. However another more rational way out will be the integrated efforts of the private sector, central government, civil society and people. However, this requires simultaneous efforts by national, local governments, civil society, and private sector and people themselves to eliminate impediments at all the levels. While central governments address policy matters and regulatory impediments nationally, local authorities and civil societies should design strategies to make appropriate interventions and regulatory changes in the city. Local experiences should be fed back to national governments to influence their support to cities, as well as for redesigning national programme.

Another thing that can be done is the site and service scheme that has been started by the government in Fourth plan and continued in seventh plan. This is a solution by which the 5 million homeless workers of Mumbai can be housed. In this scheme the government is totally responsible for providing all the services such as water, electricity, sewage, drainage, and toilets, for providing technical know how and skills, interest-free loans and for providing building materials at highly subsidized rates. First of all land is taken over under the Urban Land (Ceiling and Regulation) Act at the rate of Re1/-a square foot which is virtually free or at adequate compensation or if land is already in possession of the government it can be used directly.

Instead of This land is divided into thousands of small plots. Then no construction is actually done in the beginning, as is the case of conventional schemes. But water supply, sewage drainage and electricity are provided to each plot. Then, depending on the financial capacity of each person the worker can build his house. The advantage is even a person with a budget of 2000/-can go ahead. Secondly the house can be developed over time. Thirdly and most important, the worker has control over his house. Housing must be made fundamental right enshrined in the constitution.

Both the availability of direct finance and subsidized building materials will tremendously excite the slum dwellers in under taking the renovation and reconstruction of their houses on their own. From the table given we can see that people with different income group will be able to afford different types of shelter within there limited finances. Like People with income of as low as ₹.200/-can afford a house of cost 3,200 where the site and services has been provided by the government and the person can make a house within his or her budget. Whereas, a person with a monthly income of more than 1500, can afford a house of ₹.56, 000 made in a conventional way.

Also under the development proposal, the house will be ground and ground + one or two stories high, enabling easy repairs and maintenance directly under the control of the users. There would, therefore, be less dependency on hired skills and services.

This will encourage people's participation in decisionmaking and will inculcate a greater sense of belonging resulting in personalization of spaces and structures. While the construction of houses will be the individual's prerogative, the restructuring of the slum-layout, road, services, open spaces etc., could be a collective effort with governmental support

Development programme for each slum will have to be evolved independently and relevant guidelines fixed. Even F.S.I for each slum may vary to enable housing for all the slum-dwellers on, as–is-where–is basis. Each slum has its own peculiar situation and needs. For example what will apply for Dharavi may not be relevant for another slum in Jogeshwari and vice versa. Therefore, within the main policy framework, individual development strategies will have to be evolved. This will encourage people's participation in decisionmaking.

PROMOTE SUSTAINABLE DEVELOPMENT IN FRINGE AREAS

Control of Development on Fringe Areas: In metropolitan cities and mega cities, urban development is mostly in new settlement areas and new activity centres with planned infrastructures and facilities in the fringe areas to accommodate the increasing population and activities.

Unplanned urban sprawl grows around such centres on the agricultural lands taking advantage of the nearby facilities and infrastructure. In such cases, from an environmental perspective, regulations for protecting the agricultural and vacant lands by restricting developments and the stipulations of the regulations may be as below.

- No use, other than agriculture or irrigation facilities, is permitted.
- Existing water bodies to be preserved.
- No new building or extension of any existing building exceeding the height of 3.75 metres shall be allowed subject to the total covered area of 50 sq. m.
- The minimum front and side open spaces shall be 2 metres and the minimum rear open space shall be 5.00 metres.

Redevelopment of Blighted Pockets in the Central Area: Blighted pockets of low key commercial areas are observed within the core areas which, due to the small sizes and multiple land ownerships, do not get redeveloped as per the existing regulations. If these areas can be redeveloped in a planned manner much of the demand for commercial floor spaces can be served. For the redevelopment of such areas incentives towards land assembly by amalgamation of plots and additional floorspace ratios need to be given. The regulations in this respect may be:-

1. For land assembly exceeding one acre in size, the additional floorspace ratio would be 20 per cent above the permissible limit.
2. In case of land assembly of less than one acre the additional floorspace would be 10 per cent above the permissible limit.
3. In such cases the developments should confirm the zoning regulations.

Compulsory Rainwater Harvesting in New Area Development: Private developments in the form of sub-division of mother plots (for plotted developments and for apartments) is taking place in the fringe areas and adjoining municipal and non-municipal areas. There are regulations in most of the plans which vary according to the size of the mother plots and the regulations specify the minimum width of roads, the percentage of open spaces, the land for physical and social infrastructures *viz.* drainage, water supply (pump house and water treatment plants), sewerage (sewage treatment plants or oxidation ponds), school, health centre, market, milk booth, post office, power substation etc. In order to comply with the present efforts towards utilization of natural resources by rainwater harvesting and ground water recharging, the regulations for subdivision should include the mandatory provision of community pools of sufficient size so that the rain water from the area can be stored in such pools. The water may be supplied to the community for uses such as gardening, car washing etc. Adapting physical planning to promote sustainable development: efficient infrastructure planning.

Prescription of street alignments for regional roads in fringe areas: The regional roads (National Highways, State Highways or District Roads), connecting a city with the hinterland are often constricted in the fringe areas due to lack of scope for widening owing to dense developments and abutting built up areas. To avoid such situations where the regional roads pass through vacant areas in the fringe of the city, advance actions for prescription of street alignments may be made without acquiring land. The proposed right-ofway as per future requirements may be prescribed and the regulations may be as below.

- For any development on the adjoining plots on the regional roads, the owner/developer would have to make a setback following the proposed right-of-way line and the owners/developers would be allowed the same floorspace as they were eligible for the original plot.

- In such cases after the alignment is notified no subdivision of the adjoining plots would be allowed.
- In cases where the plot size is such that no development is possible by allowing the set back, the local body would have to acquire it.

Dispersal facilities around transport nodes: The railway stations, the regional bus terminals/stops are the important transport nodal points of the urban areas. These areas get congested with dense unplanned commercial and residential developments and in course of time become too congested for easy dispersal of passenger and vehicular traffic. Given the urban growth rates future public transport will carry larger volumes of passengers. Therefore, the areas required for dispersal facilities will need to be increased.

Where such areas are already congested, redevelopment plans are to be prepared by the local body and the redevelopment actions may be initiated, including through private-public partnership projects. In less pressured situations regulations for control of development should be made at least for the area within 200 metres on all sides. In such areas provision should be made for adequate parking facilities for different categories of vehicles including the parking and loading/unloading facilities for transit and paratransit vehicles.

Adequate width of the connecting roads, exclusive roads for pedestrians or grade separated pedestrian facilities should be made. In order to achieve these, specific plans should be prepared indicating the future right-of way of the roads, the parking areas for different categories of vehicles, the pedestrian-only roads and the integration with the railway station or the bus terminal. The regulations in such areas may include the following:

- The Floor Area Ratio (FAR) for buildings of different use categories and means of access would be half of the permissible FAR in other areas.
- The compulsory provision of parking spaces for buildings of different use categories would be double of that required in other zones.
- No new cinema halls, theatres and entertainment centres would be allowed within the area.
- For buildings with retail commercial in the ground floor, the minimum front open space would be 5 metres.

Environment protection around relocated hazardous uses: For implementing the development plans, the non-conforming uses located in a scattered way are required to be relocated in the specified areas in the fringe within a stipulated period. Such uses may be the obnoxious and hazardous industries, tanneries etc. Normally, such areas for relocation are selected beyond the city limits and in the vacant and agricultural lands.

When such relocation of activities takes place, unplanned developments adjoining such centres occur and gradually these areas grow. To avoid further environmental hazards, the relocation areas should be provided with a buffer zone where no developments other than agriculture and pisciculture are permitted. In this regard, regulations of the Pollution Control Board are to be followed. But in the development plans there should be specific regulations in respect of the buffer zones. The regulations in this respect may be:-

- The area covered by 200 meters on all sides from the boundary of such areas would be designated as Buffer Zone.
- No developments other than agriculture, pisciculture and plantation of trees would be allowed within this zone.
- The existing residential uses within the Buffer Zone would have to be relocated within a stipulated period.

Adapting physical planning to promote sustainable development: conservation of water resources and waste management

Protection of Water Fronts: The water fronts (sides of rivers, canals, lakes and big ponds) in many cities are encroached by unauthorized users and developed in an unplanned manner.

These water fronts need to be protected to ensure proper drainage, and access for open-air recreation, water transportation and protection against soil erosion. Area within 100 metres from the banks should be designated as Water Front zone and specific regulations should be prescribed. The regulations for such zone may include:-

- No new building within 30 meters from the edge of the banks would be allowed.
- In the area lying between 30 metres and 100 metres from the edge of the banks no building more than 5.00 metres in height and 30 metres along the waterfront would be allowed. In case of buildings on stilts the maximum height of the buildings shall be 6.50 metres.
- There shall be a linear gap of 50 metres between two buildings alongside the water front.

Environment protection around solid waste disposal sites: Solid waste management is one of the most critical problems of cities.

The locations of the intermediate collection sites and the final disposal grounds need special attention in consideration of the environment hazards of the nearby localities. The intermediate collection sites are generally located within or near the settlements and therefore need to have a buffer zone. This buffer zone should cover at least 30 metres on all sides.

The regulations in this respect may be:-

1. The intermediate collection site may be designated as Inner Disposal Zone.
2. The area should be provided with boundary walls of at least 3 metres high on three sides.
3. The actual dumping area should be circumscribed by two to three rows of trees in the buffer zone.

Forest Management and Use

Value of the Forests

Timber holds first place among the forest products of New Guinea and Fiji and may do so in the future in the other continental islands, as is generally true on the continents.

On the oceanic volcanic islands, however, the native forests bear very few species or individual trees of such size and quality as are suitable for commercial timber and experiments are constantly progressing with introduced plants. The aborigines use wood for house posts, paddles, canoes and sundry minor articles, for which individual trees are selected when needed.

In Hawaii the chief value of the Forest Reserves is in relation to watersheds, because of the demands of the sugar and pineapple plantations and of urban communities and the same probably also holds true for the other high islands under more intensive use.

Where there is mangrove vegetation, it is extensively exploited for fuel and in Fiji is under a 40-year management cycle, as we have seen.

On most of the islands the main use of secondary growth is for firewood and charcoal. For fence posts, highly important in all grazing regions, the naturalized Prosopis chilensis is one of the chief sources of supply.

There is no pulp industry of importance, although recent developments in the use of bagasse are significant. Rubber has been tried in the southwestern islands, but not successfully. Minor forest products are of no more than local importance. For the New Guinea native the principal value of the forest lands is as agricultural soil and once the grasses take over, he moves on, or vanishes.

Ownership and Administration

Organized forestry, private or governmental, exists in only a few of the island groups. During the Japanese administration of Micronesia, forestry activities were accelerated, with local sawmill operations, minor exports to Japan and a certain amount of reforestation, especially with Casuarina equisetifolia. The present forestry situation in American Samoa and Micronesia has recently been surveyed.

New Caledonia, Fiji (where a Forest Department was established in 1938) and Hawaii have, or have had, some government administration, with Hawaii far in the lead.

In Hawaii a Board of Commissioners of Agriculture and Forestry has existed since 1903. Its activities have centered largely around the establishment of reserves almost entirely for watersheds, the elimination of the hordes of feral mammals, fencing, a very elaborate planting programme that has involved a vast number of alien forest species and the controversial practice of introducing game animals. In the early days, forest plantings were sometimes made in total disregard of basic silvical principles and failures were excessive. For a long time, success was gauged on survival and rapid growth and undoubtedly this is a chief factor in the case of a timber species that is to be harvested.

For self-perpetuating forests, however, this policy may be very deceptive. An intensive report is much to be desired on all these forest plantings of the past, not only with regard to the survival of planted individuals, but also as to whether different species are capable of spreading naturally. Some species may be found to act as "nurse crops" that is, to prepare the way for the introduction of another semi-natural plant community closer to the original self-perpetuating forest.

Utilization

The original uses of the forest were generally unorganized and unplanned. The natives knew their trees and chose carefully the species and individuals best suited for house posts, canoes, paddles, fishnet floats and other articles to meet their daily needs. The breadfruit was recognized as one of the most valuable of timber trees (propagated vegetatively and existing in endless clonal strains), but was seldom cut, because its fruits were used for food. Coconut also served numerous purposes. Other trees of the strand were selected and many species in the coastalplain forests of the high islands were discriminately chosen, although reports concerning the same species from different island regions vary markedly. Before World War II organized forestry and forest exploitation can hardly be said to have existed in Oceania. There were a few sawmills on the larger islands, but they served immediate local needs only.

During the war exploitation was stepped up to a high pace to serve the armed forces, especially in the larger Melanesian islands. As in so many tropical regions, the number of species here is great and bewilderingly complex and many of the species have native names only and are unknown to scientific classification. The wartime operations helped to advance our knowledge of the dendrology and physical characteristics of these forests farther than throughout all previous history, but unfortunately most of such information exists only in unpublished reports and in the minds of the foresters who were directly involved.

Research

The forestry and agricultural organizations are carrying forward only limited programs of basic forestry research. Usually these organizations are under pressure to serve immediate needs and hence their investigations are oriented toward the planting of exotic tree species of proven worth elsewhere and toward the control of actively destructive factors, such as feral mammals. On the other hand, scientific research in Oceania is beginning to advance rapidly along general lines and this should benefit forestry in the long run.

Forestry in Oceania involves the management of lands originally or potentially covered with trees and such products of forest land as water and wildlife may locally be more important than commercial timber. For these reasons a sound forestry programme must go beyond the range of conventional silvicultural activities.

It must include interpretations of the vegetation of pre-European and pre-native times and also serious studies of the remaining samples of natural and semi-natural vegetation, which in some instances have very desirable characteristics. The artificially induced forest types, such as those from plantings, should also be investigated with regard both to their continuing or self-perpetuating characteristics and to their values in other respects than for timber production. Because of the extraordinary complexity of the native and introduced floras and because of the wide range of distinctive environmental conditions within relatively small areas, forestry in Oceania offers unsurpassed challenges to the ingenuity of the practical researcher.

LAND OWNERSHIP AND FARM STRUCTURE

OWNERSHIP OF U.S. LAND

The land surface of the United States covers 2.3 billion acres. Private owners held 61 per cent in 2002, the Federal Government 28 per cent, State and local governments 9 per cent, and Indian reservations 3 per cent. Virtually all cropland is privately owned, as is three-fifths of grassland pasture and range and over half of forestland. Federal, State, and local government holdings consist primarily of forestland, rangeland, and other land. Most land in Federal ownership—largely in the West—is managed by the Department of the Interior (68 per cent) and the Department of Agriculture (28 per cent).

Farm operators do not own all the land used in agriculture. According to the 1999 Agricultural Economics and Land Ownership Survey (AELOS), farmers held 58 per cent of the land in farms in 1999. These landowning farmers also made up 58 per cent of the 3.4 million farmland owners. Non-operator landlords accounted for the remaining 42 per cent of land in farms. Ninety-five per cent of non-farm landlords were individuals/families or partnerships. Of these unincorporated landlords, 55 per cent were at least 65 years old. Many non-farm landlords have a historic connection to farming. Among the people who have exited farming or inherited farmland since the number of farms peaked during the Great Depression, a number have retained ownership of some or all their land.

Farm Numbers, Farm Types, and Conservation Programmes

The number of farms has declined dramatically since its peak of 6.8 million in 1935, with most of the decline occurring during the 1940s, 1950s, and 1960s.

The decline in farm numbers has levelled off since the 1970s. By 2002, 2.1 million farms remained. The remaining farms have a much larger average acreage, but averages mask differences among farms. Today's farms range from very small retirement and residential farms to industrialized operations with sales in the millions. Part of this diversity stems from the very low sales threshold ($1,000) necessary for an operation to qualify as a farm for statistical purposes.

One way to address the diversity of farms is to categorize them into more homogeneous groups. The farm typology developed by ERS identifies five groups of small family farms (sales less than $250,000): limited-resource, retirement, residential/lifestyle, farming-occupation/low-sales, and farming-occupation/high-sales. The typology also includes large family farms, very large family farms, and non-family farms. In addition, very small farms (sales less than $10,000) make up more than half of all farms. Very small farms account for a particularly large share of farms in the limited-resource (72 per cent), retirement (76 per cent), and residential/lifestyle (76 per cent) groups. Production, however, is concentrated among larger farms; small farms account for only 27 per cent of the total value of production.

The smallness of most farms has implications for conservation and the environment. An ERS study found that smaller corn farms are less likely to use conservation tillage than are larger farms. The practice is more practical for larger farms because they have more acres over which to spread the cost of new or retrofitted equipment necessary to adopt conservation tillage. Small farms whose operators are retired or farm part-time are also less likely to adopt conservation tillage, possibly because of hesitancy to change familiar production practices. Small farms, however, participate widely in the Conservation Reserve Programme (CRP) and the Wetlands Reserve Programme (WRP).

DISTRIBUTION OF CONSERVATION PROGRAMME PAYMENTS BY TYPE OF FARM

These farms harvest most of the land planted to programme commodities and therefore receive three-quarters of commodity programme payments. However, CRP and WRP—the two major conservation programmes—are targeted at particular types of land, not commodities. Since small farms own 70 per cent of the land held by farms, they play a large role in natural resource and environmental policy. Retirement, residential/lifestyle, and low-sales farms account for nearly two-thirds of conservation payments and a similar share of the land farmers enrolled in the CRP and WRP. Participating farmers in each of the three groups tend to enroll large shares of their land in these programmes: 46 per cent of the land operated on retirement farms, 28 per cent on residential/ lifestyle farms, and 23 per cent on low-sales farms. In contrast, enrollment ranges from 5 to 9 per cent for participating high-sales, large, and very large farms.

Because their main job is off-farm, residential/lifestyle operators are limited in the amount of time they can spend farming. As a result, residential/lifestyle farmers find CRP and WRP attractive, since these programmes require little time. Given their life-cycle position, many retired farmers have land available to put into conservation uses. The same forces may also be acting on low-sales operators, who average 57 years of age and may be scaling down their operations. If an off-farm job and advanced age are major determinants of land going into conservation uses, it may be relatively easy to get smaller farms to enrol land in the programmes. Getting larger farms to enrol more of their land might require higher payments, if the opportunity cost of idling their land is higher.

Land Tenure

Farm operators leased 38 per cent of their total farmland in 2002, down from 40 per cent in 1997 and 43 per cent in 1992, according to the census of agriculture. This decline may reflect increasing rental costs as parcels of land become smaller. Parcels of farmland available to rent tend to become subdivided with time due to division among heirs. Smaller parcels increase transaction costs to operators assembling land to expand their operations. Still, rented land as a share of total farmland is higher than the 35-per cent rate that prevailed in the 1950s and 1960s.

About 38 per cent of all farms rented land in 2003, 32 per cent as part owners and 6 per cent as tenants. Land leasing has changed from a way for beginning farmers to enter agriculture to a way for established farmers to access additional land. Renting allows farms to expand without the debt and commitment of capital associated with ownership.

In fact, about 17 per cent of very large family farms are tenants, a larger percentage than in any other group. Conventional wisdom holds that farmland owners have a long-term interest in their land and thus are more likely than renters to adopt conservation practices. Soule and others (1999 and 2000) found this to be true among corn farmers, at least in the adoption of conservation practices that provide only long-term benefits, such as grassed waterways and strip cropping. The situation was different for conservation tillage, which can increase profits in the short run by maintaining or increasing yields while reducing machinery, fuel, and labour costs.

Cash-renters are less likely than owner-operators to use conservation tillage, but share-renters appear to act like owner-operators in adopting conservation tillage. Share-renters may have an incentive to adopt conservation tillage, if the landlord bears some of the costs that may increase under conservation tillage, such as herbicide expenditures. Share-landlords are also more likely to be involved in management decisions than cash-landlords, which may make share-renters act more like owners.

LAND USE: ENVIRONMENT AND THE SUSTAINABILITY

Land-use changes can affect the environment and the sustainability of production. Because impacts on the environment—including erosion, water quality, and wildlife habitat—are typically not reflected in private profit calculations, land-use choices that are optimal for an individual may not be optimal for society. This difference suggests the possibility of public policies that more closely align land-use decisions with social objectives. The allocation of a fixed land base among competing uses is determined by the relative returns to the different uses, which vary according to land quality and location. A landowner seeking to maximize profits will allocate a land parcel to the use that yields the highest expected economic return, after the costs of conversion. As relative returns change along with market conditions, technological advancements, or government policies, land-use patterns tend to adjust accordingly. Land-use change is dynamic. With the exception of urban land, changes occur to and from major land uses. For example, 44 million acres left the cropland and pasture category from 1992 to 1997 while 21 million acres shifted into the category, resulting in a net loss of 23 million acres.

MAJOR LAND USES

This series contains acreage estimates of major uses by region and State, coinciding with each census of agriculture from 1945 through 2002. Because Alaska and Hawaii have very little crop area, we focus on the contiguous 48 States. The total land area of the 48 contiguous States is approximately 1.9 billion acres, with an additional 365 million acres in Alaska and a little over 4 million acres in Hawai.

Grassland pasture and range, the largest use of land, accounted for 584 million acres (31 per cent) of the 48 States in 2002. This compares with 636 million acres in the mid-1960s. Due to improvements in the forage quality and productivity of grazing lands, less pasture and range is needed to sustain grazing herds. The inventory of domestic animals, particularly sheep, has also been declining in recent years, further reducing pasture/range demand.

Forest-use Land

Table. Major uses of land, United States, 2002[1]

Land use	48 States Million acres	US	48 States % of total	US
Cropland[2]	441	442	23.3	19.5
Grassland pasture and range	584	587	30.8	25.9
Forest-use land[3]	559	651	29.5	28.8
Special uses[4]	153	297	8.1	13.1
Urban	59	60	3.1	2.6
Miscellaneous other land	97	228	5.1	10.1
Total land area[5]	1,894	2,264	100.0	100.0

Note:

[1]See Major Land Uses for estimates of major uses by region and State, coinciding with each census of agriculture, from 1945 through 2002.

[2]All land in the crop rotation (used for crops, used for pasture, idle cropland). Includes about 34 million acres idled under the Conservation Reserve Programme.

[3]Total forest land as classified by the U.S. Forest Service minus an estimated 98 million acres of forested land used for parks, wildlife areas, and other special uses.

[4]Rural transportation areas, land used primarily for recreation and wildlife purposes, various public installations and facilities, farmsteads, and farm roads/ lanes. Excludes urban land in contrast to Major Land Uses, Aggregate Data.

[5]Distributions by major use may not add to totals due to rounding.

Forest-use land, the second largest major use, declined from about 32 per cent of total land in 1945 to about 30 per cent in 2002. A broader category, all land with forest cover, comprised 33 per cent of the land base in 2002. While forest-use land increased 1 per cent between 1997 and 2002, it declined from 612 million acres in 1964 to 559 million acres in 2002. Much forest-covered land is in "special uses" that prohibit forestry uses such as timber production. Forested land in these special uses increased from 23 million acres in 1945 to about 98 million acres in 2002.

Cropland comprises the third largest use of land, covering 23 per cent of the contiguous States in 2002. Since 1945, cropland ranged from a high of 478 million acres in 1949 to a low of 441 million acres in 2002. Total cropland has trended downward since the late 1960s, and decreased by 13 million acres (3 per cent) from 1997 to 2002. The total cropland base includes cropland used for crops, cropland used for pasture, and cropland idled. These components vary more than total cropland. Since 1945, the amount of cropland used for crops has ranged fromas much as 383 million acres in 1949 and 1982 to a minimum of 331 million acres in 1987. Total acreage used for crops exhibited two major cycles between 1945 and 1987, with cropland moving from idle to crop use and back again. Cropland used for crops increased from 331 to 349 million acres over 1987-97, and then declined to 340 million acres in 2002, about 5 per cent below the average acreage for 1910-97. Since 1945, cropland used for pasture varied from 47 million acres in 1945 to 88 million acres in 1969.

LAND ALIENATION AND PAUPERIZATION

The colonial state imposed the land laws based on this worldview on the traditional communities. This imposition affected the dominant castes as well as the tribal communities. But many of the former had access to education and other modern inputs. So they had some preparation to deal with the changes. Most traditional tribes, on the contrary, lived on mineral and forest rich land that the colonialist required as raw materials. That turned the imposition of the formal system on the informal societies into an unequal encounter. Land alienation from the traditional to "modern" communities was a consequences since the latter were unable to deal with the changes imposed on them.

This unequal encounter continues to be the basis of a disjunction and of conflicts between the two systems because the colonial laws continue to be in force in the country. One of its consequences is environmental degradation. The legal system that recognises only individual ownership is a major cause of land loss and environmental degradation. Since the CPRS are not recognised as their sustenance, the communities depending on them cannot prevent outsiders from encroaching on that land. For example, in Tripura in North Eastern India, the tribal proportion has declined from 58 per cent in 1951 to 31 per cent in 2001 because immigrants have encroached on 60 per cent of their community owned land with the help of individual-based laws. Equally important is loss of forests which catered to many needs of the tribal and other rural poor communities. The state handed many of them over to industry as raw material. They were treated as sources of profit and destroyed with no concern for their dependants or for conservation. That impoverished people (Gadgil 1989.

The third source of land loss is acquisition for development projects. The law that empowers the state to acquire land recognises only individual ownership. More than 25 million hectares have been used in India for such projects 1947-2000, around 14 million of them forest and other CPRs. Their inhabitants, most of them tribal and other rural poor like fish and quarry workers are considered encroachers and are not compensated and often not even counted among the displaced (Fernandes 2008: 92).

Often records of the CPRs are not kept since they are considered state property and their inhabitants are encroachers. For example, according to official accounts, in Assam the state used 159,017.37 hectares of land for development projects and displaced 343,262 persons from them 1947–2000. The reality is 1.9 million persons displaced from 567,281.29 hectares (Fernandes and Bharali 2006: 107). More than 1.5 millions displaced persons and 410,261 hectares were not counted because according to the law these CPRs are state property and their inhabitants are encroachers with no right to live there.

The Vicious Circle

One can mention many other modes of land alienation. The above examples are given only to show the processes that lead to alienation of the people's livelihood. Because of the unequal nature of the encounter, also the reaction of these systems to the problems that the process causes differs. That too is based on their worldview on land and the natural resources all of whose dependants feel the negative impact of the transition from the traditional to the modern economy and new values. But the rural poor, particularly the tribes and other forest dwellers feel its impact more than the remaining groups do because it is an attack on their tradition of judicious use of resources and on the systems they had developed to manage land, forests and CPRs as their renewable sustenance.

Loss of their sustenance begins the vicious circle of impoverishment that forces the dependants of these resources to overexploit them and cause further environmental degradation and more poverty. As the former Brazilian President Fernando Henrique Cardoso (1998) said, the first danger to the environment from people's impoverishment is loss of biodiversity and linked to it, loss of the values through which the communities depending on it had managed the resource as renewable. Studies show that loss of this value system or ideology is basic to the vicious circle that leads to further environmental degradation.

But reaction to this process differs according to the class one belongs to and one's ideology or culture. To the urban middle class land alienation and environmental degradation are loss of their recreational spaces while to the rural, particularly tribal, communities it results in loss of their livelihood and consequent impoverishment from which follows further land alienation and destruction of more natural resources. Conflicts are a natural consequence of this contradiction.

The first step of this process is impoverishment of the economic status they are reduced to by the alienation of their sustenance. It begins with landlessness. Then comes joblessness. For example, studies of families displaced by development projects show that in Andhra Pradesh in South India, the proportion of the landless rose from 10.9 per cent before the project to 36.5 per cent after it and in Assam in the Northeast from 15.56 to 24.38 per cent. Even among those who retain land, the average area owned declined, for example in Assam from 1.2 to 0.6 hectares per family. In every state most small and marginal farmers became landless, and medium farmers joined the ranks of small and marginal farmers. They also witnessed a decline in the support mechanisms such as the number of irrigation ponds and wells, poultry, cattle, and draught animals that used to supplement their agricultural income declined.

Joblessness is the next step. The land and other resources that are alienated from them used to provide them work. They lose this resource with no alternative to take its place. Joblessness resulting from it takes two forms. The first is lower access to work and the second is downward occupational mobility. In Andhra Pradesh, for example, 83.72 per cent of the land losers used to work on their land or elsewhere before its loss. After land loss access to work declined to 41.61 per cent. In West Bengal it declined from 91.02 to 53.18 per cent and in Assam from 77.27 to 56.41 per cent. The second is downward occupational mobility. In most states, more than 50 per cent of the land losers who were cultivators before it became landless agricultural labourers or daily wage earners after land loss. Also displacement can continue as a result of environmental degradation. For example, a new industry often forces people to move out of its neighbourood because after its construction environmental or other consequences such as fly ash and dust generated by the thermal, aluminium, nuclear, cement and other plants destroy the land around it and render it unusable. Its dependants cannot sustain themselves on it and are forced to move out. Also the noise and dust pollution and constant blasts in the coalmines often force people to leave their homes.

Absorbing a New Culture

The changes do not remain external but enter the community itself through the internalisation of the dominant culture. The major change is the culture the community in general and its elite in particular internalise, of viewing their sustenance as commodity alone. It is seen firstly in the demand the leaders make that individual ownership become the norm in their communities. For example, in the Garo tribe of East Garo in Meghalaya in Northeast India the leaders accepted the culture of individual ownership in the 1980s. A study two decades later shows that 30 per cent of the tribal families in this district had become landless since their elite had monopolised much of their land. These changes also have gender implications. As stated above, even the matrilineal societies are patriarchal. Their leaders absorbs the culture of greater patriarchy and express it in their land relations. That can be seen among the Garo who are a matrilineal tribe but individual ownership is through men. Among the Khasi of Megalaya who too are a matrilineal tribe, the male leaders who control the village council exploit their power to their own advantage and turn community-owned land into their private property (Mukhim forthcoming). Such change of gender attitudes is seen in other tribes too in the manner in which men interpret their customary law and property relations in their own favour.

Communities thus deprived of their resources absorb the same culture in another form. The first is the vicious circle of viewing their resources as a commodity alone. Once they are deprived of their resource and are impoverished, for sheer survival they overexploit the same resource for an income. For example, studies in all the tribal areas show that once they lose their land, the deprived families fall back on their forests that they had preserved for centuries and cut trees for sale as firewood or timber, and cause more deforestation.

The second to view their own bodies as a commodity. For example, 49 per cent of the families displaced by development projects in West Bengal and 56 per cent in Assam pulled their children out of school in order to turn them into child labourers. Women began to view their bodies only as a source of income. Because of it prostitution grew enormously among the families that had lost their land. All these instances point to a major change in subaltern culture. These communities lose hope in their future and think only of the present. As a result, children who are an asset for the future become commodities only for the present and are used as a source of income for survival. The same is the view of women's bodies. In other words, women and children become commodities more than men do.

This chapter which is an overview of the changes in land relations, has shown the new culture that grown as their result. It shows that imposition of another culture on a traditional group can result in a culture that is destructive of a community in general and of women in particular. The solution is not either going back to their tradition by opposing modernisation or absolutising the modern system. One cannot prevent all individual ownership either. One has to find an alternative in beginning with the tradition community values and combining them with the traditional community. Tradition has to be modernised and not replaced completely.

FARM FORESTRY: LAND AVAILABILITY, TAKE-UP RATES AND ECONOMICS

The target set by the Irish Government is to increase the forest cover to 17 per cent of the land area of the country by the year 2030. This involved an annual afforestation level of 25,000 ha to the year 2000 and 20,000 ha thereafter to the year 2030. The target was almost achieved in 1995 but planting levels have fallen far short since, even though substantial financial incentives were put in place.

IMPLICATIONS

Failure to reach the overall target by 2030 will result in failure to reach the critical mass of forest output required to support a viable timber industry. Since the employment creation potential of large timber mills is not very high, it is essential that significant value added accompanies whatever timber output is achieved in order to boost employment. In the absence of achieving the afforestation targets listed in the Strategic Plan for Forestry, the contribution of the forestry sector to the growth targets of the National Development Plan will be less than expected and the objectives set out regarding forestry in the CAP Rural Development Plan will not be achieved.

Background

The study objectives were to examine the factors:

- Influencing land availability for forestry,
- Slowing down or accelerating the rate of afforestation and
- Affecting the economic return from farm forestry.

The amount of land becoming available for afforestation via the market has declined substantially in recent years. Land transfers are via gift or inheritance in the vast majority of cases. Land becoming available (non market) for forestry at time of change of ownership was not examined but a survey of landowners opinions was used to study the factors influencing decisions to plant. In this study the economic returns from forestry were compared with the returns from existing farm enterprises using linear programming techniques. The technique as applied in this study is aimed at maximising total farm gross margin from all available resources thereby arriving at the optimum mix of enterprises (including forestry). The main assumptions of the economic study were as follows:

- Returns to forestry were calculated using a 10 per cent discount rate.
- The gross margin system is used to compare returns from forestry with agricultural enterprises.
- No economic value was given to the amount of carbon dioxide fixed by growing trees, and
- Farm labour was valued both at minimum wage and at average industrial wage rates.

The discount rate normally used by those in the forestry sector is 5 per cent. Fixed costs are proportionally much higher in agriculture than in forestry. Forestry is long-term and all costs are variable in the long term so perhaps a net figure might be more suitable for comparison purposes.

Findings

Land Availability and Take-up Rate

Landholders attitude to forestry are becoming more positive. The unfavourable responses to forestry were based mainly on pragmatic rather than cultural issues, *e.g.* small farm size, land quality, competing EU payments. The main reason for planting was the very favourable income from forestry premium payments on land that had limited other uses. Forestry on good farmland was not favoured but was a definite competitor to agricultural enterprises on land marginal for farming and/ or situated some distance away from the main farmyard. Afforestation was mostly associated with large farm size. The study did not examine the question of cutting back in farm enterprises (livestock numbers) which is often associated with old age and/ or ill health. The demographic profile of those in the sample with farm forests was the same as in the National Farm situation.

Economic Returns

Opportunities for off-farm employment and levels of remuneration can determine the choice of farm enterprise and the rate of afforestation. Off-farm earnings at or near industrial wage rate levels may result in increases in the area planted often to the exclusion of cattle and sheep enterprises at individual farm level. Since the decision to plant is for all time, economic factors alone are often not the only criteria for decision-making. Where off-farm jobs are not available, forestry will compete with farm enterprises only on farms where there is land surplus to that required to maximise REPS, compensatory allowance, and extensification payments.

However, even where no off-farm jobs are available, forestry will always compete with drystock enterprises operated at moderate and low levels of efficiency. The study gives a clear message that a switch to forestry can improve overall farm and household income for many farmers depending on their circumstances. The findings of the study are important pointers for Teagasc staff involved in the Opportunities for Farm Families Programme.

11

Non-Timber Products of Forestry

SUPPLY OF TIMBER: IMPORTS AND EXPORTS

The net imports and exports of European countries (average data, calculated from the returns of recent years). The only timber-exporting countries of Europe are Russia, Sweden, Norway, Austria-Hungary and Rumania; all the others either have only enough for their own consumption, or import timber. Great Britain and Ireland import now upwards of 10,000,000 tons a year, Germany about 4,600,000 tons and Belgium about 1,300,000 tons. Holland, France, Portugal, Spain and Italy are all importing countries, as also are Asia Minor, Egypt and Algeria. The west coast of Africa exports hardwoods and imports coniferous timber. The Cape and Natal import considerable quantities of pine and fir wood. Australasia Net Imports and Exports of European Countries. These net imports are received from non-European countries. They consist chiefly of valuable hardwoods, like teak, mahogany, eucalypts and others.

Exports hardwoods and some Kauri pine from New Zealand, but imports larger quantities of light pine and fir timber. British India and Siam export teak and small quantities of fancy woods. The West Indies and South America export hardwoods and import pine and fir wood. The United States of America will not much longer be a genuine exporting country, since they import already almost as much timber from Canada as they export. Canada exports considerable quantities of timber. The Dominion has still a forest area of 1,250,000 sq. m., equal to 38% of the total area and giving 165 acres of forest for every inhabitant. Although only about one-third of the forest area can be called regular timber land, Canada possesses an enormous forest wealth, with which she might supply permanently nearly all other countries deficient in material, if the governing bodies in the several provinces would only determine to stop the present fearful waste caused by axe and fire and to introduce a regular system of management. As matters stand, the supplies of the most valuable timber of Canada, the white or Weymouth pine, are nearly exhausted, the great stores of spruce in the eastern provinces are being rapidly destroyed and the forests of Douglas fir in the western provinces have been attacked for export to the United States and to other countries. Taking the remaining stocks of the whole earth together, it may be said that a sufficient quantity of hardwoods is available, but the only countries which are able to supply coniferous timber for export on a considerable scale are Russia, Sweden, Norway, Austria and Canada. As these countries have practically to supply the rest of the world and as the management of their forests is far from satisfactory, the question of supplying light pine and fir timber, which forms the very staff of life of the wood industries, must become a very serious matter before many years have passed.

Unmistakable signs of the coming crisis are everywhere visible to all who wish to see and it is difficult to over-state the gravity of the problem, when it is remembered, for instance, that 87% of all the timber imported into Great Britain consists of light pine and fir and that most of the other importing countries are similarly situated.

In some of these countries little or no room exists for the extension of woodland, but this statement does not apply to Great Britain and Ireland, which contain upwards of 12,000,000 acres of waste land and 12, 500,000 acres of mountain and heath land used for light grazing. Onefourth of that area, if put under forest, would produce all the timber now imported which can be grown in Britain, that is to say, about 95% of the total.

THE USES OF WOOD

The invention of metal working, first in bronze, then in iron, profoundly influenced man's relation to the forest. The operation of smelting created a technical use for fuel, hitherto needed chiefly for domestic purposes. Improved cutting tools speeded up the clearing of forests and added immeasurably to the ease of wood utilization, since better tools meant easier shaping of wood into useful articles. This in turn created a heavier draft than ever upon the forest, particularly for the construction of dwellings, public buildings and ships. The advent of framed structures to replace laboriously built stonemasonry and perishable huts of mud and wattle or rushes and thatch marked a most significant contribution of the forest to human advancement.

It should be noted that rapid progress of the ceramic arts— glass, pottery, brick and tile manufacture—and of such simple chemical arts as brewing and the manufacture of lye and dyestuffs all called for an expansion in the use of fuel. But it was the invention of steel, an alloy of iron and carbon, which was most devastating to the forests of Europe. For this process charcoal was the essential source of carbon. Armament and empire went hand-in-hand and the age of Charlemagne is no more notable for its military exploits than for its wholesale destruction of forests for the manufacture of steel. An incidental, but important, by-product of such destruction has been the easier conquest and domestication of forest-dwelling tribes, thus deprived of their shelter.

ATTEMPTS TO COMPENSATE FOR THE STRONG INROADS ON THE FORESTS

There was, however, a conserving influence in the feudal military pattern. Forests were valued as hunting preserves for royalty and nobility. Thus the region of Avernus, which Virgil mentions as heavily forested, was later denuded except for the hunting preserves of the kings of Naples. Both on the Continent and in England the chief areas where forests were protected against the insatiable demand for charcoal and timber were those which, like the New Forest, were reserved for sport and recreation of the ruling class.

Meanwhile there was general ignorance of some of the less obvious functions of the forests, though Plato had linked the deforestation of the Grecian hills with the drying of the ancient springs. In 1609 Enrico Martinez stated that the washing of mud down into the Valley of Mexico and the danger of flood had been greatly increased by the destruction of forests and other plant cover on the highlands surrounding the basin. He referred to the hills as "descarnados," literally de-fleshed or stripped to the bone.

Scientific evidence as to the part played by forests in building and stabilizing the soil and regulating the flow of water is a product of fairly recent times and still incomplete. Although forested areas are obviously humid areas, their water economy becomes less efficient after clearing. It has been maintained by some authorities that the presence of forests actually increases rainfall.

This was at one time the subject of considerable debate between the United States Forest Service and the Weather Bureau. It was maintained by the former that evaporation from the forest makes an important contribution to rainfall farther inland. The weight of opinion seems to be now that the chief source of precipitation comes from the ocean. The relationship of forests to moisture, while of great importance, is less obvious and direct.

Delicate Relationship of Soils to Forests

The part played by forests in soil formation offers some peculiar problems, because forests, as we have said, generally occur in relatively moist regions. Here water supply and facilities for transportation may encourage heavy concentrations of population and rapid expansion of agriculture. However, the soil formed beneath forests tends to be much shallower than that in the grasslands and to be underlaid by leached mineral subsoil. It is generally acid as well. Such soil when cleared yields heavy crops for a few years, but unless it is handled with great skill, the rich, shallow top layer is easily destroyed by oxidation and erosion. When this happens, there is a rapid loss of fertility, leading to deterioration of farm economy or to costly programmes of fertilization.

On more level and sandy soils such cost may be offset by the nearness of good markets, but rougher lands become the site of submarginal farms or are abandoned to second-growth forest under conditions where forest management is often difficult. Closely connected with the fact that forest soils usually offer a narrower margin for agriculture is the circumstance that on many of the poorer soils trees constitute the most profitable crop under conditions of good management. An exception occurs on certain types of glacial soil, which are rich in minerals and can be restored by skilful management.

Soils in moist, tropical forest regions present an especially difficult problem. Here the thin humus layer is rapidly destroyed by exposure, while the heavy rains tend to dissolve out nutrient minerals. Owing to the high temperature, destructive bacterial action is very rapid once the protecting forest cover is removed. Some progress has been made in transforming these soils into well-managed tropical pasture lands.

However, because of the great variety of valuable products that can be obtained from tropical trees, it would seem that much more attention should be given to types of land use that depend upon the forest or upon skilful combination of tree crops with other crops, such as coffee, which can be grown in their shade.

The increasing pressure of world population in the temperate zones and the availability of extensive areas of tropical forest land make these problems especially important at this time.

Vital Relationship to Water

The value of forests in the protection of stream sources has long been recognized, whether tacitly or explicitly. The utility of the lower river basins in China and India is largely dependent upon the heavy forest cover in the vast mountain area that separates those two countries. The setting up of great public forest reserves in the United States has in view not only the future supply of timber but the protection of watersheds. This problem, however, has its complications.

While it is generally agreed that forested headwaters do regulate and conserve stream flow, it has been shown that, where a large volume of flow is required for domestic uses, the presence of cleared areas, suitably protected by vegetation, may materially increase the amount of water available for runoff and immediate use.

The Complex Problem of Fire

There is a similar complication in the relation of fire to forests. While fire, along with clearing and pests, remains a great destroyer of forest and must be combatted effectively, fire can also be a useful tool for the forester. It has been demonstrated that the prudent use of fire is an important means of maintaining and improving the Southern forests of longleaf pine in the United States. Certain valuable species, such as the lodgepole pine of the Rocky Mountains, require the heat of forest fires to release their seeds from the cones. While forest fires have always been occasioned by such natural causes as lightning or even volcanic eruptions, man causes most of the destructive fires of modern times. Much of this is due to carelessness.

On the other hand, much is a direct heritage from the ancient practice of clearing the forests by fire. In many places, notably in Africa and in the southern United States, this practice has become crystallized into popular ritual, the woods are fired regularly and the most diverse reasons are given for the practice, which is asserted to improve the grass for cattle and to control noxious insects and even human diseases. That it does "green up" the woods there can be no doubt, but the best of woods pasture is very inferior to the best-managed grass and legume pasture.

Insect and Fungus Damage

Destructive as fire is at the present time, insects and fungus pests are more so. It is possible that danger from these sources has been intensified by breaking the continuity of the great forests that once covered the eastern part of the American continent. There is, however, abundant evidence that, even under natural conditions, forests were constantly subjected to violent disturbances by many natural forces, notably high wind as well as fire and pests.

Effect of Types of Ownership

The pattern of forest ownership has changed during the course of history and still varies according to the prevailing conception of property rights. Thus the American Indian had no sense of private property in the forests, although a general group priority for hunting and other purposes was recognized. In the tropical islands of the South Pacific, the ownership of coconut palms is recognized and allocated and during World War II military personnel who might become lost and forced to forage for food were advised to leave chits for the coconuts on certain islands, so that recompense could be made to the proper owner.

In the eastern Mediterranean area, the ownership of single olive trees may be shared, each owner claiming a certain sector, thus greatly complicating the business of improved orchard management. In Mexico the right of private exploitation of forests may be bestowed by concession and the laws against illegal felling of large trees are strict. However, it is the custom of the natives to cut out portions of the living tree for firewood bit by bit until it falls, when it becomes the property of anyone who can salvage it.

In parts of western Europe, in addition to public forests there are extensive private holdings. These, however, are subject to strict regulations as to management, which make government, in effect, a responsible party in the enterprise. In North America, in spite of the extensive reservation of government forests, the bulk of forest land is under private ownership. Until recently this has led to ruthless exploitation—a tendency now being reversed, especially in the case of large corporate owners who see the importance of a continuing supply of timber.

Because of the long period required for the maturity of harvestable timber and the frequent pressure upon private owners to raise immediate funds, private ownership of the bulk of woodlands poses difficult and challenging economic problems. The ratio of labour costs to the value of the wood and other forest products likewise must be considered. The European peasant does not hesitate to gather faggots or bundles of twigs for fuel. On the other hand, at the present time in the United States, it is often difficult to find anyone to cut cull trees, even though given the wood for sale as fuel.

Changing Uses of Forest Products

In the days of wooden sailing ships the possession of adequate forest supplies was a major factor in naval power. Oak and cypress and, in particular, tall, straight mast timbers were essential. So were framing timbers for houses, until structural steel became available. At first it would seem that with the development of metal and other structural materials the pressure on forests would be less. The contrary is the case. Not only does wood still have many technical functions in our civilization, but the variety of uses for which it is indispensable is increasing.

The great field of plastics, instead of lessening the demand for wood, has augmented it, since cellulose is a necessary ingredient in many plastics. Likewise, the insatiable demand for paper of all kinds has enlarged rather than decreased the need for wood. Thanks to technological progress, many kinds of wood which were formerly worthless for that purpose can now be used for pulp.

An interesting if minor example of the irreplaceable properties of wood is found among the Eskimos. The willow wood, which is the chief kind available to them, cannot by itself be made into bows, but when laminated with other materials lends itself well to such use. Consequently the Eskimo, before the days of firearms, traveled long distances to get supplies of this otherwise not very useful wood.

A significant phase of the use of wood in technology is afforded by the changing industrial picture due to the growing scarcity of wood. The ornate and tasteless architecture of the early post-Civil War period was closely related to the fact that at that time the white pine forests of Wisconsin and Michigan were being rapidly exploited. Under the compulsion to find markets the timber industry actually did a great deal, through the distribution of architectural plans, to promote the extravagant use of wood.

The notable severity of more modern designs, while partly traceable to an improvement in public taste, can be related as well to the increasing scarcity of a once abundant building material. Communities which supported great planing and cabinet mills in the days of abundant forests lost them, sometimes without understanding why, when raw materials became scarce. These mills were replaced by factories using smalldimension materials for boxes, handles, staves and hoops—until even the steady supply of small and inferior lumber was exhausted.

Exacting Demands for Wood on Forest Resources

So great is the continuing pressure on forest resources today that, wherever transportation is available, cutting rather generally exceeds the annual increment of merchantable timber. Reserves exist chiefly where distance or topography renders them difficult of access. Vast tropical areas of forest exist, but present their own peculiar problems.

Toward the equator, the number of species in the forest community increases rapidly, so that one encounters not merely the problems of dense growth and of difficult access, but mixtures of many kinds of trees within the same small area. These trees differ so much among themselves in physical properties that profitable mass harvesting is far less simple than in more temperate regions. Because of this, the tropical forests must be harvested, if at all, for widely differing purposes.

Among the more hopeful approaches that are being made to this problem are experiments in the manufacture of tropical plywood, in which woods of very different textures, densities and strengths can be satisfactorily combined. In any event, the harvesting of tropical timbers on a wide scale is likely to occur in the near future. Whether this will be done with more thought to a continuing supply than has been the case in temperate regions remains to be seen. A sensible world economy would certainly require it. Lumber is, of course, but one of many forest products. The heaviest use of wood, the world over, is still for fuel. In underdeveloped countries or regions where coal is lacking, much of this tree fuel is in the form of charcoal, a far more compact source of energy than the untreated wood and one which frequently affords twice the heat value. However, much of this charcoal is prepared by primitive and wasteful methods which do not conserve the various valuable distillates produced in the charring process.

In addition to lumber, fuel and pulp for paper and plastics, enormous amounts of wood are required for such special products as excelsior, matches, spools, tool handles and the like. Forests are also important sources of raw materials for the chemical industry. Native rubber, resins, gums, oils, dyes, drugs and aromatics belong in this category. While many of them can be produced in artificial plantations, the cheapness of labour and land in tropical forest areas makes the wild product a significant factor in the world market. Anyone familiar with the food habits of primitive forest dwellers knows that there are considerable possibilities for sustenance from this source It is estimated that the coconut palm alone has several hundred technical uses among native peoples, apart from the obvious one of food.

Manifold Possibilities for Wood Utilization

One of the most intriguing phases of forest utilization lies in the rare and unique qualities possessed by certain woods for particular, highly specialized purposes. The instances that could be cited are legion, including, for example: tough, straight-grained ash for medieval lances and modern tool handles; butter-like pearwood for exquisite carvings such as those of Grinling Gibbons; end grain ivory-like box for wood engraving; unsplittable lignum vitae and gum for mallets, house rollers and bowling balls; bitter quassia, which imparts its flavour and medicinal qualities to water placed in bowls of this material; teak and cypress, so valuable for the decking of ships; dogwood for "glats" or wedges, used in splitting rails and firewood in the days when steel was scarcer than now—and so on.

Although such uses, like the uses of medicinal and food plants, were discovered before the days of modern science, it is of interest to note that the rich variety of tropical woods is now being re-explored in laboratories-as for example at Yale-in the hope of finding substitutes for the ever scarcer woods of familiar commerce, as well as of finding uses that are quite new.

Vast Implications of the Forest for Human Culture

The significance of forests to mankind goes far deeper than economic utility, whether direct, as in the case of usable forest products, or indirect, as in that of watershed protection. Forests have a powerful, though often intricate, relation to the more intangible aspects of human life.

That forests give aesthetic pleasure needs no particular emphasis. Poets and artists have made this clear enough. More is involved, however, than the simple fact that forests can delight the eye and gratify the body with their cooling shelter. At least one of Lincoln's biographers has intimated that the melancholy of that great man was partly a product of the gloom and shadow of the forest that helped condition his childhood. This may be pure guess, but there is no doubt that a prolonged stay in the tall twilight of the Engelmann spruce of the High Rockies induces a mood that is vastly relieved when one descends from them and emerges into the foothills to look out over the broad expanse of sunlit plain.

The violent deforestation of the Mexican uplands following the Spanish Conquest was accomplished by axe and fire and consolidated by goats and other cattle brought from Europe. But there is testimony that the destruction was swifter than it might have been because of the Spanish craving for a landscape resembling that of their own treeless homeland. Forgetting alike that much of the poverty of the Spanish peninsula was due to its having been deforested and overgrazed and that much of the wealth that remained was due to tree crops such as cork, olive and citrus fruits, the conquerors allowed themselves to repeat ancient and costly errors.

If the forest, by presence or absence, can be so deeply involved in the human emotions, it is not surprising to find it likewise involved in religious symbolism and practice. Worn, but still beautiful, is the line "the groves were God's first temples." Even though the Judaeo-Christian tradition stems from pastoral lands, its literature is rich in symbolism connected with the forest—the tree of life, the tree of the knowledge of good and evil, the wooden Cross itself.

The use of wood in altar sacrifice, the hearth as a symbol of home and worship and ashes of wood in the ceremony of grief and repentance, are all familiar and ancient.

Among the Greeks not only forests, but also individual trees, were personified as the dwelling places of god and demigod. In the Orient, crowded for living space as it is, groves surround the temples and it is believed that it was in such groves that the living fossil, the ginkgo tree, now so much valued for its beauty in this country, was preserved from extinction.

In the Druidic worship of western Europe, as also in the robust Thor worship of the ancient Norsemen, the forest played an intrinsic part. The mistletoe was sacred in both-with a shaft of mistletoe the gentle Freya was killed by the mischievous Loki. Our use of Christmas greens and trees stems from the ancient Teutonic festivals that brightened the season of long night, during which we celebrate the birth of Christ.

Even the mood of gloom and depression that the deep shadow of the forest may induce is akin to the feeling of awe and reverence. This the primeval forest clearly inspired among the ancients-as it continues to do today—an effect not only evident in religious belief, but in the inseparable fields of poetry, music and art.

NON-TIMBER FOREST PRODUCTS IN THE STATE ECONOMY

Historically, the trend of using forests as a source of revenue was a part of colonial policy. When land tax could not be raised any further, forest was taken as an alternate source for exploitation with impunity. As a result, the revenue exploitation policy measure led to deforestation. Unfortunately today, depletion of forest cover is attributable to relentless pressures arising from ever-increasing demand for fuelwood, fodder, small timber etc, inadequacy of protection measures, diversion of forestland to non-forest uses without ensuring complementary afforestation and essential environmental safeguards, and more importantly, the tendency to look upon forests as a revenue earning resource instead of a livelihood resource of the forest-dependent poor. Orissa has rich potential of various NTFPs, besides timber. Therefore, Orissa forests are important source of non-tax revenue. An overview of the annual revenue incurred from timber and fuelwood, varieties of NTFPs (including sal seed) bamboo, kendu leaf suggests that revenue earnings from timber has registered a sharp decline from 42.4 per cent in 1985-86 to 5.23 per cent (of total forest revenue) in 1999-2000. This is how our timber – oriented forest management policy strategy performed during last one and half decades. A similar decline also in fuelwood, NTFPs and bamboo does not exclusively attribute to fast depletion of forest cover over years.

Because, bulk of fuelwood, various NTFPs, small timber, fodder etc are used/ consumed by the forest dwellers, and some are sold in the local markets, which are not computed in the state's revenue income.

Faulty NTFP policy on collection, trade and disposal, processing and value addition, stringent forest laws, State control over trade, obsolete forest Acts and regulations, lack of pluckers friendly policies, revenue friendly policy strategy as well as sustainable management strategy, disorganised trade, informal as well as unstructured market conditions, the recent emerging community management restrictions etc prevent the primary gatherers in varieties of ways, resulting in forest potentials to remain un-exploited both from the accessible as well as inaccessible areas.

Of all, forest products, kendu leaf trade appears to be very lucrative, and registers a steady increase in terms of revenue from 26.8 per cent in 1985-86 to 78.1 per cent in 1999-2000 of the total forest revenue. Though kendu leaf production potential in the State is around 7 lakh quintals, its production over years has not increased substantially (not exceeded 5 lakh quintals) due to lack of an aggressive trade policy, lack of investible funds, restricted market avenues in and outside the State, and possibly due to the State control over kendu leaf trade.

NATIONALISED PRODUCTS

As regards all nationalised products; such as, kendu leaf, bamboo and sal seed, the meagre revenue are specifically on account of:

- Hindrances to volume of trade with the reduction in the number of legal buyers that prevents free flow of goods, and delays payments to the gatherers.
- Non-payment of legitimate dues to the primary kendu leaf collectors in time and wages to the labourers in bush-cutting areas.
- State monopoly control through OFDC and TDCC, the government has created private monopolies (which seem to be illegal and arbitrary, since no tenders were invited before bestowing monopolistic rights on UFP Ltd)
- Un-remunerative piece meal basis wages to labourers engaged in drying and storing and also to the binders,

- As compared to Andhra Pradesh, Orissa leaves are of better quality, - yet pluckers get lower wages.
- Lack of adequate competition among the auction holders (insiders and outsiders forming secret cartel) at the sales centre resulting in lower auction price, - thus, meagre revenue from such trade, and also stocks get piled up for years due to timely non-disposal.
- Absence of value addition activities/processing due to limited beedi manufacturing companies in the state at the private level (not any at the initiative of the government), and also absence of beedi manufacturing industries.
- Lack of regular market studies before market strategies are drawn, and also no aggressive trade practice followed so far.
- Absence of a policy strategy that could make kendu leaf trade commercially viable
- Lack of pluckers' friendly strategy for ensuring lesser harassment, mandatory purchases against instant payments at the phadi houses, insurance cover of the pluckers and grant of bonus like Madhya Pradesh – no sharing of royalty with pluckers – no group insurance scheme etc.
- Major institutions like OFDC and TDCC (confronted with growing liabilities, overstaff,) have been massive failures in trading activities.
- Exploitation of bamboo cutters by OFDC as well as Paper Mills.
- Migration of bamboo cutters to neighbouring States in search of jobs
- Apathetic attitudes of Paper Mill owners towards the bamboo cutters
- Absence of welfare measures in favour of bamboo cutters, and also non-provision of bamboos to local artisans at the concessional rates.
- Frequent changes in the policy concerning sal seed with respect to procuring agencies, and lack of availability of investible funds in time for procurement.
- Lack of transport facilities, timely purchase, dissemination of government declared price of the nationalised products to the grassroots level at the right time.

FOREST LAWS AND REGULATIONS

Indeed, a number of forest laws and regulations in Orissa have been identified as major hurdles in NTFP trade. Some of these pertain to issues related to ownership rights over forestlands and produce, accessibility, forms of disposal, processing and value addition, marketing arrangements as well as procurement and price fixation etc. Absence of adequate attention to marketing infrastructure also has resulted in the under utilisation of existing forest potential in the State.

Precisely, some of the existing forest laws and provision in the Acts that have influenced the efficiency of procurement, marketing and processing/value addition are:

- Schedule of Rate for Forest Produce in Orissa, 1977
- Supply of bamboo to artisans including Co-operative Societies, Orissa Rules, 1980
- Orissa Timber and Other Forest Produce Transit Rules 1980
- Orissa Forest (Control and Trade) Product Act 1981, and
- Orissa Forest (Control and Trade) Rules 1983.

The following are some of the factors responsible for the failure of NTFP trade in Orissa to contribute substantial revenue to the State exchequer:

- Procurement prices declared by the Price Fixation Committee at the State/district level are not in tune with market conditions.
- Non-recognition and non-inclusion of labour costs pertaining to identifying, drying, sorting, grading and chain of other economic activities including primary processing result in lower collections from inaccessible and difficult terrains.
- Absence of Women Tribal-Co-operative Societies or large number of women organisations undermine the role of tribal women in NTFP collection, processing as well as marketing jeopardising revenue to the State.
- The Orissa Kendu Leaf (control and Trade) Act and the Orissa Forest Produce (Control and Trade) Act 1981 and so also, OFC (Control and Trade) Rules 1983 pose threats to livelihood sustenance of primary gatherers in varieties of ways.

Stringent restrictions on the marketability of certain products like kendu leaf, mahua flower on the private lands (as per provisions in the Act) have created and encouraged illegal and unfair trade practices.

- Certain provisions in the Forest Acts and the subsequent amendments to these in 1987 are not only contradictory, but also confusing. However, due to nationalisation in 1983, the grant of permissions to private parties for sal seed collection have violated the basic norms of nationalisation.
- Provisions in forest laws, and so also the regulations to check marketing of various NTFPs, kendu leaf, mahua flower, salseed etc are inadequate, obsolete and inappropriate, since these do not ensure sustainable management of forest produce, revenue interest of the state exchequer and welfare interests of the primary gatherers.

A close scrutiny of the political economy of NTFP management in Orissa suggests that the economic, ecological/environmental sustainability considerations have not only been undermined, but also have been overshadowed by the political ideology of different political parties in governance over the years resulting in inappropriate and unrealistic policies and actions. The policy strategies and marketing infrastructure have proved inadequate and inappropriate. Most of the major NTFPs have numerous alternative markets, besides those agencies/institutions recognised by the Government of Orissa by the Forest Acts from time to time.

In practice however, the State policy and revenue earning strategy/ mechanism have proved suicidal to State's own interest. The best examples of this are mahua seed and tamarind which have monopolistic buyers, who offer lower prices for these products compared to alternative market agencies operating within the State and across the borders. The high prices in the neighbouring States for such products have resulted in significant outflow of these to neighbouring states. Evidently, in Bihar and Madhya Pradesh taxes and levies on mahua flower (*madhuca indica*) and Tamarind (*tamarindus indicus*) are lower. In such a situation, higher taxes and duties in Orissa have not only affected the livelihood of primary collectors adversely, but have also provided wider scope for smuggling their products in the nearby informal markets across the border. This issue of differential prices of the NTFPs across neighbouring States has proved detrimental to Orissa. Therefore, lower prices and lack of incentives have adversely affected revenue prospects in Orissa despite nationalisation. In a historic policy resolution on 31st March 2000, (Vide No.5503/F&E) the Government of Orissa decided to grant 68 NTFPs to Gram Panchayats (GPs) in the scheduled areas in terms of ownership and control in order to make procurement, processing and marketing at the Panchayat level so as to benefit the primary gatherers in a big way. But in the non-scheduled areas, the GPs were granted control (ownership is not vested) over procurement, processing and marketing of NTFP, so as to ensure greater benefits to the forest dwellers. But, no GP, whether situated within or outside the scheduled are a will have ownership over NTFP produced in R.F, forest areas under Wildlife Sanctuaries and National Parks, which are outside the limits of revenue villages. Thus, GPs do not have the right to grant lease/license to any individual or agency for collection of NTFPs from RF and National Parks. Such a policy decision is no doubt a legend in the history of management of precious forest resource. More importantly, the provision of control of natural resource by the grassroots level democratic body (GP) could not only effectively ensure sustainability of the resource use, but also could adequately take case of the livelihood interests of the primary gatherers.

But, whether GPs (burdened with varieties of rural development activities) with poor infrastructure, scarce investible funds, lack of commercial expertise could really regulate and manage procurement and trade of NTFPs effectively to benefit the poor gatherers is a moot point. However, with a view to empowering the GPs to regulate the procurement and trade of NTFPs effectively and providing a sound and effective legal framework for implementing the scheme of delegation of powers and functions (with respect to NTFPs) to

GPs, the Government of Orissa also have proposed to formulate a set of Rules under the Orissa Gram Panchayat Act, besides amending the existing Orissa Timber and Other Forest Produce Transit Rules, 1980.

Further, pending such legal changes delegating to the GPs, the Government have also decided to delegate the District Collector of each district to fix the minimum procurement prices of 68 NTFPs (enlisted for regulation by the GPs). The minimum procurement prices fixed at the district level should be given wide publicity and the GPs, Panchayat Samitis and Zilla Parishads are required to be informed accordingly for ensuring greater benefits to the primary gatherers (Government of Orissa Resolution no 16467/F&E,dt12,Oct 2001).

ROTATION OF TIMBER HARVEST

FIRE ROTATION

Whereas previously we have considered the problem of optimal rotation of timber harvesting while accounting for non-timber amenity values, now we consider an alternative rotation scheme. This involves the use of fire to maximize the persistence of endangered species whose populations peak in a midsuccessional stage of a forest ecosystem, much as the wild turkey and grouse in the previous discussion. One such example is eastern bristlebirds in the U.S. (Pyke, Saillard, and Smith, 1995) with Johnson (1992) and Whelan (1995) providing more extended discussions and cases. Stochastic dynamic programming has been used to study optimal fire rotation systems by Possingham and Tuck (1997) and by Clark and Mangel (2000). Clark and Mangel consider an endangered population wherein habitat quality is given by q(t) since the time of the last fire, r is the litter size, s_a is the probability that an adult survives in the absence of fire, s_j is the probability that a juvenile survives in the absence of fire, and N(t) is the adult population in time t since a fire. The population equation after a fire then becomes $N(t+1) = [s_a + s_j rq(t)]N(t)$.

Letting $r = 2$, $s_a = 0.7$, $s_j = 2$, with q(t) reaching a maximum between five and ten years, Clark and Mangel (p. 178) find the trajectory of average population to follow that shown in Figure below. Letting a fitness parameter, f, be the percent of the population (both adult and juvenile) that survives a burn, and letting $f = 0.8$, Clark and Mangel study a case over time of 20 years and population that reaches a maximum of 50 but which must kept at least as great as 3. They compute at each time t the maximum probability of the survival of the species based on starting a fire or not starting a fire for a given population size. Their solution is depicted in Figure below, which divides the time-population space into zones of starting a fire or not starting a fire.

FIRE ROTATION AND MANAGEMENT

The problem of fire rotation and management has become highly controversial among forest managers within the United States, with the issues going well beyond those of preserving endangered species and involving the costs of the fires themselves and their degree of general destructiveness. Muradian (2001) argues that the relationship between fire frequency and vegetative density is one of multiple states, allowing for the possible of catastrophic dynamics. This follows rather closely the argument of Holling (1973) regarding the tradeoff between resilience and stability. Thus, traditionally policy in the U.S. was to attempt to fight all fires that appeared on national forest or park lands. However, the truly catastrophic fires that have broken out in several national parks, most famously in Yellowstone Park during the 1990s, have made policymakers aware that not allowing any fires at all leads to a dangerous accumulation of underbrush and dead branches and trunks that can lead to a much greater fire when one finally breaks out. The short term stability of fighting all fires leads to the longer term decline in resilience of the forest to catastrophic fire. So a new policy of actively starting fires to maintain resiliency in the forests has been adopted, although this has also become controversial since one of these got out of control in Arizona and ended up destroying property.

Pest Management

Holling (1965, 1973) initially posed his hypothesis mentioned above after contemplating the dynamics of spruce-budworm outbreaks in western Canadian coniferous forests. Such outbreaks occur in a fairly regular pattern approximately every 40 years or so. Among those looking at this have included May (1977), Ludwig, Jones, and Holling (1978), with Casti (1989) and Rosser (1991) putting the argument into an explicit context of catastrophe theory. What is involved is essentially a three-level predator-prey model, with the budworms feeding on the tree leaves, which grow larger as the trees grow larger, and migratory birds limiting the budworm population by preying on them. The trigger mechanism for the periodic outbreak is that there is an upper limit to the ability of the birds to concentrate in the trees, while the budworms can keep increasing with the leaf size. So, as the bird population becomes limited at a crucial level, they cease being able to limit the budworms which then break out into a rapid increase that in turn triggers a crash in the tree population and thus also a subsequent crash in the budworm population.

This set of solutions is depicted in Figure below, with the zone of multiple equilibria and associated catastrophic hysteresis loops being that of an infected forest. Holling in particular (1986) has discussed at length policy responses to this problem. Whereas many policymakers are inclined to spray the budworms, this tends to happen to late in the cycle. When they have become visible they are already in the epidemic phase and spraying simply holds the system in that very unstable state. Holling focuses on the larger system, especially the idea of encouraging greater bird population to constrain the budworms. This led him to consideration of how events at great distances might affect the system, *e.g.* how a failure to maintain wetlands in the U.S. that are used by the birds when they migrate might trigger an outbreak of the budworms by reducing the bird population below a critical size. For Holling this was example represents the very essence of "local surprise and global change" in ecosystems.

Patch Size Management

Finally let us consider the problem of the size of cut areas in forests, which is closely related to the sizes of patches within forests. It has long been known that timber harvesters prefer to harvest by cutting large clearcuts that are then replanted with a single species of all the same age. This is the least expensive method of harvesting for a pure lumber producer unconcerned about any other amenity values of the forest. However, it is known that large clearcuts can reduce the maximum size of patches in a forest and that the survival of species may depend on there being sufficiently large patches to sustain the more fragile species. More particularly it has been argued that there is a nonlinear relationship between habitat destruction (or fragmentation) and largest patch size. Below a certain threshold of patch size there is a relative sudden collapse of population for the fragile species.

The basic situation involved here. It combines figures found in the above references with the private cost of timber harvesting. The horizontal axis represents the size of the cuts and the vertical axis represents quantities of value units, assuming these can be estimated for the species affected by the timber harvesting. Line A represents the benefits per forest of not cutting at a certain scale, the value of the species preserved at that scale of patch-size of cutting, which shows the nonlinear and catastrophically dropping off aspect. Line B shows the private costs of timber harvesting per forest, which steadily decline with the size of the cut. Clearly there is a zone of sizes where it would be socially superior to cut although these would entail higher costs for the private timber harvester. Unsurprisingly this issue is one that continues to be very controversial in forestry management.

We have reviewed a variety of complex ecological-economic problems associated with dynamically managing forests around the world. Needless to say we have barely scratched the surface of these issues and it must be noted that we have mostly dealt with fairly stylized cases or specific examples. Many cases and situations may appear to be very different from the ideas presented here. We must also note that we have largely avoided any detailed discussion of issues arising from conflicts or ambiguities about property rights or access, although these are very serious matters in the traditional communities living in the tropical rain forests, and are also issues even in the temperate forests in the more high income countries such as Canada and the United States. We began by reviewing the basic literature on optimal rotation of a forest being harvested solely for timber use, resulting in the Faustmann solution. This was modified by considering the analysis of Hartman, which allows for accounting for non-timber amenities of the forest, including grazing, hunting, fishing, recreation, social values of traditional communities, carbon sequestration, and more general existence and aesthetic values. A central issue involves the fact that these other amenities may exhibit complicated time patterns over the life of a forest that do not correspond directly with the growth rate of the trees, the factor that underlies decisionmaking about timber harvesting by a private owner for whom timber is the sole value of interest. This leads to the possibility of multiple equilibria and considerable dynamic complications. These complications have led to great difficulties for actual decisionmakers responsible for the management of forests that have multiple uses, as in the national forests of the United States.

We also considered a further set of management issues, notably fire rotation, pest management, and patch size management in regard to the size of cuts made during timber harvesting. In all of these cases the presence of nonlinearities and discontinuities impose heightened difficulties for forest managers. The presence of critical thresholds in all of these cases is a pervasive phenomenon, and one that poses deep problems not easily solved. Although we did not examine cases involving chaotic or other more erratic dynamics in forestry management, such phenomena are possible. However they would tend to operate over relatively long time scales, unlike for much shorter-lived biological populations. For forests the more dramatic and compelling problems arise from the discontinuities that are studied more by catastrophe theory, collapses of species populations, sudden collapses of entire ecosystems due to fire or outbreaks of pests, or the more insidious damage of badly managed or timed timber harvesting. Dealing with these problems will challenge forest managers for the foreseeable future.

12

Forests Ecosystem and Environment

TERM OF ECOSYSTEM

A system is a group of parts that interact through one or more processes. The term ecosystem was introduced and defined by Tansley (1935), who as "a fundamental organizational unit of the natural world that includes both organisms and their spatial environment." Ecosystems have since been defined in various ways, and at different spatial and temporal scales. Some ecologists define ecosystems on the basis of biotic organisms, populations, or communities. For example, Hutchinson (1978) considered the ecosystem to be the environmental context in which population or community dynamics occur. Others define ecosystems in terms of their abiotic characteristics and processes. For example, Lindeman (1942) defined ecosystems as "...the system composed of physical, chemical, and biological processes active within a space/time unit." Regardless of whether the emphasis is on biotic components or abiotic characteristics and processes of ecosystems, both remain integral to the concept of ecosystem. Rowe (1961) emphasized this when he defined ecosystems as "...a three dimensional segment of the earth where life forms and the environment interact."

Wetland ecosystems have been defined in a variety of ways by researchers, resource managers, and regulatory authorities, depending on their specific needs and objectives. In the applied world of regulation, planning, and management, wetlands are usually defined in terms of their physical, chemical, and biological characteristics such as hydrologic regime, soil type, and plant species composition. For example, in classifying wetlands for mapping, inventory, and other purposes, Cowardin *et al.* (1979) defined wetlands as "...lands transitional between terrestrial and aquatic systems where the water table is usually at or near the surface or the land is covered by shallow water..." that are characterized by the presence of hydrophytic vegetation, hydric soils, and surface water during the growing season. Wetlands are often biodiversity 'hotspots', as well as functioning as filters for pollutants from both point and non-point sources, and being important for carbon sequestration and emissions.

The value of the world's wetlands are increasingly receiving due attention as they contribute to a healthy environment in many ways. Wetland functions are defined as the normal or characteristic activities that take place in wetland ecosystems or simply the things that wetlands do. Wetlands perform a wide variety of functions in a hierarchy from simple to complex as a result of their physical, chemical, and biological attributes. For example, the reduction of nitrate to gaseous nitrogen is a relatively simple function performed by wetlands when aerobic and anaerobic conditions exist in the presence of denitrifying bacteria. Nitrogen cycling and nutrient cycling represent increasingly more complex wetland functions that involve a greater number of structural components and processes. At the highest level of this hierarchy is the maintenance of ecological integrity, the function that encompasses all of the structural components and processes in a wetland ecosystem. Wetlands are one of the most productive of all ecosystems, and carry out critical regulatory functions of hydrological processes within watersheds. Regulating water quality, water levels, flooding regimes, and nutrient and sedimentation levels are a few of these processes. As with any natural habitat, wetlands are important in supporting species diversity and have a complex of wetland values. Moreover, the pattern of seasonal variation of the wetland affects the bird population fluctuation. Even small wetlands are extremely important to the conservation of biodiversity because they provide critical breeding habitat where dispersed populations can exchange genetic material, reducing the risks of extinction.

The present review is aimed at providing in a nutshell, the distribution of wetlands, the value of Wetlands, the causes and consequences of the loss of wetlands and their conservation status with special reference to India.

Management of Ecosystem

Practical ecosystem management usually involves maintaining a natural or artificial homeostasis in which the end product is of benefit to man, and in which violent or pathologic imbalances can be controlled. An example of a natural ecosystem which man might wish to maintain for esthetic or recreational value would be a wilderness area or National Park. Here the most important consideration is to insure that natural processes are permitted to continue. In a forest this would mean, for example, that fire, if already a natural part of the ecosystem, be permitted to occur at natural frequency and intensity.

Several recent studies have shown that certain forests depend upon intermittent burning to recycle nutrients and minerals. In the lowland conifer forests of Alaska, if fire is excluded a thick carpet of moss may accumulate and raise the permafrost level. This encourages the growth of black spruce, a species with little food or timber value. Browsing animals such as deer, moose and bear cannot survive on black spruce. They depend on the Tarai fires to maintain a suitable cycle of vegetation. Many foresters now feel that the underbrush and leaf litter in the Ponderosa pine forests of western United States should be removed by light ground fires every few years to maintain soil fertility, to prevent excessive accumulation of organic matter in the form of cellulose and also to prevent more devastating fires that destroy the entire forest.

In the pine forests of the South, very efficient fire suppression techniques allowed dangerous accumulation of combustible materials, and a pine fungus disease was favoured in the accumulated litter. In all of these forests, proper management should not exclude all fires, but should prevent totally devastating fires. These examples illustrate the need for understanding natural processes in ecosystems in order to maintain them properly.

The Everglades of Florida provide another example of the importance of understanding natural ecosystem processes before the system can be properly managed or maintained. The unique flora and fauna of the Everglades depends upon the proper balance of fresh and saline water flowing through its channels. If a significant decline in fresh water input occurs, as has been taking place due to the diversion of fresh water to the growing megalopolis of Miami, numerous important species of plants and animals may die and the characteristic features of the system may be destroyed. In times of drought, many animals depend upon alligator wallows as a source of water. These are pools hollowed out by alligators, and they tend to retain water longer than other parts of the swamp. If alligators decline through shooting or any other.

It is increasingly important to understand the dynamics of ecosystem, their patterns of succession and evolution, and their patterns of succession and evolution, and their patterns of diversity and stability. E.P. Odum has written a major review of these topics and has shown that ecosystem may be characterized as pioneer, developmental and mature. Various stages within this continuum possess certain properties of production, respiration, community structure, nutrient cycling, homeostasis, etc. For example, young developmental stages of an ecosystem tend to have greater gross production in relation to respiration, but lower species diversity and less stability than mature stages.

Thus, developmental stage to be favoured in agricultural practice, but they are also more vulnerable to ecologic damage or catastrophe. We will explore these relationships in more detail throughout subsequent chapters after various components of the ecosystem are considered seperately, diversity and stability. E.P. Odum has written a major review of these topics and has shown that ecosystem may be characterized as pioneer, developmental and mature.

Various stages within this continuum possess certain properties of production, respiration, community structure, nutrient cycling, homeostasis, etc. For example, young developmental stages of an ecosystem tend to have greater gross production in relation to respiration, but lower species diversity and less stability than mature stages. Thus, developmental stage to be favoured in agricultural practice, but they are also more vulnerable to ecologic damage or catastrophe. We will explore these relationships in more detail throughout subsequent chapters after various components of the ecosystem are considered seperately.

Water and Forested Ecosystems

Ecologists consider water to be the defining part in an ecosystem, including the forest ecosystem. Water shapes the physical landscape through erosion Undulating forest surrounds meadows, lakes, and rivers of the Charlevoix Conservation Area, a coastal watershed in Quebec, Canada. This region, which illustrates a high-quality forested watershed, has been designated a biosphere by the United Nations Educational, Scientific and Cultural Organization (UNESCO). and deposition. It also shapes the biological parts of the ecosystem by its presence or absence; its quantity and quality; and its occurrence and distribution. The water cycle plays a key role in ecosystem functions and processes. Forests, in turn, are vital to the water cycle and to water quality. In essence, the forest acts like a giant sponge, filtering and recycling water. Approximately 80 per cent of U.S. fresh-water resources are estimated to originate in forests, which cover one-third of the U.S. land area.

Tree leaves intercept water from rain, snow, and fog; the leaves also release water back to the atmosphere by evapotranspiration. Tree roots extract water from the soil while helping hold the soil in place. Forested land reduces the surface impact of falling rain through interception and delay of water reaching the surface. Forestland also decreases the amount and velocity of storm runoff over the land surface. This in turn increases the amount of water that soaks into the ground, a portion of which can ultimately recharge underlying aquifers. Conversely, water from hydraulically connected surficial aquifers may enter streams and wetlands, helping to maintain their water levels during dry periods.

Forests and the Hydrologic Cycle

The surface water in a stream, lake, or wetland is most commonly precipitation that has run off the land or flowed through topsoils to subsequently enter the waterbody. If a surficial aquifer is present and hydraulically connected to a surface-water body, the aquifer can sustain surface flow by releasing water to it. In general, a heavy rainfall causes a temporary and relatively rapid increase in streamflow due to surface runoff. This increased flow is followed by a relatively slow decline back to baseflow, which is the amount of streamflow derived largely or entirely from groundwater.

During long dry spells, streams with a baseflow component will keep flowing, whereas streams relying totally on precipitation will cease flowing. Generally speaking, a natural, expansive forest environment can enhance and sustain relationships in the water cycle because there are less human modifications to interfere with its components. A forested watershed helps moderate storm flows by increasing infiltration and reducing overland runoff. Further, a forest helps sustain streamflow by reducing evaporation (*e.g.*, owing to slightly lower temperatures in shaded areas). Forests can help increase recharge to aquifers by allowing more precipitation to infiltrate the soil, as opposed to rapidly running off the land to a downslope area.

Riparian Areas

The riparian zone is broadly defined as the area between a body of water and the upland parts of the landscape that are rarely flooded except under the most extreme conditions. But the term also can refer more specifically to the immediate streamside area. Riparian areas represent less than 10 per cent of most forest ecosystems, yet these areas often are the most productive portions. Compared to upland regions, riparian areas have more water available; the vegetation is more robust; the soils are deeper; the timber often is of higher quality; and the waterbodies have more shade. The riparian zone also may include wetlands bordering streams and lakes. This combination of factors makes riparian areas among the most heavily used portions of a forest. Riparian and wetland areas provide abundant and reliable forage for wildlife, as well as transportation corridors. They also may receive heavy human use for recreation.

Riparian zones also are attractive destinations for logging and for livestock grazing; as a result, riparian areas in forests are sometimes heavily damaged, especially in the forests of the arid American Southwest. Fortunately, riparian areas respond well to good management practices.

Aquatic Biodiversity

Forest lands and waters are vitally important in maintaining biodiversity and providing habitat for fish and wildlife, including threatened or endangered aquatic species. In the United States, over one-third of national forest lands are critical for maintaining aquatic biodiversity and protection of listed species. For aquatic species, watersheds provide the basic unit of any conservation strategy. Many watersheds also contain isolated habitats with unique characteristics producing a high potential for rare species. Some species occur only near a single spring or in a single stream within a given watershed. Lands set aside to protect these unique habitats also benefit the entire watershed and its ecosystem.

Biological Diversity Conservation Functions

There is no strict divide between "wild" and "domesticated" species important for food and livelihoods. Many wild plant species and populations that have been considered to be wild are in fact carefully nurtured by people. A similar continuum exists for animal species that use agroecosystems as habitat, nesting grounds and food. Whilst not necessarily the subject of conscious management by herders or farmers, many wild species thrive in, or are dependent on, agroecosystems. In general the more structurally and biologically complex the agroecosystems, the more diverse the forms of wildlife. For example:

- The systems of shifting cultivation common in Asia have long been considered to be damaging to biological diversity in particular. However, given the opportunity, shifting cultivators preserve wild resources. Studies in Asia have concluded that most of the mature forests in this region are not virgin forests, but merely old forests that have reached a relatively stable dynamic state after some earlier clearing by human or natural means. Under traditional systems of shifting cultivation which speed up natural succession, wildlife flourishes, with elephants, wild cattle, deer, and wild pigs all feeding in the abandoned fields. Tigers, leopards and other predators are in turn attracted by the herbivores. Older fields contain a high proportion of fruit trees that attract primates, hornbills, squirrels and a variety of other animals.
- Long term research in the Lowland of west Poland shows that a mosaic of landscape structure of small cultivated fields, shelterbelts, meadows and small ponds helps maintain biological diversity (and many other functions such as enhanced water storage). Mammal, amphibian, reptile, insect diversity are enhanced and the number of bird species is positively correlated with the diversity index of the landscape.

Climate Functions

Although agricultural and the atmosphere interact in many ways, the links between climate and weather, and agricultural biodiversity can be rather complex.

At the global scale, the distribution of individual plants and animals, vegetation and crops is conditioned by available climatic resources such as solar radiation, which controls the production potential, and by rainfall, which determines to what extent the radiant energy can actually be used by plants for their growth. Indeed, it is for these reasons that climatic classifications largely coincide with vegetation maps. At the local scale, types of landscapes and vegetation, including crop and crop-vegetation mixes contribute towards modifying the local climates by directly affecting wind patterns, rates of evaporation, rainfall interception (effective rainfall), etc. This in turn conditions the development of vegetation and crop canopies which can be said to create their own microclimate, resulting from the interaction of plants with the general climate. Shelter belts, or the use or large tree belts to protect tropical plantation crops from cyclones, provide clear examples in which people and communities derive direct advantage from these landscape features.

Many examples demonstrate the benefits of maintaining minimum agrobiodiversity in the face of climate variability. Recent droughts in some southern African countries for example, have shown that mixes of local varieties planted over several weeks have the potential to better resist unusual patterns of rainfall variability (*e.g.* early-season drought) than some modern varieties planted on the "optimum dates". In fact, there appears to be a link between crop biodiversity and relatively low but regular production, one of the keys to food security.

Similarly, atmospheric pollution has been shown to interact with agro-ecosystem functions, both positively (nutrients, such as nitrates and sulphur) and negatively (toxic compound like tropospheric ozone and heavy metals). Given that the response to these substances varies enormously across the spectrum of species, they have the potential to modify patterns of biological diversity. Agriculture also contributes towards the emission of some of the most significant "greenhouse" gases (in terms of global warming potential, GWP). Some studies have suggested for example, that increases in the area of permanently or quasi-permanently flooded rice cultivation account for a significant proportion of the increase in net methane emissions. The increased specialisation of ruminant production based on high yielding breeds has also significantly contributed to global methane emissions (methane is produced by anaerobic digestion in animals).

An extreme case would be the enhanced biogenic emissions of carbonylsulphide associated with increasing cultivation of high sulphur crops such as rape. Oxidation of carbonylsulphide in the stratosphere leads to the production of sulphate aerosols that influence the intensity of ultra violet radiation reaching the earth's surface, potentially affecting the dynamic functions of agricultural biodiversity. Volatile organic compounds such as terpenes and isoprenes are produced and released into the atmosphere by many plant species, especially in agroecosystems dominated by Mediterranean shrubs, eucalyptus and conifers. By influencing the oxidation capacity of the troposphere, these volatile compounds influence the abundance and distribution of trace gases such as ozone. In almost all cases however, many of the these effects are marginal when compared with the climatic effects of land use change, including deforestation, which have until recently constituted one of the main non-industrial sources of carbon dioxide

Functions in the Water Cycle

There are few experimental studies exploring the links between agricultural biodiversity and water. However, available evidence shows that agricultural biodiversity plays a crucial role in cycling water from the soil to the atmosphere and back. It also has measurable impacts on water quality. Agroecosystems with different species assemblages and plant architectures result in differences in the amount of precipitation intercepted, the proportion of precipitation converted to stem flow, and the proportion of precipitation that infiltrates the soil rather than running off. At the landscape level, the types, relative abundances and relative spatial locations of agro-ecosystem types affect the amount of water moving from one point to another. For example, conversion of vegetation within a watershed from forest or shrub land to less structurally and biologically complex grassland is known to influence stream flow out of the watershed, in both temperate and tropical systems.

At the functional group level, the root structure, phenology and physiology of different plant species important for food and agriculture have direct implications for the quantity and timing of water transfer to the atmosphere *via* evapotranspiration. Individual plant species differ in their resistance to water stress, their efficiency of water uptake from the soil, and so on. Genetic variations among crop varieties (differences in water use efficiency, stomatal resistance...) also influence these processes. At the landscape level, evapotranspiration from agroecosystems can have an effect on relative humidity and microclimate downwind.

In both terrestrial and aquatic environments, the plant and animal components of agricultural biodiversity also function to alter water quality by performing various filtration, uptake and excretory processes. These functions all affect the composition and concentration of dissolved gases, solutes and particulates. Species level differences in physiology can positively or negatively affect water quality. However, in most cases a greater diversity of biological organisms (from microbes to fish and macrophytes) leads to a higher quality of water for human consumption and use.

Changes in Policy Environment

REDD+ Expectations

Probably one of the more notable short-term changes in the policy arena is the discussion of GHG emissions reduction through REDD+ and management, conservation and restoration of forest carbon stocks. Large sums of money have been pledged against the demonstrable reduction of GHG emissions through REDD+, but so far, no international agreement has been reached on emissions reduction targets for developing countries. Further, in many pilot projects, measurable results have been interesting but financial benefits limited. REDD+ expectations are manifold, depending on the interest group. Some of these expectations are justified, others not, and most are probably too ambitious. Implementation of REDD+ strategies will have to deal with most, if not all, of the challenges mentioned in this chapter. At the same time it will require the implementation of a monitoring system, the extent and detail of which has not yet been agreed upon. While this has serious implications, the current (international and national) political environment is set to enable projects and countries alike, to meet at least some of these challenges. For the forest manager much of the challenge lies in adjusting management practices in favour of carbon accumulation, while at the same time maintaining biodiversity, recognizing the rights of indigenous people and contributing to local economic development.

Changes in Legislation

In Latin America, many countries implemented new forest legislation in the period between 1995 and 2000. While in some countries this was based on a thorough analysis of the forest sector, in others it was more in response to different pressure groups and based on changes in neighbouring countries.

In some countries (for example Costa Rica), new legislation was relatively successful in achieving the objective of forest conservation, although reducing forest use for timber production considerably (Louman, in print). In others, it has been difficult to implement new legislation if unaccompanied by other measures and if the process was not participatory and consultative.

More recently, countries have realized that they have better results when their new legislation is developed using more participative processes (for example in the DRC and Honduras). However, these processes are too young to be able to assess the true success in terms of increased implementation of legislative requirements.

Climate change will increase the challenge of designing and implementing new legislation that considers new international agreements, conflicts of interest in forest areas, as well as the need for coordination with other sectors. This may involve legislation on land and forest tenure, indigenous rights, the production of fuels and land use planning including restricting the access and use of certain areas or of some species, due to the risk of climate change impacts or the need of soil and water protection or maintenance of biological corridors. In revising forest legislation, it is important to consider all related legislation, so that, for example, legislation or policies oriented at increasing forest area on private land is not nullified by policies or legislation that define forest land as 'un-used' or 'luxury possessions', taxing them relatively heavily or even threatening to expropriate the owners.

Social Responsibility Requirements

Concerns for sustainable development, for the deterioration of the environment and of social relations, as well as for the negative effects of climate change at different scales are influencing market decisions. This can above all be noticed in agricultural product markets, where buyers are looking for products that meet specific environmental and/or social standards. Some banana plantation owners that export to the European market, for example, have started to invest in forest land for conservation and carbon emissions compensation.

New standards have just recently been developed to monitor and evaluate carbon dioxide equivalent emissions from livestock farms in Costa Rica, while the COOPEDOTA coffee cooperative was recently declared carbon neutral. These new developments pose interesting opportunities, more research is required to determine how these mechanisms can be used to improve the maintenance of other ecosystem services (such as water regulation and biodiversity maintenance), strengthen the adaptive capacity of natural and human systems and complement conservation and sustainable use of the existing forest areas within the agricultural landscapes.

Opportunity Costs of Land Use

Meeting REDD+ expectations has much to do with being able to identify the opportunity costs of local actors when they choose forest conservation and management rather than other land uses. Many of the REDD+ cost analyses are based on compensation for lost opportunities, although it has been found that forest conservation on private lands does not only occur for financial reasons.

If lands surrounding forests have high opportunity costs, there is the likelihood of increased pressure to convert those forests to the adjacent land use in order to make them more profitable.

Opportunity costs may vary due to variations in market prices of the crops cultivated, government policies that subsidize agricultural inputs or the exportation of the outputs, or policies favouring the production of biofuel. The forest user or owner does not easily influence these factors.

As a group, in particular, if acting within the framework of REDD+, it may be possible to influence legislation, reduce the unequal treatment of forests as compared to agricultural crops, thus making forest management more competitive with other forms of land use.

Uncertainty and risk management in Forest Climate

Climate change projections for the future involve a series of uncertainties. It is still not sure what emission scenario will best reflect reality, how these emissions change climate, in particular in relation to the distribution of precipitation or what other factors may play a role in influencing local vegetation and how local vegetation will react to climate and other factors. Thus, forest management for climate change has to deal with a range of uncertainties.

The challenge is to reduce those uncertainties and to design management systems that can deal with unexpected changes. Uncertainty and risk management options may involve monitoring systems (*e.g.* climate, biodiversity, production, and social impacts), early warning systems, working groups that analyze the implications of data obtained through monitoring, mechanisms dealing with risk of income loss, appeal systems for unpopular decisions as well as free prior and informed consent of indigenous and local communities.

Flexible adaptive management approaches need to be a part of any management strategy that involves risk and uncertainty. Such strategies will need to include a set of tools, rather than one specific approach, to be able to switch from one to another tool, depending on local conditions, changes in those conditions, and success of already applied tools.

FORESTRY AND BIODIVERSITY

The National Development Strategy provides relevant information on the forestry sector in Guyana. Of the total estimated forest area of 65,000 square miles (169,000 km^2), 34,000 square miles (87,800 km^2) lie within the gazetted State Forest boundaries.

The forest resources are characterised by the following:

- Heterogeneity - there are over 100 tree species
- Relatively few species that are of commercial importance
- The small average size of forest trees
- Most of the commercial timber species are dense heavy hardwoods, which according to the Forestry Sector National Development Strategy, make up an average of 80 per cent of the exploited species.

Approximately 2.5 million hectares of forest lands are considered not exploitable for timber with present technology. The total volume of standing timber in the exploitable forest area is estimated at more than 350 million cubic metres, of which hardwoods account for just less than 90 per cent. An area of 3.6 million hectares of forested land is accessible for exploitation, and approximately 2.4 million hectares have been allocated for harvesting. Many rivers that could provide access to the forests are not navigable because of waterfalls and rapids. The forests that are closest to navigable water have been logged for commercial species.

The forestry sector employs about 20,000 people and produces some 218,000 cubic metres of timber annually. Foreign exchange generated by forest products exports doubled during 1994 to approximately US$15 million. The sector is again set to double its export earnings by mid-1996 if plywood exports reach and maintain their target of 10,000 cubic metres per month.

There are seventeen (17) concessionaires operating under Timber Sales Agreements (TSAs). The TSAs are issued for areas >60,000 acres (24,000 ha). The large concessionaires have significant investments in plant and equipment and convey exclusive harvesting rights for 15-25 years. Most of the concessionaires concentrate on logging the endemic greenheart (*Ocotea rodiaei*), and eight of the concessionaires export regularly. All the concessionaires have integrated logging and sawmill operations in the interior, concentrated in the Essequibo and Demerara areas.

Small scale loggers have operated with State Forest Permissions (SFPs), generally one year in term, which grant rights to a specified volume of timber within a prescribed area. There are at present 486 SFPs for areas <20,000 acres (8,100 ha) covering approximately 4,126,230 acres (1,669,801 ha). SFPs were usually issued to smaller operators who produce for the domestic market. About 1.2 million hectares have been covered by SFPs and most of the log production flows to small sawmills concentrated in the Berbice and Demerara areas. Minor forest operators also worked with SFPs in the dry evergreen forests of the Demerara area close to Georgetown, Linden, and the populated coastal settlements.

Monitoring of forestry operations by the Guyana Forestry Commission (GFC) is only nominal because of shortages of staff and equipment, limited funding and absence of a good data base. Large scale concessionaires, small scale loggers, and minor forest products operators still pursue forestry activities with virtually no monitoring by the GFC. The environmental impacts of logging vary with the size of the concession and the conditions attached to the logging permits. Each stage of the logging activity has a separate impact on land, soil, and water. Because of lack of monitoring and regulation, the environmental impacts of logging activities can only be described in qualitative terms, and the sources often disagree as to the seriousness of the various impacts. The following are perceived to be the main impacts from logging activities.

Exploitation of the Greenheart

Greenheart is the best known timber species and is of such intense commercial interest that foresters do not harvest other species in those areas where the greenheart is most concentrated and of best quality. It accounts for only 1.5 per cent of the stand merchantable volume but provides nearly 40 per cent of the total volume of roundwood production. Because of lack of monitoring, conclusive evidence of over-harvesting of the greenheart is not available, but ongoing studies may reveal the true status of this species.

Until recently, efforts to commercialise other species in export markets, to take the pressure off the potentially dwindling greenheart resource, have been only partially effective. Only smaller producers selling on the domestic market have harvested a significant proportion of other species. The high cost of shipping from Guyana constrains exports of species other than the greenheart to North America. Such costs are higher than shipping these same products from Africa and the Pacific. In the case of the greenheart, strong market demand overcomes these factors. Port facilities are also inadequate (though they are being improved), causing costly delays in loading and only small vessels can take a full load. Recently, certain private sector initiatives suggest that marketing possibilities for other species and for non-tree forest products may have improved. The largest and most recent concessionaire, the Barama Company Limited, has established an integrated logging and plywood production system based on harvesting about twelve plywood species. Barama's operation represents a technological and commercial breakthrough for the utilisation of large quantities of lesser known species and more intensive utilisation of forests. The company contracted the Edinburgh Centre for Tropical Forests (ECTF) to undertake monitoring of its environmental impacts and research to benefit its operations.

Impacts on Forest Ecosystems

Concessionaires are required to submit Forest Management Plans (FMPs) as a condition of the TSA, but they have not observed this requirement in the past. Therefore, the long term sustainability of the selective harvesting system used is unknown. Several actions of loggers provide cause for concern. Careless felling and extraction due to under-skilled, poorly supervised, chain saw operators and skidder drivers can result in unnecessary damage to the remaining stand, which is likely to result in lower harvests next time around. Seed trees are not usually retained, wildlife important to seed dispersal are not safeguarded, protective buffer strips along watercourses are not always respected and production demands defer to the speed of the operation rather than to selectivity of harvesting. With one exception, there are no restricted areas within logging concessions that conserve representative areas of productive forest types in their unlogged condition. Consequently, comparison of the ecological condition of the logged forests with the unlogged, once the first full cutting cycles are completed, will not be possible, thereby hampering monitoring of compliance with the FMP.

Impacts on Soils and Rivers

The main impacts of forestry exploitation on rivers and streams are: increased turbidity caused by soil erosion from logging, increased BOD from the discharge of organic waste from sawmilling, and oil pollution from the discharge of petroleum products.

GFC has already issued regulations to protect rivers from the effects of logging wastes, which are automatically included in each FMP. The regulations require the maintenance of 50-metre buffer strips of forest along the river banks. Nevertheless, in some cases when such buffer strips are established, the river banks are demolished by the missile dredges of largely unregulated gold miners. Consequently, the logging waste often slips into the river causing turbidity, with consequent adverse impacts on aquatic life and on the navigability of the rivers. GFC has not yet recommended procedures for the safe storage of oil and fuel away from watercourses nor does it have the capacity to monitor such storage effectively. Proper disposal of sawmill waste has long been an intractable problem. About 60 per cent of the average saw log remains in the yards as waste in the form of slabs, ends, and sawdust. Most mills heap this waste on the riverbanks and it eventually spills over or is pushed into the water, raising BOD levels and hampering aquatic life. The Essequibo area is estimated to generate 50-60 thousand cubic metres of sawmill waste each year.

Recently, some concessionaires have started exploring the possibility of utilising the waste as a source of energy. (A pilot project (No. 34) for such conversion was proposed in the NFAP.) Currently, two steam producing boilers fueled by sawmill waste power the Willems Timber and Trading Limited mill at Kaow Island. The Company has also experimented with producing charcoal from sawmill ends in portable kilns. A. Mazaharally Sawmill Limited has acquired a turbine generator to produce electricity from its sawmill wastes. Current efforts at using sawmill waste as a fuel have made little impact on the problem of river contamination, but there may be scope for the conversion of sawmill waste into briquettes using wood densification technology. Forestry exploitation, as practised in here, does not lay bare large expanses of soil or lead to serious soil erosion and land slides at all the logging sites. For economic reasons, concessionaires avoid logging in excessively wet conditions, when the soil is most prone to erosion. The forestry research programme at the Barama concession includes studying the impact of forest operations on soil properties, with a specific focus on soil compaction, erosion and loss of fertility. Tropenbos has been conducting an ecological and forestry research study at the DTL concession at Mabura Hill on the impacts of logging activities on soil properties. The results of such studies are not yet known but will be made available to GFC so that the findings can be incorporated into forestry policy.

Forest Fires

Incidences of illegally set forest fires have caused losses of forest resources. The principal causes of such fires are untended charcoal burning pits and vandalism. The damage from these forest fires could be contained if specific areas were designated for charcoal burning at each camp site and if permittees of the SFP, TSA and WCL were required to report, and, where possible, to attempt to put out fires within forested areas. Monitoring, especially during the dry season, could be the dual responsibility of concessionaires and the local communities.

Forest Management

The management of the forests has not been sufficiently studied to generate a proven silviculture system. In-depth inventories are lacking as are data on growth either in the undisturbed natural forest or in logged-over areas.

The Government emphasised its interest in promoting sustainable forestry development in Guyana through the preparation of the National Forestry Action Plan (NFAP) in 1989. A round-table meeting of the donor community in February 1992, resulted in donor pledges for ten priority projects from the NFAP totalling US$8.6 million. Implementation of the NFAP has continued with the recent appointment of a national coordinator. CIDA agreed to fund an Interim Forestry Project (IFP) that began in 1989, as a bridge between NFAP preparation and implementation. Meanwhile, with assistance from Germany, Government is proceeding to formulate and implement a forest land-use policy, related legislation and an appropriate administrative structure to ensure the sustainable use of its forest resources.

As a further expression of its commitment to protection of the tropical rainforest, the Guyana Government advised the Commonwealth Heads of Government Meeting in October 1989, that the country would set aside 360,000 hectares of its Amazon rainforest for a pilot research project under Commonwealth auspices. Since then the Commonwealth Secretariat and the Global Environment Facility (GEF) have begun to finance the establishment of an International Centre for Research and Training for the Sustainable Management of Tropical Forests in the Iwokrama rainforest. This research project will investigate ways that the tropical rainforest can maintain desired levels of biological diversity while supporting economic activity.

BIODIVERSITY

In recognition of the significance of its biodiversity assets, Guyana signed the UN Convention on Biological Diversity during the Earth Summit of 1992. The Convention commits signatories to adopt regulations to conserve their biological resources. In this context, as stated in the NEAP: "the Government is committed to saving biodiversity, studying biodiversity and using biodiversity sustainably and equitably. The Government is also aware of the need to ensure that the ownership of intellectual property rights, including knowledge and customary and traditional practices of local people, is adequately and effectively protected. However, to date, Guyana lacks specific legislation to facilitate such actions."

Although our wealth in biological diversity is unquestionable, there is a general paucity of information on its exact nature and extent. However, some 8,000 species of flora, of which half are endemic, have been identified in the biogeographic Guiana region. Guyana provides habitats for a variety of fauna and is deemed to have one of the richest mammalian faunas of any comparably sized area in the world. There are nearly 1,200 vertebrates, of which 728 are birds, 198 mammals, 137 reptiles and 105 amphibians. Of these, CITES currently lists 44 as in danger of extinction. The avifauna in its habitat in the widespread rain and seasonal forests is known to be rich. Nevertheless, there is a paucity of data about the country's reptiles, amphibians and fish; only three surveys approved by CITES have been done in the past ten years: two for caimans and one for boid snakes.

Guyana's forests have abundant wildlife, but there are no reliable population surveys of commercial and other species. Therefore, there is no measurement of whether wildlife harvests exceed sustainable levels, nor whether and when closed harvest seasons should be established annually for commercial species. Wildlife exports were estimated at US$800,000 in 1992, mostly from the sale of birds, particularly parrots and macaws. Guyana is the fifth largest exporter of birds in the world. Besides the seventeen authorised exporters of wildlife, the trade is a major source of income for thousands of trappers (mostly Amerindians), intermediaries, carpenters who build holding stations, cages and export boxes, and farmers who provide food for the birds and animals. Operating without the benefit of population or biological surveys, Government devised, with CITES and the World Trade Monitoring Unit, an empirical export licence formula to set export quotas.

In December 1992, Government decided not to issue any licences for wildlife exports in 1993 as a prelude to passage of the Conservation of Wildlife Bill. Despite a general lack of public awareness about wildlife issues, there is a strong lobby in and outside Guyana against the wildlife trade, a trade that generates considerable export revenues as well as domestic income and employment. Government has put in place a system for training wardens and monitoring the wildlife trade, in order to fully comply with the pertinent international conventions. Arrangements also have been made with the San Diego Wildlife Park for continuing assistance in this area. Given these advances, Government decided to lift the wildlife export ban in September 1995.

The sand and shell beaches between the Moruka river mouth and Waini Point on the northwest coast are the nesting grounds for four species of marine turtles: the leatherback, *Dermochelys coriaceae*; the hawksbill, *Eretmochelys imbricata*; the olive ridley, *Lepidochelys olivacea* and the green turtle, *Chelonia mydas*. Despite legislation to protect the turtles, intensive exploitation of the turtles and their eggs for food has resulted in ever decreasing populations and the threat of their extinction. To protect the turtles, Government has required that turtle exclusion devices (TEDs) be installed on shrimp nets. In addition, the Government will work with communities of artisanal fisherman to help them develop economic alternatives to hunting turtles and their eggs, and to educate them in the vulnerability of the turtle population to that kind of predation. Studies on various topics related to biodiversity have been conducted in specific areas by the World Wildlife Fund (WWF), Conservation International, the Smithsonian Institute, Global 2000, and the U.K. Natural Resources Institute. Most of these studies emphasise the need for an established system of national parks, by which the extensive biodiversity resources can be nurtured and protected.

National Parks and Protected Areas

Government is committed to ensuring the integrity of forest systems, the conservation and protection of selected forest areas with high species diversity as genetic reservoirs for the future, the allocation of outstanding natural areas for recreational purposes, and the preservation of the country's historical and cultural heritage. This commitment is confirmed in the NEAP. The National Parks Commission Act of 1977 gives management authority to the National Parks Commission (NPC), but the NPC is under-funded and more oriented to urban recreational parks.

The Protected Areas project in the NFAP was given high priority and pledges of funding at the international round-table in February 1993. Such a system will incorporate ongoing work to identify the places of special natural, scientific, and cultural interest.

The NFAP calls for the protection of the Kaieteur National Park and 14 other natural areas, including a biosphere reserve in the southwest (for which a Guyana Biosphere Reserve Bill has already been drafted) and a World Heritage Site at Mt. Roraima. Conservation International completed a rapid assessment of the Kanuku mountains and the EEC financed a study for the creation of a protected area in the Kanuku Mountains and adjoining savanna areas of the Rupununi region. Consultations with Amerindian communities in these areas will be ongoing as their involvement and agreement will be critical to the success of these protected zones.

Kaieteur National Park is the only legally established protected area in the country. Legislation establishing Kaieteur was passed in 1929 and the Kaieteur National Park Act of 1973 provides the legal framework for its constitution and management.

With no land-use planning in effect, the park is not demarcated on the ground and only one park ranger safeguards the ecological integrity of the entire protected area. As presently constituted, the park comprises the falls, the greater part of the gorge below, and part of the Potaro river above the falls to the south. Currently, the designated area counts with only minimal infrastructure. Full authority over the park is not clearly defined as the GGMC, GFC, and the Land and Surveys Commission each have different responsibilities in the park.

WATERSHEDS

Forest cover in the watersheds helps the infiltration of rainwater into the ground which then charges aquifers; the forest cover protects against flash flooding and soil erosion. Some forest cover has been lost to competing activities, such as bauxite mining, agriculture, and harvesting of fuelwood and poles. The watersheds in the coastal plain and in the sandy rolling lands that supply the conservancies have not been protected or managed for water production. The forests nearest to urban centres and the coast have been heavily exploited for fuelwood by household and industrial users and have also suffered repeated wildfires from charcoal and agricultural production. The wallaba (eperua) forest of the White Sands peneplain, which has been harvested for telephone and electricity poles, has been degraded to such an extent that regeneration of the original dry evergreen forest is virtually nonexistent. As much as 200,000 hectares are believed to be unable to regenerate spontaneously.

Most of the water courses from the watersheds are also subject to competing demands: for drinking and irrigation water and as receptacles for domestic and industrial waste. Consequently, much of the coastal plain's supply of potable and irrigation water is believed to be polluted. Deforestation may also explain the more frequent and less predictable flooding of the coastal plain. While no clear picture emerges of the extent of the deforestation, potential pressures from logging could have serious consequences for the critical watersheds unless preventive measures are taken ahead of time.

FOREST CANOPY STRUCTURE AND ITS ECOLOGICAL FUNCTIONS

Wind river slide Forest structure, the spatial arrangement of both live and dead tree and plant material, strongly influences the spatial patterns of forest co-habitants due to the fundamental organisation of food, shelter, and space. Structure is closely linked with composition, age, and history, including disturbance. Components of forest structures are leaves, reproductive parts, branches, trunks, butts, roots, and dead wood, and the airspace among them. G. Parker wrote an excellent review and synthesis in the 1995 Forest Canopies text, which I use as the basis for this lecture. I summarise the general structural features and microclimates peculiar to forest canopies, compare how some forests differ in these characteristics, and explore how structure affects microclimate. I focus on structure and environment of closed, continuous forests.

Several themes: 1) forest canopy structure has been poorly defined, and rarely represented to allow cross-site comparison; 2) measurements of microclimate usually focus on mean values, at a few locations and short time scales - variation has not been assessed; 3) studies on the relation of structure and function are uncommon. Lots of theory, but little measured.

DEFINITIONS OF CANOPY STRUCTURE

Canopy definitions Canopy is combination of all leaves, twigs, and small branches in a stand of vegetation; the aggregate of all the crowns. The canopy is a region as well as a collection of objects. Forest canopy structure is the organisation in space and time, including the position, extent, quantity, type and connectivity of the aboveground components of vegetation. It is often useful to consider the open spaces between canopy elements and the atmosphere contained within and between crown as part of the canopy. Terms Many terms have been used in the past: Physiognomy for shapes of individual crowns; architecture for growth patterns and forms of stems; organisation for statistical distribution of canopy components; texture to the sizes of crown units composing the overstory. Units of canopy structure: usually, crowns of trees, but ultimately, is leaves and twigs. But often deal with statistical distribution of millions of leaves. Many scales are evident: foliage may be climbed or clustered; crowns are grouped into stands; stands into landscapes. Descriptors Many descriptors: eg. Maximum tree height (hmax) or mean height (h), number or biomass density of elements (stems ha-1); canopy cover (fraction of sky not covered by canopy); or leaf area index, ratio of total one-sided leaf area to projected ground area (LAI, m2/m3). Less common are specifying 3-D organisation of canopy elements. Almost always described by mean conditions, not an assessment of variation.

Quantification of Canopy Structure

White profile diagram For many years our view of forests has been two-dimensional (2-D) and the structure and dynamics of forest ecosystems have been studied and analysed using data expressed as stem maps that indicate the X and Y coordinates of individual trees along with species and size information (*e.g.*, diameter at breast height). "Stand structure" usually referred to the species composition and tree size distribution of forest stands, and sometimes included information on the 2-D spatial distribution of trees and tree height. Because humans are confined to the ground, we have been unable to study in detail the 3-D structure of forests including the forest canopy. Instead, we inferred tree growth from diameter increment at breast height, and competitive interactions among trees from analysis of the relationship between horizontal spatial distribution and diameter growth or mortality patterns. However, we have always known that the dynamics of forest ecosystems, including growth and competitive interactions among individual trees, occur in the canopy and not at breast height. Canopy access tools have provided the means to quantify canopy structure in a more 3-d way.. Early characterisations of canopy structure were caricatures of the crowns of larger trees of forests - profile diagrams. Oldeman and others did more sophisticated images. But they tend to reflect only the peculiarities of the plot and provide little quantification of the vertical organisation of the whole.

Leaf distribution – jess Whole canopy Lz (leaf-height density) can be estimated by assembling structural measurements of individual crowns made from observations from the grown or harvested stems. Lots of measurements in crop plants, very few for whole forests. This shows vertical stratification of leaf distribution for an eastern deciduous forest, gathered with crane data. Fish eye Optical point measurements more common. Hemispheric fisheye photography uses potential light environment at a point to assess canopy structure. Several devices now estimate LAI from in-canopy light measurements, relying on Beer's law and the absorbance of light.

Remote sensing has done a lot. Use the spectral quality of canopy light, the ratio of red/far red light transmitted through the canopy. Several measures calculated from combining different reflectance bands relate to the amount of green canopy biomass, such as the "normalised difference vegetation index (NDVI) or "greenness" index. Index takes advantage of the strong reflectance in the near infrared but weak reflectance in the red wavelengths of green canopies. Other remote sensing techniques use a similar approach, with sensors of different wavebands on several satellite platforms. (LIDAR) Also from a profiling airborne laser - to sense the elevation of both the ground and canopy, yielding the contour of canopy height over a long transect. So advances in quantifying and visualising canopy structure is growing in sophistication.

Old growth messy The term "structural complexity" was coined as an integrative concept to represent the complex 3-D structure of old-growth forests. However, many of the measures and indices used to characterise structural complexity such as species composition, tree-size distribution and abundance of snags and woody debris are derived from 2-D, ground-based measurements. Ishii young old forest One of the objectives for developing indices of structural complexity is to quantitatively distinguish old-growth forests from younger stands and to establish criteria for enhancing old-growth forest structure in managed stands for conservation purposes, such as creating wildlife habitat. In order to meet such management objectives, we must integrate various aspects of forest structure including canopy and below-ground processes into future ecosystem management strategies.

VERTICAL ORGANISATION

Canopy elements can be non-uniformly distributed with height. This pattern derives from species differences in growth form and shade tolerance, and stand developmental stage. Jess species distribution At its simplest, we can use an example from mixed deciduous forest. Vertical sorting of species leaf area. This is a foliage height profile for an Appalachian mixed species forest, giving the percentage of leaf area for the major species.

More generally, the vertical organisation of microclimate, structures, and biota in forests is a recurring theme in scientific investigations and forest description. For example, Leaf characteristics such as size, shape, mass, inclination, chlorophyll content, N content, and photosynthetic capacity vary within a tree crown along gradients of light and other microenvironmental conditions so that the individual plant maximizes carbon gain. Vert strat definition One aspect of this is the concept of vertical stratification. Stratification proposes predictable vertical separation of canopy components such as forest leaves and other structures, species, or individual organisms into distinct horizons, layers or gradients. Long history of vertical organisation. Early naturalists, such as Allee (1949) saw stratification in the big picture, as a general phenomenon of animal and plant communities in aquatic (freshwater lakes, oceans, inter-tidal zones) and terrestrial (grasslands, deserts, forests) environments.

Smith (1973) concluded that stratification optimises light utilisation, CO_2 concentrations, pollination and dispersal, reduces predation on flowers, fruits and leaves, and increases structural integrity of the forest. Strict adherence to the proposition of stratification has been criticised as too limiting when in fact there are ecological gradients in three dimensions from forest floor through the canopy that are complex mosaics of biota, microclimate, gaps, and the growth, mortality, and development of trees.

Horizontal Variation

Light gap Forests are not spatially uniform, but are horizontally heterogeneous at various scales. Most work has dealt with foliage-free spaces. Light gaps are holes in the canopy extending to the forest floor that permit the penetration of unscattered light (Runkle and Canham). Gaps of various sizes originate from a variety of causes. Lots of work done on this, as it influences bird flight, regeneration, seed germination. Crown shyness In some forests, individual subcrowns and crowns are clearly separate, with vegetation free borders in between.

This "crown shyness" is most common in single-species and single-cohort stands, and on windy sites. Probably maintained by wind-induced abrasion between adjacent crowns. "Crown asymmetry", where the crown centre is offset from the stem base, results from plasticity in the directional growth of tree crowns. Broad-leaved trees show great plasticity in crown growth that allows trees to grow towards open areas of the canopy and avoid competition from neighbouring crowns. Crown asymmetry can buffer negative effects of crown competition, reducing tree mortality and increasing the mean and variation in tree size within stands. Coniferous trees have less plasticity in crown form and directional growth of the crown.

Temporal Changes

Light env over year Canopy structure changes seasonally in all forest, but is most dramatic in deciduous stands. But even evergreen forests, the quantity of leaf area varies over the year. Gen stand development More substantial changes occur on a succession time scale. Total amount stabilises, but its vertical and horizontal distribution change slowly. Bob vp stands This difference has been shown through comparative studies of 2-D stand structure. At the individual tree level, can be seen.

Jess images of stand ages But at the stand level, can also be quantified. Species composition and tree size distributions become more diverse with increasing stand age and specific structural elements such as large, old trees and snags characterise older stands

Deterministic Processes that Drive Development of Canopy Structure

In early stages of stand development, deterministic processes such as timing of establishment following disturbance, height-growth rate, and crown interactions determine canopy structure. In mixed-species natural forests, differences among species in timing of establishment and initial height-growth rates result in vertical stratification of species within the canopy. Early-successional, fast-growing species can establish soon after disturbance, reach the upper canopy, and dominate during early stages of succession.

The vertical development of canopy structure with increasing stand age can be inferred by comparing stands of different ages, *i.e.*, a chronosequence approach. Bob vp leaves In Douglas-fir and western hemlock forests of the Pacific Northwest Coast of North America, development of vertical canopy structure during early-successional stages begins with the dominance of the fast-growing, pioneer species, Douglas-fir, in the upper canopy of mixed-species stands. In late-successional stands, canopy height reaches over 70 m. Douglas-fir continues to dominate in the upper canopy as more shade-tolerant species such as western hemlock and western red cedar invade the mid- to lower-canopy. This results in the development of a deep, continuous canopy comprising both early- and late-successional species As forests mature, canopy height reaches maximum and species differences in height-growth rate become less important in determining structural development.

Species with similar levels of shade-tolerance will occupy similar positions in the canopy. Late-successional species that can reach the upper canopy eventually catch up and take the place of less shade-tolerant, early-successional species in the upper canopy. However, in regions where there are few physical limitations to canopy height (*e.g.*, typhoons and poor soil conditions), physiological limitations to height growth and crown expansion may reduce competition among the tallest trees, allowing early successional species to coexist in the upper canopy with the late-successional species. For example, in the old-growth Douglas-fir–western hemlock at the Wind River Canopy Crane Research, mild climate and abundant rainfall allow canopy trees to reach heights over 60 m. In this forest, upper-canopy trees (tree height > 40 m) of all species have attained maximum crown size and show very little crown expansion growth. In the absence of crown competition, long-lived pioneer species such as Douglas-fir may be able to coexist with the late-successional species in the upper canopy.

STOCHASTIC PROCESSES AND DEVELOPMENT OF STRUCTURAL COMPLEXITY

With increasing stand age, stochastic or random processes such as mortality of individual trees that create gaps in the canopy and small-scale disturbances that cause damage and die-back of crowns play increasingly important roles in creating structural complexity of the forest canopy. As trees reach maximum size, limitations to crown expansion in the upper canopy enhance structural complexity of the canopy surface. In Douglas-fir–western hemlock forests, gaps created in the upper canopy after individual tree mortality are not filled by neighbouring trees and the upper-canopy surface becomes increasingly heterogeneous with increasing stand age. Many trees in old-growth forests show evidence of past damage and regrowth, such as forks and crooks in the main stem. In tropical forests and monsoon regions that are frequently affected by windstorms and typhoons, crown damage is commonly observed. oughts, fungal infections, insect outbreaks, and forest fires can also cause defoliation and die-back of the crown and are often followed by regrowth. Stochasticity of small-scale disturbances followed by regrowth of the crown adds variability to the otherwise deterministic architecture of trees and enhances structural complexity of the forest canopy.

Reiteration contributes to prolonging tree longevity by reproducing dead and dying crown components. Many long-lived, late-successional species can reiterate architectural units and maintain the crown, in contrast to short-lived early-successional species which tend to have less ability to reiterate crown components. Reiteration of various architectural units ranging from shoots and twigs to entire branches and vertical axes (reiterated trunks) has been observed in some large, old trees of long-lived species, including redwoods and Douglas-fir. Understory trees of European beech, a shade-tolerant, late-successional species, maintain the crown by means of reiteration when growth is suppressed due to limited light conditions. In old Douglas-fir trees, reiteration enhances structural complexity of the crown by increasing branch size variability. Reiteration also contributes to enhancing structural complexity by creating specific structural features such as reiterated trunks, fan-shaped clusters of epicormic branches, and platform-shaped forks within branches, making the crown of each tree "highly individualistic and irregular

Marbled murreletWhy is this important? These developmental processes of canopy structure drive and enhance various ecological functions such as community dynamics and stand productivity. Spotted owl Development of structural complexity enhances biodiversity of forest ecosystems by creating specific structural elements that provide food and habitat for other organisms.

Forest Micro-Environmental Gradients

Mv cloud Canopy microclimate is ultimately determined by the stand macroclimate; the rhytms of change above and within the forest are set by the cycles of annual and diurnal heating and by the movements of air masses and clouds. Very short term events (time scale of less than a minute) are important in exchange process and ventilation of canopy layers. Some environmental variables are influenced by broadscale canopy features (wind), whereas others (light) are depended on the local arrangements of elements. The vertical pattern of microenvironmental conditions within forests is important because it influences the distribution of forest biota, behaviour of vertebrates, the development and growth of tree structures, amount of gas exchange and water release by forest leaves, infection potential for numerous tree parasites, invasiveness of lianas into tree crowns, growth and productivity of epiphytes, biological activity levels of microbes, and numerous other aspects of ecosystem function. The forest influences microclimate, and microclimate influences how and where the forest will grow, so that the interaction of the two results in measured patterns in a dynamic state.

The three-dimensional microenvironment (light, humidity, temperature, and wind) of forests is spatially heterogeneous based on composition and structure of the forest. Wind distribution Wind, for example, has higher peaks in the upper canopy, than down near the forest floor. In general, wind is rapidly decelerated in the layer just above the forest The velocity profile in this layer is commonly described as though the wind were reacting to a rough surface displaced above the ground by a distance d. This is equivalent to the mean height of the momentum absorption, with a gradient controlled by the roughness of the surface.

Both the roughness and the displacement height of canopies depend on the amount and distribution of canopy material, and also on wind speed itself. Estimates are often based on the canopy height. In some stands, wind speeds do not decline monotonically with depth, but have a secondary max in the lowermost canopy levels. This is seen in stands of simple structure that lack vegetation layers at the bottom, or at forest boundaries, where winds may blow through for distances equal to several canopy heights.

The canopy acts as a filter of high frequency gusts, arresting small-scale fluctuations, but permitting the penetration of large eddies. The depth to which eddys penetrate depends on canopy density, strength of the eddy, stability of the canopy air column. Much of the total transport occurs during a small fraction of the time. Periods of relative quiescence are punctuated with gusts that can penetrate deeply. With high-frequency sensors, rapid vertical motions and temperature deviations may be observed almost simultaneously at several canopy levels. Trace gases and particle concentrations have relatively weak gradients within the canopy, but mean concentrations are typically lower in the understory than in the overstory. For CO_2, however, the active layer of the canopy is an enormous sink, and CO_2 concentrations are often slightly depressed in the overstory during the daytime. The ground is a source due to root and soil respiration and decomposition. A pronounced CO_2 max develops in the understory late at night, especially under stable conditions.

Light is perhaps the most influential and complex of all canopy microclimatic variables. Most microenvironmental factors correlate with light intensity. Therefore, the effect of microclimate on plant physiology and growth as well as on animal behaviour and occurrence is difficult to separate from that of light alone.

This makes light a suitable universal indicator for just about every aspect of forest canopy ecology, but it is very difficult to measure in three-dimensional space. Parker proposed a vertical subdivision of canopies into three zones based on the patterns of the mean and variance of vertical light transmittance; bright, transition, and dim. The bright zone (upper canopy) is characterised by high transmittance and low variability, the transition zone (mid canopy) is where transmittance is most variable and the mean changes rapidly with height, while the dim zone (lower canopy) is characterised by low transmittance and variability.

Bibliography

A. Kannan, M. Ravichandran and S. Bhoopathi: *Environmental Management : Issues in Common Property Resources (CPRs) in India*, Abhijeet Publication, Delhi, 2011.

C.V. Jayamani and R. Vasanthagopal: *Environmental Management : From Ancient to Modern Times*, New Century Publications, Delhi, 2012.

D.R. Khanna, A.K. Chopra, Vikas Singh, R. Bhutiani and Gagan Matta: *Environmental Management*, Daya Publication, Delhi, 2013.

G.L. Maliwal: *Handbook of Environmental Management*, Agrotech Publication, Delhi, 2006.

H.K. Pathak and M. Thomas: *Environmental Management and Business Strategy*, Cyber Tech Publication, Delhi, 2011.

Hussain, Majid: *Environmental Management in India*, Manak Publication, Delhi, 1997.

I.V. Murali Krishna and Valli Manickam: *Environmental Management: A Primer for Industries*, BS Publications/BSP Books, Delhi, 2015.

J. Sathya and M. Ravichandran: *Environmental Management : An Economic Approach to Pollution Control in Sago Industry*, Abhijeet Publication, Delhi, 2010.

Lingaraj Patro: *Environmental Management System*, Sonali Publication, Delhi, 2010.

M C Metti: *Environmental Management in Hospitality*, Anmol Publication, Delhi, 2008.

M Ravichandran and S Boopathi: *Environmental Management : Issues in Potable Water in Rural Tamil Nadu*, Concept Publication, Delhi, 2007.

M. Anji Reddy: *Geoinformatics for Environmental Management*, BS Publication, Delhi, 2004.

M. Arora: *Environmental Management of Toxic and Hazardous Chemicals*, IVY Publishing, Delhi, 2001.

N K Uberoi: *Environmental Management*, Excel Books, Delhi, 2001.

N.K. Singh and Ashok Kumar: *Environmental Management : Global Concern*, S.K. Publication, Delhi, 2011.

Naresh Chandra Saxena, Gurdeep Singh and Rekha Ghosh: *Environmental Management in Mining Areas*, Scientific Publication, Delhi, 2013.

P.C. Mishra and Ashutosh Naik: *Environmental Management in Coal Mining and Thermal Power Plants (Professor Rebati Charan Das Commemoration Volume)*, ABD Publication, Delhi, 2003.

Padmanabh Dwivedi: *Environmental Pollution and Environmental Management*, Scientific Publication, Delhi, 2004.

Paras Diwan and Parag Diwan: *Environmental Management Law and Administration (Readings and Cases)*, Deep & Deep Publication, Delhi, 1998.

Peter Gomes Dayal and C K Nambian: *Environmental Management and Designs for the Sustainable Development, Vols. 1 to 2*, Dominant Publication, Delhi, 2009.

R K Khitoliya: *Environmental Management and Conservation (2 Vols-Set)*, APH Publication, Delhi, 2008.

S A Abbasi and K B Chari: *Environmental Management of Urban Lakes with Special Reference to Oussudu*, Discovery Publication, Delhi, 2008.

S Bhatt & Akhtar Majeed: *Environmental Management and Federalism : The Indian Experience*, Uppal Publication, Delhi, 2002.

S.W. Bunting, P. Edwards and N. Kunda: *Environmental Management Manual : East Kolkata Wetlands*, Manak Publication, Delhi, 2011.

T. V. Ramachandra and Vijay Kullkarni: *Environmental Management*, TERI, 2009.

T.K. Chandrabhanu: *Environmental Management*, Global Publication, Delhi, 2010.

V K Sinha: *Global Change and Environmental Management*, Vital Publication, Delhi, 2007.

Index